# THE LAKES OF NEW MEXICO

# The Lakes of New Mexico

## A Guide to Recreation

Andy Sandersier

University of New Mexico Press
*Albuquerque*

A Coyote Book

Library of Congress Cataloging-in-Publication Data

Sandersier, Andy, 1918–
    The lakes of New Mexico : a guide to
recreation / Andy Sandersier. — 1st ed.
        p.   cm. — (A Coyote book)
    Includes indexes.
    ISBN 0-8263-1714-6
    1. Lakes — New Mexico — Recreational use
— Directories. 2. Lakes — New Mexico —
Recreational use — Guidebooks. 3. Fishing —
New Mexico — Directories. 4. New Mexico —
Guidebooks. I. Title. II. Series: Coyote books
(Albuquerque, N.M.)
GV191.42.N6S36   1996
917.89—dc20                         96-9107
                                       CIP

# CONTENTS

## Zone Divisions, Vicinities, and Lakes

### Zone 1: Northwest Area

### Zone 2: Northeast Area

# ACKNOWLEDGMENTS

My decision to produce this book was generated many years ago when I first took residence in New Mexico. An avid fisherman and camping enthusiast, I could find no organized guide to some of the more remote lakes of the state, and during my trips to the lakes (which I managed to find by trial and error), I often discovered upon arrival that many of the accesses were either not suitable for passenger cars or were reached by trail only. Some of the lakes were private and not for public use, some were without facilities. My feeling was that persons venturing into unknown areas should be aware of access and facilities before they go.

I kept a diary of each destination that I visited. This book is a compilation of notes, observations, photographs, hand-drawn maps, and research made on personal visits to each lake and vicinity, and interviews with personnel of the Forest Service, the Department of Game and Fish, chambers of commerce, state parks personnel, townspeople and whenever possible, town mayors, Indian tribal governors and tribal rangers of the Indian pueblos. Certain historical facts in the vicinity narratives come to me by word-of-mouth, promotional brochures, historical roadside markers, and the above mentioned interviews and conversations, and their accuracy was verified through extensive reading of New Mexico history. The preparation of this book has, from beginning to end, been a one-man project. I employed no researchers, photographers, or cartographers.

I am indebted to my friend Elvin Smith, who contributed generously of his time and wisdom in guiding me to some of the more remote areas and reading portions of the manuscript. I am grateful to numerous others whose unselfish cooperation has vastly improved my own efforts. My good friends Loré and Van White shared the hospitality of their Taos Chalet with me on my several day-explorations of the "Enchanted Circle," and Jeff Newquist who helped me over some of the hurdles of computer techniques necessary for the preparation of this book. Luke Shelby, Assistant Chief of Urban

Fisheries, New Mexico Department of Game and Fish, was always available to answer some of my many questions, and at the request of the University of New Mexico Press, he reviewed the entire manuscript and provided invaluable and updated information on the stocking policy of the Game and Fish Department. (This information is of great benefit to anglers who can now anticipate the quality and size of catch in the lakes that they plan to visit.) I owe special thanks, too, to Jack Samson, former Editor-in-Chief, *Field and Stream,* who read the manuscript and provided the Foreword for this book, and to my editor Larry D. Ball of The University of New Mexico Press, whose helpful guidance through the book's design and final preparation made its publication possible.

Finally, I am especially indebted to the many people who responded to my requests for information and who have given me the benefit of their knowledge. Some went to the trouble of sending me detailed, well-considered memoranda, from which I derived great profit. I list some of their names with my deep thanks: Lisa B. Romero, Albuquerque District Corps of Engineers; Derrick Dunlap, Park Ranger, Corps of Engineers, Cochiti Dam; Gene Onken, District Forest Ranger, Canjilon Ranger District; Criss Wacondo and Roger Fragua of the Jemez Recreation Areas; Española Valley Chamber of Commerce; David E. Esquibel, Supt., El Vado Lake State Park; Farmington Chamber of Commerce; Buck and Bonnie Stevens, Fenton Lake State Park; Tom Watts, Biologist, Jicarilla Apache Indian Reservation; Los Alamos Chamber of Commerce; Zandra Beadle, USDA/Forest Service; Mike Maddox, Navajo Lake State Park; Gordon Denipah, Tribal Ranger, San Juan Tribal Lakes; Governor Pete Martinez and Irene Tse-De Folwell, San Ildefonso Pueblo; Jim Snyder, Tribal Ranger, Santa Clara Lakes; Bernie Trujillo, Sandia Lakes; Fidencio Shije, Tribal Ranger, Zia Pueblo; Charles Jordan, Park Manager, Clayton Lake State Park; Levi Garcia, Park Manager, Chicosa Lake State Park; Tina Kemether, Supt., Conchas Lake State

Park; Marshall Garcia, Park Manager, Cimarron Canyon State Park; Richard Grothe, Park Ranger, Cimarron Canyon State Park; Joaquin Valdez, Park Ranger, Rio Costilla Cattle & Livestock Association Park; Las Vegas Chamber of Commerce; George Adelo, Mayor of Pecos; Jerry D. French, Refuge Manager, Maxwell National Wildlife Refuge; Joseph Griego, Coyote and Morphy State Parks; Linda Stoll, Park Supt., Pecos National Historical Park; Ray Casados, Park Manager, Fenton Lake State Park; Red River Chamber of Commerce; Arthur Baca, Park Manager, Santa Rosa State Park; Santa Rosa Chamber of Commerce; Robert Mumford, Park Ranger, United States Army Corps of Engineers, Santa Rosa Lake; Miles A. McInnis, Southeast Area Fisheries Manager, Department of Game and Fish; Belen Chamber of Commerce; Christine Dawson, Park Technician, Bottomless Lakes State Park; Adrean Gonzales, Park Manager, Harry McAdams State Park; Thomas E. Rickels, Park Ranger, Harry McAdams State Park; Joe Christopherson, Park Manager, Manzano State Park; Socorro County Chamber of Commerce; Ernest Jaquez, Southwest Area Fisheries Manager; Charles N. Sundt, District Forest Ranger, Glenwood Ranger District; Michael G. Gardener, District Forest Ranger, Reserve Ranger District; Pamela Dickerson, Special Projects Director, State Parks and Recreation Division.

# FOREWORD

Only someone who has grown up in the vast state of New Mexico and has been associated with the outdoors can fully appreciate the scope of this fine book. Author Sandersier has accomplished what a great many people who have hunted, fished, and camped here for decades have hoped would take place for a long time. There are road maps and atlas notations galore concerning the many lakes of New Mexico, but nothing in the literature can compare with the detailed descriptions of these lakes or the intricate directions needed to get there found in this book.

Years ago the late Robert Pettingell, editor and publisher of an outdoor magazine called *Fly & Shell*—published in Albuquerque in the late 1940s—put out a series of fishing maps for the state. While they were well done and sold state-wide, they were not in the same class as this excellent publication.

In 1989 The University of New Mexico Press published an excellent book by Ti Piper entitled *Fishing in New Mexico*. Piper, a premiere fisherman himself, did a marvelous job describing the many rivers and lakes in the state in which there was fishing, but that book is aimed solely at fishermen—as good as it is. Andy Sandersier's Herculean endeavor, which took more than seven years to complete, is the definitive travel book on the lakes of the nation's fifth largest state. What makes this book so fascinating to me—who moved to New Mexico in 1930 as a small boy—is that the author has discovered and painstakingly described lakes I did not know existed! It is even more surprising since I was once public relations director for the New Mexico Department of Game and Fish and traveled over most of the state continuously.

Those of you reading this book who are new to the state or who have been here some time but have never explored the lakes, should take a few moments to view this publication. New Mexico has lakes hidden far up in high mountains that were known only to our Indians, early trappers and field men of the Game Department, Forest Service, and Fish and Wildlife Service. They are covered with snow half the year and are only free of ice for a few months in the summer.

There are natural and man-made lakes in the foothills of half a dozen mountain ranges that have been seen by only a few people: ranchers, Indians, and backpackers. In addition, the state's vast desert regions are pock-marked by small, remote lakes—reachable only by dirt roads. There are lakes so small they are really only ponds—or a series of ponds—made by beaver damming up streams. They are known only to ranchers and a few federal and state trappers. There are lakes on many of the state's Indian reservations and pueblos that are so remote that—until only recently—they were known only to the Indians themselves. This not-withstanding, there is hardly a lake, pond, impoundment, or ranch tank that has not been ferreted out by this dedicated writer and revealed in this book.

I have known Andy Sandersier for more than thirty years, and though I knew him as a serious, honest, hard-working professional, I had no idea he would be as dedicated to a long-range project of this magnitude as he has been. Believe me, *The Lakes of New Mexico: A Guide to Recreation* is a must for the library of any serious fisherman, hiker, backpacker or just plain tourist seeking to view the many beautiful lakes of this lovely land.

Jack Samson
Former Editor-In-Chief
*Field and Stream*

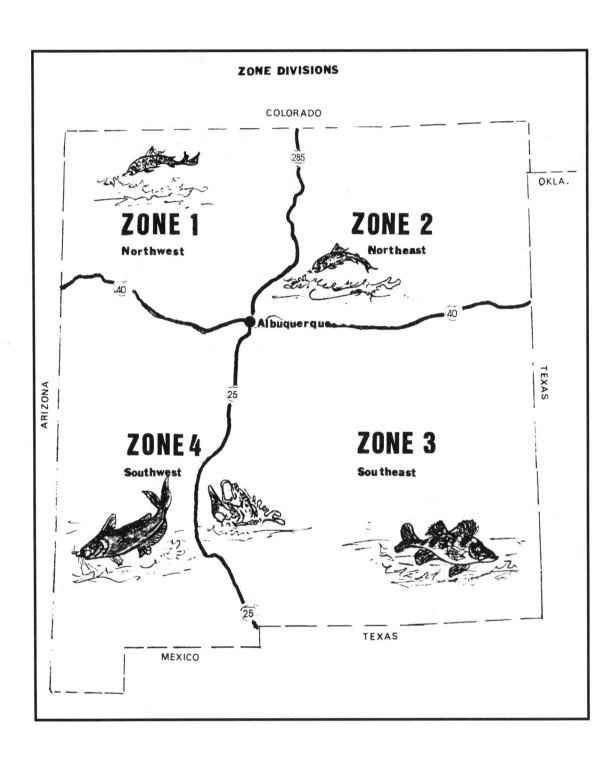

ZONE DIVISIONS

# INTRODUCTION

In the months of planning this book and during the personal visits to each area included in the project, I was determined to keep this guide simple and straightforward and not let non-essential facts clutter and defeat its intent to be a guide; a simple, concise book containing information and directions for the traveler. Now and again I allowed some history of interest to seep into the narrative, but I've tried diligently to let brevity be my guide.

The primary purpose of this book is three-fold:

1. To provide a rapid method for the user to pinpoint the location of a lake and its vicinity
2. To show its proximity to New Mexico's largest and most populated city, Albuquerque, and its approximate distance from a few major cities bordering the state
3. To acquaint the reader with the particular area's facilities and privileges

It is for the family. Where difficult access to a lake is encountered, it is noted in the indices so that sudden surprises to the frail or less adventurous can be avoided. I have sectioned the state into four zones (see Zone Divisions map on page x). An overview map of each Zone and a list of the lakes located in that Zone precede each section of this guide.

An index lists the lakes alphabetically for quick referral to each one's proper Zone, page references, and accessibility from its nearest town or village. In certain instances, some lakes border different Zones but are close to each other. In such cases all these lakes are listed together. This affords the user of this guide an instant awareness of a lake's proximity to that vicinity.

With the stream angler in mind (although this book is not intended to be a treatise on fishing), I've included some streams and tributaries worthy of note, which flow either upstream or downstream from the lake. It should also be mentioned here that most trout lakes are stocked with catchable trout unless otherwise noted in the lake descriptions or in the tables that follow.

I hope you will enjoy many excursions and adventures in this beautiful Land of Enchantment as you follow this guide.

A.S.

# ZONE 1

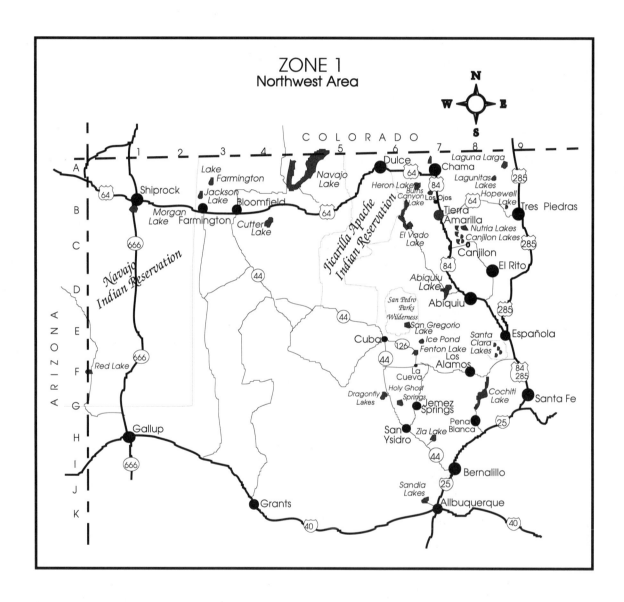

# ZONE 1

AREA NORTH OF I-40 TO THE COLORADO BORDER AND WEST OF I-25 AND
U.S. 285 TO THE ARIZONA BORDER

## Table of Distances (to vicinity)

| VICINITY (lake access from nearest town) | Map Key | Albuquerque | Farmington | Las Cruces | Clayton | Hobbs |
|---|---|---|---|---|---|---|
| **Albuquerque** | K7 | --- | 182 | 223 | 273 | 315 |

Tingley Beach Lake, p.6 (SW Albuquerque Zone 4)
Sandia Lakes, p. 8
Isleta Lakes, p. 10 (S.E. Albuquerque, Zone 3)

| | | | | | | |
|---|---|---|---|---|---|---|
| **San Ysidro** | H6 | 41 | 141 | 264 | 314 | 356 |

Zia Lake, p. 14
Holy Ghost Springs, p. 16
Dragon Fly Lakes, p. 18

| | | | | | | |
|---|---|---|---|---|---|---|
| **Jemez Springs** | G7 | 59 | 159 | 282 | 332 | 374 |

Fenton Lake, p. 22
Ice Pond, p. 24

| | | | | | | |
|---|---|---|---|---|---|---|
| **Cuba** | F6 | 80 | 90 | 303 | 354 | 396 |

San Gregorio Lake, p. 28

| | | | | | | |
|---|---|---|---|---|---|---|
| **Peña Blanca** | H8 | 40 | 191 | 263 | 243 | 355 |

Cochiti Lake, p. 32

| | | | | | | |
|---|---|---|---|---|---|---|
| **Los Alamos** | F8 | 93 | 193 | 316 | 228 | 342 |

Los Alamos Dam, p. 36

| | | | | | | |
|---|---|---|---|---|---|---|
| **Española** | E9 | 84 | 174 | 307 | 209 | 333 |

Santa Cruz Lakes, p. 40
Santa Clara Lakes, p. 42
San Ildefonso Lakes, p. 44
Nambe Falls Lake, p. 46
San Juan Tribal Lakes, p. 48

| | | | | | | |
|---|---|---|---|---|---|---|
| **Abiquiu** | E8 | 106 | 152 | 329 | 231 | 353 |

Abiquiu, p. 52

| | | | | | | |
|---|---|---|---|---|---|---|
| **Canjilon** | C8 | 131 | 143 | 354 | 287 | 380 |

Canjilon Lakes, p. 56
Nutrias Lakes (Trout Lakes), p. 58

| | | | | | | |
|---|---|---|---|---|---|---|
| **Tierra Amarilla** | B7 | 150 | 124 | 373 | 268 | 399 |

El Vado Lake, p. 62
Heron Lake, p. 64

## Table of Distances (to vicinity)

| VICINITY (lake access from nearest town) | Map Key | Albuquerque | Farmington | Las Cruces | Clayton | Hobbs |
|---|---|---|---|---|---|---|
| **Los Ojos** | B7 | 152 | 122 | 375 | 270 | 401 |

Burns Canyon Lake, p. 68

| | | | | | | |
|---|---|---|---|---|---|---|
| **Tres Piedras** | B9 | 132 | 172 | 355 | 191 | 384 |

Hopewell Lake, p. 72
Lagunitas Lakes, p. 70
Laguna Larga, p. 70

| | | | | | | |
|---|---|---|---|---|---|---|
| **\*Dulce** (Jicarilla Apache Reservation Lakes) | A6 | 176 | 88 | 409 | 288 | 409 |

*Dulce Lake, p. 74,78
*La Jara Lake, p. 77,78
*Mundo Lake, p. 79
*Stone Lake, p. 79
*Embom Lake, p.79
*Hayden Lake, p.79

Note: Asterisks denote tribal lakes on Jicarilla Apache Indian reservation.

| | | | | | | |
|---|---|---|---|---|---|---|
| **Bloomfield** | B3 | 169 | 13 | 392 | 389 | 484 |

Navajo Lake, p. 82

| | | | | | | |
|---|---|---|---|---|---|---|
| **Farmington** | B3 | 182 | --- | 405 | 376 | 497 |

Farmington Lake, p. 86
Jackson Lake, p. 88

| | | | | | | |
|---|---|---|---|---|---|---|
| **\*Shiprock** (Navajo Reservation Lakes) | B1 | 215 | 33 | 438 | 343 | 539 |

*Morgan Lake, p. 94
*Asaayi Lake, p. 94
*Red Lake, p. 95
*Todacheene Lake, p. 95
*Berland Lake, p. 96
*Aspen Lake, p. 96
*Whiskey Lake, p. 96
*Chuska Lake, p. 96
*Cutter Lake, p. 96
*Horse Lake, p. 80
*Stinking Lake (Burford Lake), p. 80

**Note: Asterisks denote Navajo Tribal lakes.**

# In the Vicinity of Albuquerque

## *Albuquerque*

*There are three lakes in the vicinity of Albuquerque: TINGLEY BEACH LAKE (in Southwest Albuquerque Zone 4), SANDIA LAKES (just outside the city limits), ISLETA LAKES (just outside the city limits, located in Zone 3).*

Albuquerque is New Mexico's largest city, containing approximately one-third of the state's population. It was founded in 1706 by New Mexico Governor Francisco Cuervo y Valdes. It began as a small Spanish settlement of the Rio Abajo, or lower river district, with its traditional plaza and a church surrounded by adobe houses. The original church, San Felipe de Neri, is still in use today. It is the oldest church in Albuquerque and has continuously served the community without interruption since 1706. It was originally founded and served by the Franciscan friars. This parish church has been served successively by the secular clergy of Durango, Mexico (1817), the Jesuit fathers and brothers (1868), and since 1966 has been administered by the secular clergy of the Archdiocese of Santa Fe.

Visitors from all over the country stop to see its gardens and architecture and to shop in the old adobe shops for Native American art, jewelry, crafts and New Mexican/Spanish cuisine. Old Town, as it is now called, is the oldest of the neighborhoods and one of the most visited attractions. It has maintained its distinct personality, embracing three cultures: Indian, Spanish, and Anglo. To insure its sense of tradition and charm, a zoning ordinance was enacted in the late 1940s to preserve its appearance. Apparent everywhere in Old Town is the Native American influence, especially in the food, crafts, and clothing.

When the Atchison, Topeka, and Santa Fe Railroad arrived in Albuquerque in April of 1880, in order to avoid what is now Old Town they laid the track east of the town and the Rio Grande. A new Albuquerque then grew up around the railroad station, and there emerged two towns: the original one, now called Old Town, and the new town of Albuquerque.

Albuquerque is still a fast-growing city. Its population is approaching half a million. At an elevation of 5,400 feet, it has all the conveniences of any large city. It is a tourist's delight, with its two huge shopping malls—Coronado and Winrock—located close to each other and conveniently situated near modern freeways, a major university (The University of New Mexico), and many fine restaurants and lodgings. Albuquerque has also become famous for its tram lift. It is the longest aerial tram in the country, stretching 2.7 miles along Sandia Peak. The lift rises 3,700 feet from the base of the mountain to the top, where there is a restaurant and ski area. The imposing grandeur of the Sandia Mountains is spectacular from morning to sunset, as light and shadows play across the rock face, cross-hatched with side canyons, changing its moods. They provide the perfect backdrop for the largest city in this Land of Enchantment, New Mexico.

*Tingley Beach*

# TINGLEY BEACH LAKE

Tingley Beach is a twelve-acre lake located in the southwestern part of Albuquerque near the Rio Grande Park Zoo. It is situated on an old meander bend in the former flood plain of the southwest valley. When the Spanish arrived in the 1700s, large groves of cottonwoods covered the valley floor. These cottonwoods provided valuable fuel and building timbers. By the middle of the nineteenth century almost all were cut down. The linear configuration of Tingley Beach is the result of the levee and drain ditch construction. These early efforts were to control floods and improve drainage of potentially arable farmlands adjacent to the Rio Grande. In the early 1930s, the Rio Grande Conservancy drained the marshes and built drains that confined the river to its present channel. In 1933 Mayor Clyde Tingley convinced the Conservancy district to rearrange its levees and divert water into a small lake. The Conservancy Park was then developed as a municipal bathing beach, with Tingley Drive as its access. Its facilities included a slide, boat dock, diving platforms, bath houses, and a snack bar. Due to poor quality of the water, the beach was permanently closed in the late summer of 1952. However, fishing and model boating activities are still enjoyed, and other plans are under way to consider providing snack bar and paddle boat concessions at the lake.

In 1976 and 1977 the lake was dredged, cleaned, deepened, and relined. Many improvements have since been implemented, and today it is one of the most heavily fished areas in the state. Rainbow trout are stocked every other week between November and March. Channel catfish are stocked during the spring each year to supplement fish in the pond during the spring and summer months. These catfish weigh one and a quarter pounds and measure fifteen to sixteen inches long, and the bag limit is two catfish per day. This is called the Big Cat Program. It was started in 1993 by the New Mexico State Game and Fish Department to provide greater fishing opportunities during the spring and summer months. Tingley Beach is one of only seven lakes in New Mexico that are included in the Big Cat Program (see page 344, Warm-Water Fishing Regulations, for the other six).

## Directions from Albuquerque

From East Albuquerque go west on old Highway 66, now Central Avenue (past Broadway it becomes West Central). Go fourteen blocks to Laguna Blvd., turn left or south, then follow road as it veers sharply to the left and becomes Kit Carson Ave. Turn right on Alcalde, then continue to Tingley Drive and Tingley Beach Lake.

If approach is from the west side of Albuquerque, just after crossing the Old Town Bridge, turn right or south on to Tingley Drive. Tingley Drive skirts the entire lake. A complete circuit of the lake measures 1.7 miles.

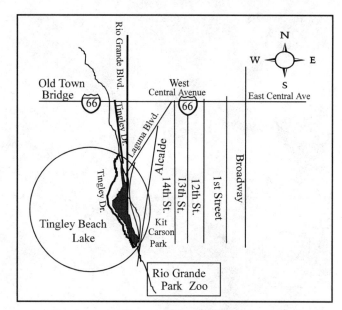

| | |
|---|---|
| **Surface acres:** 12 | **Distance from Albuquerque:** In Albuquerque |
| **Elevation:** 5,000 feet | **Location:** Just west of the Rio Grande Zoo |
| **Max. trailer size & fee:** No camping | **Fish species:** Stocked winter trout, sunfish, |
| **Time limit:** No camping | channel catfish (part of Big Cat Program, |
| **Mailing address:** None | see page 344, Warm-Water Regulations) |
| **Police emergency tel. #:** 911 | **Season:** All year |
| **Medical emergency Tel. #:** 911 | |

## ACTIVITIES AND FACILITIES

| | NO | YES | Proximity to Lake in Miles | | NO | YES | Proximity to Lake in Miles |
|---|---|---|---|---|---|---|---|
| Bait and supplies | X | | | Airplane runway | X | | |
| Boat gas | X | | | Bottled gas | X | | |
| Boat ramp | X | | | Cafe/snack bar | X | | 1/2 |
| Boat rental | X | | | Chemical toilets | | X | |
| Camping | X | | | Drinking water | X | | |
| Fire pits | X | | | Electrical hook-up | X | | |
| Fire places | X | | | Flush toilets | X | | |
| Firewood | X | | | Grocery store | X | | |
| Fishing | | X | | Handicapped access | X | | |
| Golf | X | | 1/4 | Ice | X | | 1/2 |
| Hiking | X | | | Laundry | X | | |
| Marina | X | | | Lodgings | X | | |
| Picnicking | | X | | Pit toilets | X | | |
| Riding | X | | | Playground | X | | 1/8 |
| Scuba diving | X | | | Restaurant | X | | 1/2 |
| Stables | X | | | Sanitary disposal | X | | |
| Swimming | X | | | Sewer Hook-up | X | | |
| Tables | | X | | Shelters | X | | |
| Telephone | X | | | Shopping | X | | 1 |
| Tennis | X | | | Showers | X | | |
| Tent sites | X | | | Trailer space | X | | |
| Winter sports | X | | | Water hook-up | X | | |

**Special Rules and Regulations**

**Fishing:** State fishing license required

**Catch limit:** Trout, 6 per day; catfish, 2 per day; see Warm-Water Regulations, page 344

**Boating:** No boats or floating devices permitted

**Other:** Dogs must be kept on leash; no alcoholic beverages permitted

*Sandia Lakes*

# SANDIA LAKES

Sandia Lakes and Recreation area is located just half a mile northwest of the Albuquerque city limits, off U.S. Highway 85. It is a forty-acre park located along the Rio Grande. The park is surrounded by a mature cottonwood bosque and is well maintained and operated by the Sandia Pueblo. Sandia Pueblo was one of the Indian pueblos that participated in the Pueblo Revolt of 1680. The uprising was against Spanish domination and religious oppression. In this revolt, the pueblos as far south as Isleta united under the leadership of a San Juan Indian named Juan Popé. It marked the first time a European nation was ever driven from a New World colony, in defeat. After the revolt and victory over Spanish domination, the Sandia Indians moved to higher grounds as a protection against Apache raids. In 1742 they returned and settled permanently at their original home, Sandia Pueblo.

In the 1960s, the lake area was leased to a private individual who developed it into a private sports and fishing lodge. After its deterioration in the 1970s and 1980s, the pueblo resumed control, restored and improved it, then opened its facilities to the public on a fee basis.

There are three lakes in the complex. Two of the lakes are four surface acres each in size, and a third lake, newly constructed, contains approximately eleven surface acres. It is about fifteen feet deep. This larger lake was opened for use in the spring of 1992. All the lakes are well stocked with rainbow trout, channel catfish, and largemouth bass.

Since the lakes are nestled in a cottonwood bosque and located on the Pacific Flypath, they serve as a sanctuary and stopover for ducks, snow geese, sandhill cranes, and pheasants on their winter journey south. Because of its proximity to New Mexico's largest city, Albuquerque, plus its excellent day-use facilities, Sandia Lakes and Recreation Area is becoming one of the most popular and convenient fishing lakes in the Albuquerque district.

## Directions from Albuquerque

Take I-25 north to Exit 234 (Tramway Exit). Go west on Tramway one and a half miles, then north on NM 313 (U.S. 85) one mile to Sandia Lakes and Recreation Area sign. Turn left on a good gravel entrance road to the office for permit and fee payment. (The 4th St. or 2nd St. approach may also be taken.) No state fishing license is required.

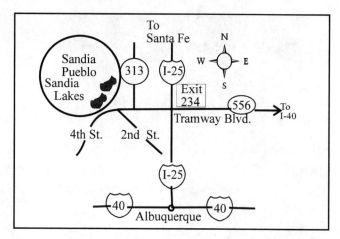

| | |
|---|---|
| **Surface acres:** 20 | **Distance from Albuquerque:** 1 mile |
| **Elevation:** 5,021 feet | **Location:** 1 mile northwest of city limits (15 min. |
| **Max. trailer size & fee:** No overnight | from downtown Albuquerque) |
| **Time limit:** No overnight | **Fish species:** Stocked rainbow trout, catfish, and |
| **Medical emergency tel. #:** At office | largemouth bass |
| **Police emergency tel. #:** At office | **Season:** Year round, sunrise to sunset |

## ACTIVITIES AND FACILITIES

| | NO | YES | Proximity to Lake in Miles | | NO | YES | Proximity to Lake in Miles |
|---|---|---|---|---|---|---|---|
| Bait and supplies | | X | | Airplane runway | X | | |
| Boat gas | X | | | Bottled gas | X | | |
| Boat ramp | X | | | Café/snack bar | | X | |
| Boat rental | X | | | Chemical toilets | | X | |
| Camping | X | | | Drinking water | | X | |
| Fire pits | | X | | Electrical hook-up | X | | |
| Fire places | X | | | Flush toilets | X | | |
| Firewood | X | | | Grocery store | X | | |
| Fishing | | X | | Handicapped access | | X | |
| Golf | X | | | Ice | | X | |
| Hiking | | X | | Laundry | X | | |
| Marina | X | | | Lodgings | X | | |
| Picnicking | | X | | Pit toilets | X | | |
| Riding | X | | | Playground | | X | |
| Scuba diving | X | | | Restaurant | X | | |
| Stables | X | | | Sanitary disposal | X | | |
| Swimming | X | | | Sewer hook-up | X | | |
| Tables | | X | | Shelters | | X | |
| Telephone | | X | | Shopping | X | | |
| Tennis | X | | | Showers | X | | |
| Tent sites | X | | | Trailer space | X | | |
| Winter sports | X | | | Water hook-up | X | | |

Full facilities in city limits, within one mile of lake.
### Special Rules and Regulations
**Fishing:** Adults, $8.00; children (5-17), $6.00; children under 5 with adult, free; seniors (60+), $6.00
**Special fee:** 2 hours before closing, adults, $4.00; children, $3.00; seniors $3.00 (4 fish catch limit)
**Catch limit:** Adults, 8 fish; children (5-17), 8 fish; seniors (60+) 8 fish
**Boating:** No boats or floating devices permitted
**Other:** Picnicking fee: adults, $2.00; children, $1.00; seniors, $1.00; no camping or overnight stay

*Isleta Lakes*

# ISLETA LAKES

Isleta Lakes and Recreation Area is located thirteen miles southwest of Albuquerque, just beyond the city limits, on the Isleta Indian Reservation. The historic Isleta Indian Pueblo has been located at the same site since before the Spanish conquistador Coronado visited the southwest in 1540. It is southernmost of the nineteen Indian pueblos of New Mexico and is said to have derived its name from the frequent floodings of the Rio Grande that surrounded the village, giving it the appearance of a little island. It is a farming community set in a fertile valley, noted for the excellence of its crops and orchards. The Pueblo itself, with a population of 3,500, is situated three and a half miles southwest of Isleta Lakes, off Highway 47.

The three lakes were constructed in 1970 and dug to a depth of fourteen to sixteen feet. They are fed from sub-surface water and are surrounded by grasslands and wooded bosques (cottonwood groves). Two of the lakes are stocked with rainbow trout, largemouth bass, and channel catfish. According to Carl Lujan, the General Manager of the Isleta Lakes and Recreation Area, the third lake is not stocked but does contain bass and channel catfish.

The lakes offer recreational opportunities for family picnicking, with excellent camping facilities, a playground, and a softball field. There are forty RV sites available adjacent to Sunrise Lake. These are well equipped and maintained facilities with electric and water hook-ups, barbecue pits, and conveniently located sanitary facilities. Also available are 100 sites for "primitive type" camping for tents and campers. Birdwatchers and photographers, too, find Isleta Lakes an enjoyable place to visit, since it is located on the Pacific Flypath. Canadian geese, snow geese, sandhill cranes, and ducks stop over to rest on their flight to the warmer regions of the south.

## Directions from Albuquerque

Take I-25 south to Exit 215. Follow exit to Isleta road marker. This puts you on NM 47. Proceed on NM 47 for about a mile to the Isleta cut-off and Isleta Lakes direction sign. Go one mile to the lakes, on a good road. Stop at the first building and parking area for permit and fee payment. No state fishing license is required to fish Isleta Lakes. An Isleta Tribal permit is required.

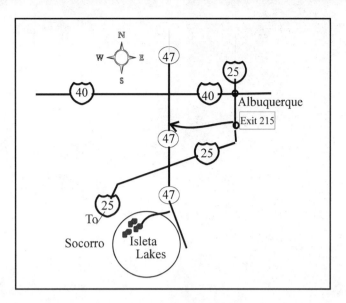

| | |
|---|---|
| **Surface acres:** 28 | **Distance from Albuquerque:** 13 miles |
| **Elevation:** 5,000 feet | **Location:** On the Isleta Indian Reservation; |
| **Max. trailer size:** 40 feet | 13 miles southwest of Albuquerque and the Big I |
| **Time limit:** 14 days | **Fish species:** Rainbow trout, catfish, and bass |
| **Mailing address:** Box 383, Isleta, N.M. 87022 | **Season:** All year |
| (505) 834-7359 | **Camping:** All year |
| **Medical emergency tel. #:** At office | **Police emergency tel. #:** At office |

## ACTIVITIES AND FACILITIES

| | NO | YES | Proximity to Lake in Miles | | NO | YES | Proximity to Lake in Miles |
|---|---|---|---|---|---|---|---|
| Bait and supplies | | X | | Airplane runway | X | | |
| Boat gas | X | | | Bottled gas | X | | |
| Boat ramp | X | | | Café/snack bar | | X | |
| Boat rental | X | | | Chemical toilets | X | | |
| Camping | | X | | Drinking water | | X | |
| Fire pits | | X | | Electrical hook-up | | X | |
| Fire places | | X | | Flush toilets | | X | |
| Firewood | X | | | Grocery store | | X | |
| Fishing | | X | | Handicapped access | | X | |
| Golf | X | | | Ice | | X | |
| Hiking | | X | | Laundry | | X | |
| Marina | X | | | Lodgings | X | | |
| Picnicking | | X | | Pit toilets | | X | |
| Riding | X | | | Playground | | X | |
| Scuba diving | X | | | Restaurant | X | | |
| Stables | X | | | Sanitary disposal | | X | |
| Swimming | X | | | Sewer hook-up | | X | |
| Tables | | X | | Shelters | | X | |
| Telephone | | X | | Shopping | X | | |
| Tennis | X | | | Showers | | X | |
| Tent sites | | X | | Trailer space | | X | |
| Winter sports | X | | | Water hook-up | | X | |

### Special Rules and Regulations

**Fishing fee:** Adults, $5.00; children under 12, $2.50
**Catch limit:** Adults, 8; children under 12, 4; no limit for bluegill or carp
**Boating:** No boats or floating devices permitted

# In the Vicinity of San Ysidro

## *San Ysidro*

*There are three small lakes in the vicinity of San Ysidro, all on Indian Reservations and operated by the pueblos: Zia Lake (on the Zia Pueblo), Holy Ghost Springs (Jemez Pueblo), Dragon Fly Lakes (Jemez Pueblo)*

San Ysidro was one of the early Spanish communities established in New Mexico. It is a small village of about two hundred people. It is located at the southern edge of the Jemez Mountains on NM 44 at an elevation of 5,460 feet above sea level. Like so many of the early communities, the residents and their properties are located close to, and along, the main highways, with restaurants, gas stations, and other services conveniently accessible for the traveler.

San Ysidro was an important crossroads to northwestern and north central New Mexico. It was on the trail linking Santa Fe and Albuquerque with Cabezon and Chaco Canyon. It was also on the supply route for Fort Wingate and Fort Defiance. Later, a buckboard drawn by mules and known as the Star Line Transportation Company, connected Santa Fe with Prescott, Arizona, with a main stopover in San Ysidro.

Surveys show that on average more than 4,000 cars daily travel on Highway 44 south of San Ysidro. Many recreational activities can be reached from San Ysidro to the west as well as to the north and east. Along with fishing, hunting, cross-country skiing and camping, the many archaeological sites, mineral springs, and religious festivals attract thousands of visitors and tourists annually. The Feast Day of its patron saint, San Ysidro Labrador, has been celebrated every year since 1786, when the King of Spain granted the land to the village. The patron saint, San Ysidro, is the protector of the farmers and called on for his blessing of spring plantings and protection from drought. He is one of the most popular saints among Spanish American worshippers.

Zia Lake is seventeen miles northwest of Bernalillo and five miles southeast of San Ysidro, off NM 44, on the Zia Reservation. Holy Ghost Springs is located eighteen miles northwest of San Ysidro, off NM 44; Dragon Fly is five miles farther, off NM 44.

*Zia Lake*

# ZIA LAKE

Zia Lake is a thirty-acre lake on the Zia Reservation located on the north side of the Jemez River, two and a half miles west of the pueblo, lying at an elevation of 5,450 feet. The reservation lies on the upper Sonoran Life Zone with its characteristic vegetation of native grasses, juniper, cactus, and sagebrush, while piñon, ponderosa pine and Douglas fir thrive in the higher elevations. The lake, stocked with rainbow trout and catfish, is open year round for fishing and picnicking. It is a well maintained and patrolled recreation area, sheltered in a scenic, serene setting. The public is welcome to use the facilities, but no picture taking is permitted.

It is approximately thirty-five miles from Albuquerque and about sixty miles southwest of Santa Fe. Archaeological findings trace the people of Zia as direct descendants of the Anasazi Civilization. The present site of Zia was settled about A.D. 1250, and it has been occupied continuously to the present time. It is one of the nineteen pueblos within New Mexico. The first Spanish expedition to arrive in the Jemez Valley in 1541 found five villages associated with Zia Pueblo. One of the five villages had eight plazas and a population of over 5,000. By 1690, as a direct result of Spain's rule, the population declined to fewer than three hundred. The trend of a decreasing population was reversed in the 1920s, and today the population is well over seven hundred.

On the reservation is a Cultural Center that exhibits local arts and crafts, a convenience store, and a laundromat. Just five miles west of the reservation, in San Ysidro, are service stations, grocery stores, and fast food restaurants. Other conveniences, accommodations, and restaurants are located seventeen miles east, in Bernalillo.

## Directions from Albuquerque

Take I-25 north to Bernalillo. Take the off-ramp west on NM 44 and go seventeen miles to Zia Reservation. Stop at the Tribal Office for permit and fee payment.

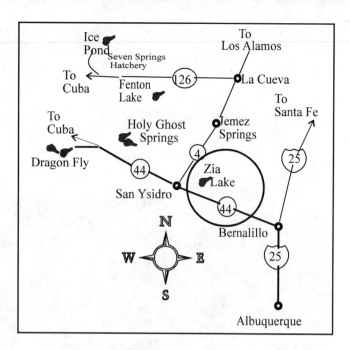

| | | |
|---|---|---|
| **Surface acres:** 30 | **Distance from Albuquerque:** 35 miles | |
| **Elevation:** 5,450 feet | **Location:** 17 miles west of Bernalillo; 5 miles east | |
| **Max. trailer size:** No camping or trailers | of San Ysidro | |
| **Mailing address:** Pueblo of Zia, Gen. Delivery, | **Fish species:** Catfish, rainbow trout, perch, | |
| San Ysidro, NM 87053 (505) 867-3304 | bluegill, and bass | |
| **Police emergency tel. #:** At Tribal Office | **Season:** 1 April-30 November, Open sunrise to sunset | |
| **Medical emergency tel. #:** At Tribal Office | **Fee:** Pay at Tribal Office (See Rules below) | |

## ACTIVITIES AND FACILITIES

| | NO | YES | Proximity to Lake in Miles | | NO | YES | Proximity to Lake in Miles |
|---|---|---|---|---|---|---|---|
| Bait and supplies | | X | | Airplane runway | X | | 30 |
| Boat gas | X | | | Bottled gas | X | | |
| Boat ramp | X | | | Café/snack bar | X | | 5 |
| Boat rental | X | | | Chemical toilets | X | | |
| Camping | X | | 10 | Drinking water | X | | |
| Fire pits | | X | | Electrical hook-up | X | | |
| Fire places | X | | | Flush toilets | X | | |
| Firewood | X | | | Grocery store | | X | |
| Fishing | | X | | Handicapped access | X | | |
| Golf | X | | 16 | Ice | X | | 5 |
| Hiking | X | | | Laundry | | X | |
| Marina | X | | | Lodgings | X | | 17 |
| Picnicking | | X | | Pit toilets | | X | |
| Riding | X | | | Playground | X | | |
| Scuba diving | X | | | Restaurant | X | | |
| Stables | X | | | Sanitary disposal | X | | |
| Swimming | X | | | Sewer hook-up | X | | |
| Tables | | X | | Shelters | | X | |
| Telephone | | X | | Shopping | X | | |
| Tennis | X | | | Showers | X | | |
| Tent sites | X | | | Trailer space | X | | |
| Winter sports | X | | | Water hook-up | X | | |

Stores and services in San Ysidro and in Bernalillo.
**Special Rules and Regulations**
   **Fishing fees:** Adults, $4.00; children under 12, $2.00
   **Catch limit:** Adults, 8; children, 4; no bass less than 10 inches
   **Boating:** Row boats or canoes only; no motors; fee for your own boat, $5.00
   **Other:** No picture taking or alcoholic beverages permitted

*Holy Ghost Springs*

# HOLY GHOST SPRINGS

Holy Ghost Springs is located 18.7 miles northwest of San Ysidro, and a mile off NM 44. The access to the three one-acre lakes that comprise this delightful recreation area is via a good gravel road. The complex is owned and managed by the Jemez Pueblo and contains shelters with tables. Construction is under way to equip the area with camping facilities that will include electric and water hook-ups. The estimated completion date is spring of 1995. The lakes are stocked with rainbow trout, catfish, and bass. The lakes are open to public use on weekends, but after the construction project is complete, plans for daily use are being considered.

Visible from the lakes is Cabezon Peak, about fifteen miles off NM 44. Cabezon Peak is a volcanic stem that towers about 2,000 feet from the Rio Puerco Valley floor and is part of the Ojo del Espiritu Santa ("spring of the Holy Ghost") Land Grant. The Ojo del Espiritu Santo Land Grant was one of the largest land grants in New Mexico. The grant was awarded to the Luis Maria Baca family in the 1700s by the Spanish government, but Indian raids forced the Baca family from the land. About a hundred years later in a land claim settlement, the United States Government purchased the land from the Baca family, then turned it over to the Jemez Indians as part of the land settlement.

The name, Holy Ghost Springs, came from an oft-told tale that in the early days of the settlement, a man standing guard after dinner, saw what appeared to be a spiralling mist rising from a nearby canyon. Rushing into camp he shouted "El Espiritu Santo! El Espiritu Santo!" The aroused camp tracked down the spirals and found a spring, which they named for the apparition. These are the springs that feed the Holy Ghost Springs.

## Directions from Albuquerque

Take I-25 north to Bernalillo. Turn west on the Farmington/Cuba exit. Proceed on NM 44, past the town of San Ysidro and go eighteen miles to the Holy Ghost Springs sign. Turn right through entrance gate and drive on dirt road about one mile to lakes. Fee and regulations are posted at lakes and a tribal warden is on duty to collect fee.

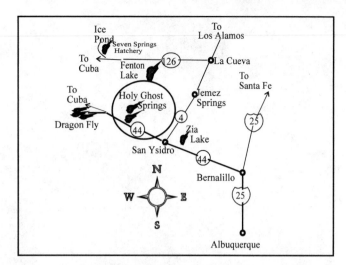

| | |
|---|---|
| **Surface acres:** 3 lakes, total about 6 acres | **Distance from Albuquerque:** 57 miles |
| **Elevation:** About 6,000 feet | **Location:** 18 miles west of SanYsidro |
| **\*\*Max. trailer size :** No camping, but plans are under way to provide overnight camping by 1995; table below reflects facilities as of 1994. | **Fish species:** Rainbow trout, bass, and catfish<br>**Hours:** 10 A.M. to sundown, Saturdays and Sundays only, until further notice |
| **Mailing address:** Pueblo of Jemez, Walatowa Recreation Area, NM 87024 (505) 834-7238 | **Season:** May-October<br>**Police emergency tel. #:** In San Ysidro, 18 miles |

## ACTIVITIES AND FACILITIES

| | NO | YES | Proximity to Lake in Miles | | NO | YES | Proximity to Lake in Miles |
|---|---|---|---|---|---|---|---|
| **Bait and supplies** | X | | | **Airplane runway** | X | | |
| **Boat gas** | X | | | **Bottled Gas** | X | | |
| **Boat ramp** | X | | | **Cafe/snack bar** | | X | |
| **Boat rental** | X | | | **Chemical toilets** | | X | |
| **Camping** | X | | | **Drinking water** | X | | * |
| **Fire pits** | | X | | **Electrical hook-up** | X | | * |
| **Fire places** | | X | | **Flush toilets** | X | | |
| **Firewood** | X | | | **Grocery store** | X | | 18 |
| **Fishing** | | X | | **Handicapped access** | | X | |
| **Golf** | X | | | **Ice** | X | | 18 |
| **Hiking** | X | | | **Laundry** | X | | |
| **Marina** | X | | | **Lodgings** | X | | |
| **Picnicking** | | X | | **Pit toilets** | | X | |
| **Riding** | X | | | **Playground** | X | | * |
| **Scuba diving** | X | | | **Restaurant** | X | | 18 |
| **Stables** | X | | | **Trash cans** | | X | * |
| **Swimming** | X | | | **Sewer hook-up** | X | | * |
| **Tables** | | X | | **Shelters** | | X | |
| **Telephone** | X | | | **Shopping** | X | | |
| **Tennis** | X | | | **Showers** | X | | |
| **Tent sites** | X | | * | **Trailer space** | X | | * |
| **Winter sports** | X | | | **Water hook-up** | X | | * |

*Food, stores and fuel in San Ysidro, 18 mi.
**Special Rules and Regulations**
   **Fishing:** Jemez tribal permit
   **Fees:** Adults 18-59, $8.00; children 5-17 and seniors 60+, $6.00
   **Special evening rates (5:00 P.M.-8:00 P.M.):** Children and seniors, $3.00; adults, $4.00
   **Catch limit:** For adults, children and seniors, 8; Evenings: adults, children, and seniors, 6
   **Boating:** No boating or floating devices permitted
   **Other:** Overnight camping area with hook-ups was planned for late 1994 or 1995; for information on progress, call (505) 834-7238

# DRAGON FLY

Dragon Fly is one of the three recreation areas owned and managed by the Jemez Pueblo. It is one mile off NM 44, five miles northwest of the Holy Ghost Springs Recreation Area and twenty-three miles northwest of San Ysidro. Like Holy Ghost Springs, it is spring-fed and stocked with rainbow trout, catfish, and bass. It contains two lakes with shelters, fireplaces, and pit toilets. Plans are under way to install camping facilities and extend hours of usage. The complex is open weekends from 10 A.M. to sundown.

## Directions from Albuquerque

Take I-25 north to Bernalillo. Turn west on Farmington/Cuba cut-off on NM 44. Proceed on NM 44 past San Ysidro twenty-three and a half miles. Look for Dragon Fly sign on left side of road. Turn in to entrance and drive about one mile on dirt road to lakes. A warden is on duty to collect fee. (The entrance gate is five miles northwest of the Holy Ghost Springs entrance gate.)

No NM state fishing license is required at Dragon Fly, but a tribal permit is required.

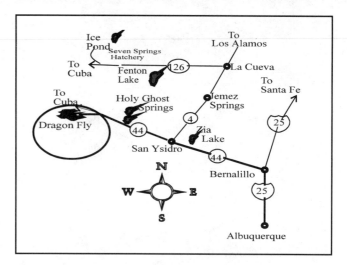

| | | |
|---|---|---|
| **Surface acres:** 2 lakes, about 1 acre each | | **Distance from Albuquerque:** 62 miles |
| **Elevation:** 6,000 feet | | **Location:** 24 miles west of San Ysidro |
| **Max. trailer size & fee:** No camping, but | | **Fish species:** Rainbow trout, and catfish |
| plans underway to provide overnight camping | | **Hours:** 10 A.M.-8 P.M. Sat. and Sun. only |
| by 1995; table below reflects facilities in 1994. | | **Season:** May-October |
| **Mailing address:** Pueblo of Jemez, Walatowa Rec- | | **Medical emergency tel. #:** In San Ysidro |
| reation Area, NM 87024 (505) 834-7238 | | **Police emergency tel. #:** In San Ysidro |

## ACTIVITIES AND FACILITIES

| | NO | YES | Proximity to Lake in Miles | | NO | YES | Proximity to Lake in Miles |
|---|---|---|---|---|---|---|---|
| Bait and supplies | | X | | Airplane runway | X | | |
| Boat gas | X | | | Bottled gas | X | | |
| Boat ramp | X | | | Café/snack bar | | X | |
| Boat rental | X | | | Chemical toilets | X | | |
| Camping | X | | | Drinking water | *X | | |
| Fire pits | | | | Electrical hook-up | *X | | |
| Fire places | | X | | Flush toilets | X | | |
| Firewood | | X | | Grocery store | X | | *24 |
| Fishing | | X | | Handicapped access | | X | |
| Golf | X | | | Ice | X | | |
| Hiking | | X | | Laundry | X | | |
| Marina | X | | | Lodgings | X | | |
| Picnicking | | X | | Pit toilets | | X | |
| Riding | X | | | Playground | X | | |
| Scuba diving | X | | | Restaurant | X | | *24 |
| Stables | X | | | Trash cans | | X | |
| Swimming | X | | | Sewer hook-up | *X | | |
| Tables | | X | | Shelters | | X | |
| Telephone | X | | | Shopping | X | | |
| Tennis | X | | | Showers | X | | |
| Tent sites | | X | | Trailer space | *X | | |
| Winter sports | X | | | Water hook-up | *X | | |

*Restaurants, stores, and services in San Ysidro, 24 miles.
**Special Rules and Regulations**
   **Fishing:** Tribal permit only
   **Fees:** Adults (18-59), $8.00; children (5-18) and seniors 60+, $6.00
   **Special evening rates (5 P.M.-8 P.M.):** Children and seniors, $3.00; adults, $4.00
   **Catch limit:** 8 fish per day; evenings (5 P.M.-8 P.M.), 4 fish
   **Other:** Overnight camping and hook-ups were planned for late 1994 or 1995; check with pueblo, 834-7235, for progress and days of lake usage

# In the Vicinity of Jemez Springs

### *Jemez Springs*

*There are two lakes in the vicinity of Jemez Springs: Fenton Lake and the Ice Pond*

Jemez Springs is located in the Jemez Mountains within an hour's drive from Albuquerque. It is an incorporated village, with a population of about 475, lying at an elevation of 6,400 feet. To get there from Albuquerque, take I-25 north to Exit #242, for Farmington. Turn west on to NM 44 to San Ysidro, then right on NM 4, and go eighteen miles to Jemez Springs. The drive to Jemez Springs from San Ysidro is pleasant and colorful as you pass through a series of communities, small farms, and pasture lands. Along the way, one is momentarily surprised by a half-mile stretch of red rock formations, softly sculptured by the wind. Their ever-changing shades of red—from brilliant to muted purple—is hypnotic, as sun and shadows play across their surface. A short distance farther north is Jemez Pueblo, which has been occupied continuously since 1696. Visitors are welcome in the pueblo, but permission to take pictures is required. During the warm season of spring and summer, roadside stands are set up by the Indians from the pueblo to sell their tamales, fried bread, and round loaves of bread baked in outdoor ovens. Continuing north through Jemez Canyon (*el cañon de San Diego*), many travelers pause at about four-fifths of a mile north of mile post 11 to see if they can spot the outline of a robed figure near the top of the cliff wall on the west side of the highway. The tale is told that long ago, while a band of besieged Indians were fighting off assailants from the top of the bluff, their patron saint, St. James, suddenly appeared. Their assailants made a fast retreat when they spotted the apparition. The image, said to be that of St. James, appears to be etched on the wall of the cliff below.

Jemez Springs is a vibrant community with a modern fire station, a police station, a community library, an arts and crafts club, and a medical clinic staffed by two Nurse Practitioners, and an emergency Medical Technician. Also available in emergencies is the Jemez Valley Medical System Inc., started in 1974 to develop teams of paramedics to cover the Jemez area.

Well worth visiting is the Via Coeli Monastery at the northern end of the village, famous for its beautiful gardens, art treasures, and its use as a rest retreat for Catholic priests. The Jemez State Monument, just across the road from the monastery, marks the ruins of the old Jemez Mission, built around 1617 under the direction of Spanish priests. It is one of the best examples of seventeenth-century Spanish mission architecture in this part of the country. A mile up the road is Soda Dam, an interesting stop for travelers. It is a natural formation of calcium carbonate deposits that formed a dam. The water in this area is highly mineralized; hot mineral springs are prevalent throughout the Jemez Mountains, and it is the deposits from these thermal springs that precipitate out to form the dam.

In and around Jemez Springs there are many recreational opportunities, which offer excellent camping and picnic facilities, hunting, fishing, cross-country skiing and hiking. Just four miles north of Soda Dam, off NM 4, are five camping or picnic grounds, all within a two-mile stretch. Continue on for eighteen miles, and you will reach Fenton Lake. Four miles farther, off NM 126, you will reach Seven Springs Fish Hatchery and the Ice Pond.

*Fenton Lake*

# FENTON LAKE

Fenton Lake is a twenty-five-to-thirty-acre lake, seventy-five miles northwest of Albuquerque, on the site of the old Fenton Homestead. It lies north of Jemez Springs, thirty miles southwest of Los Alamos and sixty-five miles southwest of Santa Fe. Fenton Lake is surrounded by the colorful peaks of the Jemez Mountains, heavily wooded in ponderosa pine. Both the lake and stream fishing around Fenton Lake makes Fenton one of the most popular fishing lakes and camping retreats in New Mexico. The lake and surrounding streams contain natural brown trout and are stocked with rainbow trout by the New Mexico Department of Game and Fish. Fenton Lake is well maintained and operated by the New Mexico State Parks and Recreation Division.

In the 1940s it was established as a Wildlife Refuge for the protection of waterfowl. In 1956 the lake was formed by damming the Cebolla River. Many deer, turkeys and elks inhabit the area. It is also a natural habitat for muskrats, tassel-eared squirrels, beavers, red-winged blackbirds, swallows, ducks, and coots. Tall wildflowers border the roads: white and yellow primroses, bee balm, scarlet penstemon, yarrow, bush poppies. Green grass is everywhere, complementing in color, the lichen-spotted boulders on the mountainside.

More than thirty camping and picnic sites are scattered along a two-and-a-quarter-mile stretch southwest of the lake, with conveniently placed chemical toilets, serviced by state park personnel. The Fenton Lake area is a favorite winter sports place for ice fishing, cross-country skiing, and dog sled racing. A well-maintained cross-country ski trail, which serves as a hiking trail in summer, is next to the main camping area just past the dam. There is a special fishing access for the handicapped. There is a boat ramp, but only hand-powered boats are permitted on the lake.

## Directions from Albuquerque

Go north on I-25 and go sixteen miles to Bernalillo, then take Exit 142, west on NM 44 twenty-four miles to San Ysidro. Turn north onto NM 4. Drive through Jemez Springs, then eight miles to La Cueva. Turn west onto NM 126 and go eight miles to Fenton Lake. (The paving on NM 126 ends one mile east of arrival at the lake. During heavy rains or after thawing snow, four-wheel-drive or high-clearance vehicles are advised.)

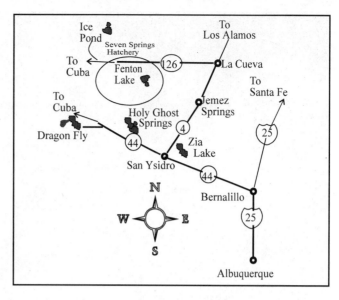

| | | |
|---|---|---|
| **Surface acres:** 25-30 | **Distance from Albuquerque:** 75 miles |
| **Elevation:** 7,680 feet (2377 meters) | **Location:** 21 miles northwest of Jemez Springs |
| **Max. trailer size:** 40 ft | |
| **Time limit:** 14 days | **Fish species:** Stocked with catchable rainbow |
| **Mailing address:** P.O. Box 555, Jemez | trout, and populated with natural brown trout |
| Springs, NM 87025 (505) 829-3630 | **Season:** 1 April-31 March |
| **Medical emergency tel. #:** 829-3591 | **Camping:** 1 April-30 November |
| **Police emergency tel. #:** 829-3555 | **Fee:** Posted at entrance |

## ACTIVITIES AND FACILITIES

| | NO | YES | Proximity to Lake in Miles | | NO | YES | Proximity to Lake in Miles |
|---|---|---|---|---|---|---|---|
| Bait and supplies | X | | 8 | Airplane runway | X | | |
| Boat gas | X | | 8 | Bottled gas | X | | 8 |
| Boat ramp | | X | | Café/snack bar | X | | |
| Boat rental | X | | | Chemical toilets | | X | |
| Camping | | X | | Drinking water | | X | |
| Fire pits | | X | | Electrical hook-up | | X | |
| Fire places | | X | | Flush toilets | | X | |
| Firewood | X | | 8 | Grocery store | X | | 8 |
| Fishing | | X | | Handicapped access | | X | |
| Golf | X | | | Ice | X | | 8 |
| Hiking | | X | | Laundry | X | | 8 |
| Marina | X | | | Lodgings | X | | 8 |
| Picnicking | | X | | Pit toilets | | X | |
| Riding | X | | | Playground | X | | |
| Scuba diving | X | | | Restaurant | X | | 8 |
| Stables | X | | | Sanitary disposal | X | | |
| Swimming | X | | | Sewer hook-up | X | | |
| Tables | | X | | Shelters | X | | |
| Telephone | | X | | Shopping | X | | |
| Tennis | X | | | Showers | X | | |
| Tent sites | | X | | Trailer space | | X | |
| Winter sports | | X | | Water hook-up | X | | |

*Gas, food, tackle, and fishing license in La Cueva, 8 miles.
**Special Rules and Regulations**
   **Fishing:** New Mexico Department of Game and Fish regulations apply; see Fishing Proclamation for other details
   **Bag limit:** 6 per day, see New Mexico Fishing Proclamation or Fishing Regulations, page 343
   **Boating:** Boats restricted to those without motors or sail
   **Other:** No firearms permitted; no swimming allowed; hunting in National Forest only

*The Ice Pond*

# THE ICE POND

The Ice Pond is a small one-and-a-half-acre fishing pond at the Seven Springs State Fish Hatchery, operated by the New Mexico Department of Game and Fish. At the hatchery is a visitors center, open from 7 A.M. to 7 P.M., seven days a week, year round. Here, you will find the only native cutthroat brood stock in the state. No camping or fishing is permitted on the hatchery grounds, but next to the fish brooding area is the Ice Pond, stocked with rainbow trout from the hatchery and populated with native browns. Although the Ice Pond is within sight of the hatchery complex, it bears a quiet sense of remoteness. Grasses, untrimmed and dense, slope to the pond's calm waters, which reflect the sky and forested mountainside of piñon, ponderosa pine, and spruce.

This was a favorite fishing hole for fishers until late 1991 when it was limited to a children's pond. Before the age limit was restricted to children under twelve years of age, it experienced heavy pressure, especially during weekends and holidays.

The Rio Cebolla flows through this area, and the many beaver ponds along the way provide anglers with fishing opportunities. Just a short distance west of the hatchery and the Ice Pond, off NM 126, is a quiet, enchanting picnic and camping area with a few tables, fire pits, and a swift-running stream. There are many other undeveloped camp and picnic sites scattered along the entire length of the Rio Cebolla. The primary access to these camp and picnic sites is via NM 126 and FR 314 via unsurfaced single-lane roads. During wet and inclement weather, four-wheel-drive vehicles or high-clearance pickup trucks are advised.

## Directions from Albuquerque

Follow the same route that you would take to Fenton Lake. Then go past Fenton Lake, three and a half miles to Seven Springs Hatchery. Turn right into Hatchery complex, past the brooding ponds to the Ice Pond.

Primitive campgrounds are located west of the entrance, off NM 126. (To review complete route from Albuquerque, see Fenton Lake directions on page 23.)

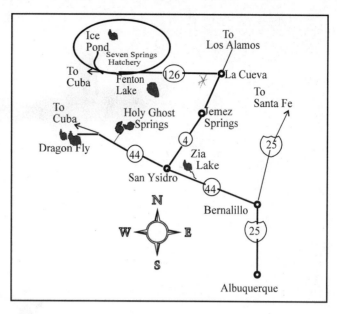

| | |
|---|---|
| **Surface acres:** 1 1/2-Acres | **Distance from Albuquerque:** 79 miles |
| **Elevation:** 8,000 ft. | **Location:** 22 miles northwest of Jemez Springs; |
| **Max. trailer size:** No trailers permitted | 8 miles west of La Cueva |
| **Time limit:** No overnight | **Fish species:** Stocked rainbow trout, natural |
| **Mailing address:** N.M. Dept. of Game and Fish, | brown, and fry |
| Mountain Rt., Jemez Springs, NM 87025 | **Season:** Year round; 8 A.M. to 5 P.M. |
| **Police emergency tel. #:** At hatchery | **Medical emergency tel. #:** 829-3740 |

## ACTIVITIES AND FACILITIES

| | NO | YES | Proximity to Lake in Miles | | NO | YES | Proximity to Lake in Miles |
|---|---|---|---|---|---|---|---|
| Bait and supplies | X | | | Airplane runway | X | | |
| Boat gas | X | | | Bottled gas | X | | |
| Boat ramp | X | | | Café/snack bar | X | | 8 |
| Boat rental | X | | | Chemical toilets | X | | |
| Camping | X | | 1/4 | Drinking water | X | | |
| Fire pits | X | | 1/4 | Electrical hook-up | X | | |
| Fire places | X | | 1/4 | Flush toilets | X | | |
| Firewood | X | | | Grocery store | X | | 8 |
| Fishing | | X | | Handicapped access | | X | |
| Golf | X | | | Ice | X | | 8 |
| Hiking | | X | | Laundry | | | 8 |
| Marina | X | | | Lodgings | X | | 22 |
| Picnicking | | X | | Pit toilets | X | | |
| Riding | X | | | Playground | X | | |
| Scuba diving | X | | | Restaurant | X | | 8 |
| Stables | X | | | Sanitary disposal | X | | |
| Swimming | X | | | Sewer hook-up | X | | |
| Tables | X | | | Shelters | X | | |
| Telephone | | X | | Shopping | X | | |
| Tennis | X | | | Showers | X | | |
| Tent sites | | | 1/4 | Trailer space | X | | 1/4 |
| Winter sports | | X | | Water hook-up | X | | |

*Bait and tackle, gas, food, and lodgings in La Cueva, 8 miles.

**Special Rules and Regulations**
    **Fishing:** Limited to children up to 12
    **Bag limit:** 4 fish
    **Boating:** No boats or floating devices permitted
    **Other: Hours:** 8 A.M. to 5 P.M., no fee, fishing also allowed on Rio Cebolla

# In the Vicinity of Cuba

## *Cuba*

*In the vicinity of Cuba is the San Pedro Parks Wilderness, and within its forty-one thousand acres, framed by a beautiful spruce and pine forest, is one lake: San Gregorio Lake*

Cuba is located fifty-five miles northwest of Bernalillo on NM 44 between Bernalillo and Farmington. It is a trading community for the Navajos, Jicarilla Apaches, and the surrounding farmers, and sheep and cattle ranchers. It is now an important tourist center for campers, sportsmen, and mountain vacationers. The land around Cuba offers many recreational opportunities and has become a favorite place for hunters, fishermen, backpackers and winter sports enthusiasts. About three miles east of Cuba, NM 126 enters the Santa Fe National Forest and the border of the San Pedro Wilderness and Clear Creek Campground, where a forested trail goes half a mile to San Gregorio Lake, cradled at an altitude of 9,400 feet. NM 126 also continues on to the many recreational areas of the Jemez Mountains, including Fenton Lake, the Ice Pond, Seven Springs Fish Hatchery, and Jemez Springs.

Since its first Spanish settlement more than two hundred years ago, the Cuba area has remained the scenically appealing place it is today. In 1769, The San Joaquin del Nacimiento Land Grant permitted settlement of a large parcel of land at the base of the Señorito Mountains, known as the Nacimientos, near the headwaters of the Rio Puerco. (In Spanish, *nacimiento* is the word for birth, or nativity, but it also

means spring or source.) This is possibly the source of the name, *Nacimiento*, referring to the settlement's location at the headwaters of the river. After the post office was established in 1877, the name of the town was changed to Cuba, Spanish for *tank or trough*, which has a similar reference to its location and may also account for the derivation of its name.

The San Joaquin del Nacimiento Land Grant consisted of about thirty-six families, who were all closely related to each other. They comprised prominent names in New Mexico history, like Atencio, Luna, Manzanarez, Martinez, Gonzales, Romero, Lucero, Salazar, Varela, and Cisneros. The town has a wild, stormy history of daily raids by Navajo, Apache, and Ute Indians on the Spanish settlement that farmed in the area. The raiding Indians finally forced the original settlers to move out, and it was not until almost a century later, when a treaty with the Navajos was signed, that the settlers returned. In 1872 after the treaty took effect, a new settlement was established.

There are many services for tourists in Cuba: gas stations, motels, restaurants, grocery stores, fishing and camping supplies, a good medical clinic, a library, a newspaper, and a good school system. Worth seeing is the old Young's Hotel, one of the oldest buildings in Cuba in its original state. Its primitive interior is reminiscent of times long past.

At the southern end of town is a National Forest Service Ranger Station, where visitors wishing to enter the Santa Fe National Forest and the San Pedro Parks Wilderness can obtain entry permits and information.

*San Gregorio Lake*

# SAN GREGORIO LAKE

San Gregorio is one of those delightful surprises that one is likely to come across in the Jemez Mountains. It is a thirty-two-to-forty-acre lake astride the headwaters of Clear Creek, atop the huge San Pedro Mountain Plateau, at an altitude of 9,400 feet. It is nestled in a blue spruce forest, on the slope of Nacimiento Peak, within the 41,000-acre preserve of the San Pedro Parks Wilderness Area. San Gregorio Lake is one of the few lakes in New Mexico, at an altitude of almost 10,000 feet, that can be reached within a half-mile by car. A half-mile hike on a good, well-maintained forested trail leads you to its blue waters and excellent fishing for stocked cutthroat and rainbow trout.

Adjacent to the large parking area at the entrance to the trail that leads to the lake is a large picnic area and campground. Its excellent facilities are maintained by Department of Game and Fish personnel. It is a very popular lake for fishermen,

and the campgrounds are busy on weekdays and on weekends. This man-made wonder was formed by damming Clear Creek. It was constructed in 1958 by the New Mexico Department of Game and Fish, funded through fishing license bond funds and federal aid to fisheries. The Forest Service and the Department of Game and Fish work together to give sportsmen the maximum in hunting and fishing pleasure in this area. San Gregorio Lake can be reached from Fenton Lake on NM 126, but the road is impassable during inclement weather and during winter. The best access is via Cuba on NM 126. A good paved road turns into an improved gravel road for the last three miles to the parking area and campground. There are no stores or concessions at or near the lake. If necessary, picnic supplies or other needs can be purchased in Cuba before entering the San Pedro Parks Wilderness.

## Directions from Albuquerque

Take I-25 to Bernalillo, and turn west on off-ramp to NM 44. Continue on 44 to San Ysidro. At San Ysidro you can continue on NM 44 to Cuba, turn right on NM 126 (at the Fina gas station), and go ten miles to the cut-off of NM 126 and Forest Road 70. Turn left on FR 70, and go three miles. There is a large campground and parking area at the end of the road. Access to the lake from this point is by way of a half-mile hike on a good trail. (This alternate route to San Gregorio Lake by way of Cuba is a better access to the lake than the route through the Ice Pond and the Seven Springs Fish Hatchery. NM 126 from that area is treacheous during bad weather, and four-wheel-drive vehicles are advised.)

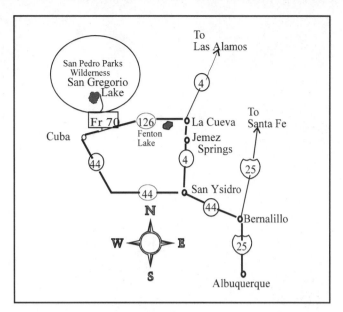

| | |
|---|---|
| **Surface acres:** 32 | **Distance from Albuquerque:** 79 miles |
| **Elevation:** 9,400 feet | **Location:** 14 miles northeast of Cuba in the |
| **Max. trailer size:** 16 feet (In campground 1/2 mi.) | San Pedro Wilderness |
| **Time limit:** 14 days | **Fish species:** Rainbow and cutthroat trout |
| **Mailing address:** None | **Season:** 1 April-31 March, depending on accessibility, |
| **Police emergency tel. #:** None | determined by weather conditions |
| **Medical emergency tel.:** None | |

## ACTIVITIES AND FACILITIES

| | NO | YES | Proximity to Lake in Miles | | NO | YES | Proximity to Lake in Miles |
|---|---|---|---|---|---|---|---|
| Bait and supplies | X | | | Airplane runway | X | | |
| Boat gas | X | | | Bottled gas | X | | |
| Boat ramp | X | | | Café/snack bar | X | | |
| Boat rental | X | | | Chemical toilets | X | | |
| Camping | X | | 1/2 | Drinking water | X | | |
| Fire pits | X | | 1/2 | Electrical hook-up | X | | |
| Fire places | X | | 1/2 | Flush toilets | X | | |
| Firewood | X | | | Grocery store | X | | |
| Fishing | | X | | Handicapped access | X | | |
| Golf | X | | | Ice | X | | |
| Hiking | | X | | Laundry | X | | |
| Marina | X | | | Lodgings | X | | |
| Picnicking | | X | | Pit toilets | X | | 1/2 |
| Riding | X | | | Playground | X | | |
| Scuba diving | X | | | Restaurant | X | | |
| Stables | X | | | Sanitary disposal | X | | |
| Swimming | X | | | Sewer hook-up | X | | |
| Tables | X | | 1/2 | Shelters | X | | |
| Telephone | X | | | Shopping | X | | |
| Tennis | X | | | Showers | X | | |
| Tent sites | X | | 1/2 | Trailer space | X | | 1/2 |
| Winter sports | X | | | Water hook-up | X | | |

*Full facilities available in Cuba (gas, food, and lodgings).
**Special Rules and Regulations**
   **Fishing:** Same rules apply as in state Fishing Proclamation; state fishing license required
   **Bag limit:** 6 fish; 6 in possession
   **Boating:** No motors
   **Other:** No camping at lake; good campground and facilities adjacent to parking area, half a mile from the lake

*The Church of
Nuestra Señora de Guadalupe
Peña Blanca, New Mexico*

# In the Vicinity of Peña Blanca

## Peña Blanca

*In the vicinity of Peña Blanca there is one lake:
COCHITI LAKE*

Peña Blanca is a ranching and farming community eight miles north of I-25, northwest of Albuquerque, and twenty-three miles southwest of Santa Fe. The original land grant was awarded by the King of Spain to Juan Montes Vigil in 1745. Thirteen years later, for a purchase price of 500 pesos, Vigil sold the land to Jose Miguel de la Peña, a descendant of one of the original Mexican colonists who arrived in New Mexico with de Vargas in 1690. In 1770, twelve years after he bought the land from Vigil, Jose Miguel de la Peña established his ranch, known as El Rancho de Jose Miguel de la Peña, later referred to as El Rancho de la Peña, evolving to its present name, Peña Blanca.

Today, Peña Blanca is commonly identified with the politically renowned Montoya family. It is the birthplace of the late Senator Joseph M. Montoya, who rose through local, county, and state offices to the federal office of United States Senator. The drive to, and through, Peña Blanca on NM 22 is a pleasant and scenic cottonwood-lined route. In the center of the village, the old Catholic church of Nuestra Señora de Guadalupe, with its high ceiling and massive adobe walls, was built by the villagers. It was plastered by the townspeople each year to preserve it, but in August of 1985, after a broken water pipe went undetected and leaked for two days, the rear of the church collapsed. After a study was made on repairing the damage, the church council decision was to replace the 108-year-old

structure. The new church was completed and the first mass was celebrated 12 December 1987, on *Our Lady of Guadalupe Feast Day.* The original bells were saved and adorn the tower of the new church.

Just up the highway, past this church and to the left, is another church. It is a very small and very old church of the Penitentes, St. Francis of Assisi. The villagers call it *La Morada ("bruise").* The Penitentes are a conservative Catholic society most active in the late 1800s and early 1900s and still active in some parts of northern New Mexico. The Penitentes expressed their religion and atonement of sin through suffering, by abuse of their bodies by flagellations and mock crucifixions. These extreme rites of penance were condemned by the officials of the Catholic Church, who banned the group's practices. The official condemnation drove the brotherhood underground until 1947, when the Archbishop accepted their practices as part of the Church, with the understanding that the penances would not include deliberate abuse of the body and cause physical harm. Today, most of the ceremonies and simulations of the procession of Christ to Calvary are symbolic. The actual crucifixions of the past are symbolized by the one chosen to represent Jesus being tied to a cross, then raised for a brief display, then taken down. Finally, there is a procession to the chapel or *morada.*

The town of Peña Blanca has a gas station, a small grocery store, a post office, and a bait shop. There are no lodgings available for visitors.

NM 22 continues another three miles to the Cochiti Dam Stilling Basin, then a mile up the road to the Cochiti Pueblo turn-off. It continues a mile farther to the town of Cochiti Lake on the left and the lake entrance on the right.

*Cochiti Lake*

# COCHITI LAKE

Cochiti Lake is approximately seven miles long with twenty-one miles of shoreline and has a maximum depth of eighty-five feet, at permanent pool elevations. The dam is one of the eleven largest earthfill dams in the world, spanning more than five miles across both the Santa Fe River and the Rio Grande drainages. The dam is on Cochiti Indian Pueblo land. It was built and is operated by the Army Corps of Engineers as a flood and sediment control project for the Middle Rio Grande Basin. First-time visitors are shocked when they catch the first sail-spangled glimpse of the lake, as the road approach over a rise, almost without warning except for a sign and caution light warning of *"Lake Ahead!!,"* segues into a steep grade that becomes the launching ramp for the many boat-laden trailers that frequent the lake daily.

On a summer day, the lake is dotted with boats of all sizes and types. Dozens of windsurfers find the winds of Cochiti favorable almost any time of the day. Because of its proximity to New Mexico's largest city, Albuquerque—only about an hour's drive away—Cochiti has become one of the most popular fishing and boating lakes in the state. It is a *"no-wake"* lake, stocked by the New Mexico Department of Game and Fish with rainbow trout. The lake also contains walleye, catfish, bluegill, crappie, and largemouth bass. Though Cochiti Lake is a day-use area with no overnight camping permitted, a full-facility campground is less than a quarter of a mile from the water's edge. Scattered throughout the surrounding canyons are many other camping and picnicking areas.

Adjacent to the lake is the resort town of Cochiti Lake. It is on pueblo land, leased to the town by Cochiti Pueblo. The town has a small shopping center. An eighteen-hole golf course, just two miles away, is well maintained and operated by the pueblo. The attractive and secured marina at the lake is also operated by the pueblo.

## Directions from Albuquerque

Take I-25 north to junction of NM 22. Take Exit 259 west, and go eight miles to and through Peña Blanca. Three miles farther is the Stilling Basin of Cochiti Dam, then two miles farther is the lake entrance on the right, and the village of Cochiti on the left. Distance via Peña Blanca on NM 22 off I-25: fifteen miles.

**(From Santa Fe** take I-25 south to the junction of NM 16. Take NM 16 until it intersects with NM 22. Turn right on 22 to the lake. (Distance from I-25, twelve miles.)

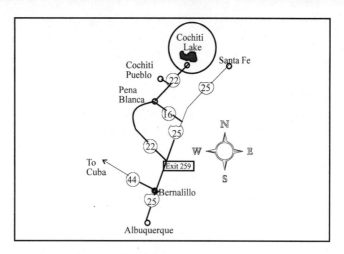

| | |
|---|---|
| **Surface acres:** 1,200 | **Distance from Albuquerque:** 50 miles |
| **Elevation:** 5,500 feet | **Location:** 50 miles northwest of Albuquerque, 40 miles south- |
| **Max. trailer size:** 40 feet | west of Santa Fe, 14 miles from junction of I-25 and NM 22 |
| **Time limit:** 14 days | **Fish species:** Rainbow trout, walleye, catfish, |
| **Mailing address:** Box 1238, Peña Blanca, NM 87041 | bluegill, crappie, largemouth bass, northern pike |
| **Police emergency tel. #:** At Ranger Office | **Season:** All year |
| **Medical emergency tel. #:** At Ranger Office | **Camping:** 11 April–11 October; no fee in winter |

## ACTIVITIES AND FACILITIES

| | NO | YES | Proximity to Lake in Miles | | NO | YES | Proximity to Lake in Miles |
|---|---|---|---|---|---|---|---|
| **Bait and supplies** | | X | 1/4 | **Airplane runway** | X | | |
| **Boat gas** | | X | 1/4 | **Bottled gas** | X | | |
| **Boat ramp** | | X | | **Café/snack bar** | | X | |
| **Boat rental** | | X | | **Chemical toilets** | | X | |
| **Camping** | | X | 1/4 | **Drinking water** | | X | 1/4 |
| **Fire pits** | | X | 1/4 | **Electrical hook-up** | | X | 1/4 |
| **Fire places** | | X | 1/4 | **Flush toilets** | | X | 1/4 |
| **Firewood** | X | | 1/4 | **Grocery store** | | X | 1/4 |
| **Fishing** | | X | | **Handicapped access** | | X | |
| **Golf** | X | | 2 | **Ice** | | X | 1/4 |
| **Hiking** | | X | | **Laundry** | X | | 1/4 |
| **Marina** | | X | | **Lodgings** | X | | |
| **Picnicking** | | X | | **Pit toilets** | | X | |
| **Riding** | X | | | **Playground** | | X | 1/4 |
| **Scuba diving** | | X | | **Restaurant** | X | | |
| **Stables** | X | | | **Sanitary disposal** | | X | 1/4 |
| **Swimming** | | X | | **Sewer hook-up** | X | | |
| **Tables** | | X | 1/4 | **Shelters** | | X | 1/4 |
| **Telephone** | | X | | **Shopping** | X | | |
| **Tennis** | | X | 1/4 | **Showers** | X | | |
| **Tent sites** | | X | 1/4 | **Trailer space** | | X | 1/4 |
| **Winter sports** | X | | | **Water hook-up** | | X | 1/4 |

*No camping at lake. Camping, store, food, 1/4 mile from lake, as noted above

**Special Rules and Regulations**

**Fishing:** All New Mexico state regulations apply, Fishing Proclamations available from all vendors

**Catch limit:** 6 fish; Fishing Proclamation available from fishing license vendors throughout state

**Boating:** A "no-wake lake"; state boating laws and Corps of Engineers Regulations apply; copies of Regulations are available at the Corps Information Center or any State Park Office

**Other:** Swimming, snorkeling, and scuba diving are permitted at your own risk, except where prohibited by signs or buoys

# In the Vicinity of Los Alamos

## *Los Alamos*

*Tucked away in a remote part of town, in an obscure and beautiful setting of tall spruce and ponderosa pines there is a charming and trout populated reservoir: Los Alamos Reservoir*

Never did Ashley Pond, a Detroit businessman, dream when he founded the Los Alamos Ranch School for Boys in 1918 that twenty-five years later it would become the birthplace of the world's first atom bomb. The Los Alamos Ranch School for Boys was hidden on the eastern slope of the Jemez Mountains, on the Pajarito Plateau, 7,300 feet above sea level, where boys studied the classics and hiked, fished, and rode horseback in the surrounding area.

In the closing months of 1942, during World War II, the United States conducted an extensive search for a location to establish a laboratory research site to produce an atomic bomb. Because of its highly secret nature, several requirements had to be met regarding its location. Isolation and an ideal year-round climate were the first priorities along with such factors as roads, railroads, ease of access to testing grounds and available housing. The Los Alamos Ranch School met all requisites, so in 1942 it was chosen by the Manhattan District, United States Corps of Engineers. The school's buildings were converted into laboratories, creating the secret "Atomic City," whose perimeters were guarded around the clock by men on horseback, uniformed patrols, and manned watchtowers.

After the mission was completed, and with the resulting defeat of Japan, politicians and scientists realized that the work that began during the war must be harnessed for peace-time use. Thus, the research installation expanded its interests and responsibilities and now devotes a large part of its efforts to the peaceful application of space exploration and atomic energy.

Today, Los Alamos is an incorporated city-county with two main residential and commercial areas: Los Alamos and White Rock. It is a community of 20,000 people. There are deep canyons, spanned by bridges, and well-maintained roads, landscaped streets, and modern buildings and homes with well-kept lawns. Stands of ponderosa, piñon pine, and spruce blanket the mountains and mesas bordering the town. There are roads that snake through some of the most beautiful parts of the Santa Fe National Forest.

There is something for everyone in Los Alamos County. There are slopes for the skier— whether beginner, intermediate, or expert. Cross-country skiing is there too, practically at one's doorstep. Excellent camping, fishing, hunting, picnicking, and hiking are available. Some of these recreational opportunities and their facilities are within the city limits. The recreation facilities include an eighteen-hole championship golf course, tennis courts, and swimming pools. There are many horseback riding trails, playing fields for soccer, baseball, and softball for all ages. Many civic, cultural, and arts activities are also available. There are several shopping areas, and a wide variety of goods and services are available, all close to hotel accommodations and restaurants within town.

Since 1957, Los Alamos has been an "open city." There is no restriction on entering or leaving town by the several access roads. Entry to technical areas is controlled, however, and some of the laboratory buildings are not open to the public.

*Los Alamos Lake*

# LOS ALAMOS RESERVOIR

*Seclusion, wrapped in pine and gentle silence*

Los Alamos Reservoir is a charming two-acre lake, hidden in a gorgeous canyon surrounded by a densely wooded pine forest. It is a quiet and remote lake, within the city limits yet seemingly miles from anywhere. It is a well-populated lake, stocked with rainbow trout by the Department of Game and Fish, and is well worth the trip to enjoy not only the beauty of the setting but the drive through this scenic part of the Santa Fe National Forest.

The access road to the lake is primitive and rough—rock-strewn and deeply rutted—but the final destination after a mile-and-a-half drive is rewarding. Due to its primitive access, passenger cars are not recommended during inclement weather. There are no facilities for camping or picnicking, but there are two chemical toilets at the lake, and a pleasant day can be spent here with a carry-in picnic basket. It is a carry-in and carry-out area, with no garbage service. However, camping and picnicking facilities are just a short distance away and scattered throughout this most beautiful part of the Santa Fe National Forest.

In its isolated beauty, it is hard to believe that you are just minutes away from the busy town of Los Alamos. This proximity to Los Alamos makes the visit conveniently close to other recreational opportunities that are available in the town and the surrounding forest.

## Directions from Albuquerque

Take I-25 to Santa Fe. On the approach to Santa Fe take Exit 282 and connect with 84/285 toward Española. Watch for the junction of NM 502. Turn west on NM 502 to Los Alamos, eighteen miles west. In Los Alamos, take Trinity Drive. After passing the fire station (on right side of the street) go about one block beyond the first light signal and turn right on the Loop Road. Follow this road as it winds down the hill and watch for an open, two section, white-pipe gate at the bottom of the hill on the opposite side of the road. Go through this gate. This road is a primitive, rough, rock-strewn, bumpy road, not recommended for passenger cars during inclement weather, but well worth the one-and-a-half-mile distance to this charming little lake.

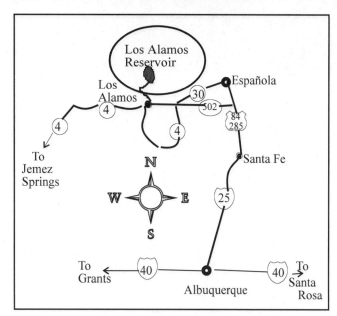

| | | |
|---|---|---|
| **Surface acres:** 2 | | **Distance from Albuquerque:** 95 miles |
| **Elevation:** 7,000 feet | | **Location:** West side of Los Alamos, off the Loop Road |
| **Max. trailer size & fee:** No trailer parking | | |
| **Time limit:** No camping area | | **Fish species:** Stocked rainbow trout |
| **Mailing address:** None | | **Season:** All year, weather permitting |
| **Police emergency tel. #:** In Town | | **Medical emergency tel. #:** In town |

## ACTIVITIES AND FACILITIES

| | NO | YES | Proximity to Lake in Miles | | NO | YES | Proximity to Lake in Miles |
|---|---|---|---|---|---|---|---|
| Bait and supplies | X | | | Airplane runway | X | | |
| Boat gas | X | | | Bottled gas | X | | |
| Boat ramp | X | | | Café/snack bar | X | | |
| Boat rental | X | | | Chemical toilets | | X | |
| Camping | X | | | Drinking water | X | | |
| Fire pits | X | | | Electrical hook-up | X | | |
| Fire places | X | | | Flush toilets | X | | |
| Firewood | X | | | Grocery store | X | | |
| Fishing | | X | | Handicapped access | X | | |
| Golf | X | | | Ice | X | | |
| Hiking | | X | | Laundry | X | | |
| Marina | X | | | Lodgings | X | | |
| Picnicking | X | | | Pit toilets | X | | |
| Riding | X | | | Playground | X | | |
| Scuba diving | X | | | Restaurant | X | | |
| Stables | X | | | Sanitary disposal | X | | |
| Swimming | X | | | Sewer hook-up | X | | |
| Tables | X | | | Shelters | X | | |
| Telephone | X | | | Shopping | X | | |
| Tennis | X | | | Showers | X | | |
| Tent sites | X | | | Trailer space | X | | |
| Winter sports | X | | | Water hook-up | X | | |

*Full facilities in Los Alamos.

**Special Rules and Regulations**

    **Fishing:** New Mexico Department of Game and Fish Regulations apply; see Fishing Proclamation page 343

    **Catch limit:** See Fishing Proclamation, or see page 343

    **Boating:** Not permitted

*Camel Rock*
*Carved and eroded by wind and rain,*
*Camel Rock is one of the most*
*photographed sites in New Mexico*
*(Fifteen miles south of Española off*
*U.S. 285)*

# In the Vicinity
# of Española

## *Española*

*There are five lakes in the vicinity of Española; since Española borders both Zone 1 to the west, and Zone 2 to the east, all five lakes in its vicinity are listed together so that one may be aware of the lakes' proximity while in this area. With the exception of Santa Cruz Lake, the following lakes are operated and maintained by the pueblos: Santa Cruz Lake (Zone 2, east of Española), Santa Clara Lakes (Zone 1, west of Española), San Ildefonso Lake (Zone 1), San Juan Tribal Lakes (Zone 1), Nambe Falls Lake (Zone 2).*

Española is located in the beautiful Española Valley, at an elevation of 5,595 feet. It has a population of 12,200. It is eighty-six miles north of Albuquerque and twenty-four miles northwest of Santa Fe. Its central location, between the 12,000-feet altitude of the Jemez Mountains, to the west, and the 13,000-feet Truchas Peaks, to the east, provides easy access to the spectacular and diverse recreation, historical areas, and archaeological sites of northern New Mexico.

Española was established in the 1880s as a stop on the Denver and Rio Grande Railroad. The town has grown to be the commercial center of the Española Valley. It once was the home of dinosaurs, whose remains are still being found near Abiquiu, just a few miles to the north. In 1855, Congress appropriated $30,000 to import camels to the southwest territory. Almost one hundred camels were imported to the area, but the experiment was unsuccessful due to the lack of interest and

acceptance of the strange animals' peculiarities. The tale is told that a weary camel stopped to rest next to the Tesuque Pueblo and, too tired to move on, turned to stone. It now stands on the west side of U.S. 285, sculpted by the wind and rain, and is one of the most photographed sites in New Mexico. More than a thousand years ago, the ancient Anasazi Indians settled in this valley. Their ruins stand today in the cliff dwellings at Puye, just ten miles west of Española, on NM 602. Their descendants still live in Santa Clara Pueblo, the location of the Puye dwellings, and in the other Indian pueblos scattered throughout the Española Valley.

In 1598, the Spanish, led by Juan de Oñate, settled near San Juan Pueblo. Five miles north of Española, across the river from San Juan Pueblo, a cross marks the site of the pueblo that the Spanish took over and established as the first capital of New Mexico. After the coming of the railroad in the 1880s, the three cultures of Indian, Spanish, and American blended. Their evidence and influences still pervade the Española Valley in the languages spoken, in the religion, and in the food. In Española, there are grocery stores, medical facilities, motels, and restaurants. Within an hour's drive from Española are perhaps the best hunting, fishing, boating and skiing in New Mexico. A mile east of Española is Santa Cruz, the second oldest villa in New Mexico, founded in 1695. The Holy Ghost Church in Santa Cruz was one of the most important churches in New Mexico. Its many examples of religious art of the eighteenth century are worth visiting.

*Santa Cruz Lake*

# SANTA CRUZ LAKE

Santa Cruz Lake is a man-made lake operated by the Bureau of Land Management. It provides much of the water for the valley farms. It is located in the foothills of the Sangre de Cristo Mountains, ten miles east of Española, thirteen miles east of Pojoaque, and about four miles south of Chimayó. Santa Cruz Lake is a popular lake for anglers, picnickers, campers, and boaters. There are forty-two picnic shelters with fire places. Also provided are camp sites, toilets, a boat launching ramp, and drinking water.

The town of Santa Cruz is located about one mile east of Espanola on NM 76. It was founded in 1695 and is the oldest villa in New Mexico. The Holy Cross Church in Santa Cruz is worth a visit. It was one of the most important churches in New Mexico during the eighteenth century and was the center of religious and social life at that time. The church attracts many visitors to see its display of early religious art. Also worth a visit is the quaint, picturesque, and famous village of Chimayó. Visitors are attracted all year long to the Santuario de Chimayó Church. It is one of the finest examples of Spanish colonial church architecture and church art. On Good Friday, as many as 30,000 people walk from outlying towns and villages on a religious pilgrimage to the Santuario. Many tales have been told of miraculous cures owed to the dirt found in the back anteroom behind the church altar. The church was built from 1816 to 1819 by Bernardo Abeyta as a family chapel, and the Santuario has become a legendary shrine.

## Directions from Albuquerque

Take I-25 to Pojoaque. At junction of 285/503 turn east on NM 503. Follow signs to Santa Cruz. Continue through the small town of Condiyo. Turn left on NM 596 to the lake. The lake is approximately three miles from Condiyo on a good, but winding, steep descending road to the lake.

NOTE: Chimayo is about three miles northwest of Condiyo, reached by NM 520.

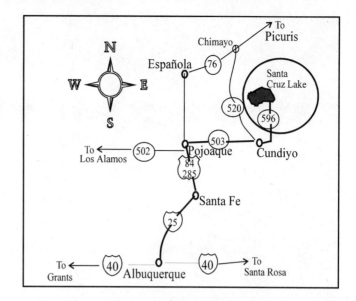

| | | |
|---|---|---|
| Surface acres: 120 | Distance from Albuquerque: 94 miles |
| Elevation: 7,000 feet | Location: 10 miles east of Española; 13 miles |
| Trailer fee: none | northeast of Pojoaque |
| Time limit: 14 days | Fish species: Rainbow trout, and wild brown trout |
| Mailing address: 224 Cruz Alto Rt., Taos 67571 | Season: All year, weather permitting; no ice fishing |
| (505) 758-8851 | |

## ACTIVITIES AND FACILITIES

| | NO | YES | Proximity to Lake in Miles | | NO | YES | Proximity to Lake in Miles |
|---|---|---|---|---|---|---|---|
| Bait and supplies | | X | *10 | Airplane runway | X | | |
| Boat gas | X | | | Bottled gas | X | | *10 |
| Boat ramp | | X | | Café/snack bar | X | | *10 |
| Boat rental | | X | | Chemical toilets | | X | |
| Camping | | X | | Drinking water | | X | |
| Fire pits | | X | | Electrical hook-up | X | | |
| Fire places | | X | | Flush toilets | X | | |
| Firewood | X | | | Grocery store | X | | *10 |
| Fishing | | X | | Handicapped access | | X | |
| Golf | X | | | Ice | X | | * |
| Hiking | | X | | Laundry | X | | * |
| Marina | X | | | Lodgings | X | | *10 |
| Picnicking | | X | | Pit toilets | | X | |
| Riding | X | | | Playground | X | | |
| Scuba diving | X | | | Restaurant | X | | * |
| Stables | X | | | Sanitary disposal | X | | |
| Swimming | X | | | Sewer hook-up | X | | |
| Tables | | X | | Shelters | | X | |
| Telephone | | X | | Shopping | X | | * |
| Tennis | X | | *4 | Showers | X | | |
| Tent sites | | X | | Trailer space | | X | |
| Winter sports | X | | | Water hook-up | X | | |

*Full facilities for food and lodgings are in Pojoaque and Española

**Special Rules and Regulations**

**Fishing:** State fishing license required; regulations apply; see Fishing Proclamation

**Catch limit:** 6 trout; for other information see Regulations on page 343

**Boating:** "No-wake" lake

**Other:** No ice fishing allowed

*Santa Clara Lakes*

# SANTA CLARA LAKES

A trout's jump ripples the placid waters of Nana Ka Pond, one of the four lakes in the Santa Clara Canyon, owned and operated by the Santa Clara Pueblo. The canyon is considered one of the most beautiful canyons in New Mexico. Along its twenty-mile length, from the eastern rim of the Valle Grande to Santa Clara Pueblo at the edge of the Rio Grande, are stands of cottonwoods, willows, box elders, grassy meadows, and the Santa Clara Creek. The Indian-owned portion of Santa Clara Creek extends approximately nineteen miles due west of Santa Clara Pueblo.

The entrance to the canyon is at the Santa Clara Pueblo by way of a paved road off NM 30, two miles south of Española. The developed portion of the canyon begins approximately eleven miles west of the pueblo. Here, a Ranger stationed at the entrance to the lakes issues permits and collects fees for camping, picnicking, and fishing.

Thick growths of ponderosa, piñon pine, and spruce border the winding, improved dirt road leading to the forested upper half of the canyon. Twenty-six beautiful grassy picnic areas and campgrounds dot a five-mile stretch along a creek that abounds with beaver ponds, which attract flocks of visitors on weekends. The first two lakes lie at an elevation of 6,700 feet. The third lake, Nana Ka, is nestled in a beautiful woodland setting. Heavily wooded Tsichoma Lake, at an elevation of 8,000 feet is the uppermost, and last of the four lakes. In the Tewa language, *tsichoma* means *"obsidian covered mountain."* (According to Tribal Ranger, Jim Singer, Santa Clara Canyon is a crater formed by a volcano. Its activity, millions of years ago, accounts for the obsidian in the area.) No camping is permitted at Tsichoma Lake. It is for fishing and picnicking only.

## Directions from Albuquerque

Ttake I-25 through Santa Fe. Two miles south of Española take a paved cut-off road (NM 30). Turn southwest on NM 30 to the NM 5 cut-off. Turn west on NM 5. (You will pass by the Puye cliff dwellings.) Follow direction signs to the lakes' entrance. A tribal ranger will collect camping, picnicking, sightseeing and fishing fees at the entrance. From the entrance gate to the uppermost lake is about a ten-minute drive.

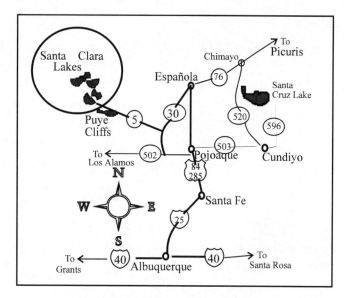

| | |
|---|---|
| **Surface acres:** 4 lakes, total 120 acres | **Distance from Albuquerque:** 82 miles |
| **Elevation:** Lake #4 (Nana Ka) 8,600 feet | **Location:** On NM 5; 4 miles southwest of |
| **Trailer fee:** $10.00 per night | Española |
| **Time limit:** 24 hours or until noon next day | **Fish species:** Rainbow trout |
| **Mailing address:** Santa Clara Pueblo, | **Season:** 1 April-31 October, 7 A.M.-8 P.M |
| P.O. Box 580, Española, NM 87532 | |
| (505) 753-7326 | |

## ACTIVITIES AND FACILITIES

| | NO | YES | Proximity to Lake in Miles | | NO | YES | Proximity to Lake in Miles |
|---|---|---|---|---|---|---|---|
| Bait and supplies | X | | *4 | Airplane runway | X | | |
| Boat gas | X | | | Bottled gas | X | | *4 |
| Boat ramp | X | | | Café/snack bar | X | | |
| Boat rental | X | | | Chemical toilets | | X | |
| Camping | | X | | Drinking water | | X | |
| Fire pits | | X | | Electrical hook-up | X | | |
| Fire places | | X | | Flush toilets | X | | |
| Firewood | | X | | Grocery store | X | | *4 |
| Fishing | | X | | Handicapped access | X | | |
| Golf | X | | *4 | Ice | X | | *4 |
| Hiking | | X | | Laundry | X | | *4 |
| Marina | X | | | Lodgings | X | | *4 |
| Picnicking | | X | | Pit toilets | X | | |
| Riding | X | | | Playground | X | | |
| Scuba diving | X | | | Restaurant | X | | *4 |
| Stables | X | | | Trash cans | | X | |
| Swimming | X | | | Sewer hook-up | X | | |
| Tables | | X | | Shelters | | X | |
| Telephone | | X | By Radio | Shopping | X | | |
| Tennis | X | | *4 | Showers | X | | *4 |
| Tent sites | | X | | Trailer space | | X | |
| Winter sports | X | | | Water hook-up | X | | |

*Stores, gas, food, and lodgings in Española, 4 miles west.

**Special Rules and Regulations**

    **Fishing:** Adults, $8.00; children $4.00; hours: 6 A.M. to sunset; no minnows for bait

    **Catch limit:** Adults, 8 fish; children, 4 fish

    **Boating:** No boating; no swimming or wading

    **Sightseeing:** $8.00 Price subject to change; check with Tribal Office for other information

*San Ildefonso Lake*

# SAN ILDEFONSO LAKE

San Ildefonso Lake is a four-and-a-half-acre fishing lake located about half a mile west of the plaza in San Ildefonso Pueblo. The lake is stocked twice a month with rainbow trout and catfish by the Mescalero National Fish Hatchery. Fishing is permitted in the lake area only. There is no overnight camping permitted, but picnic shelters, grills, water, and restroom facilities are available. Daily permits can be obtained at the lake or at the Ranger's Office within the pueblo.

San Ildefonso Pueblo is a charming pueblo with the Rio Grande to the south and the Jemez Mountains to the west. Its ancestors originally came from the ancient Anasazi community of Mesa Verde in southern Colorado. Later, around A.D. 1300, they moved to the Rio Grande Valley. North of the pueblo lies Black Mesa, where in 1694 the villagers joined forces with neighboring pueblos, and courageously defended themselves against the Spanish reconquest.

San Ildefonso was once the home of the famous potter, Maria Martinez. Using the coil method and local clay, she developed the matte-finish black-on-black pottery that brought national fame to the pueblo. Her work is highly valued and is displayed in museums throughout the country. This pottery-making process is described at the San Ildefonso Pueblo Museum, where other exhibits of arts and crafts and the history of the pueblo are exhibited.

The several gift shops, selling pueblo pottery, jewelry, books, paintings, baskets, kachinas, and beadwork, are open to the public from 10 A.M. to 5 P.M. daily.

## Directions from Albuquerque

Go north on I-25 to Santa Fe. Continue north on U.S. 84/285. Drive twenty-six miles to Pojoaque and junction of NM 502. Turn left on NM 502 to San Ildefonso Pueblo. The Pueblo entrance is about six miles farther to the right.

Stop at the Ranger's office for permit and fee collection. The lake is half a mile west of the Plaza.

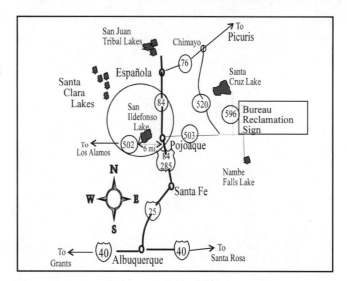

| | |
|---|---|
| **Surface acres**: 4 1/2 | **Distance from Albuquerque**: 91 miles |
| **Elevation**: 6,800 feet | **Location**: 32 miles northwest of Santa Fe in |
| **Max. trailer size & fee**: No camping | San Ildefonso Pueblo |
| **Time limit**: No overnight stays | **Fish species**: Rainbow trout and catfish, |
| **Mailing address**: Pueblo of San Ildefonso, | stocked bi-monthly by the Mescalero National |
| Rt. 5, Box 315A, Santa Fe, NM  87501; | Fish Hatchery |
| (505) 455-2273 | **Season**: March-October |

## ACTIVITIES AND FACILITIES

| | NO | YES | Proximity to Lake in Miles | | NO | YES | Proximity to Lake in Miles |
|---|---|---|---|---|---|---|---|
| **Bait and supplies** | X | | | **Airplane runway** | X | | |
| **Boat gas** | X | | | **Bottled gas** | X | | |
| **Boat ramp** | X | | | **Café/snack bar** | X | | |
| **Boat rental** | X | | | **Chemical toilets** | X | | |
| **Camping** | X | | | **Drinking water** | | X | |
| **Fire pits** | | X | | **Electrical hook-up** | X | | |
| **Fire places** | | X | | **Flush toilets** | X | | * |
| **Firewood** | X | | | **Grocery store** | X | | * |
| **Fishing** | | X | | **Handicapped access** | | X | |
| **Golf** | X | | | **Ice** | X | | * |
| **Hiking** | X | | | **Laundry** | X | | |
| **Marina** | X | | | **Lodgings** | X | | |
| **Picnicking** | | X | | **Pit toilets** | | X | |
| **Riding** | X | | | **Playground** | X | | |
| **Scuba diving** | X | | | **Restaurant** | X | | * |
| **Stables** | X | | | **Sanitary disposal** | X | | |
| **Swimming** | X | | | **Sewer hook-up** | X | | |
| **Tables** | | X | | **Shelters** | | X | |
| **Telephone** | X | | 1/2 | **Shopping** | X | | |
| **Tennis** | X | | | **Showers** | X | | |
| **Tent Sites** | X | | | **Trailer space** | X | | |
| **Winter sports** | X | | | **Water hook-up** | X | | |

*Indian Arts and Crafts, shops, and supplies sold near pueblo plaza.

**Special Rules and Regulations**

   **Fishing fee:** Adults, $5.00; children (6-12), $3.00; children  (under 6), free; senior citizens, $3.00
   **Catch limit:** Adults, 8 fish ; children (6-12), 8 fish ; children  (under 6), 4 fish
   **Boating:** No boats or floating devices permitted; fishing in lake only; no camping

*Nambe Falls Lake*

# NAMBE FALLS LAKE

Nambe Falls Lake is a picturesque sixty-acre lake, owned and operated by Nambe Pueblo. The lake is located in the mountains above the pueblo. Nambe Pueblo has been inhabited for seven hundred years. Of the two hundred original pre-colonial buildings in the Pueblo, only a couple of dozen still remain. Contemporary buildings have replaced them near the site of the original pueblo. Approximately four hundred people live on the 19,000-acre pueblo, which is nestled on the slopes of the Sangre de Cristo mountain range, only twenty miles from Santa Fe. The pueblo is noted for its micaceous pottery, woven belts, and beadwork. Several gift shops and artist's studios within the pueblo attract visitors daily. One of the studios operates a training center, where students and the general public can learn the creative process of carving and other arts and crafts.

Outdoor recreational activities draw hundreds of visitors to the lake and recreational site lying amid rolling piñon pine-dotted hills. A fifteen-minute hike from the main picnic area, visitors can view the Nambe Falls. It is a spectacular scenic wonder, of a waterfall making a three-tiered plunge into Nambe Reservoir above the falls. The dam was built by the Bureau of Reclamation. Here, visitors can camp and picnic.

The park is well equipped with grills, electric hook-ups, water, toilets, and picnic tables. The lake is stocked with rainbow and cutthroat trout. Motorless boats, limited to a maximum length of fourteen feet, are permitted, and there is a handicapped access at the boat ramp. Camping and picnicking at the lake shore are permitted, but no fires are allowed on the shoreline.

## Directions from Albuquerque

Take I-25. Go fifteen miles north of Santa Fe on U.S. 84/285 to the junction of NM 503, and turn right. Drive three miles east on NM 503 to the Bureau of Reclamation sign for Nambe Falls Road. Drive another mile to gate to Nambe Falls Lake. Fees are collected at the gate. Continue about five miles farther to the lake. Access is by way of a good road, but the last quarter-mile is dirt and intermittently rough and partly paved.

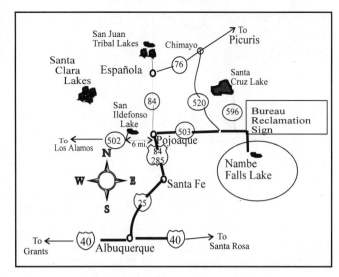

| | |
|---|---|
| **Surface acres:** 60 | **Distance from Albuquerque:** 93 miles |
| **Elevation:** 6,600 feet | **Location:** In the mountains above the Pueblo. |
| **Max. trailer size & fee:** Any size,  $7.00 per night | 34 miles northeast of Santa Fe |
| **Time limit:** 5 days | **Fish species:** Rainbow trout, stocked by Mescalero National Fish Hatchery |
| **Mailing address:** Nambe Pueblo Government Office, | |
| Rt. 1, Box 117 BB, Santa Fe, NM 87501 | **Season:** 10 March-28 September |
| (505) 455-2304 | **Hours:** summer, 6 A.M.-9 P.M.; fall, 7 A.M.-7 P.M. |

## ACTIVITIES AND FACILITIES

| | NO | YES | Proximity to Lake in Miles | | NO | YES | Proximity to Lake in Miles |
|---|---|---|---|---|---|---|---|
| **Bait and supplies** | | X | | **Airplane runway** | X | | |
| **Boat gas** | X | | | **Bottled gas** | X | | |
| **Boat ramp** | | X | | **Café/snack bar** | | X | |
| **Boat rental** | X | | | **Chemical toilets** | | X | |
| **Camping** | | X | | **Drinking water** | | X | |
| **Fire pits** | | X | | **Electrical hook-up** | | X | |
| **Fire places** | | X | | **Flush toilets** | X | | |
| **Firewood** | X | | | **Grocery store** | | X | |
| **Fishing** | | X | | **Handicapped access** | | X | ramp |
| **Golf** | X | | | **Ice** | | X | |
| **Hiking** | | X | | **Laundry** | X | | |
| **Marina** | X | | | **Lodgings** | X | | |
| **Picnicking** | | X | | **Pit toilets** | | X | |
| **Riding** | X | | | **Playground** | | X | |
| **Scuba diving** | X | | | **Restaurant** | X | | |
| **Stables** | X | | | **Trash Cans** | | X | |
| **Swimming** | X | | | **Sewer hook-up** | X | | |
| **Tables** | | X | | **Shelters** | | X | |
| **Telephone** | | X | | **Shopping** | X | | |
| **Tennis** | X | | | **Showers** | X | | |
| **Tent sites** | | X | | **Trailer space** | | X | |
| **Winter sports** | X | | | **Water hook-up** | | X | |

Gift shops and some food supplies available in Pueblo.
Small store at gate for bait, tackle, ice, picnic supplies and cold drinks.

**Special Rules and Regulations**

**Fishing:** Adults, $5.00 per day; senior citizens and children, $3.00 per day; season, adults, $40.00; children $30.00; senior citizens, $35.00

**Catch limit:** Adults and seniors, 10 fish; children 7 catches

**Boating:** Non-motorized boats, 14 feet and under, $7.00 per day.

**Other:** Camping, $7.00 for first night; each extra night, $4.00; picnicking; $5.00 per car (over 4, $2.00 per person)

**Sightseeing:** $2.00 per person (all fees subject to change)

*San Juan Tribal Lakes*

# SAN JUAN TRIBAL LAKES

There are three lakes on the San Juan Tribal Lakes and Recreation Complex. Its location is at the northern end of Española within its city limits (about a quarter-mile north of Red's Steak House). Its proximity to the many facilities in Española catering to tourists makes it a convenient place for fishing and picnicking for individuals, families, special groups, or company gatherings. Shelters and tables are located throughout the area with conveniently placed pit toilets, tables, grills, and a children's playground. The lakes are stocked with rainbow trout, catfish, and largemouth bass, eight to twelve inches in size.

With a population of about 1,200, it is the largest of the Tewa-speaking pueblos. It is the headquarters for the eight northern pueblos, and was the home of the famous Indian leader Popé, who led the Pueblo Revolt against the Spanish in 1680. San Juan Pueblo is not only the first capital of the New Mexico Territory, established in 1598 by General Don Juan de Oñate, but is also the first capital established by Europeans in the continental United States.

It is a picturesque pueblo near the confluence of the Rio Grande and Chama Rivers: a community of high-walled adobes with streets that wind beneath cottonwoods and poplars. Tourists are welcome and invited to shop in the many stores for their traditional crafts of tourquois and silver jewelry, weavings, and their famous brown-and-red pottery with its traditional symbols etched into the surfaces. Open 9 A.M. to 2:30 P.M. is an Indian restaurant that prepares and serves the finest in traditional Indian foods. There is a Shell gas station, and fishing, picnicking, and other supplies are also available in the pueblo.

## Directions from Albuquerque

Take I-25 north to the junction of U.S. 84/285. Continue on to Española. About a mile north is a sign on the west side of the highway, marking the entrance to the San Juan Tribal Lakes.

The access road to the lakes is a narrow and winding dirt and gravel road that ends at one of the three lakes, where a tribal ranger on duty issues fishing permits and collects the fee.

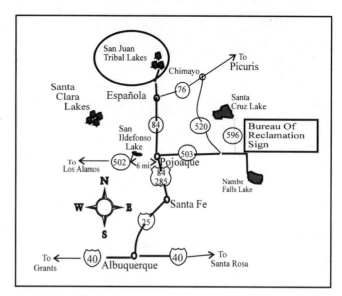

| | | |
|---|---|---|
| **Surface acres:** 3 lakes, total about 12 acres | **Distance from Albuquerque:** 85 miles | |
| **Elevation:** 5,595 feet | **Location:** 1 mile north of downtown Española, | |
| **Max. trailer size & fee:** No camping | within the city limit | |
| **Time limit:** No overnight | **Fish species:** Rainbow trout, bass, and catfish | |
| **Mailing address:** P.O. Box 1099, | **Season:** All year | |
| San Juan Pueblo, NM 87566 (505) 852-4213 | | |

## ACTIVITIES AND FACILITIES

| | NO | YES | Proximity to Lake in Miles | | NO | YES | Proximity to Lake in Miles |
|---|---|---|---|---|---|---|---|
| Bait and supplies | X | | | Airplane runway | X | | |
| Boat gas | X | | | Bottled gas | X | | |
| Boat ramp | X | | | Café/snack bar | X | | |
| Boat rental | X | | | Chemical toilets | X | | |
| Camping | X | | | Drinking water | X | | |
| Fire Pits | X | | | Electrical hook-up | X | | |
| Grills | | X | | Flush toilets | X | | |
| Firewood | | X | | Grocery store | X | | |
| Fishing | | X | | Handicapped access | | X | |
| Golf | X | | | Ice | X | | |
| Hiking | X | | | Laundry | X | | |
| Marina | X | | | Lodgings | X | | |
| Picnicking | | X | | Pit toilets | | X | |
| Riding | X | | | Playground | | X | |
| Scuba diving | X | | | Restaurant | X | | |
| Stables | X | | | Trash cans | | X | |
| Swimming | X | | | Sewer hook-up | X | | |
| Tables | | X | | Shelters | | X | |
| Telephone | X | | | Shopping | | X | |
| Tennis | X | | | Showers | X | | |
| Tent sites | X | | | Trailer space | X | | |
| Winter sports | X | | | Water hook-up | X | | |

Groceries and supplies in Española and Pojoaque.

**Special Rules and Regulations**

    **Fishing:** Adults, $7.00; children under 12, $4.00; senior citizens, $4.00

    **Catch limit:** Adults, 8 fish; children, 4 fish

    **Boating:** No boating permitted

    **Other:** Sightseeing/picnic $2.50; No firearms; no hunting or trapping allowed

# In the Vicinity of Abiquiu

## *Abiquiu*

*In the vicinity of Abiquiu and located northwest of this small village is one lake: Abiquiu Lake*

The village of Abiquiu lies twenty-three miles north of Española on U.S. 84. It is a farming community planned like many of the old settlements of that time. Its church, the old Mission Santo Tomás, reconstructed in 1938 on its original site, is in the center of a town consisting of a plaza surrounded by adobe buildings. It was first settled by the Spanish in 1747 on the site of a Tewa Pueblo ruin that is believed to have been abandoned two centuries earlier. The people living in this area were referred to as *genizaros* (people of mixed tribal backgrounds with Spanish surnames). They go back to the years of Indian raids by Plains Indians upon villages, whose women and children were captured and either traded or sold to the Spanish colonists who christianized them and used them as laborers and servants. Through the years, a mixture of Spanish and Indian blood and loss of their tribal identity were the results. In 1778, Abiquiu served as a stage for travelers to the new village of Los Angeles in California and also as an outfitting and supply point for traders and trappers

Today, Abiquiu is identified with Georgia O'Keeffe, the famous artist, whose works are known the world over and whose beautiful paintings were inspired by the brilliant colors of the sandstone formations of the mesas and cliffs near the village. The O'Keeffe house is about fourteen miles north of the village and within sight of the Ghost Ranch Visitors Center. The Ghost Ranch is an interesting place to visit while in this area. The Ghost Ranch Museum is maintained by the National Forest Service. It is a free public museum, displaying exhibits of Indian artifacts, dinosaur fossils, and animals indigenous to the area.

Just before reaching the Ghost Ranch Visitors Center, a side jaunt to Christ in the Desert Monastery, where the Benedictine monks built their center in 1964, is worth visiting. The monks welcome visitors here to their guest house to spend a night or just a day to see their gardens or their bee cultivations. Visitors can attend mass in the church, and guests can participate in the prayers and even join in the everyday labor performed by the monks. There is a gift shop for visitors, offering arts and crafts of the monks' weavings, woodworkings, and carvings. The church is a modern structure of high glass walls blending with the colors of the surrounding landscape. Access to the monastery is by a winding, bumpy road, a distance of thirteen miles along the Chama River.

*Abiquiu Lake*

# ABIQUIU LAKE

Abiquiu Dam is framed in a colorful setting of brilliant red sandstone formations of mesas and cliffs. It is part of the Corps of Engineers water resources development plan for the Rio Grande Valley. It was designed and built under the supervision of the U.S. Army Corps of Engineers in 1963 to control the sediment and flood waters of the Rio Chama, one of the most sediment-laden and largest tributaries of the Rio Grande. The dam controls the snow and rain run-off of a two-thousand-square-mile mountainous watershed and has resulted in a lake of four thousand surface acres, providing excellent boating, water-skiing, picnicking, camping, and fishing opportunities. The fishing at Abiquiu is excellent, with several cold- and warm-water species. The southern portion of the lake is inhabited by warm-water species of fish, while it contains a mixed population of warm and cold water species further north to cold-water species in the extreme northern end.

The facilities are excellent at Abiquiu Dam. There are fifty-four camp sites, fifteen tent camping sites, a group shelter, smaller shelters with picnic tables, a shower building, restrooms, water faucets, grills, picnic tables, and two boat ramps. There is no charge to use the boat ramp or the day-use facilities, but fees are charged for overnight camping and use of electrical hook-ups. The Riana Recreation Area, for summer camping, is equipped with restrooms, drinking water, showers, and a sanitation station. There are picnicking facilities for groups and families in the Cerrito, Riana, and Overlook areas. Some sites are covered to provide shade and protection from rain and are equipped with tables and cooking grills. On the Rio Chama below the dam there are campgrounds, picnic sites, and rest rooms. Road access to the lake is by way of good paved roads.

## Directions from Albuquerque

Take I-25 north to Española and the junction of U.S. 84/285. Proceed on 84 to Abiquiu and take the NM 96 cut-off (this is thirty miles northwest of Española). Then proceed on NM 96 seven miles to Abiquiu Dam. (The road is paved all the way to the lake.)

There are no stores or food concessions at the lake. Camping, picnic, and fishing supplies are available in Abiquiu.

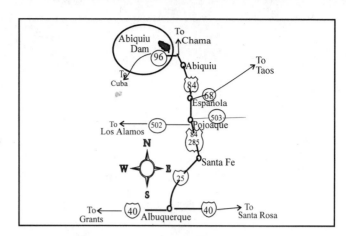

| | | | |
|---|---|---|---|
| **Surface acres:** 4,000 | | **Distance from Albuquerque:** 113 miles | |
| **Elevation:** 6,380 feet | | **Location:** 7 miles northwest of Abiquiu | |
| **Max. trailer size & fee:** 40 feet; $4.00 per night; | | **Fish species:** Cutthroat, German brown trout, | |
| tent sites, $2.00 per night; 14 day time limit | | kokanee salmon, bluegill, smallmouth and | |
| **Mailing Address:** Abiquiu Dam Resident Office, | | largemouth bass, walleye, crappie and catfish; | |
| P.O. Drawer D, Abiquiu, NM 87510 | | stocked with 3-inch fingerling rainbows and | |
| **Police emergency tel. #:** 753-2277 | | sub-catchable and catchable yellow perch | |
| **Medical emergency tel. #:** 753-7111 | | **Season:** All year | |

## ACTIVITIES AND FACILITIES

| | NO | YES | Proximity to Lake in Miles | | NO | YES | Proximity to Lake in Miles |
|---|---|---|---|---|---|---|---|
| **Bait and supplies** | X | | 7 | **Airplane runway** | X | | |
| **Boat gas** | X | | 7 | **Bottled gas** | X | | 7 |
| **Boat ramp** | | X | | **Café/snack bar** | X | | 7 |
| **Boat rental** | X | | 7 | **Chemical toilets** | | X | |
| **Camping** | | X | | **Drinking water** | | X | |
| **Fire pits** | | X | | **Electrical hook-up** | | X | |
| **Fire places** | | X | | **Flush toilets** | | X | |
| **Firewood** | X | | 7 | **Grocery store** | X | | 7 |
| **Fishing** | | X | | **Handicapped access** | | X | |
| **Golf** | X | | | **Ice** | X | | 7 |
| **Hiking** | | X | | **Laundry** | X | | 7 |
| **Marina** | X | | | **Lodgings** | X | | 7 |
| **Picnicking** | | X | | **Pit toilets** | | X | |
| **Riding** | X | | | **Playground** | | X | |
| **Scuba diving** | | X | | **Restaurant** | X | | 7 |
| **Stables** | X | | | **Sanitary disposal** | | X | |
| **Swimming** | | X | | **Sewer hook-up** | X | | |
| **Tables** | | X | | **Shelters** | | X | |
| **Telephone** | | X | | **Shopping** | X | | 7 |
| **Tennis** | X | | | **Showers** | | X | |
| **Tent sites** | | X | | **Trailer space** | | X | |
| **Winter sports** | X | | | **Water hook-up** | | X | |

Nearest services: stores, lodgings, restaurants in Abiquiu, 7 miles.

**Special Rules and Regulations**

**Fishing:** State fishing license required; see Fishing Proclamation

**Catch limit:** Trout, 10 per day; crappie daily bag, minimum size 10 inches (limit 20); see page 344

**Boating:** No boats within 200 feet of Dam; "no-wake" boating area at Cañones Creek; other areas permit water-skiing

**Other:** State Boating Regulations apply at lake; Regulations are available from the park manager at the Corps of Engineers Office at the dam

# In the Vicinity of Canjilon

## *Canjilon*

*There are two groups of lakes in the vicinity of Canjilon: Canjilon Lakes, Nutrias (Trout Lakes)*

Canjilon, *("deer antler"),* is a sparsely populated farming community set in a broad valley at an elevation of 7,800 feet. It is located three miles east of the junction of U.S. Highway 84 and NM 115, and just nineteen miles southeast of Tierra Amarilla.

Canjilon was settled by the followers of the Spanish conquistador, De Vargas. Its residents are descendants of the original settlers and were activists in the land grant movement. They still regard the land as rightfully theirs and resent any restrictions imposed on them by the Forest Service.

The town has a post office, a gas station, and a general store where picnicking, fishing, and other supplies can be purchased. On the approach to Canjilon on NM 115, visitors can stop at the Canjilon Ranger Station for information on the lakes and road conditions. NM 115 is a good, double-laned, paved highway that goes directly to the village, where a direction sign points to Canjilon Lakes. The first four miles to the lakes are pocked with deep potholes and deteriorated, but the route improves, allowing easy access to the lakes' parking area.

*Canjilon Lakes*

# CANJILON LAKES

*One of the two "lower" Canjilon Lakes*

It was an early morning in mid-September when field guide Elvin Smith and I reached the sparsely populated village of Canjilon. Turning north at the direction sign pointing to Canjilon Lakes, a once-paved road pocked with deep and wide potholes, slowed our speed to a crawl for the next four miles. Then the pavement turned into a hard-packed dirt/gravel road that narrowed and wound its way up the southeastern slope of Canjilon Mountain, passing through alpine meadows and colorful wildflowers. To the right, a profusion of cottonwood trees, starting to don their fall colors, hid from view the Canjilon River that parallels the road. Autumn comes early here in these high mountains, and very soon its briskness will bring swaths of reds, russets, and gold to the landscape.

Canjilon Lakes were originally formed by beaver dams, then improved and developed by the Forest Service in 1949. The six small lakes of two to four acres each are maintained by the Forest Service and stocked with rainbow trout by the New Mexico Department of Game and Fish. Although the Department stopped stocking cutthroat trout in 1969, cutthroat may still occur. Campers have a choice of two campgrounds near Canjilon Lakes: *Lower* or *Middle*. There are thirty-four camping units with a daily fee of $5 per camping unit. Tables, grills, toilets, drinking water by faucet, parking for trailers, tent sites, a garbage service, and uncut fuelwood are all available. The lakes and campgrounds are surrounded by aspen and fir trees and at 10,500 feet elevation, these high mountain campgrounds provide superb views of the Jemez and Sangre de Cristo mountains and the Española Valley.

## Directions from Albuquerque

Take I-25 north to Santa Fe. Take Exit 282 and connect with 285/84 north to Española, then take 84 and go twenty-one and a half miles north of Abiquiu Dam to Canjilon cut-off. Turn right on NM 115 and go three miles to Canjilon Village, then turn left at the direction sign to Canjilon Lakes. From this point on and for a distance of four miles, the road (which was once paved) is pocked with huge and deep potholes. It then turns into a narrow, winding, but better, dirt and gravel road the rest of the eight miles to the lakes.

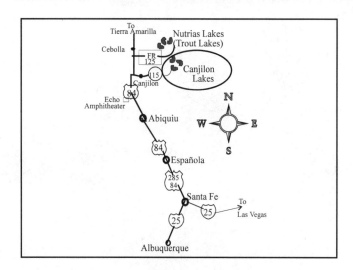

| | |
|---|---|
| **Surface acres**: 6 lakes, 2-4 acres; total 18 acres | **Distance from Albuquerque**: 142 miles |
| **Elevation**: 9,700 feet | **Location**: 12 miles northeast of Canjilon, with access |
| **Max. trailer size & fee**: 14 feet; $5.00 daily fee | from Forest Roads 559 and 129 |
| **Time limit**: 14 days | **Fish species**: Native cutthroat and rainbow trout |
| **Mailing address**: Box 488, Canjilon, NM 87515 | **Season**: Memorial Day-15 October |
| **Camping**: 34 camping units; 6 picnic units; tables, | **Police emergency tel. #:** In Canjilon village |
| toilets, grills, and drinking water available | |

## ACTIVITIES AND FACILITIES

| | NO | YES | Proximity to Lake in Miles | | NO | YES | Proximity to Lake in Miles |
|---|---|---|---|---|---|---|---|
| Bait and supplies | X | | 12 | Airplane runway | X | | |
| Boat gas | X | | 12 | Bottled gas | X | | |
| Boat ramp | X | | | Café/snack bar | X | | |
| Boat rental | X | | | Chemical toilets | | X | |
| Camping | | X | | Drinking water | | X | |
| Fire pits | | X | | Electrical hook-up | X | | |
| Fire places | | X | | Flush toilets | X | | |
| Firewood | | X | | Grocery store | X | | 12 |
| Fishing | | X | | Handicapped access | X | | |
| Golf | X | | | Ice | X | | 12 |
| Hiking | | X | | Laundry | X | | |
| Marina | X | | | Lodgings | X | | |
| Picnicking | | X | | Pit toilets | | X | |
| Riding | X | | | Playground | X | | |
| Scuba diving | X | | | Restaurant | X | | |
| Stables | X | | | Trash cans | | X | |
| Swimming | X | | | Sewer hook-up | X | | |
| Tables | | X | | Shelters | X | | |
| Telephone | X | | 12 | Shopping | X | | |
| Tennis | X | | | Showers | X | | |
| Tent sites | | X | | Trailer space | | X | |
| Winter sports | X | | | Water hook-up | X | | |

Gas, grocery store, fishing supplies in Canjilon, 12 miles.

**Special Rules and Regulations**

    **Fishing:** State Regulations apply; See Fishing Proclamation for latest fees and rules

    **Catch limit:** 6 trout; New Mexico Game and Fish Department Regulations apply

    **Boating:** Oars or electric motors only

    **Other:** Due to primitive road access, recreational vehicles over 22 feet not recommended

*Nutrias (Trout Lakes)*

# NUTRIAS (TROUT LAKES)

*First of the three Trout Lakes at the end of Forest Road 125*

Nutrias Lakes, also known as Trout Lakes, is a series of three lakes totaling about twenty acres. They are located on the northwestern side of the Canjilon Mountains at the headwaters of Nutrias Creek, cradled at an elevation of about 9,300 feet in a beautiful, serene forest of fir, spruce, pine, and aspen. It is an especially colorful location when the aspen leaves turn to gold. Trout Lakes contain a population of native cutthroat and brook trout. The upper lakes are stocked with three-inch fingerling rainbows and some catchables by the New Mexico Department of Game and Fish. The lower lake is stocked with all catchable rainbows.

The best access to the lakes is a mile south of the small community of Cebolla, which has a gasoline station and a store, where picnicking and fishing supplies can be purchased. The access road is reached by U.S. Highway 84, two miles north of the Canjilon cut-off. Here, U.S. 84 junctions with FR 125. Turn east on FR 125 and go eleven miles on a primitive road. The road deadends at the first Trout Lake. (This road is not recommended for passenger cars during inclement weather.) An uphill trail at the north end of the first lake leads to the largest of the lakes. The other lakes are small ponds and a few beaver ponds.

The Trout Lakes Family Campground is open from Memorial Day through 15 October. It is a no-fee campground with tables, grills, uncut fuelwood, toilets, and tent sites. There are no drinking water or garbage services available. It is a pack-in and pack-out campground, and due to primitive access recreation vehicles over sixteen feet in length are not recommended.

## Directions from Albuquerque

Take I-25 north and on approach to Santa Fe take the 282 exit and connect with U.S. 285/84 north to Española. Take 84 to Abiquiu and continue north for twenty-three and a half miles to FR 125 cut-off. Turn right and follow signs eleven miles to Trout Lakes on a dirt/gravel road.

NOTE: Should you be returning to Highway 84 from the Canjilon Lakes area, a direction sign indicates twenty-three miles to Nutrias (Trout Lakes). Though one may be tempted to take this route to Trout Lakes, this is a very rough, primitive road, not recommended for passenger cars, especially in wet weather.

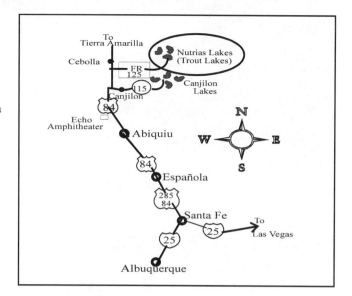

| | |
|---|---|
| **Surface acres:** 5 lakes, total 20 acres | **Distance from Albuquerque:** 140 miles |
| **Elevation:** 9,300 feet | **Location:** 11 miles east of Cebolla; best access |
| **Max. trailer size & fee:** 16 feet, no fee | is via FR 125 off 84, 2 miles N of Canjilon cut-off |
| **Time limit:** 14 days | **Fish species:** Native cutthroat, rainbow, and |
| **Mailing address:** P.O. Box 488, Canjilon, NM 87515 | brook trout; see stocking policy, page 343 |
| **Police emergency tel. #:** In Cebolla | **Season:** Memorial Day-15 October |
| **Medical emergency tel. #:** In Cebolla | |

## ACTIVITIES AND FACILITIES

| | NO | YES | Proximity to Lake in Miles | | NO | YES | Proximity to Lake in Miles |
|---|---|---|---|---|---|---|---|
| Bait and supplies | X | | *11 | Airplane runway | X | | |
| Boat gas | X | | | Bottled gas | X | | |
| Boat ramp | X | | | Café/snack bar | X | | |
| Boat rental | X | | | Chemical toilets | | X | |
| Camping | | X | | Drinking water | X | | |
| Fire pits | | X | | Electrical hook-up | X | | |
| Fire places | | X | | Flush toilets | X | | |
| Firewood | | X | | Grocery store | X | | *11 |
| Fishing | | X | | Handicapped access | | X | |
| Golf | X | | | Ice | X | | |
| Hiking | | X | | Laundry | X | | |
| Marina | X | | | Lodgings | X | | |
| Picnicking | | X | | Pit toilets | | X | |
| Riding | X | | | Playground | X | | |
| Scuba diving | X | | | Restaurant | X | | |
| Stables | X | | | Trash cans | | X | |
| Swimming | X | | | Sewer hook-up | X | | |
| Tables | | X | | Shelters | X | | |
| Telephone | X | | *11 | Shopping | X | | |
| Tennis | X | | | Showers | X | | |
| Tent sites | | X | | Trailer space | | X | |
| Winter sports | X | | | Water hook-up | X | | |

*Picnic, fishing, gas, and food supplies in Cebolla.

**Special Rules and Regulations**

**Fishing:** New Mexico Department of Game and Fish Regulations apply

**Catch limit:** 6 trout (effective 1 April 1995-31 March 1998); see latest Fishing Proclamation

**Boating:** Oars or electric motors only

**Other:** Due to primitive road access, recreational vehicles over 16 feet, not recommended

*County Court House*
*Tierra Amarilla, New Mexico*
*(Scene of the 1967 Reies Tijerina*
*Land Grant shootout)*

# In the Vicinity of Tierra Amarilla

## *Tierra Amarilla*

*There are two lakes in the vicinity of Tierra Amarilla: El Vado Lake, Heron Lake*

Tierra Amarilla is the seat of Rio Arriba County, once the home of Spanish, then later Mexicans who farmed the area in 1832, after Mexico awarded a land grant to Juan Martinez and his eight children. At that time it was known as Las Nutrias, named after the many beaver ponds that abound in the nearby streams. Later it was called Tierra Amarilla, which translated from Spanish means *"yellow earth,"* referring no doubt to the yellow earth in the vicinity. Tierra Amarilla lies at an elevation of 6,800 feet off U.S. 84, about twelve miles south of Chama, in a picturesque valley edged by the slope of the San Juan Mountains.

Tierra Amarilla has a turbulent history of murderous outlaw gangs that operated in the area, marauding Indians, and quarrels with the Federal Government over land rights. In 1967 the County Courthouse was the scene of a shootout. The incident gained national attention when Reies Lopez Tijerina, a land grant activist, and his followers took over the County Courthouse to call attention to his argument that the land around Tierra Amarilla belonged to the original grantees and their descendants, not to the present owners, whom he claimed acquired it fraudulently. The incident erupted into violence; shooting broke out and a Sheriff's deputy was injured. The military quelled the disturbance, and Tijerina was jailed then later exonerated. To this day, the residents of the town regard the land in dispute as rightfully theirs.

It is a depressed town, lacking in accommodations for the tourist, but Chama, only twelve miles to the north, has everything needed in supplies, restaurants, and lodgings.

*El Vado Lake*

# EL VADO LAKE

El Vado Lake is a state park, containing a 3,200-surface-acre lake at an elevation of 6,902 feet. It was built in 1935 by the Middle Rio Grande Conservancy District to control the spring runoff for agricultural use, and to impound the waters of the Chama and Brazos Rivers above the lake. It is over a mile wide and four miles long and lies west of Tierra Amarilla on NM 112, situated in a scenic setting of evergreen-covered mesas in a region noted for its farming and sheep-raising ranches. The region has a violent past of outlaw gangs and gunfighters, Indian raids and murders. Names like Ike Stockton and Charlie Allison operated here with their outlaw gangs, and made the local news frequently.

El Vado Lake is an excellent trout and salmon fishing lake, well stocked with fingerling and fry rainbow trout. The lake also contains lake trout, kokanee salmon, and browns. The park has fifty improved camp sites near the boat ramp on A and B Loops, where there is a small marina, and some of the camp sites provide double and group shelters. Other camp sites are equipped with trash cans, tables, grills, a comfort station, fresh tap drinking water, twenty-one electric and water hook-ups, chemical toilets, and modern restrooms with flush toilets. Located south of the boat ramp at Loop C, there are over thirty semi-improved sites and many primitive camp-sites west of the lake. There are also convenience stores, restaurants, a motel, a graveled airstrip, telephones and a playground.

El Vado is a favorite lake for water-skiing, and for those who prefer the quiet waters of a "*no-wake*" lake, a hiking trail and a good road connects the northern end of El Vado Lake to the southern end of Heron Lake.

## Directions from Albuquerque

Drive north on I-25 to Exit 285 and connect with 84/285. Drive through Santa Fe and at Española connect with 84 to Tierra Amarilla. From Tierra Amarilla drive one and a third miles to the junction of U.S. 84 and NM 112. Turn west on NM 112 on a good-double lane highway. Go thirteen miles to a state park sign, turn right, and go four and a half miles to the lake. It is a good dirt/gravel road access.

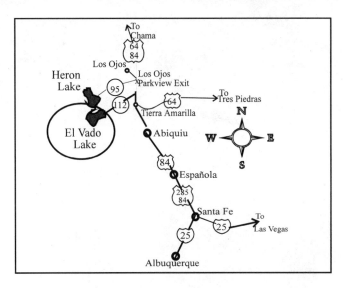

| | | |
|---|---|---|
| **Surface acres:** 3,200 | **Distance from Albuquerque:** 165 miles |
| **Elevation:** 6,902 feet | **Location:** 15 miles southwest of Tierra Amarilla |
| **Max. trailer size & fee:** 40 feet; site, $7, electric, $4 | on NM 112 |
| **Time limit:** 14 days | **Fish species:** Stocked with fingerling and fry |
| **Mailing address:** El Vado Lake State Park, | rainbow trout; populated with lake trout, |
| P.O. Box 156, Tierra Amarilla, NM  87575 | kokanee salmon, cutthroat trout, and browns |
| | **Season:**  Year round; see fishing season below |

### ACTIVITIES AND FACILITIES

| | NO | YES | Proximity to Lake in Miles | | NO | YES | Proximity to Lake in Miles |
|---|---|---|---|---|---|---|---|
| Bait and supplies | | X | | Airplane runway | | X | |
| Boat gas | | X | | Bottled gas | | X | |
| Boat ramp | | X | | Café/snack bar | | X | |
| Boat rental | | X | | Chemical toilets | | X | |
| Camping | | X | | Drinking water | | X | |
| Fire pits | | X | | Electrical hook-up | | X | |
| Fire places | | X | | Flush toilets | | X | |
| Firewood | X | | | Grocery store | | X | |
| Fishing | | X | | Handicapped access | | X | |
| Golf | X | | | Ice | | X | |
| Hiking | | X | | Laundry | X | | |
| Marina | | X | | Lodgings | | X | |
| Picnicking | | X | | Pit toilets | | X | |
| Riding | X | | | Playground | | X | |
| Scuba diving | | X | | Restaurant | | X | |
| Stables | X | | | Trash cans | | X | |
| Swimming | | X | | Sewer hook-up | X | | |
| Tables | | X | | Shelters | | X | |
| Tennis | X | | | Shopping | X | | |
| Tent sites | | X | | Showers | X | | |
| Water skiing | | X | | Trailer space | | X | |
| Winter sports | | X | | Water hook-up | | X | |

A grocery store, gas, and snack bar are available about 1/2 mile from cut-off to lake.

**Special Rules and Regulations**

  **Fishing:** New Mexico Department of Game and Fish Regulations apply; see Fishing Proclamation

  **Catch limit:** 6 trout; kokanee salmon; 12 per day; see page 343 for other regulations

  **Boating:** No restrictions,  boaters must observe general boating courtesy

  **Other:** Special kokanee salmon season, 1 November-31 January

*Heron Lake*

# HERON LAKE

*Twilight at Heron . . . the stillness, the silence, the serenity*

With its marina and 135 improved camping sites, some with water and electric hook-ups, and its numerous unimproved sites, set in a beautiful 4,000-acre ponderosa- and fir-forested state park, Heron Lake has become one of the most popular lakes in New Mexico. It is a full-facility lake catering to almost any recreational interest. It is a *"no-wake"* lake and a favorite among fishermen, boaters, and windsurfers. Standard New Mexico state park fees apply for camping and day use. Fees are posted at the entrance to "use areas," or are available from any state park office.

Heron Lake was built in 1972 as part of the San Juan–Chama Diversion Project, which employed several miles of tunnels to divert early spring run-offs from the western watershed to impound the water at Heron Lake for timely release into the Rio Chama and finally into the Gulf of Mexico.

North of the Tourist Center, the New Mexico sailing club operates a small marina at the Willow Creek input. There is also a boat ramp at Willow Creek and another on the west side of the dam. The Visitors Center near the entrance to the park provides visitors with interpretive exhibits and the lake's history, and also provides restrooms for the convenience of tourists. Other recreational opportunities include hiking trails, winter ice fishing and cross-country skiing. The lake is stocked with rainbow trout frys and kokanee salmon, and also contains some cutthroat and brown trout. The Willow Creek tributary is also popular with anglers.

## Directions from Albuquerque

Take I-25 north. On the approach to Santa Fe, take Exit 282 and connect with 84/285 to Española and take U.S. 84 north. Drive one and two tenths miles north of Tierra Amarilla and turn west on NM 95, then go six miles to the lake. Highway access to lake is excellent. State Park fees apply.

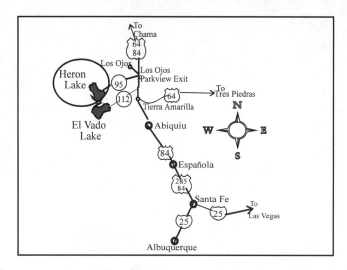

| | | |
|---|---|---|
| **Surface acres**: 5,900 | **Distance from Albuquerque**: 157 miles |
| **Elevation**: 7,316 feet | **Location**: 10 miles west of Tierra Amarilla off NM 95 |
| **Max. trailer size and fee**: 40 feet; $7.00 per night | **Fish species**: Stocked with rainbow fry; contains |
| **Time limit**: 14 days | lake, cutthroat, brown trout, and kokanee salmon |
| **Mailing address**: P.O. Box 31, Rutheron, NM | **Season**: 1 April-31 March |
| 87563 (505) 588-7470 | **Kokanee fishing,** 1 November-31 January |
| **Emergency tel. #**: At visitor center | |

## ACTIVITIES AND FACILITIES

| | NO | YES | Proximity to Lake in Miles | | NO | YES | Proximity to Lake in Miles |
|---|---|---|---|---|---|---|---|
| **Bait and supplies** | | X | | **Airplane runway** | X | | |
| **Boat gas** | | X | | **Bottled gas** | | X | |
| **Boat ramp** | | X | | **Café/snack bar** | | X | |
| **Boat rental** | | X | | **Chemical toilets** | | X | |
| **Camping** | | X | | **Drinking water** | | X | |
| **Fire pits** | | X | | **Electrical hook-up** | | X | |
| **Fire places** | | X | | **Flush toilets** | | X | |
| **Firewood** | X | | | **Grocery store** | | X | |
| **Fishing** | | X | | **Handicapped access** | | X | |
| **Golf** | X | | | **Ice** | | X | |
| **Hiking** | | X | | **Laundry** | | X | |
| **Marina** | | X | | **Lodgings** | | X | |
| **Picnicking** | | X | | **Pit toilets** | | X | |
| **Riding** | X | | | **Playground** | X | | |
| **Scuba diving** | | X | | **Restaurant** | | X | |
| **Stables** | X | | | **Sanitary disposal** | | X | |
| **Swimming** | | X | | **Sewer hook-up** | | X | |
| **Tables** | | X | | **Shelters** | | X | |
| **Tennis** | X | | | **Shopping** | X | | |
| **Tent sites** | | X | | **Showers** | X | | |
| **Water skiing** | X | | | **Trailer space** | | X | |
| **Winter sports** | | X | | **Water hook-up** | | X | |

*Full facilities, stores, and accommodations in Chama.
**Special Rules and Regulations**
    **Fishing:** New Mexico Department of Game and Fish Regulations apply; see Fishing Proclamation
    **Catch limit:** 10 per-day; kokanee, 12 per-day in addition to trout; other regulations, page 343
    **Boating:** A "no-wake" lake; trolling speed only
    **Other:** A full-facility lake; good trout fishing in surrounding streams

# In the Vicinity of Los Ojos

## *Los Ojos*

*In the vicinity of Los Ojos, two miles north of Tierra Amarilla and ten miles south of Chama, there is one lake: Burns Canyon Lake*

Nearly two hundred years ago, Spanish settlers brought sheep and floor looms to their southwest frontier outposts in the Chama Valley. The pastures for their sheep were plentiful in this lush valley, but surviving the harshness of the winters and the isolation of the mountains demanded a life style of self-reliance and cooperation with each other.

To survive in this environment, the settlers honed their skills and divided their labor between family members. Some worked as spinners, some as carders, and others became skillful weavers. Cooperation with other families became a way of life. This cooperation extended to sheep breeding as well as wool spinning. Wool cloth was made for export by mule train to mining camps farther north. Spanish caballeros dressed themselves in colorful and elegant serapes, and the area around the historic town of Los Ojos became a center of the weaving industry in the Chama Valley. Today its history is evident in the Tierrra Wools Showroom, located in a century-old building in the center of town. It is a tourist attraction, famous for its quality wool weavings of hand-dyed colors passed down from generation to generation, and where visitors are invited to see weavers and dyers at work, using the same basic type of looms and methods as did their ancestors nearly two hundred years ago.

Burns Canyon Lake is about two miles from the village of Los Ojos, where a glimpse of the past permeates the entire village. Fishing and food supplies can be purchased here on the way to the lake.

*Burns Canyon Lake*

# BURNS CANYON LAKE

Burns Canyon Lake is a fifteen-acre lake on the Parkview Fish Hatchery owned by the Department of Game and Fish. The lake is located half a mile from the Parkview Hatchery site and two and a half miles southwest of the Los Ojos/Parkview exit off U.S. 84. A mile from the cut-off exit, and two miles north of Tierra Amarilla, is the small, quaint village of Los Ojos, where fishing supplies and food for picnicking are available.

Burns Canyon Lake is accessed by a primitive road. During inclement weather, four-wheel drive vehicles are recommended. The road ends at a parking area, where a turnstile gate allows entrance to the lake. The lake is about forty yards away from the parking area but is not visible from there since it is located behind an incline in the terrain. The lake lies at an elevation of 8,000 feet and is surrounded by spruce, fir and aspen, especially colorful in the fall.

Burns Canyon Lake is stocked with rainbow trout. There are no picnicking facilities, no camping or boating is permitted, and access to surrounding areas is restricted. The only facility available is one vault toilet in the parking area. A posted sign indicates rules to observe while using this no-fee area.

## Directions from Albuquerque

Take I-25 north. Before reaching Santa Fe, take Exit 282. Connect with 285/84, follow this route, and connect north on 84. About two miles past Tierra Amarilla turn left (west) at the Los Ojos/Parkview exit. Continue for one and a half miles to the Fish Hatchery sign, which indicates the site of the hatchery to the left. Burns Canyon Lake is straight ahead, about one mile, on a good gravel road that dead-ends at a parking area. The lake is not visible from the parking area, as it is on a rise fifty yards beyond a turnstile entry gate in the parking area.

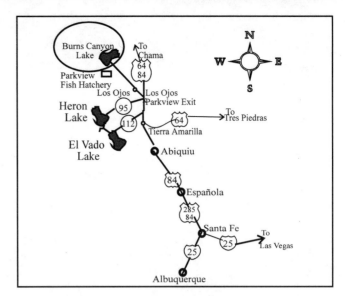

| | |
|---|---|
| **Surface acres:** 15 acres | **Distance from Albuquerque:** 155 miles |
| **Elevation:** 8,000 feet | **Location:** 4 1/2 miles NW of Tierra Amarilla; |
| **Max. trailer size & fee:** No camping | 2 miles west of the small village of Los Ojos |
| **Time limit:** No camping | **Fish species:** Trout |
| **Mailing address:** P.O. Box 25112, Santa Fe, NM 87504; | **Season:** 1 April-31 October; daylight only |
| (505) 588-7307 | |
| **Police emergency tel. #:** At hatchery | |

## ACTIVITIES AND FACILITIES

| | NO | YES | Proximity to Lake in Miles | | NO | YES | Proximity to Lake in Miles |
|---|---|---|---|---|---|---|---|
| Bait and supplies | X | | | Airplane runway | X | | |
| Boat gas | X | | | Bottled gas | X | | |
| Boat ramp | X | | | Café/snack bar | X | | |
| Boat rental | X | | | Chemical toilets | X | | |
| Camping | X | | | Drinking water | X | | |
| Fire pits | X | | | Electrical hook-up | X | | |
| Fire places | X | | | Flush toilets | X | | |
| Firewood | X | | | Grocery store | X | | 1 |
| Fishing | | X | | Handicapped access | X | | |
| Golf | X | | | Ice | X | | 1 |
| Hiking | X | | | Laundry | X | | |
| Marina | X | | | Lodgings | X | | 12 |
| Picnicking | X | | | Pit toilets | | X | |
| Riding | X | | | Playground | X | | |
| Scuba diving | X | | | Restaurant | X | | |
| Stables | X | | | Sanitary disposal | X | | |
| Swimming | X | | | Sewer hook-up | X | | |
| Tables | X | | | Shelters | X | | |
| Telephone | X | | 1 | Shopping | X | | |
| Tennis | X | | | Showers | X | | |
| Tent sites | X | | | Trailer space | X | | |
| Winter sports | X | | | Water hook-up | X | | |

Lodgings and restaurants are 10 miles north in Chama. Stores, bait and tackle in Los Ojos.

**Special Rules and Regulations**

    **Fishing:** New Mexico Department of Game and Fish Regulations apply; see Fishing Proclamation

    **Catch limit:** 6 trout. See current Fishing Proclamation for detailed regulations

    **Boating:** No boats or floating devices permitted

    **Other:** No camping or picnicking facilities available; pack-in and pack-out

# In the Vicinity of Tres Piedras

## *Tres Piedras*

*There are three lakes in the vicinity of Tres Piedras:
Hopewell Lake, Lagunitas Lakes, Laguna Larga*

One doesn't think of Tres Piedras in tourist terms. It is just a small village that started as a lumber and ranching settlement in 1879, alongside three huge granite extrusions from which the village gets its name Tres Piedras, Spanish for "three rocks."

Tres Piedras is located at the junction of U.S. Highways 64 and 285. From Albuquerque, it is reached via U.S. 285 north and from Taos via U.S. 64 west and across the spectacular Rio Grande Rift, an awesome split in the earth's crust, which resulted in the Rio Grande Rift Basin. It is filled with thousands of feet of alluvium from the bordering mountains and lava flow from the depths of the earth, exposing 650 feet of earth in the Rio Grande Gorge at the bridge crossing. The approach to Tres Piedras from the west at Tierra Amarilla is a spectacular and scenic forty-mile drive through a pine,

aspen, and oak forest of the Brazos Range, where the highway ascends to over 10,000 feet in places and is closed during the heavy snows of winter.

The area around Tres Piedras is home to an abundance of wild game that includes elk, mule deer, antelope, beaver, rabbit, and numerous species of other wild game. It has been a favorite hunting region for Indians of the past and for hunters enjoying the sport today. A few gas stations and stores accommodate travelers and sportsmen who frequent the area. A Ranger Station is located on U.S. 64 just a short distance west of the U.S. 285 intersection. Helpful information and maps can be obtained here regarding points of interest in the area and road conditions to the outdoor recreation spots. It is advisable to stop here before driving on unimproved roads in the mountains, especially during inclement weather. On our visit to Lagunitas Lakes and Laguna Larga, the road conditions were too muddy and rough to allow entry to the lakes or the campgrounds.

*Hopewell Lake*

# HOPEWELL LAKE

Hopewell Lake is an attractively wooded nineteen-acre lake located nineteen miles west of Tres Piedras off U.S. Highway 64. It lies at an elevation of 9,400 feet above sea level. The lake was created by construction of a dam across Placer Creek by the New Mexico Department of Game and Fish, through a permit from the United States Forest Service. Boats restricted to oars or electric motors are permitted. It contains lake-bred brook trout and is regularly stocked with rainbow.

Access to Hopewell Lake from the west is by way of U.S. 64 at Tierra Amarilla. The easiest access is from the east at Tres Piedras, where the appoach is by way of U.S. 64, an excellent double-lane paved highway, wooded on both sides in ponderosa pine, scrub oak, piñon, cedar, and aspen,

ablaze with color in the fall. The lake is visible from the highway. The scenic drive down the winding gravel turn-off road to the lake is lined with wildflowers and stands of blue spruce, Douglas fir, Edelman spruce, and aspen. Care must be taken on this road during inclement weather, when mud and deep ruts that result from spring snow thaws make the use of four-wheel drive high-clearance vehicles necessary. No camping is permitted around the lake, but a no-fee primitive campground above the lake offers trailer and camper sites. Its facilities include chemical toilets, attractively screened by a lattice of tree-limb cuttings. Tables, grills, and trash cans are also provided. There are no electric or water hook-ups, nor is there drinking water.

## Directions from Albuquerque

Take I-25 north through Santa Fe. Continue to Española and connect with U.S. Highway 285 north to Tres Piedras, then take U.S. 64 west and go nineteen miles to Hopewell Lake. The lake is off the highway and is accessed by gravel roads that may be rough during wet weather.

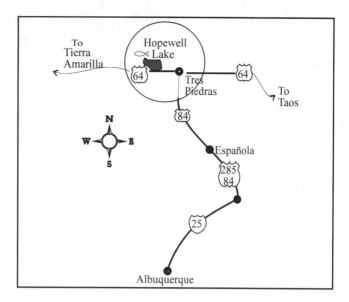

| | | |
|---|---|---|
| **Surface acres:** 14 | **Distance from Albuquerque:** 170 miles |
| **Elevation:** 9,400 feet | **Location:** 19 miles west of Tres Piedras |
| **Max. trailer size & fee:** Oversize not advised | **Fish species:.** Rainbow and brook trout |
| **Time Limit:** 14 days; no fee | **Season:** 1 April-31 March |
| **Mailing address:** U.S. Forest Service, 517 Gold S.W., Albuquerque, NM 87102, 758- 8678 | |
| **Medical emergency tel. #:** 911 | **Police emergency tel. #:** 911 |

## ACTIVITIES AND FACILITIES

| | NO | YES | Proximity to Lake in Miles | | NO | YES | Proximity to Lake in Miles |
|---|---|---|---|---|---|---|---|
| Bait and supplies | X | | | Airplane runway | X | | |
| Boat gas | X | | | Bottled gas | X | | |
| Boat ramp | X | | | Café/snack bar | X | | |
| Boat rental | X | | | Chemical toilets | | X | |
| Camping | | X | | Drinking water | X | | |
| Fire pits | | X | | Electrical hook-up | X | | |
| Fire places | | X | | Flush toilets | X | | |
| Firewood | X | | | Grocery store | X | | |
| Fishing | | X | | Handicapped access | | X | |
| Golf | X | | | Ice | X | | |
| Hiking | | X | | Laundry | X | | |
| Marina | X | | | Lodgings | X | | |
| Picnicking | | X | | Pit toilets | | X | |
| Riding | X | | | Playground | X | | |
| Scuba diving | X | | | Restaurant | X | | |
| Stables | X | | | Trash cans | | X | |
| Swimming | X | | | Sewer hook-up | X | | |
| Tables | | X | | Shelters | X | | |
| Telephone | X | | | Shopping | X | | |
| Tennis | X | | | Showers | X | | |
| Tent sites | | X | | Trailer space | | X | |
| Winter sports | X | | | Water hook-up | X | | |

Services and stores in Tres Piedras, 19 miles.

**Special Rules and Regulations**

**Fishing:** State fishing license required

**Catch limit:** 6 fish; 6 in possession

**Boating:** Restricted to oars or electric motors at trolling speeds

**Other:** No camping around lake; camping above lake, by road and within walking distance

# In the Vicinity of Dulce and the Jicarilla Apache Reservation

## *Dulce*

*Dulce is the gateway to the Jicarilla Apache Indian Reservation and the lakes within the reservation boundaries. The following are the most popular stocked lakes open to the public with tribal permit: \*Dulce Lake, \*La Jara Lake, \*Mundo Lake, Enbom Lake, Stone Lake. Pictures of the asterisked lakes above typify the lakes on the Jicarilla Reservation and are detailed on the following pages. The regulations and facilities for boating, camping, and fishing on page 76 apply to all of the lakes.*

Since 1821, Dulce has been the tribal headquarters and trading center of the Jicarilla Apache Indian Reservation. The reservation's latest purchases and acquisition of 94,000 acres of private ranch lands include the El Poso ranch, the Theis ranch, and the Willow Creek ranch that abuts Heron Lake to the east. The Jicarilla Reservation is comprised of almost one million acres, an area straddling the Continental Divide, twenty-five miles wide between Farmington and Chama, and extending south from the Colorado state line for approximately seventy miles. Heavily timbered mountains, canyons, and wide valleys of Douglas fir, ponderosa pine, spruce, and scrub oak make up the northern half of the reservation, while in the southern half rolling hills, colorful sandstone bluffs, and deep mesa canyons of piñon pine, ponderosa pine, and juniper grace the landscape. Within this magnificent mountainous country the Jicarillas developed and maintain a paradise for fishermen and hunters. The abundant ponds and lakes provide a haven for nesting and migrating waterfowl; unsurpassed hunting for bear, turkey, and fishing for trophy trout makes the reservation one of the finest sports areas in northwest New Mexico.

The reservation can be reached from Albuquerque by way of NM 44 and NM 537, or from Farmington by way of U.S. Highway 64. There is a 5,000-foot all-weather paved airstrip in Dulce, where the 2,617 residents of the reservation are concentrated. Dulce offers a full array of accommodations for visitors and sportsmen. There are service stations, motels, restaurants, gift shops, and a modern shopping center—all conveniently located to give easy access to all the lakes and hunting areas. The Best Western Jicarilla Inn offers the finest in accommodation, with luxurious rooms, and a restaurant and lounge with excellent cuisine and service. There is also a gift shop that displays original Indian arts and crafts.

# LAKES OF THE JICARILLA RESERVATION

Excellent trout fishing is available in six reservation lakes and along the scenic Navajo River. The lakes are stocked annually with rainbow, brown, and cutthroat trout. A tribal permit is required to fish and camp around the lakes. Picnic tables, grills, and shelters are available at most of the lakes.

The lakes and ponds also provide a haven for nesting and migrating waterfowl. Waterfowl hunting is permitted with a duck stamp and tribal permit. Hunting for bear and turkey is also permitted, but bear hunting requires a guide.

## Jicarilla Reservation

### Boating, Camping, and Fishing Regulations

These regulations apply to all reservation lakes open to the public.

The lakes open to fishing and boating require a Jicarilla tribal permit, but do not require a New Mexico fishing license. Fishing permits are available at the Jicarilla Fish and Game Department in Dulce or in Albuquerque from Charlie's Sporting Goods.

**Season:** Year round, half an hour before sunrise to half an hour after sunset

**Catch limit:** 12 years of age and over, 8 fish daily or 16 in possession; children under 12 years, 4 fish daily or 8 in possession

**Taking of fish:** No nets or traps allowed; fishing permitted with one pole only, limited to two hooks; no float jugs or trotlines allowed, no chumming or night fishing; no minnows either dead or alive can be used as bait; no game fish, frogs, or water dogs can be used as bait; carp may be taken at Stone Lake with gigs (no bag limit on carp); all grass carp caught at Dulce Lake must be returned to lake alive

**Boats:** Any size boat with motor not exceeding 35 horsepower and not to exceed 5 mph, or trolling speed; boats restricted to electric power or oars only; boaters must comply with the New Mexico boat safety requirements; only fishermen with fishing permits are allowed to use boats on Jicarilla waters

**Camping:** Permitted on all lakes; facilities are limited; no campfires allowed on any of the lakes during winter time; no camping within 150 feet of the bank of any Jicarilla water; no littering or pollution of any Jicarilla lakes or streams permitted

**Fees:** Since fees are subject to change, it is advisable to check with Jicarilla Department of Game and Fish for current fees; for information write or call: Jicarilla Game and Fish Department, Box 546, Dulce, New Mexico 87528, (505) 759-3255

**Lakes open to fishing:** Stone Lake, Hayden Lake, Enbom Lake, Dulce Lake, La Jara Lake, Mundo Lake. Horse Lake is restricted to Jicarilla tribal members, employees, and Dulce residents.

## Directions from Albuquerque

Take I-25 north to Bernalillo to Exit 142 and connect with NM 44. Go northwest through Cuba, then at the junction of NM 537 continue north through the Jicarilla Apache Reservation. NM 537 connects with U.S. 64 about eleven miles south of Dulce, headquarters of the reservation.

From Farmington Dulce is reached via U.S. 64 East.
From Chama Via U.S. 64 West.

### Distances from Dulce to the major lakes
Mundo Lake: 5.3 miles via J 8
Enbom Lake: 12.8 miles via J 8
Stone Lake: 18.6 miles via J 8
Dulce Lake: 4.8 miles via U.S. 64
La Jara Lake: 15.0 miles via U.S. 64 and NM 537

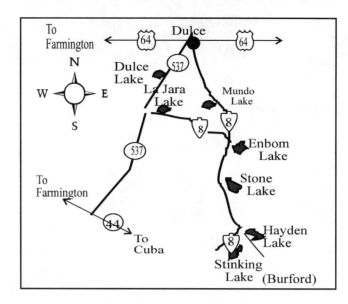

| | |
|---|---|
| **Surface acres:** Lakes vary in size up to 75 acres | **Distance from Albuquerque:** 176 miles |
| **Elevation:** 6,500-9,500 feet | **Location:** Northwestern New Mexico, south of Dulce |
| **Max. trailer size:** Check with Tribal Office for accessibility to lakes with trailers | |
| **Mailing address:** Jicarilla Dept. of Game and Fish, Box 546, Dulce, NM 87528 (505) 759-3255 | **Fish species:** Rainbow and cutthroat trout |
| | **Season:** Year round, 1/2 hour before sunrise to 1/2 hour after sunset |

## ACTIVITIES AND FACILITIES

| | NO | YES | Proximity to Lake in Miles | | NO | YES | Proximity to Lake in Miles |
|---|---|---|---|---|---|---|---|
| Bait and supplies | X | | * | Airplane runway | X | | * |
| Boat gas | X | | | Bottled gas | X | | |
| Boat ramp | X | | | Café/snack bar | X | | * |
| Boat rental | X | | | Chemical toilets | X | | |
| Camping | | X | | Drinking water | X | | * |
| Fire pits | | X | | Electrical hook-up | X | | |
| Fire places | | X | | Flush toilets | X | | |
| Firewood | X | | | Grocery store | X | | * |
| Fishing | | X | | Handicapped access | X | X | |
| Golf | X | | | Ice | X | | * |
| Hiking | | X | | Laundry | X | | * |
| Marina | X | | | Lodgings | X | | * |
| Picnicking | | X | | Pit toilets | | X | |
| Riding | | X | | Playground | X | | |
| Scuba diving | X | | | Restaurant | X | | * |
| Skiing (water) | X | | | Sanitary disposal | X | | |
| Swimming | X | | | Sewer hook-up | X | | |
| Tables | | X | | Shelters | X | | |
| Telephone | X | | * | Shopping | X | | * |
| Tennis | X | | | Showers | X | | |
| Tent sites | | X | | Trailer space | | X | |
| Winter sports | X | | | Water hook-up | X | | |

*Lodgings, stores, services in Dulce.
**Special Rules and Regulations**
  **Fishing:** Fishing on all lakes permitted with tribal permit; See Regulations, page 76
  **Catch limit:** 8 fish, 16 in possession
  **Boating:** On all lakes; restricted to electric motors or oars, not to exceed trolling speeds
  **Other:** Primitive campgrounds; see Regulations, page 76

*Dulce Lake*

# Dulce Lake

Dulce Lake is an attractive seventy-four-acre lake. It is the largest of the Jicarilla lakes and visible off U.S. Highway 64, four miles west of the town of Dulce. There is a small fishing pier on the lake with some tables and camping sites. A launch ramp for boats, which are limited to oars or electric trolling motors, is available. During the winter of 1992–93, few fish survived in Dulce Lake due to low water levels that caused abundant weed growth and reduced oxygen supply for the high fish density. The lake was stocked in the following spring with 5,000 twelve- to thirteen-inch rainbows and 35,000 six-inch rainbows, so catchable trout looks promising for future seasons. As on all Jicarilla lakes, a tribal permit is required for fishing, boating, and camping. It is advisable to contact the Jicarilla Game and Fish Department at (505) 759-3255 for current road and lake conditions. See page 76 for fishing, camping and boating regulations. These regulations apply to all the lakes on the Jicarilla Reservation. The table on page 77 details the facilities offered by most of the Jicarilla lakes.

# La Jara Lake

La Jara lake is a fifty-five-acre lake on the Jicarilla Apache Indian Reservation fifteen miles south of Dulce off NM 537. A good gravel road allows easy access to its banks. Camping and picnicking facilities include tables and a pit toilet. Boats are permitted, but power is restricted to oars or electric trolling motors not to exceed five miles per hour. (See Boating Regulations page 76.)

Because of a low water level going into the winter of 1992–93, La Jara Lake experienced winter kill resulting in loss of most of the trout. The lake was restocked in April of 1993 with 30,000 six-inch trout after a good water level was achieved by the spring run-off. The rapid growth of trout made for excellent fishing during the summer and fall months.

As on all Jicarilla lakes it is advisable to contact the Jicarilla Game and Fish Department at (505) 759-3255 for current road and lake conditions. (See page 76 for Regulations.)

*La Jara Lake*

# Mundo Lake

Mundo Lake is a sixty-acre lake, 5.3 miles south of Dulce, attractively bordered by mountains forested in pine and easily accessed off paved Jicarilla highway J-8. Although some of the lakes in this high country of harsh winters have suffered winter-kill, there has never been a winter kill at Mundo Lake. It is stocked with rainbow and brown trout, channel catfish, and cutthroat. The abundance of fish and size of the catch (one brown measuring twenty-six inches and weighing over seven pounds) has made this lake a favorite for fishermen. Mundo Lake sits off the paved highway, where a turn around area is provided. A camping and picnicking area with tables, fire pits, and pit toilets is located at the lake just below this turnaround area. (See page 76, for Regulations.)

*Mundo Lake*

# Stone Lake

Stone Lake is 18.6 miles southeast of Dulce, reached by Jicarilla Highway J-8. It is situated in a colorful setting, where excellent fishing makes this one of the favorite fishing lakes on the reservation. It is also the site of the Stone Lake Fiesta, held annually on 14–15 September, when Apache families gather at the traditional fiesta grounds adjacent to Stone Lake. On this gala occasion, tepees are erected, campfires are lit, and rodeos, foot races and traditional dances in colorful ceremonial dress are staged. Tourists are welcome at this event. In the past, a modern lodge at Stone Lake accommodated sportsmen and tourists, but it is no longer in operation. Overnight accommodations are available in Dulce.

Stone Lake has had a good population of fifteen- to seventeen-inch rainbow and cutthroat trout, but due to winter weather extremes that may effect fish survival, it is advisable to contact the Jicarilla Game and Fish Department at (505) 759-3255 for current conditions of this lake and others on the reservation. Camping is permitted at the lake that provides limited facilities. Boats restricted to electric motors limited to 5 miles per hour, or trolling speeds are permitted. (See Boating Regulations on page 76.)

# Enbom Lake

Enbom Lake is a small, shallow, and weedy lake located 12.8 miles south of Dulce. It is prone to suffer winter kill, but in April of 1993 it was stocked with 5,000 rainbows resulting in good catchable rainbows in the summer and fall.

Enbom Lake is reached off Jicarilla Highway J-8 and is accessed by a good gravel road. Because of its low water level, boating is best by hand-powered boats. Canoes are most adaptable to Enbom. Camping and picnicking facilities include tables, fire pits, and pit toilets. As is general on all Jicarilla Lakes, it is advisable to contact the Jicarilla Game and Fish Department in Dulce for current conditions and accessibility or call (505) 759-3255 for information.

# Hayden Lake

Stocking of Hayden Lake was discontinued a few years ago due to the low water level. Stocking of rainbows was tried in the spring of 1992, but none survived the winter. In the spring of 1993, the water level was raised substantially by the spring run off, and the lake was stocked with 15,000 six-inch rainbows. The aeration system was reactivated, and it is hoped that the water level will be maintained to support a trout population. It is advisable to check with the Jicarilla Department of Game and Fish for current conditions at Hayden and other Jicarilla lakes.

# Horse Lake

Fishing at Horse Lake is reserved for Jicarilla tribal members, Dulce residents, and tribal employees. In the spring of 1993, a sampling showed nearly all of the rainbows stocked in 1992 suffered winter kill. Another stocking of the lake was done in the fall of that year, and these fish survived. A higher water level that rose to the spillway the following spring, five feet higher than the previous fall, resulted in excellent fishing the following year. Hopefully the higher water level will be maintained for continued fish survival. It is advisable to check with the Jicarilla Department of Game and Fish for current conditions.

# Stinking Lake (Burford Lake)

Stinking Lake is reserved for hunters during the fall hunting season. No fishing is permitted on the lake.

*Field Guide Elvin Smith stands in front of original Salmon house and birthplace of his mother in 1898*
*Salmon Ruins Archaeological Site and Museum*
*Bloomfield, New Mexico*

# In the Vicinity of Bloomfield

## *Bloomfield*

*In the vicinity of Bloomfield, and fifteen miles northeast of Blanco there is one lake: Navajo Lake*

Bloomfield is located on the San Juan River in northwestern New Mexico at the junctions of NM 44 and U.S. 64. It has a population of 6,462 and lies at an elevation of 5,395 feet above sea level. Bloomfield is a ranching and farming community situated in the center of an oil- and gas-producing region, whose industries provide many of the jobs and revenues for the community.

Bloomfield had its beginnings in the late 1800s as a trading post set up by an army general whose name was Porter, after whom the town was originally named. Later the name was changed to Bloomfield. Bloomfield has known turbulent times. It was here that the infamous outlaw from the Lincoln County War, Port Stockton, was hired as a peace officer, but his criminal ways led to his dismissal. He resumed his outlaw activities; terrorizing the town with stagecoach hold-ups, shootings, and cattle rustlings. Stockton was killed in 1881 by a sheriff hunting for a gunslinger Stockton was hiding. The shootings and violence continued for some years until the lawlessness finally settled down, and Bloomfield became the trading center for farmers and ranchers in the area.

An interesting place to visit while in the Bloomfield area is the Salmon Ruins Archaelogical Site and Museum, located just two miles west of Bloomfield on U.S. 64. It is one of the largest of the Anasazi villages built by people of the Chaco Canyon in the eleventh century. Visitors can tour Salmon Ruins by trails and view the many artifacts recovered from the ruins now on display in the adjacent museum. The photograph above shows the original home of George Salmon, who homesteaded the property before the turn of the century. It was also the birthplace of field guide Elvin Smith's mother in 1898. This home was restored by the San Juan County Historical Society. Bloomfield has adequate accommodations for tourists as well as grocery stores, restaurants, and service stations.

*Navajo Lake*

# NAVAJO LAKE

Navajo Lake is a 15,610-acre lake with 150 miles of piñon pine-dotted shoreline and sandstone mesas. It is set within the 17,959-acre Navajo Lake State Park. Navajo dam was constructed in 1962 to provide flood control water storage, recreation, and a game and fish habitat. The dam is almost three-quarters of a mile long and 400 feet high, and is operated by the Bureau of Reclamation. The lake's recreational facilities were constructed by the National Park Service and are maintained and managed by the states of Colorado and New Mexico. Navajo Lake is fed by spring thaws of the snowpack from the San Juan Mountains. Most of the park is in New Mexico and is divided into three recreational areas: Pine River, Sims Mesa Site, and San Juan River, where huge cottonwoods line its banks and where the surrounding hills are home to a large variety of deer, elk, rabbits, and other wildlife. The lake contains both cold- and warm-water species of fish. The lake is stocked with rainbow frys and five-inch fingerlings, and contains an abundant population of brown trout, kokanee salmon, smallmouth and largemouth bass, crappie, bluegill, channel catfish, and northern pike. Pine River and Sims Mesa Site boast a marina with docks and a boat ramp, a bait and tackle shop, a picnic ground, a developed campground with electric and water hook-ups, a dump station, flush toilets and showers, and a general store. The San Juan River site has picnic grounds, campgrounds, and three and a half miles of catch-and-release quality waters—an angler's paradise. Navajo Lake permits boats of all sizes and is open all year. It is a popular lake for water-skiing, windsurfing, swimming, and scuba diving.

## Directions from Albuquerque

Take I-25 north to Cuba/Farmington exit at Bernalillo. Continue northwest on NM 44 to Bloomfield, then go nine miles east on U.S. 64 to Blanco. Turn north on NM 511 and follow signs to Navajo Dam. All roads are paved allowing easy access.

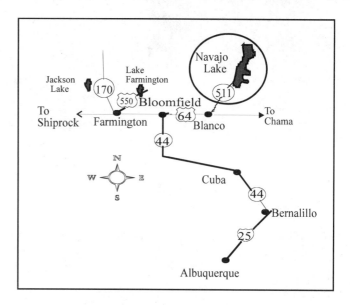

| | | |
|---|---|---|
| **Surface acres:** 15,610 | **Distance from Albuquerque:** 195 miles | |
| **Elevation:** 6,085 feet | **Location:** 15 miles northeast of Blanco; 24 miles | |
| **Max. trailer size & fee:** 40 feet; park fees posted | northeast of Bloomfield | |
| **Time limit:** 14 days | **Fish species:** Rainbow and brown trout, kokanee | |
| **Mailing address:** 1448 NM Highway 511, | salmon, largemouth and smallmouth bass, | |
| No.1 Navajo Dam , NM 87419  (505) 632-2278 | channel catfish, bluegill, crappie, and northern pike | |
| **Police emergency tel. #:** 911 | **Season:** 1 April-31 March  (Kokanee, 1 Oct.-31 Dec) | |

## ACTIVITIES AND FACILITIES

| | NO | YES | Proximity to Lake in Miles | | NO | YES | Proximity to Lake in Miles |
|---|---|---|---|---|---|---|---|
| Bait and supplies | | X | | Airplane runway | | X | |
| Boat gas | | X | | Bottled gas | X | | |
| Boat ramp | | X | | Café/snack bar | | X | |
| Boat rental | | X | | Chemical toilets | | X | |
| Camping | | X | | Drinking water | | X | |
| Fire pits | | X | | Electrical hook-up | | X | |
| Fire places | | X | | Flush toilets | | X | |
| Firewood | | X | | Grocery store | | X | |
| Fishing | | X | | Handicapped access | | X | |
| Golf | X | | | Ice | | X | |
| Hiking | | X | | Laundry | X | | |
| Marina | | X | | Lodgings | X | | |
| Picnicking | | X | | Pit toilets | | X | |
| Riding | X | | | Playground | | X | |
| Scuba diving | | X | | Restaurant | | X | |
| Stables | | X | | Sanitary disposal | | X | |
| Swimming | | X | | Sewer hook-up | | X | |
| Tables | | X | | Shelters | | X | |
| Telephone | | X | | Shopping | X | | |
| Tennis | X | | | Showers | | X | |
| Tent sites | | X | | Trailer space | | X | |
| Winter sports | X | | | Water hook-up | | X | |

## Special Rules and Regulations

**Fishing:** State fishing license required; see page 343 for license requirements

**Catch limit:** 10 trout per day; kokanee salmon, 12 per day, 24 in possession; see Fishing Proclamation for special regulations and special waters (page 343)

**Boating:** No restrictions on size or mode of power

**Other:** Camping with full facilities on three sites

# In the Vicinity of Farmington

## *Farmington*

*There are two lakes open to public use in the vicinity of Farmington: Farmington Lake, Jackson Lake*

Farmington is located in the northwestern corner of New Mexico at an elevation of 5,395 feet above sea level. It is the commercial center of the Four Corners Area, less than sixty miles east of the only point in the United States common to four state corners. These are the corners of the states of Arizona, Utah, Colorado, and New Mexico. It is also the center of New Mexico's oil, gas, and uranium industries, where coal gasification plants and thermo-electric power plants supply energy to a major portion of the Southwest.

Farmington was founded in 1879 as a trade center for homesteaders, farmers, and ranchers in the area. It is now a thriving, bustling city of almost 37,000 people. It lies in a fertile valley at the confluence of the San Juan, Animas, and La Plata Rivers, which carry sixty percent of New Mexico's surface water.

Jackson Lake lies off NM 170 (La Plata Highway). Farmington Lake is the City of Farmington's water supply. Farmington has modern accommodations for visitors. It has department stores, restaurants, service stations, grocery stores, golf courses, and an airport.

*Lake Farmington*

# LAKE FARMINGTON

Lake Farmington is a 198-acre lake, located six miles northeast of Farmington. It is the City of Farmington's water supply reservoir and is populated with largemouth bass and catfish, and is stocked with rainbow trout year round, except in the month of July, which is too hot for stocking.

Lake Farmington is a day-use lake, open to fishing between the hours of 5 A.M. and 10 P.M. Swimming, motor boating, firearms, and hunting are not permitted. Picnicking is permitted only in designated areas, where there are a few trash cans. No other facilities are available.

## Directions from Albuquerque

Take I-25 north to Cuba exit. Continue northwest on 44 to junction of 64. Go west to Farmington, then north on NM 550 and follow signs about five miles to lake. Access is good by paved roads.

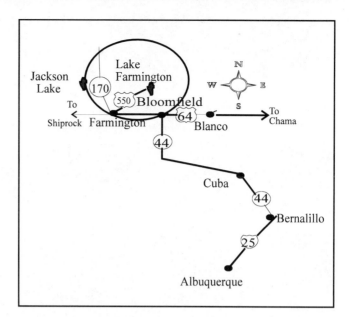

| | |
|---|---|
| **Surface acres:** 198 | **Distance from Albuquerque:** 188 miles |
| **Elevation:** 5,395 feet | **Location:** 6 miles northeast of Farmington |
| **Max. trailer size & fee:** Day use only | **Fish species:** Largemouth bass, catfish, and rainbow trout |
| **Time limit:** No camping | **Season:** All year |
| **Mailing address:** None | |
| **Police emergency tel. #:** 911 | |
| **Medical emergency tel. #:** 911 | |

## ACTIVITIES AND FACILITIES

| | NO | YES | Proximity to Lake in Miles | | NO | YES | Proximity to Lake in Miles |
|---|---|---|---|---|---|---|---|
| Bait and supplies | X | | *6 | Airplane runway | X | | *6 |
| Boat gas | X | | | Bottled gas | X | | |
| Boat ramp | X | | | Café/snack bar | X | | *6 |
| Boat rental | X | | | Chemical toilets | X | | |
| Camping | X | | | Drinking water | X | | |
| Fire pits | X | | | Electrical hook-up | X | | |
| Fire places | X | | | Flush toilets | X | | |
| Firewood | X | | | Grocery store | X | | *6 |
| Fishing | | X | | Handicapped access | X | | |
| Golf | X | | | Ice | X | | *6 |
| Hiking | X | | | Laundry | X | | |
| Marina | X | | | Lodgings | X | | *6 |
| Picnicking | | X | | Pit toilets | | X | |
| Riding | X | | | Playground | X | | |
| Scuba diving | X | | | Restaurant | X | | *6 |
| Stables | X | | | Sanitary disposal | X | | |
| Swimming | X | | | Sewer hook-up | X | | |
| Tables | X | | | Shelters | X | | |
| Telephone | X | | | Shopping | X | | *6 |
| Tennis | X | | | Showers | X | | |
| Tent sites | X | | | Trailer space | X | | |
| Winter sports | X | | | Water hook-up | X | | |

*Full facilities in Farmington, 6 miles.

**Special Rules and Regulations**

    **Fishing:** State fishing license required

    **Catch limit:** 6 fish, New Mexico Regulations apply

    **Boating:** Restricted to hand-powered boats only

    **Other:** Day use only

*Jackson Lake*

# JACKSON LAKE

Jackson Lake is a sixty-acre lake located five miles northwest of Farmington. It is owned by the New Mexico Department of Game and Fish. It is stocked with rainbow trout and also contains largemouth bass, bluegill, and channel catfish. Jackson Lake is a fishing and waterfowl habitat. Because of its proximity to the city of Farmington, and its fine fishing, it is a favorite year-round fishing and picnicking spot for local residents. It is also a pleasant place to view the many species of waterfowl, pheasants, quail, and mourning dove that inhabit the area. Many songbirds and raptors can also be seen in the river bottom. Waterfowl and dove hunting is allowed in specified areas. Signs identify the closed areas.

The dam is visible from the parking area, about two hundred yards below, and reached by either of two footpaths that wind up to the dam. The path on the left side, facing the dam, is the closest approach. Camping is not permitted at the lake, but picnic sites with limited facilities are provided around the lake.

## Directions from Albuquerque

Take I-25 north to Cuba cut-off Exit 142, then go northwest on NM 44 and connect with U.S. Highway 64 west to Farmington. Then go north on NM 170 and follow signs about five miles to lake.

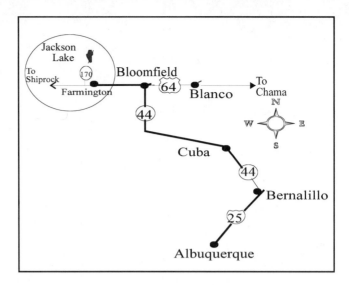

| | | |
|---|---|---|
| **Surface acres: 60** | **Distance from Albuquerque:** 185 miles | |
| **Elevation:** 5,395 feet | **Location:** 5 miles northwest of Farmington | |
| **Max. trailer size & fee:** No camping | **Fish species:** Rainbow trout, bluegill, channel catfish, and | |
| **Time limit:** No camping | largemouth bass | |
| **Police emergency tel. #:** 325-7547 | **Season:** 1 April-31 March | |
| **Medical emergency tel. #:** 911 | | |

## ACTIVITIES AND FACILITIES

| | NO | YES | Proximity to Lake in Miles | | NO | YES | Proximity to Lake in Miles |
|---|---|---|---|---|---|---|---|
| Bait and supplies | X | | * | Airplane runway | X | | |
| Boat gas | X | | | Bottled gas | X | | |
| Boat ramp | X | | | Café/snack bar | X | | |
| Boat rental | X | | | Chemical toilets | X | | |
| Camping | X | | | Drinking water | X | | |
| Fire pits | | X | | Electrical hook-up | X | | |
| Fire places | X | | | Flush toilets | X | | |
| Firewood | X | | | Grocery store | X | | |
| Fishing | | X | | Handicapped access | X | | |
| Golf | X | | | Ice | X | | |
| Hiking | X | | | Laundry | X | | |
| Marina | X | | | Lodgings | X | | |
| Picnicking | | X | | Pit toilets | | X | |
| Riding | X | | | Playground | X | | |
| Scuba diving | X | | | Restaurant | X | | |
| Stables | X | | | Trash cans | | X | |
| Swimming | X | | | Sewer hook-up | X | | |
| Tables | | X | | Shelters | X | | |
| Telephone | X | | | Shopping | X | | |
| Tennis | X | | | Showers | X | | |
| Tent sites | X | | | Trailer space | X | | |
| Winter sports | X | | | Water hook-up | X | | |

*Full facilities, stores, and services in Farmington, 5 miles.
**Special Rules and Regulations**
   **Fishing:** State fishing license required
   **Catch limit:** 6 fish; New Mexico Regulations apply
   **Boating:** No motors

# In the Vicinity of Shiprock

## *Shiprock*

*Shiprock is a Navajo town. It is the gateway to the Navajo Reservation and the lakes within the reservation's boundaries. The following are some of the lakes open by tribal permit to the public: \*Morgan Lake, \*Asaayi Lake, \*Red Lake, \*Todachene Lake, Berland Lake, Aspen Lake, Whiskey Lake, Chuska Lake, Cutter Lake. Four of these lakes (preceded by an asterisk) are typical of the Navajo lakes and are detailed on the following pages.*

Shiprock is located in northwestern New Mexico, thirty miles west of Farmington, on U.S. Highways 64 and 666. It is a Navajo town established in 1903 as a Navajo Indian Agency, or District, serving as a major trading center for the Navajo communities in the area. It is one of the five Navajo Nation geographical agencies, or districts, that comprise the Navajo Nation, whose population exceeds 210,000. The district encompasses more than 25,000 square miles, an area about the size of West Virginia; straddling the borders of New Mexico, Arizona, and southern Utah. In 1938, the five agencies were consolidated. Window Rock, Arizona, was established as a capital, where most programs and services are administrated by the Navajo Tribal Council, the largest and most sophisticated American Indian government in the United States. The reservation contains some of the most awesome and spectacular scenery in the world, providing superb recreational

opportunities for fishermen, campers, hikers, and hunters.

Today, Shiprock has grown into the Navajo Nation's largest town, and each year in early October, Shiprock attracts more than 90,000 to the Shiprock Navajo Fair. It is the oldest Navajo Tribal Fair of the Navajo fairs held on the reservation. Since 1903, the fair has been held in conjunction with the nine-day ceremony called the *Yeibechei Ceremony,* a colorful affair of arts and crafts, Indian jewelry displays, rodeos, ceremonial dances, and a chance for visitors to see colorful traditional clothing worn by the older men and women of the tribe.

A short distance southwest of Shiprock is Tse Bida'hi, pronounced, *"Tse Bitai,"* ("rock with wings"), the Indian name for Shiprock. This huge monolith is the stem of a volcano that rises almost 1,500 feet from its base and is visible from a hundred miles away. Indian legends vary as to its mythical past. All of the legends are linked to the Navajos' arrival at this spot. One tale tells of a giant bird that carried them to safety from the pursuit of enemies. Finally landing, the bird turned to stone. Another tale tells of the Navajos sailing from a distant place beyond the setting sun, landing among an unfriendly people and rescued by the Great Spirit, who transported them to safety to this spot, in a stone ship. The rock is venerated by the Navajos, and because of its religious significance climbing *Tse Bida' hi* is off-limits to visitors and tourists.

# LAKES ON THE NAVAJO RESERVATION OF NEW MEXICO

The map opposite shows the location of some of the more popular Navajo Reservation lakes in New Mexico. Most of the lakes are cradled in the beautiful Chuska Mountains located in the east-central area of the Navajo Reservation. They range from one to one thousand acres and provide excellent fishing for rainbow, brook, and cutthroat trout. These lakes and their regulations and facilities are described on pages 93-96.

## Navajo Lakes of New Mexico

### Fishing, Boating, and Camping Regulations

Daily and annual fishing, boating, and camping permits may be purchased directly from the Navajo Fish and Wildlife Office or from vendors located in border towns surrounding the Navajo Nation. For additional information and current fees contact Navajo Fish and Wildlife Office, P.O. Box 1480, Window Rock, AZ 86515 (602) 871-5338.

**Fishing permit:** Required for all persons over 12 years of age; not required for persons under 12 years of age; non-Navajos, $26.00 for annual permit

**Catch limits:** 12 years of age or older, 8 per day or in possession of trout, channel catfish, or bass; under 12 years of age, 1/2 daily bag and possession limit; Whiskey Lake is a quality water lake, bag limit, 4 fish

**Boating regulations:** Annual boat fee, $14.00; all lakes (except Morgan Lake) oars or electric motors; Morgan Lake permits boats of any size or motor type; (check with Navajo Fish and Wildlife office for current annual and daily fees for boating, fishing, and camping)

**Baits:** In trout waters, no minnows, cray fish, water dogs, alive or dead, permitted; use of only one line containing not more than two hooks; in Other Waters, all baits permitted, except minnows, dead or alive

**Camping:** Camping facilities are primitive; call Navajo Fish and Wildlife Office for current information on road conditions, and accessibility during wet weather

**Season:** 1 January-31 December (except Whiskey Lake); Whiskey Lake, 1 May-30 November

## Directions from Albuquerque

Take I-40 to Gallup. Turn right on U.S. 666. Travel north through the Navajo Reservation. U.S. 666 goes directly to Shiprock, located at the junction of U.S. 666 and U.S. 64. Shiprock is the largest town and commercial center of the New Mexico Navajo Indian Reservation. The reservation can also be reached from Farmington via U.S. 64 West.

Direction routes to lakes from Shiprock
Berland Lake: Via U.S. 666 & NM 134
Aspen Lake: Via U.S. 666 & NM 134
Chuska Lake: Via U.S. 666 near Tohatchi
Cutter Lake: Via U.S. 64, south of Blanco
Morgan, Asaayi, Red, and Todacheene
Lakes are detailed on pages 94-95

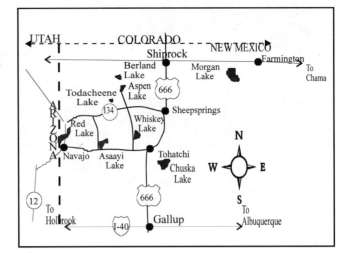

| | |
|---|---|
| **Surface acres:** 1,000-1,200 acres | **Distance from Albuquerque:** 215 miles |
| **Elevation:** 6,500-9,000 feet | **Location:** South of Shiprock |
| **Max. trailer size & fee:** Check with tribal office as rules change | **Fish species:** Rainbow, brook, and cutthroat trout |
| **Time limit:** Regulations from Navajo | **Season:** 1 January-1 December (except at Whiskey Lake); |
| Fish and Wildlife Office | Whiskey Lake season is 1 May-30 November |
| **Mailing address:** P.O. Box 1480, Window | |
| Rock, AZ, 86515 (602) 871-5338 | |

## ACTIVITIES AND FACILITIES

| | NO | YES | Proximity to Lake in Miles | | NO | YES | Proximity to Lake in Miles |
|---|---|---|---|---|---|---|---|
| Bait and supplies | X | | | Airplane runway | X | | |
| Boat gas | X | | | Bottled gas | X | | * |
| Boat ramp | X | | | Café/snack bar | X | | * |
| Camping | | X | | Drinking water | X | | |
| Fire pits | | X | | Electrical hook-up | X | | |
| Fire grills | | X | | Flush toilets | X | | |
| Firewood | X | | | Grocery store | X | | |
| Fishing | | X | | Handicapped access | | X | |
| Golf | X | | | Ice | X | | * |
| Hiking | | X | | Laundry | X | | * |
| Picnicking | | X | | Pit toilets | | X | |
| Riding | | X | | Playground | X | | |
| Scuba diving | X | | | Restaurant | X | | * |
| Skiing (water) | X | | | Trash cans | | X | |
| Swimming | X | | | Sewer hook-up | X | | |
| Tables | | X | | Shelters | | X | |
| Telephone | | | * | Shopping | X | | * |
| Tennis | X | | | Showers | X | | |
| Tent sites | | X | | Trailer space | | X | |
| Winter sports | X | | | Water hook-up | X | | |

*Lodgings, stores, and services in Shiprock.
**Special Rules and Regulations**
**Fishing:** Allowed on all lakes with tribal permit; see Navajo Regulations on page 92
**Catch limit:** 8 fish; 16 in possession
**Boating:** Restricted to oars or electric motors not to exceed trolling speeds, except at Morgan Lake, which permits any size boat and motor—gasoline or electric.
**Other:** Information on table above, typifies all lakes on the reservation; camping facilities are primitive

*Morgan Lake*

# Morgan Lake

Morgan Lake is a 1,200-acre artificial lake adjoining the Four Corners Steam-Electric Power plant off U.S. Highway 550, between Kirtland and Fruitland. It has a warm-water fish population of largemouth bass, channel catfish, bullheads, and bluegill. These fish survive on Morgan Lake waters warmed by the power plant. It is also the only Navajo Nation lake in New Mexico that permits gasoline motors. The other Navajo lake permitting gasoline engines is Many Farms Lake near Chinle, Arizona.

To reach Morgan Lake turn left off the junction of U.S. 64 and U.S. 550, and go southwest approximately thirteen miles. Leaving the paved highway, the roads are unimproved dirt roads on the northwest side of the lake, and four-wheel-drive high-clearance vehicles are recommended during inclement weather. Facilities at the lake include a concrete boat ramp, picnic tables, and some pit toilets.

Since this is a Navajo Reservation lake, no New Mexico fishing license is required. A tribal permit is required and can be obtained from the Navajo Fish and Wildlife Office or a vendor in the surrounding area.

# Asaayi Lake

Asaayi Lake is a thirty-six-acre lake lying at an elevation of 7,523 feet above sea level in the Chuska Mountains about five miles south of Crystal and thirteen miles east of the small town of Navajo. This high mountain lake is cradled in a magnificent setting surrounded by pine forests, hills, and red sandstone formations. On our arrival at Asaayi Lake on a late afternoon, the cooling breath of pine and the rising of trout on its surface in the last moments of the waning day made this lake one to be remembered.

Camping, fishing, and picnicking facilities include trash cans, tables, and pit toilets. A large parking area at the edge of the lake provides easy access for the handicapped. The parking area also serves as a boat launching area. Boats are restricted to electric trolling motors or oars. Asaayi Lake is stocked with trout, and its remote location offers seclusion for campers and fishermen. Picnic supplies, and bait and tackle are available in Navajo, thirteen miles west.

*Asaayi Lake*

# Red Lake

Red Lake is a 600-acre Navajo Reservation lake that straddles the Arizona–New Mexico border at an elevation of 7,100 feet above sea level. It is stocked with rainbow trout and northern pike. The northern pike were stocked to control the population of undesirable species of fish. Red Lake is reached from Shiprock first by way of U.S. 666, then west on NM 134 at Sheep Springs, past Crystal, then south, connecting with NM 34, which runs parallel to the lake's shore. The lake is accessed at its southern end in the small village of Navajo. At the entrance to the lake, a sign welcomes visitors with posted regulations as follows: *"Requirements: Tribal fishing permit, tribal boating permit, overnight camping permit. 24 hours fishing permitted. No swimming, no littering, no hunting."*

A general store just south of the lake in the town of Navajo has groceries, ice, soft drinks, and picnic and fishing supplies. As on all lakes on the Navajo Reservation, except Morgan Lake, no gasoline motors are permitted.

*Red Lake*

*Todacheene Lake*

# Todacheene Lake

Todacheene Lake is a four-acre lake nestled in a heavily wooded, scenic, and pristine setting. It is reached by way of State Road 134, then go south on a dirt road that also goes north to Berland and Aspen Lakes. The last three-tenths of a mile is a scenic drive on a winding, badly deteriorated, muddy, and deeply rutted road. Todacheene Lake is identified by a small sign affixed to a huge ponderosa growing alongside the road that leads to the lake.

Upon our arrival in mid-afternoon, no one was at the lake. A sense of remoteness and infinite serenity pervaded the entire scene, broken only by the splash of rainbow trout rising to the surface that mirrored the mountainside bristling with fir, pine, and larch. If ever one desires solitude, it can be experienced here in this peaceful place, wrapped in silence and bathed in the heady scent of pine.

Todacheene Lake has primitive camping sites and permits boats restricted to electric motors or oars. There are no other facilities at the lake. Groceries, bait, and tackle, are available in the town of Navajo located close to Red Lake that straddles the Arizona–New Mexico border. Navajo also has a gas station.

# Other Popular Lakes on the Navajo Reservation

## Berland Lake

A seven-acre lake at an elevation of 8,900 feet above sea level, located on the Aspen Lake road north of Crystal. It is stocked with rainbow and cutthroat trout. This high mountain lake offers great fishing and primitive camping in an alpine setting of pine and aspen.

## Aspen Lake

A one-acre lake at an elevation of 9,000 feet, located five miles south of Crystal, between Crystal and Sheep Springs. Aspen lake is stocked annually with catchable rainbows. It offers primitive camping in a forested setting of pine and aspen.

## Whiskey Lake

Unlike other Navajo Reservation lakes, Whiskey Lake is a quality water lake reserved for the management of trophy fish. Taking fish is limited to lures only. No live bait is allowed, and the catch limit is four fish. Whiskey Lake lies in a magnificent forest setting of ponderosa and aspen. It is located south of Shiprock, eight miles south of Narbona Pass off U.S. 666, and is reached by Logging Road 7170, a rough unimproved road requiring four-wheel-drive or high-clearance vehicles.

## Chuska Lake

A 100-acre lake south of Shiprock off NM 666 near Tohatchi. It is stocked with rainbows and cutthroats. As with all of the Navajo Lakes, with the exception of Morgan Lake, boats are restricted to hand-power or electric trolling motors.

## Cutter Lake

A forty-acre lake located southeast of Blanco. It is part of the irrigation canal for the Navajo Indian Irrigation Project. Its water is supplied from the Navajo Reservoir. Cutter Lake is stocked with rainbows, and kokanee salmon. It is also populated with bass and channel catfish.

# ZONE 2

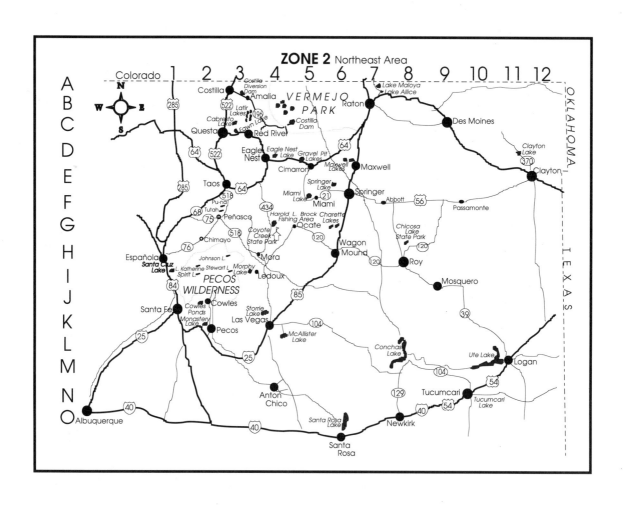

# ZONE 2

AREA EAST OF I-25 AND 84/285 TO THE OKLAHOMA/TEXAS BORDERS AND NORTH OF I-40 TO THE COLORADO BORDER

## Table of Distances (Miles to vicinity)

| VICINITY (lake access from nearest town) | Map Key | Albuquerque | Farmington | Las Cruces | Clayton | Hobbs |
|---|---|---|---|---|---|---|
| **Pecos** | K2 | 81 | 220 | 302 | 195 | 227 |
| Monastery Lake, p.102 | | | | | | |
| **\*Pecos Wilderness (Cowles)** | F4 | 101 | 242 | 325 | 215 | 247 |
| Cowles Ponds, p.106 | | | | | | |
| \*Stewart Lake, p.109 | | | | | | |
| \*Lake Katherine, p. 109 | | | | | | |
| \*Johnson Lake, p. 109 | | | | | | |
| \*Spirit Lake, p. 109 | | | | | | |
| \*Pecos Baldy Lake, p. 109 | | | | | | |
| \*Lost Bear Lake, p. 109 | | | | | | |
| \* Asterisks denote lakes located within Pecos Wilderness. | | | | | | |
| **Las Vegas** | K7 | 123 | 263 | 307 | 150 | 285 |
| Storrie Lake, p. 112 | | | | | | |
| McAllister Lake, p. 114 | | | | | | |
| **Mora** | G3 | 153 | 239 | 337 | 180 | 315 |
| Morphy Lake, p. 118 | | | | | | |
| Harold L. Brock Fishing Area, p. 120 | | | | | | |
| **Española** (see zone 1 for other lakes in this vicinity) | H1 | 84 | 174 | 307 | 209 | 303 |
| Santa Cruz Lake, p. 40 | | | | | | |
| Nambe Falls Lake, p. 46 | | | | | | |
| **Peñasco** | F3 | 121 | 234 | 332 | 142 | 343 |
| Pu-na and Tutah Lakes, p. 124 | | | | | | |
| **Questa** | C2 | 151 | 236 | 374 | 182 | 285 |
| Eagle Rock Lake, p. 128 | | | | | | |
| Cabresto Lake, p. 130 | | | | | | |
| Heart Lake, p. 127 | | | | | | |
| Red River Hatchery Pond, p. 132 | | | | | | |
| **Costilla/Amalia** | A2 | 171 | 256 | 394 | 202 | 405 |
| Costilla Diversion Dam, p. 136 | | | | | | |
| Shuree Ponds, p. 135 | | | | | | |
| Latir Lakes, p. 138 | | | | | | |
| **Red River** | C3 | 165 | 250 | 388 | 148 | 338 |
| Horse Lake, p. 141 | | | | | | |
| Lost Lake, p. 141 | | | | | | |
| Middle Fork Lake, p. 141 | | | | | | |
| Pioneer Lake, p. 141 | | | | | | |
| Goose Lake, p. 141 | | | | | | |
| Fawn Lake, p. 142 | | | | | | |

## Table of Distances (to vicinity)

| VICINITY (lake access from nearest town) | Map Key | Albuquerque | Farmington | Las Cruces | Clayton | Hobbs |
|---|---|---|---|---|---|---|
| **Eagle Nest** | D4 | 164 | 245 | 383 | 129 | 369 |
| Eagle Nest Lake, p. 146 | | | | | | |
| Gravel Pit Lakes, p. 148 | | | | | | |
| **Springer** | E6 | 190 | 293 | 374 | 83 | 323 |
| Springer Lake, p. 152 | | | | | | |
| Charette Lake, p. 154 | | | | | | |
| Miami Lake, p. 156 | | | | | | |
| **Maxwell** | D7 | 203 | 294 | 387 | 96 | 336 |
| Maxwell Lakes, p. 160 | | | | | | |
| Stubblefield Lake, Laguna Madre, p. 162 | | | | | | |
| **Raton** | B7 | 224 | 309 | 413 | 83 | 362 |
| Lake Maloya, p. 166 | | | | | | |
| Lake Alice, p. 166 | | | | | | |
| **Roy** | H7 | 199 | 339 | 383 | 89 | 227 |
| Chicosa Lake, p. 170 | | | | | | |
| **Clayton** | D11 | 273 | 376 | 414 | -- | 296 |
| Clayton Lake, p. 174 | | | | | | |
| **Santa Rosa** (see Zone 3 for other lakes in this vicinity) | O6 | 114 | 296 | 244 | 170 | 222 |
| Santa Rosa Lake, p. 178 | | | | | | |
| Tres Lagunas, p. 182 | | | | | | |
| **Newkirk** | N6 | 141 | 323 | 271 | 144 | 167 |
| Conchas Lake, p. 184 | | | | | | |
| **Tucumcari** | M10 | 173 | 355 | 303 | 111 | 200 |
| Tucumcari Lake, p. 188 (Ladd S. Gordon Wildlife Area) | | | | | | |
| **Logan** | L11 | 195 | 377 | 325 | 87 | 232 |
| Ute Lake, p. 192 | | | | | | |

# In the Vicinity of Pecos

## *Pecos*

*In the vicinity of Pecos there is one lake: Monastery Lake. Cowles, gateway to the Pecos Wilderness lakes, is twenty miles north.*

Pecos is located twenty miles east of Santa Fe on NM highway 63, lying at an elevation of 6,925 feet above sea level. It is a small historic mountain town set in a wide valley on the Pecos River at the southern edge of the majestic Sangre de Cristo Mountains, whose highest peaks rise more than 13,000 feet. Its heavily forested canyons provide some of the most scenic and pleasurable drives in New Mexico, as well as some of the best fishing and outdoor recreation areas in the state. The Pecos area draws thousands each year to fish the 150 miles of streams, and the many alpine lakes, to hunt the abundant wildlife, to hike the miles of mountain trails, and to camp in the many sites scattered throughout the area and along NM 63 north to Cowles, the gateway to the Pecos Wilderness. It is at Cowles, that trails lead to the famous peaks of Pecos Baldy, Santa Fe Baldy, Truchas Peaks, and the many lakes that shine like jewels in the cirques of the high mountain slopes. The Pecos Ranger Station is located on the highway, where visitors can obtain permits to enter the wilderness and get information on road conditions and camping facilities.

In the center of Pecos is St. Anthony's Church, whose rear faces the road and its front faces the river. It is an elaborately designed structure with a tall steeple gracing its pitched, tinned roof. Pecos has accommodations for overnight visitors. There are gas stations, restaurants, and a completely stocked general store, *Adelo's,* owned by the town mayor, George Adelo. The store has tools, camping supplies, fishing and picnicking supplies, and groceries: everything needed for treks into the wilderness. Complete services and facilities for visitors are available in Santa Fe, twenty miles west of Pecos.

Two miles south of the town is the 365-acre Pecos National Monument that preserves the multi-storied ruins of the Pecos Pueblo, one of the largest fifteenth century Indian pueblos, once home of over 2,000 Pueblo Indians, who inhabited the area long before Coronado entered the area in search of the *Golden Cities of Cibola*. It is also the site of the ruins of the Spanish *Mision de Nuestra Señora de Los Angeles de Porciúncula,* which was founded in the early 1620s by Franciscan priests and became the center of the entire community. Its purpose was to replace the political and religious way of life of the Indian with that of the Spaniard. The thick adobe walls of the mission church served as a landmark for travelers on the Santa Fe Trail. Ruts of this historic trail still exist in the vicinity. Visitors may walk through the ruins on a one-and-a-quarter-mile self-guided trail. There is an exhibit room in the visitors center that covers 10,000 years of history in the Pecos Valley, and a ten-minute film is repeated throughout the day. Guided tours are also provided to any organized group (pre-arrange two weeks in advance). The park may be reached from I-25 at Glorieta, eight miles west of the park via the town of Pecos, or the town of Rowe, three miles south of the park.

*Monastery Lake*

# MONASTERY LAKE

Monastery Lake is an oval-shaped six-acre lake set in a wide valley. It is located two miles north of the town of Pecos. About a mile past the town of Pecos, on NM 63, is the Benedictine Monastery, an interesting place to visit while in the area. About a half-mile farther north on NM 63 is a dirt/gravel turn-off road that leads four-tenths of a mile to the lake parking area.

About a thirty-yard walk from the parking area, along a nicely wooded path, is the lake. Next to the parking area is a vault toilet and another one is located about two-thirds down the path to the lake. There are no other facilities at the lake. It is a no-fee, carry-in and carry-out day-use lake. It is well worth taking the time to enjoy a picnic or day of fishing for the rainbow trout that is reared at the Lisboa Springs Hatchery, located about a mile north of the lake and stocked by the New Mexico Game and Fish Department, which leases the lake from the Benedictine Monastery. It is a secluded, man-made, spring-fed lake ringed by a forest of firs, piñon pine, juniper, ponderosas, cottonwoods, birch, and scrub oak. North of the lake are many campgrounds, some improved and well appointed, some unimproved for camping and picnicking. Many have pit toilets conveniently placed along NM 63 that heads north to Cowles, gateway to the Pecos Wilderness.

Pecos is the place to stop for needed supplies for fishing and picnicking. The town has grocery stores, bait and tackle shops, gas stations, restaurants, and motels. A New Mexico fishing license is required to fish Monastery Lake, where New Mexico Department of Game and Fish Regulations apply. A Fishing Proclamation containing these rules can be obtained from any bait and tackle shop or fishing license vendor in the state.

## Directions from Albuquerque

Take I-25 north to Santa Fe. Continue to the junction of NM 50 at Glorieta and go east through Pecos on NM 63. About one mile north, on SR 63 is the Benedictine Monastery. Continue north about a quarter of a mile past the Monastery to the Monastery Lake turn-off. Take turn-off to the left at the sign and go four-tenths of a mile on a good dirt/gravel road to the lake.

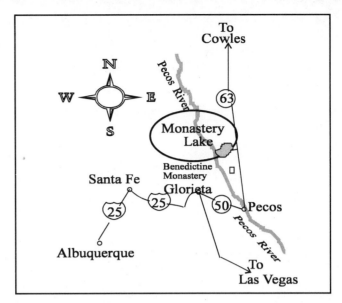

| | |
|---|---|
| **Surface acres:** 6 | **Distance from Albuquerque:** 83 miles |
| **Elevation:** 7,100 feet | **Location:** 2 miles north of Pecos |
| **Max. trailer size & fee:** No camping | **Fish species:** Rainbow trout; good fishing for browns in the |
| **Time limit:** Day use only | River along the highway |
| **Mailing address:** Lisboa Fish Hatchery, P.O. Box 25112, | **Season:** March-May; September-October, 6 A.M.-8 P.M.; |
| Santa Fe, N.M. 87504 Tel. (505) 757-6121 | November- February, 6 A.M.-6 P.M.; June-August, 6 A.M.-9 P.M. |

## ACTIVITIES AND FACILITIES

| | NO | YES | Proximity to Lake in Miles | | NO | YES | Proximity to Lake in Miles |
|---|---|---|---|---|---|---|---|
| **Bait and supplies** | X | | | **Airplane runway** | X | | |
| **Boat gas** | X | | | **Bottled gas** | X | | |
| **Boat ramp** | X | | | **Café/snack bar** | X | | |
| **Boat rental** | X | | | **Chemical toilets** | X | | |
| **Camping** | X | | | **Drinking water** | X | | |
| **Fire pits** | X | | | **Electrical hook-up** | X | | |
| **Fire places** | X | | | **Flush toilets** | X | | |
| **Firewood** | X | | | **Grocery store** | X | | |
| **Fishing** | | X | | **Handicapped access** | X | | |
| **Golf** | X | | | **Ice** | X | | |
| **Hiking** | X | | | **Laundry** | X | | |
| **Marina** | X | | | **Lodgings** | X | | |
| **Picnicking** | | X | | **Pit toilets** | | X | |
| **Riding** | X | | | **Playground** | X | | |
| **Scuba diving** | X | | | **Restaurant** | X | | |
| **Stables** | X | | | **Sanitary disposal** | X | | |
| **Swimming** | X | | | **Sewer hook-up** | X | | |
| **Tables** | X | | | **Shelters** | X | | |
| **Telephone** | X | | | **Shopping** | X | | |
| **Tennis** | X | | | **Showers** | X | | |
| **Tent sites** | X | | | **Trailer space** | X | | |
| **Winter sports** | X | | | **Water hook-up** | X | | |

Stores and accommodations in Pecos, 2 miles south.

**Special Rules and Regulations**

**Fishing:** State license required; no-fee fishing; see Fishing Proclamation

**Catch limit:** 6 trout; see Fishing Proclamation for latest possession limits

**Boating:** No boats or floating devices permitted

**Other:** Day use only; many campgrounds and picnic sites to the north along highway

# In the Vicinity
# of Cowles
# (Pecos Wilderness)

## *Cowles*
## *(Pecos Wilderness)*

The tiny village of Cowles ends at the entrance to the trails that lead to the lakes in the Pecos Wilderness. At this point, there is a large parking area, and opposite the parking area there are two small ponds reserved for children under the age of twelve, and the handicapped, called Cowles Ponds.

The lakes within the Pecos Wilderness are reached by trail only. Because many of the lakes of the Pecos Wilderness are difficult to reach in one-day trips and many entail long and strenuous hikes, such as the Trampas and Truchas Lakes, they have not been detailed in this guide. Some of the more popular lakes and some of the more popular campgrounds reached from Cowles are listed as follows: Stewart Lake, Lake Katherine, Johnson Lake, Spirit Lake, Lost Bear Lake, Pecos Baldy Lake. A map and descriptions of these lakes are on pages 108 and 109.

The Pecos Wilderness encompasses 223,333 acres of unspoiled mountain scenery, as beautiful as any to be found in New Mexico. It lies at the southern end of the Sangre de Cristo Mountains at the headwaters of the Pecos River and is protected and managed to preserve it in its natural state. It includes some of the highest peaks in New Mexico, including the 13,103 feet Truchas Peak, second highest peak in the state.

From Cowles and from Pecos, an extensive trail system leads out in all directions to the many glacier-spawned, cloud-reflecting alpine lakes, each with its own particular charm, heightened by the wonderful mountain settings ranging from rugged, wild crags to gentle sylvan slopes blanketed with wildflowers. These lakes and the miles of trout-populated streams attract thousands of campers, hikers, backpackers, mountaineers, anglers, and lovers of the outdoors. Almost all the lakes support fish, and they are stocked periodically, by helicopter, with cutthroat trout, by the New Mexico Department of Game and Fish.

The map on page 108 shows the location of some of the more popular lakes reached by trail, including some of the overnight campgrounds. Included on page 108 are some of the hazards to be expected when entering the Wilderness. Brief descriptions of the campground's facilities and the lakes reached by trail are listed on page 109.

**Note:** There are fifteen lakes in the Pecos Wilderness, but because many of the lakes are difficult to reach in one-day trips, such as the Truchas Lakes, Trampas Lakes and others in the Wilderness, they have been omitted. (Some of these lakes are mentioned on page 109.) For more complete information on planning and preparing a visit to the Pecos Wilderness, maps can be purchased from the nearest Forest Service Office.

*Cowles Ponds*

# COWLES PONDS

Cowles Ponds is located at the end of NM 63, twenty miles north of Pecos. NM 63 ends at a large parking area . The two ponds that comprise this attractive small recreation area, known as Cowles Ponds, are stocked with rainbow trout, where fishing is limited to children under twelve and the handicapped. There are nine units with potable water and there are two well-maintained restrooms.

It is a day-use area, but the large parking area across the road, the gateway to the Pecos Wilderness Area, has ample room for parking trailers and campers. From here you can reach the Iron Creek, Jacks Creek, and Panchuela overnight campgrounds by an extensive trail system. The Holy Ghost and Field Tract Campgrounds are reached from Pecos off NM 63 and Forest Roads.

## Directions from Albuquerque

Take I-25 north to Santa Fe. Continue to the junction of NM 50 at Glorieta and go east through Pecos on NM 63. Go north on NM 63 twenty miles to Cowles. Four miles before Cowles is the Terrero General Store, where picnic supplies, bait and tackle, food, and a guide service are available for those wishing to explore the Pecos Wilderness Area. Along the roadside are many private and Santa Fe National Park developed and primitive campgrounds and picnic areas.

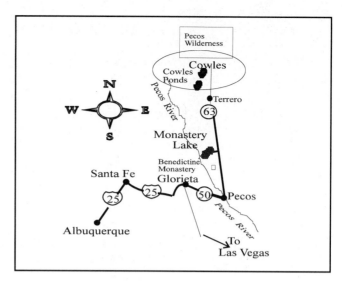

| | | |
|---|---|---|
| **Surface acres:** 2 Ponds, total about 3 acres | **Distance from Albuquerque:** 101 miles | |
| **Elevation:** 8,500 feet | **Location:** 20 miles north of Pecos; 4 miles north of Terrero | |
| **Max. trailer size & fee:** No camping | **Fish species:** Rainbow trout | |
| **Time limit:** No camping | **Season:** 1 April-31 March | |
| **Mailing address:** None | | |
| **Police emergency tel. #:** 911 | | |
| **Medical emergency tel. #:** 911 | | |

### ACTIVITIES AND FACILITIES

| | NO | YES | Proximity to Lake in Miles | | NO | YES | Proximity to Lake in Miles |
|---|---|---|---|---|---|---|---|
| Bait and supplies | X | | *4 | Airplane runway | X | | |
| Boat gas | X | | | Bottled gas | X | | |
| Boat ramp | X | | | Café/snack bar | X | | *4 |
| Boat rental | X | | | Chemical toilets | | X | |
| Camping | X | | ** | Drinking water | X | | ** |
| Fire pits | X | | ** | Electrical hook-up | X | | ** |
| Fire places | X | | ** | Flush toilets | X | | ** |
| Firewood | X | | ** | Grocery store | X | | *4 |
| Fishing | | X | | Handicapped access | | X | |
| Golf | X | | | Ice | X | | |
| Hiking | | X | | Laundry | X | | |
| Marina | X | | | Lodgings | X | | |
| Picnicking | | X | | Pit toilets | X | | ** |
| Riding | X | | ** | Playground | X | | |
| Scuba diving | X | | | Restaurant | X | | |
| Stables | X | | | Sanitary disposal | X | | ** |
| Swimming | X | | | Sewer hook-up | X | | ** |
| Tables | X | | ** | Shelters | X | | ** |
| Telephone | X | | ** | Shopping | X | | |
| Tennis | X | | | Showers | X | | |
| Tent sites | X | | ** | Trailer space | X | | ** |
| Winter sports | X | | ** | Water hook-up | X | | ** |

*Guide service, and store for picnic and fishing supplies in Terrero, 4 miles south.

**Special Rules and Regulations**

Fishing: Reserved for children under 12 and the handicapped

Catch limit: See Fishing Proclamation for special waters for children and the handicapped

Boating: No boats or floating devices permitted

Other:**Many camping facilities and picnic areas, some with pit toilets, along road from Pecos to Cowles; some private with hook-ups and some National Park managed

# The Pecos Wilderness

The Pecos Wilderness contains fifteen lakes and eight major streams with their tributaries that offer excellent fishing. An extensive trail system attracts thousands of hikers, campers, anglers, and hunters each year. It is heavily forested in ponderosa pine, Douglas fir, white fir, bristle cone-pine, aspen, and Engleman spruce in the higher areas. It has an abundant wildlife population that includes black bear, turkey, mule deer, bighorn sheep, and elk. Many of the lake basins are off-limits to overnight camping. These include Lake Johnson, Lake Katherine, Sanatiago Lake, Spirit Lake, Stewart Lake, Pecos Baldy, Truchas Lake, and Jose Vigil Lake.

The wide diversity of elevations ranging from 8,400 to over 13,000 feet, with steep slopes and cliffs, can be hazardous to backpackers, hikers, and pack animals. Visitors should be aware of the risks before entering the Wilderness and prepare accordingly. Sudden lightning and thunderstorms occur almost daily during the summer months. Inclement weather may limit access to trailheads, and snowpack may limit or even close roads to as late as mid-June. Not all trails are marked, and some turn-off junctions have no signs, increasing the possibility of a novice becoming disoriented and losing his way. In light of these conditioins, before entering the Wilderness, it is advisable to get current conditions and information from the nearest Forest Service Office. It is also recommended that you notify them of your itinerary, or leave your plans with a friend or family member. The map below shows some of the lake locations. (Because many of the lakes are difficult to reach in one-day trips, they have not been detailed in this book, but they can be located on Carson National Forest Service maps, available at the nearest Forest Service Office.)

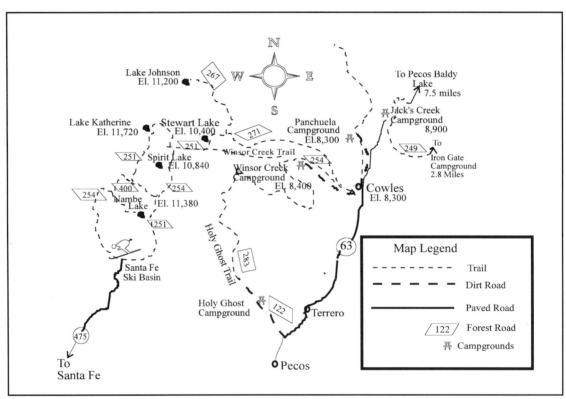

# Lakes and Campgrounds of the Pecos Wilderness

## Lakes

**Stewart Lake:** Altitude 10,400 ft. A five-acre lake, reached by the Winsor Creek Trail, six miles northwest of Cowles. Rainbow frys and cutthroat trout.

**Lake Katherine:** Altitude 11,720 ft. A twelve-acre lake at the head of Winsor Creek, reached by trail, eight miles west of Cowles, from the Winsor Creek Campground. It lies at the timberline in a gorgeous alpine setting at the foot of Santa Fe Baldy. It is stocked by helicopter with rainbow frys and cutthroat trout. It was named for a frequent visitor to the lake, Katherine Kavanaugh, owner of a guest ranch on the Pecos River.

**Johnson Lake:** Altitude 11,200 ft. A six-acre lake north of Lake Katherine, reached by Trail 267. It lies at timberline and is stocked by helicopter with rainbow frys and cutthroat trout.

**Spirit Lake:** Altitude 10,840 ft. A seven-acre lake at the head of Holy Ghost Creek, reached by Trail 257. It is stocked with rainbow frys and cutthroat trout.

**Lost Bear Lake:** Altitude 10,000 ft. A two-acre lake at the head of Pecos River above Pecos Falls, reached by Trail 456A, a steep and rough trail. The turn-off from the main Trail 456 is obscure, it can be missed if not watched for. It is stocked with rainbow frys and cutthroat trout.

**Pecos Baldy Lake:** Altitude 11,000 ft. An eight-acre lake at the base of Pecos Baldy, 8 miles from Cowles, reached by Trail 245 from Beatty's Flats. The trail is steep and climbs almost 2,000 feet in about two miles. It is not recommended for pack and saddle. Stocked with rainbow frys and cutthroat.

## Campgrounds

Trails from Cowles lead to the following campgrounds:

**Irongate:** Located four miles northeast of Cowles via Forest Road 223; no fee
*Access:* Poor; high-clearance vehicles only, parking at trailhead
*Facilities:* Fourteen units; toilets; horse corrals; no potable water

**Panchuela:** Three miles northeast of Cowles on Forest Road 305; fee, $6.00 per day per site
*Access:* Dirt road, narrow, no trailers permitted, parking at trailhead
*Facilities:* Six units; toilets; horse corrals; potable water; fishing on site

**Jack's Creek:** Two miles north of Cowles via NM 63; fee, $6.00 per day, per site
*Access:* Good; road accommodates trailers; parking at trailhead
*Facilities:* Forty-one units; toilets; horse corrals; potable water

Trails from the town of Pecos lead to the following campgrounds:

**Holy Ghost:** Sixteen miles north of Pecos via NM 63; three miles west on Forest Road 122; fee. $6.00 per day per site
*Access:* Good, on a narrow road; parking at trailhead
*Facilities:* Twenty-one units; water; toilets; no horse trailers allowed in campground or at trailhead

**Field Tract:** Ten miles north of Pecos via NM 63; fee $7.00 per day per site
*Access:* Good paved access road accommodates trailers; parking at camp site
*Facilities:* Fourteen units (6 with shelters); potable water; toilets

**Note: Stay limit at all campgrounds is 14 days. Fees and regulations are posted.**

# In the Vicinity of Las Vegas

## *Las Vegas*

*In the vicinity of Las Vegas, there are two lakes open to public fishing: Storrie Lake (6 miles north of Las Vegas on NM 518), McAllister Lake (8 miles southeast via NM 281 off NM 104)*

Las Vegas is situated on the old Santa Fe Trail in the foothills of the Sangre de Cristo Mountains. It lies at an elevation of 6,380 feet, with an Indohispanic and Anglo population of about 15,000. Las Vegas has a colorful history that dates back to 1835, when fifteen Spanish families received a grant from the Mexican Government. They constructed a plaza, which soon became the center of life and a prosperous trading center, serving the merchants, traders, ranchers, wagon trains and stagecoaches that traveled the Santa Fe Trail that connected Independence, Missouri, with Santa Fe, California, and Mexico. Las Vegas was once the most prosperous and largest commercial center in the New Mexico Territory. Everywhere you go, the color, the architecture, and the culture and history of over 150 years are in evidence. Dotting the dramatic scenery of the countryside and valleys around Las Vegas are old churches, chapels, historic buildings; and architectural treasures, which lend a special charm to the city. Some 900 of these architectural treasures have been placed in the National Register of Historic Buildings. It was from the rooftop of one of these buildings on the Las Vegas Plaza (now the Dice Apartments that face the plaza) that General Stephen Kearney, in 1846, proclaimed New Mexico as a United States Territory.

After the arrival of the railroad in 1879, a new surge of prosperity flourished, attracting many fortune seekers and notorious characters to Las Vegas. The town became one of the wildest of the wild west towns, playing host to the likes of Billy the Kid, Jesse James, Wyatt Earp, Bat Masterson, and Doc Holliday and his girlfriend Big Nosed Kate. Before his move to Tombstone, Doc Holliday owned a gambling hall and saloon and a dental office in Las Vegas. At the turn of the century, Las Vegas became the largest town and one of the most important trading and financial centers in New Mexico.

Everything a visitor wishes to do and see is in and around Las Vegas. Summer or winter, the recreational opportunities are abundant: fishing, hunting, camping, water-skiing and windsurfing, sledding, ice-skating, and cross-country skiing—all just minutes away. For those who pursue the cultural and aesthetic, there are galleries, walking tours in historic districts, and golf courses. For overnighters, Las Vegas is a full-service town with good accommodations, gas stations, stores, and restaurants serving authentic southwestern cuisine.

*Storrie Lake*

# STORRIE LAKE

Storrie Lake is a 1,100-acre reservoir within Storrie Lake State Park. It lies at an elevation of 6,500 feet. When the dam was constructed in 1919 on the Gallinas River, it created a lake whose purpose was to provide irrigation for the many farms in the vicinity, and to bring agricultural prosperity to Las Vegas and the surrounding area. The lake draws its water from ground run-off and a diversion channel from the Gallinas River.

Storrie Lake State Park straddles the Historic Santa Fe Trail, which brought the first American traders and adventurers on the overland trail from St. Louis to Santa Fe. Traces of wagon wheel ruts from stagecoaches and covered wagons are still evident here as they passed through Las Vegas to the south. The park was given state park status in 1959 and has become one of the most popular recreation spots in the area. Its location at the base of the Sangre de Cristo Mountains and its flat terrain, unobstructed by trees, allow steady winds across the lake that lure windsurfers by the droves. Their colorful sails that flit across the lake against the Sangre de Cristo Mountain backdrop are a daily invitation to photographers and sightseers. The Department of Game and Fish manages and stocks the lake with three-inch fingerling and some catchable rainbow trout. Storrie Lake also contains crappie, bullheads, and channel catfish. At the southern end of the dam is a boat ramp. The public is permitted to fish from boat or the bank. Access to the lake is by paved and a gravel road, and the campground is well maintained. Its facilities include RV sites with electric hook-ups, tent sites, shelters, tables, flush toilets, chemical toilets, hot showers, a sports field, and hiking trails. Full accommodations, grocery stores, and services are available in Las Vegas, three miles south.

## Directions from Albuquerque

Take I-25 to Las Vegas, then NM 518 north. Follow signs to Storrie Lake State Park. Good access by paved roads.

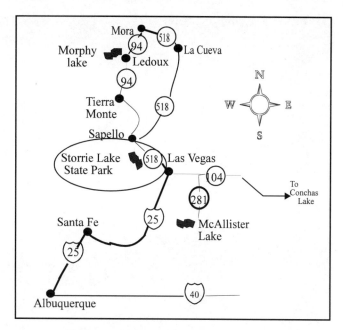

| | | | | | | |
|---|---|---|---|---|---|---|
| **Surface acres:** 1,100 | | | **Distance from Albuquerque:** 126 miles | | | |
| **Elevation:** 6,430 feet | | | **Location:** 3 miles north of Las Vegas, off NM 518 | | | |
| **Max. trailer size & fee:** 40 feet; state park fees | | | **Fish species:** Rainbow trout, crappie, bullheads, and channel catfish | | | |
| **Time limit:** 14 days; fees are posted | | | | | | |
| **Mailing address:** Storrie Lake State Park, P.O. Box 3157, Las Vegas NM 87701, (505)425-7278 | | | **Season:** 1 April-31 March | | | |

## ACTIVITIES AND FACILITIES

| | NO | YES | Proximity to Lake in Miles | | NO | YES | Proximity to Lake in Miles |
|---|---|---|---|---|---|---|---|
| Bait and supplies | X | | 3 | Airplane runway | X | | 3 |
| Boat gas | X | | 3 | Bottled gas | X | | 3 |
| Boat ramp | | X | | Café/snack bar | X | | 3 |
| Boat rental | X | | | Chemical toilets | | X | |
| Camping | | X | | Drinking water | | X | |
| Fire pits | | X | | Electrical hook-up | | X | |
| Fire places | | X | | Flush toilets | | X | |
| Firewood | | X | | Grocery store | X | | 3 |
| Fishing | | X | | Handicapped access | | X | |
| Golf | X | | 3 | Ice | X | | 3 |
| Hiking | X | | | Laundry | X | | 3 |
| Marina | X | | | Lodgings | X | | 3 |
| Picnicking | | X | | Pit toilets | X | | |
| Riding | X | | | Playground | | X | |
| Scuba diving | X | | | Restaurant | X | | 3 |
| Stables | X | | | Sanitary disposal | | X | |
| Swimming | X | | | Sewer hook-up | | X | |
| Skiing (water) | X | | | Shelters | | X | |
| Tables | | X | | Shopping | X | | 3 |
| Telephone | | X | | Showers | | X | |
| Tent sites | | X | | Trailer space | | X | |
| Winter sports | | X | | Water hook-up | | X | |

Lodgings, stores, and services in Las Vegas, 3 miles.

**Special Rules and Regulations**

    **Fishing:** State fishing license required; see Proclamation for current regulations

    **Catch limit:** 6 fish; see Fishing Proclamation for current regulations

    **Boating:** State Regulations apply

    **Other:** Use of minnows for bait illegal

*McAllister Lake*

# McALLISTER LAKE

McAllister Lake is a 100-acre lake on the Las Vegas National Wildlife Refuge about eight miles southeast of Las Vegas. The refuge is a 623-acre prime wintering ground for waterfowl, managed by the Fish and Wildlife Service. The Department of Game and Fish maintains and manages the lake and a small stretch of land around it, and stocks it with mostly sub-catchable and some catchable rainbow trout. To the west rise the majestic Sangre de Cristo Mountains with their towering peaks, lush forests, canyons, and streams, providing visitors with a scenic backdrop for a pleasurable day of fishing, boating, camping, picnicking, and birdwatching.

At the south and west ends of the lake are camping, picnicking, boat launching facilities, and vault toilets. There is handicapped access at the concrete boat ramp. Boats are limited to outboard or electric motors at trolling speeds. The nearest accommodations, service stations, and stores where picnic and fishing supplies are available are in Las Vegas.

## Directions from Albuquerque

Take I-25 to Las Vegas. From Las Vegas go east on NM 104, two miles, then south on NM 281, four miles to Refuge Office for detailed information. Continue about two miles south to lake entrance. Parking allowed at edge of lake.

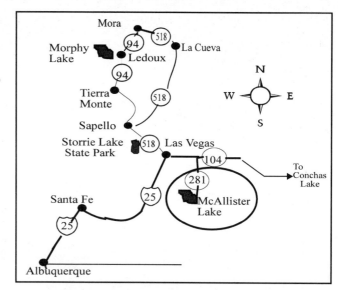

| | |
|---|---|
| **Surface acres:** 100 | **Distance from Albuquerque:** 129 miles |
| **Elevation:** 6,500 feet | **Location:** 8 miles southeast of Las Vegas via NM 104 and |
| **Max. trailer size & fee:** Any size, no fee | 281; lake access by good paved and improved gravel roads |
| **Time limit:** 10 days | **Fish species:** Sub-catchable and catchable rainbow trout |
| **Mailing address:** None | **Season:** 1 March-31 October |
| **Police emergency tel #:** 425-6771 | |
| **Medical emergency tel. #:** 911 | |

## ACTIVITIES AND FACILITIES

| | NO | YES | Proximity to Lake in Miles | | NO | YES | Proximity to Lake in Miles |
|---|---|---|---|---|---|---|---|
| Bait and supplies | X | | 8 | Airplane runway | X | | |
| Boat gas | X | | 8 | Bottled gas | X | | 8 |
| Boat ramp | | X | | Café/snack bar | X | | 8 |
| Boat rental | X | | | Chemical toilets | X | | 8 |
| Camping | | X | | Drinking water | X | | 8 |
| Fire pits | X | | | Electrical hook-up | X | | |
| Fire places | X | | | Flush toilets | X | | |
| Firewood | X | | | Grocery store | X | | 8 |
| Fishing | | X | | Handicapped access | | X | |
| Golf | X | | | Ice | X | | 8 |
| Hiking | | X | | Laundry | X | | 8 |
| Marina | X | | | Lodgings | X | | 8 |
| Picnicking | | X | | Pit toilets | | X | |
| Riding | X | | | Playground | X | | |
| Scuba diving | X | | | Restaurant | X | | 8 |
| Stables | X | | | Trash cans | X | | 8 |
| Swimming | X | | | Sewer hook-up | X | | |
| Tables | X | | | Shelters | X | | |
| Telephone | X | | | Shopping | X | | 8 |
| Tennis | X | | | Showers | X | | |
| Tent sites | | X | | Trailer space | | X | |
| Winter sports | X | | | Water hook-up | X | | |

Lodgings, services, stores in Las Vegas, 8 miles.
**Special Rules and Regulations**
   **Fishing:** State fishing license required
   **Catch limit:** 10 trout per day; see Proclamation for current regulations or page 343
   **Boating:** Outboard or electric motors at trolling speeds; permitted during season only
   **Other:** No open fires or shooting of firearms

*Cleveland Roller Mill Museum*
*Cleveland, New Mexico*
*(Just north of the city limits of Mora on NM 434)*

# In the Vicinity
# of Mora

## *Mora*

*There are are two lakes in the vicinity of Mora accessed by motor vehicle: Morphy Lake, Harold L. Brock Fishing Area*

*Three other lakes in the vicinity of Mora are reached by trail only; they are Pacheco Lake, Middle Fork Lake of Rio La Casa, and North Fork Lake.*

The town of Mora is located 153 miles north of Albuquerque at the eastern edge of the Sangre de Cristo Mountains, at the junctions of NM 94, 518, and 434. It is the county seat. It sits at an elevation of 7,200 feet above sea level and has a population of 7,000. More than a hundred years ago, Mora was the mercantile capital of the Mora Valley, which served as a gateway and distribution center to the lands and communities east of the Rockies. Mora was formally established in 1835, when a group of seventy-six Mexican settlers received a grant of land from Mexican Governor Albino Perez.

The abundant precipitation during late winter and early spring months in this area encouraged a heavy growth of pine, spruce, and fir trees. These forests provided a friendly habitat for the wildlife that abounds amidst these favorable conditions, luring trappers and fur traders in the 1850s in hope of obtaining beaver peltry and black bear skins. Then followed the ranchers and farmers, and by the mid-nineteenth century, Mora grew and prospered. Lumber mills, flour mills, and mercantile stores were built. Hotels, saloons, and dance halls flourished. As the population increased in the

1850s, the need for protection from marauding Indians increased, and Fort Union was established in 1851 to defend the new territory, the travelers along the Santa Fe Trail, and the communities that sprang up in the region. Fort Union became a strategic military post and quartermaster depot to supply other forts and the hundreds of workers at the Fort Union. This created a demand for larger and more efficient flour mills. The first of these mills was St. Vrain Mill, a massive stone building now deserted and deteriorated but still standing on the other side of the river on NM 434. Another mill, the Cleveland Roller Mill, is on NM 434, about a mile north of the city limits of Mora. It was established in 1901 and until 1947 was the last of the flour producing mills in full operation. It is a two-story adobe structure, now a museum, with its original equipment and machinery still intact. It was placed on the National Register of Historic Places in 1979. The museum includes tour guides for groups as well as self-guided tours of the mill, featuring historical and cultural exhibits focusing on the Mora Valley. Fort Union was founded where the Cimarron cut-off left the Santa Fe Trail. It was abandoned in 1891 and is also on the National Register of Historic Places.

About eighteen miles north of Mora, on NM 434, just beyond the small village of Guadalupita, is Coyote Creek State Park. It is a well-maintained park with electric and water hook-ups, pull through RV sites, group shelters, a playground, toilet facilities, a dump station, and a creek dotted with beaver ponds and populated with rainbow trout.

*Morphy Lake*

# MORPHY LAKE

Just southwest of Mora, and three miles northwest of the small town of Ledoux, at an elevation of 7,840 feet above sea level, is Morphy Lake State Park (pronounced "Murphy"). It is a twenty-five- to fifty-acre lake nestled in a small basin high in the mountains. It is the remotest and most scenic of New Mexico's state parks, a blue, shimmering mirror, reflecting a dramatic backdrop of dense stands of spruce and ponderosa pine that encircles the lake and slopes down to near the water's edge. The park is a haven of peace and solitude—a true retreat for the fisherman, camper, picnicker, and nature lover.

The three-mile access road off NM 94 to Morphy Lake State Park is steep, rough, narrow, and unimproved, winding in snake-like bends, up into the scenic mountains and valleys, past farms and pasture lands. The road is impassable during winter snows, and even in dry weather, high-clearance or four-wheel-drive vehicles are advised. Boat trailers are not recommended on this rough road. However, canoes, row boats, or kayaks can be transported by car-top to the lake, provided that boats are powered by oars or electric motors only. The difficult access to the park discourages the less adventurous from visiting this lake, making Morphy Lake a less-frequented, but very popular spot for fishermen who prefer the solitude and opportunity to enjoy excellent fishing. The lake is stocked regularly with rainbow trout and is maintained by the Department of Game and Fish. The State Parks and Recreation Division maintains recreational sites for camping and picnicking. The facilities include twenty primitive sites with picnic tables and toilets. No water is available in the park, and state park fees apply. Accommodations, services, and picnic and fishing supplies are available in Mora, seven miles northeast.

## Directions from Albuquerque

Take I-25 to Las Vegas, then go north on NM 518 through Sapello, to Tierra Monte. Connect with NM 94 north to Ledoux and follow signs to Morphy Lake, about three miles via a dirt unimproved rough access road to lake. Road not recommended for trailers or RVs. Four-wheel-drive or high clearance vehicles advised.

### From Mora

Take NM 94 south to Ledoux, to Morphy Lake direction sign, then to turn-off on FR 635, a rough, deteriorated road about three miles to lake.

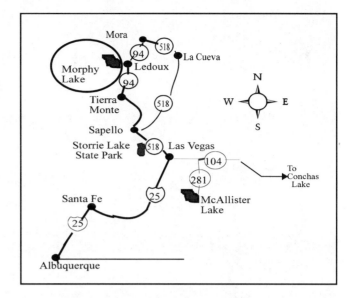

| | |
|---|---|
| **Surface acres:** 50 | **Distance from Albuquerque:** 152 miles |
| **Elevation:** 7,840 feet | **Location:** 3 miles northwest of Ledoux, 4 miles southwest of Mora |
| **Max. trailer size & fee:** Trailers not advised | |
| **Time limit:** 14 days; state park fees posted | **Fish species:** Rainbow trout |
| **Mailing address:** P.O. Box 428, Guadalupita, NM 87722, (505) 387-2328 | **Season:** 1 April-31 October |
| **Police emergency tel. #:** 911 | |

## ACTIVITIES AND FACILITIES

| | NO | YES | Proximity to Lake in Miles | | NO | YES | Proximity to Lake in Miles |
|---|---|---|---|---|---|---|---|
| Bait and supplies | X | | | Airplane runway | X | | |
| Boat gas | X | | | Bottled gas | X | | |
| Boat ramp | | X | | Café/snack bar | X | | |
| Boat rental | X | | | Chemical toilets | X | | |
| Camping | | X | | Drinking water | X | | |
| Fire pits | | X | | Electrical hook-up | X | | |
| Fire places | | X | | Flush toilets | X | | |
| Firewood | | X | | Grocery store | X | | |
| Fishing | | X | | Handicapped access | | X | |
| Golf | X | | | Ice | X | | |
| Hiking | | X | | Laundry | X | | |
| Marina | X | | | Lodgings | X | | |
| Picnicking | | X | | Pit toilets | | X | |
| Riding | X | | | Playground | X | | |
| Scuba diving | X | | | Restaurant | X | | |
| Stables | X | | | Sanitary disposal | X | | |
| Swimming | X | | | Sewer hook-up | X | | |
| Tables | | X | | Shelters | X | | |
| Telephone | X | | | Shopping | X | | |
| Tennis | X | | | Showers | X | | |
| Tent sites | | X | | Trailer space | | X | |
| Winter sports | X | | | Water hook-up | X | | |

Lodgings, services, stores in Mora, 4 miles.

**Special Rules and Regulations**

**Fishing:** State fishing license required; see License Requirements, page 343

**Catch limit:** 6 trout, State Fishing Regulations apply. (See page 343 for more details)

**Boats:** Restricted to oars or electric motors

**Other:** Rough unimproved road access; check road conditions; four-wheel-drive or high-clearance vehicles advised; not recommended for trailers or RVs; primitive camping

*Harold L. Brock Fishing Area*

# HAROLD L. BROCK FISHING AREA

The Harold L. Brock Fishing Area is comprised of a series of small ponds along Coyote Creek about a half-mile north of Coyote Creek State Park and about nineteen miles north of Mora. The ponds were created in 1987 by the State Game Commission under a lease agreement in which the Commission agreed to provide two gravelled parking lots, restrooms, and periodic stocking of the ponds and Coyote Creek, which flows along the east side of NM 434. NM 434 is a well maintained, paved, and lined highway that winds through the forested mountains that surround the scenic Guadalupita Canyon.

The ponds are visible on the east side of the highway with easy access to them and the over one mile of fishing in the stream is open to the public without a fee. A state fishing license is required, and state regulations apply. The creek and the ponds are stocked with rainbow and brown trout. There are two gravelled parking areas and restrooms, but overnight camping, fires, or shooting of firearms are not permitted. Camping is available at nearby Coyote Creek State Park to the south. A beaver dam-speckled creek with conveniently placed foot bridges to allow access to either side gushes through the park and offers good fishing opportunities for the stocked rainbow trout. Coyote Creek State Park is well maintained, with electric and water hook ups, a dump station, some pull through RV sites, sheltered camp sites, tables, fire pits, pit toilets, and a playground. State park fees apply. (See page 342 for State Park Regulations.)

## Directions from Albuquerque

Take I-25 to Las Vegas, then go north on NM 518 through Mora. Continue north on NM 434, nineteen miles to Coyote Creek State Park. The Harold L. Brock Fishing Area is half a mile north of the park and visible from the east side of the highway.

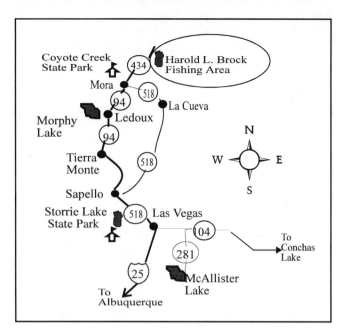

| | |
|---|---|
| **Surface acres:** 5 | **Distance from Albuquerque:** 172 miles |
| **Elevation:** 7,750 feet | **Location:** 19 miles north of Mora; 1/2 mile north |
| **Max. trailer size & fee:** No camping | of Coyote Creek State Park |
| **Time limit:** No camping | **Fish species:** Rainbow and brown trout |
| **Mailing address:** None | |
| **Police emergency tel. #:** 911 | |
| **Medical emergency tel. #:** 911 | **Season:** 1 March-31 October |

## ACTIVITIES AND FACILITIES

| | NO | YES | Proximity to Lake in Miles | | NO | YES | Proximity to Lake in Miles |
|---|---|---|---|---|---|---|---|
| Bait and supplies | X | | * | Airplane runway | X | | |
| Boat gas | X | | | Bottled gas | X | | * |
| Boat ramp | X | | | Café/snack bar | X | | * |
| Boat rental | X | | | Chemical toilets | X | | |
| Camping | X | | 1/2 | Drinking water | X | | 1/2 |
| Fire pits | X | | 1/2 | Electrical hook-up | X | | 1/2 |
| Fire places | X | | 1/2 | Flush toilets | X | | 1/2 |
| Firewood | | | 1/2 | Grocery store | X | | * |
| Fishing | | X | | Handicapped access | | X | |
| Golf | X | | | Ice | X | | * |
| Hiking | | X | | Laundry | X | | * |
| Marina | X | | | Lodgings | X | | * |
| Picnicking | | X | | Pit toilets | | X | |
| Riding | X | | | Playground | X | | 1/2 |
| Scuba diving | X | | | Restaurant | X | | * |
| Stables | X | | | Sanitary disposal | X | | 1/2 |
| Swimming | X | | | Sewer hook-up | X | | 1/2 |
| Tables | X | | 1/2 | Shelters | X | | 1/2 |
| Telephone | X | | 1/2 | Shopping | X | | * |
| Tennis | X | | | Showers | X | | |
| Tent sites | X | | 1/2 | Trailer space | X | | 1/2 |
| Winter sports | X | | | Water hook-up | X | | 12 |

*Full facilities and stores in Mora, 19 miles south.
**Special Rules and Regulations**
    **Fishing:** State fishing license required
    **Catch limit:** 6 fish; check Fishing Proclamation for current Regulations
    **Boating:** No boating or floating devices permitted
    **Other:** Coyote Creek State Park, one half-mile south has a fully developed campground

# In the Vicinity of Peñasco

## *Peñasco*

*In the vicinity of Peñasco is the Picuris Pueblo. This pueblo operates and maintains two lakes that permit public fishing, picnicking, and camping: Puna Pond, Tutah Pond*

The town of Peñasco is located about a mile south of Picuris Pueblo. It was founded in 1796 after permission was granted to three families to build a town in the valley. Three villages were built by these families. The villages sprawled eastward, eventually becoming one village, called Peñasco, taking its name from the rocky outcroppings in the area. Peñasco became the commercial center for all the ranchers and farmers of the small villages throughout the valley.

Today, remnants of the original settlements are still in evidence in the old traditional adobe structures that are scattered through the mountain valleys in the area. Peñasco is still the main center of the entire region, where, as the educational center of the valley, kindergarteners through high-schoolers are bussed into schools at the east end of town. Peñasco has gas stations, stores, and restaurants.

The Picuris Pueblo, twelve miles northeast of Peñasco and just twenty miles south of Taos, welcomes visitors to their many activities and festivals. One of the attractions is the Tri-Cultural Arts and Crafts Fair held the first weekend in July. The fair features arts and crafts, entertainment, and food representing all three cultures from northern New Mexico. The pueblo also offers tours to ruins that date back to A.D. 1250. The pueblo has a good restaurant serving native Picuris foods and American foods. There are a museum with a gift shop, a recreation complex with overnight camping sites, and two fishing ponds open to the public.

*Tutah Lake, one of the two ponds in the Pueblo of Picuris*

# PU-NA AND TUTAH PONDS

Both Pu-na and Tutah Ponds are one-acre ponds in the Pueblo of Picuris about a mile north of Peñasco. They are open to the public from 6 A.M.–7 P.M. during the summer months. No state fishing license is required, but a tribal permit is necessary to fish these ponds. The fee is $4.00 for adults (ten percent discount for senior citizens) and $3.00 for children. Both ponds are well stocked regularly with rainbow and brown trout. The catch limit is eight fish per permit. Permits are available at the museum or at the lake, where fees are collected by tribal game wardens as they make their rounds. Overnight camping sites equipped with trailer spaces, RV facilities, picnic tables, grills and toilets are also provided at Pu-na Pond (the lower pond). The fee for camping is $5.00 per night. Check current fees at the Tribal Office. The village has stores, a gift shop in the museum, and a restaurant serving native Picuris foods and American foods.

Although only twenty miles from Taos, the Pueblo of Picuris is one of the most isolated of the pueblos. It is ringed by mountains in a high secluded valley. The Picuris people have resided here more than 700 years and still conduct their religious ceremonies in kivas as they did 700 years ago. At one time, Picuris was one of the largest of the pueblos, with buildings rising five and six stories high. Each year, on the evening of 9 August ceremonies begin with a mass at the church, followed by a procession along the shrine path through the northern part of the village, to celebrate the feast day of its patron saint, San Lorenzo. The following day on 10 August the Feast Day of San Lorenzo is highlighted by dances and foot races.

## Directions from Albuquerque

Take I-25 to Santa Fe. Connect with U.S. 84/285 to Española and junction of NM 76. Turn east on NM 76 and continue northeast on this road. Go through Chimayo and continue to the intersection of NM 76 and NM 75. Turn west at the intersection, and go half a mile to Tribal Road 120. It is a paved road that leads to Picuris Pueblo.

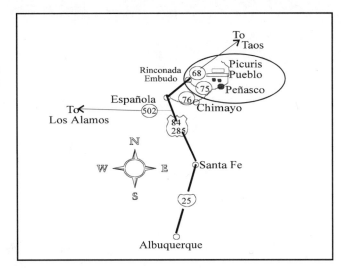

| | | |
|---|---|---|
| **Surface acres:** 2 | | **Distance from Albuquerque:** 122 miles |
| **Elevation:** 7,000 feet | | **Location:** 1 mile north of Peñasco, 20 miles south of Taos, off NM 75 |
| **Max. trailer size & fee:** No limit; $5.00 per night | | |
| **Time limit:** No limit | | **Fish species:** Rainbow and brown trout |
| **Mailing address:** P.O. Box 127, Peñasco, NM 87553, (505)587-2519/2043 | | **Season:** 6 A.M.-7 P.M. seven days a week during summer months |
| **Medical emergency tel. #:** At Tribal Office | | |

## ACTIVITIES AND FACILITIES

| | NO | YES | Proximity to Lake in Miles | | NO | YES | Proximity to Lake in Miles |
|---|---|---|---|---|---|---|---|
| **Bait and supplies** | | X | | **Airplane runway** | X | | |
| **Boat gas** | X | | | **Bottled gas** | X | | |
| **Boat ramp** | X | | | **Café/snack bar** | | X | |
| **Boat rental** | X | | | **Chemical toilets** | X | | |
| **Camping** | | X | | **Drinking water** | X | | |
| **Fire pits** | | X | | **Electrical hook-up** | X | | |
| **Fire places** | | X | | **Flush toilets** | X | | |
| **Firewood** | X | | | **Grocery store** | | X | |
| **Fishing** | | X | | **Handicapped access** | | X | |
| **Golf** | X | | | **Ice** | | X | |
| **Hiking** | X | | | **Laundry** | X | | |
| **Marina** | X | | | **Lodgings** | X | | |
| **Picnicking** | | X | | **Pit toilets** | | X | |
| **Riding** | X | | | **Playground** | | X | |
| **Scuba diving** | X | | | **Restaurant** | | X | |
| **Stables** | X | | | **Sanitary disposal** | X | | |
| **Swimming** | X | | | **Sewer hook-up** | X | | |
| **Tables** | | X | | **Shelters** | X | | |
| **Telephone** | | X | | **Shopping** | | X | |
| **Tennis** | X | | | **Showers** | X | | |
| **Tent sites** | | X | | **Trailer space** | X | | |
| **Winter sports** | X | | | **Water hook-up** | X | | |

Stores, picnic supplies in village. Camping permitted at lower lake.

**Special Rules and Regulations**

   **Fishing:** No state license required; tribal permit required; adults $4.00; children $3.00; senior citizens, $3.60

   **Catch limit:** 8 fish per permit

   **Boating:** No boats or floating devices permitted

   **Other:** Camping, picnicking, and RV facilities at lower lake (Pu-na Pond)

*Iglesia de San Antonio*
*(St. Anthony's Church)*
*(Oldest building in town of Questa,*
*built in 1873)*
*Questa, New Mexico*

# In the Vicinity of Questa

## Questa

*There are five lakes in the vicinity of Questa: Eagle Rock Lake, Cabresto Lake, Heart Lake (A 4-mile hike by trail, starting at the trailhead at Cabresto Lake. Not detailed in this book), Red River State Hatchery Pond*

Questa is a small village located in the heart of the unspoiled beauty of the Sangre de Cristos, at the junction of NM 522 and NM 38, twenty-two miles north of Taos and twelve miles west of Red River. Each year thousands of visitors are drawn to this part of northern New Mexico billed as the *"Enchanted Circle,"* whose towns include Taos, Red River, Eagle Nest, and Angel Fire. At an elevation of 7,655 feet, the "Enchanted Circle" is one of the most beautiful and scenic areas of New Mexico, offering opportunities for an unlimited variety of recreation activities throughout the year. Fishermen, nature lovers, and backpackers are drawn to the lakes and streams and to the mountain wilderness areas to hike the miles of trails and camp its many campgrounds. Photographers too, flock to the scenic areas of Mallette Canyon one mile north of Red River and fifteen miles east of Questa and to the scenic area of Midnight Canyon, just a few miles northeast of Questa, where cottonwoods and aspen are ablaze with color in autumn. The famous and popular ski areas of Taos Ski Valley, Ski Rio, Red River Ski Area, Angel Fire and Sipapu, are all within fifty miles of Questa, luring thousands each winter to some of the finest skiing in the country.

In the early 1800s, Questa was known as San Antonio del Rio Colorado (St. Anthony of the Red River). At that time, the families who lived in the area were under constant attack by Apache and Ute Indians. In 1854, in order to protect themselves from these raids, the residents built a six-foot wall around the town. In the early 1870s, when the first post office was established, the name Questa was adopted. (*Questa* means "hill," "slope," or "grade.") In 1873, the church, St. Anthony's, was built by the men and women of the village who set aside each Saturday for its construction. It is now the oldest building in Questa. It is built of five-foot-thick adobe walls in the shape of a cross. It is twenty-five feet high and has six windows. The village of Questa was officially incorporated in June of 1964.

When molybdenum mining came to Questa in the early 1920s, it was an open-pit mine. The present owners, Union Oil, are now constructing underground mines, greatly improving the appearance of the area. It is now the largest single employer in Taos County. Questa is also famous for its honey. Beekeepers in the northern part of town sell their honey from their homes. Although Questa is a small town, with a population of under 800, it offers lodgings, restaurants, service stations, and grocery stores. It is advisable to stop here for needed supplies before entering the wilderness area.

*Eagle Rock Lake*

# EAGLE ROCK LAKE

Eagle Rock Lake is a three-acre lake one mile east of Questa, on the Red River. Here, in a pristine setting at an elevation of 7,850 feet and surrounded by high, heavily forested mountains, is serenity at its supreme splendor. A quiet sense of remoteness pervades the entire scene, yet it is close to, and easily accessed from paved, NM Highway 38. Eagle Rock Lake is a day-use lake, offering no overnight camping or picnicking facilities, but it is convenient to nearby Elephant Rock Campground, a privately operated campground leased out by the Carson National Forest. The convenience of the campground's location and its facilities make this a popular fishing lake that is stocked regularly with rainbow trout.

There are many other well-maintained campground and picnic sites scattered through the entire area. Some are developed, and some are undeveloped. About a mile and a half east of Eagle Rock Lake at an elevation of 7,500 feet is the Eagle Rock Campground with sites equipped for picnicking, camping, trailer, and RV parking, tables, fireplaces, and pit toilets. It is open from April through October and the stay limit is fourteen days. Drinking water is available at the Questa Ranger Station.

For the angler, nearby Columbine Creek, just five miles east of Questa, offers some of the best cutthroat trout fishing in the area. Since there are no services or stores east of Questa until you reach Red River, it is advisable to stock up on needed food, and camping or fishing supplies in Questa, one mile west of Eagle Rock Lake.

## Directions from Albuquerque

Take I-25 north to the junction of U.S. 84/285 at Santa Fe. Continue on U.S. 84/285 north to NM 68. Continue northeast on NM 68 to Taos and connect with U.S. 64 north to NM 522. Continue north on NM 522 and go twenty-two miles to Questa. At Questa, turn east on NM 38. Go one mile to Eagle Rock Lake. The lake is visible from the highway. A large paved parking area accommodates visitors.

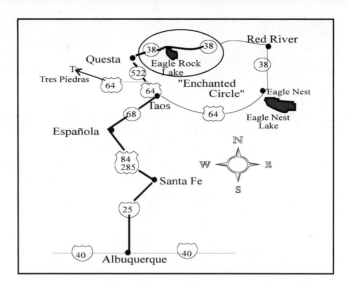

| | |
|---|---|
| **Surface acres:** 3 | **Distance from Albuquerque:** 152 miles |
| **Elevation:** 7,850 feet | **Location:** 1 mile east of Questa on NM 38 |
| **Max. trailer size & fee:** No overnight camping; camping at Elephant Rock Campground nearby; other campgrounds are along NM 38 | **Fish species:** Rainbow trout; cutthroat trout (also on Columbine Creek 4 miles east) |
| | **Season:** May–October |
| **Police emergency tel. #:** C.B. at campground | **Camping:** In campground near lake; see below |
| **Medical emergency tel. #:** C.B. at campground | |

## ACTIVITIES AND FACILITIES

| | NO | YES | Proximity to Lake in Miles | | NO | YES | Proximity to Lake in Miles |
|---|---|---|---|---|---|---|---|
| Bait and supplies | X | | | Airplane runway | X | | |
| Boat gas | X | | | Bottled gas | X | | |
| Boat ramp | X | | | Café/snack bar | X | | |
| Boat rental | X | | | Chemical toilets | X | | |
| Camping | | X | | Drinking water | | X | |
| Fire pits | | X | | Electrical hook-up | X | | |
| Fire places | | X | | Flush toilets | X | | |
| Firewood | X | | | Grocery store | X | | |
| Fishing | | X | | Handicapped access | | X | |
| Golf | X | | | Ice | X | | |
| Hiking | X | | | Laundry | X | | |
| Marina | X | | | Lodgings | X | | |
| Picnicking | | X | | Pit toilets | | X | |
| Riding | X | | | Playground | X | | |
| Scuba diving | X | | | Restaurant | X | | |
| Stables | X | | | Sanitary disposal | X | | |
| Swimming | X | | | Sewer hook-up | X | | |
| Tables | | X | | Shelters | X | | |
| Telephone | X | | | Shopping | X | | |
| Tennis | X | | | Showers | X | | |
| Tent sites | | X | | Trailer space | | X | |
| Winter sports | | X | | Water hook-up | X | | |

Table above lists facilities at Elephant Rock Campground close to lake.

**Special Rules and Regulations**

    **Fishing:** Fishing license required

    **Catch limit:** 6 fish (no more than 2 cutthroat); see Fishing Proclamation for current Regulations

    **Boating:** No boats or floating devices permitted

    **Other:** A day-use lake; many developed campgrounds with facilities in canyon west of lake

*Cabresto Lake*

# CABRESTO LAKE

Cabresto Lake is a fifteen-acre man-made lake located seven miles northeast of Questa. It is set high in the Sangre de Cristo Mountains at an elevation of 9,500 feet above sea level and is stocked with catchable rainbow trout by the New Mexico Department of Game and Fish. Because of its remote location and lightly traveled access, it offers excellent trout fishing. Cutthroat and brook trout may occur there, even though cutthroat stocking was discontinued in the early 1980s. From Questa, Cabresto Lake is reached by way of NM 38, connecting with FR 134, and finally swinging left on FR 134A, two miles to the lake. From this point the route is a narrow, single-lane, unimproved rough road that climbs and winds steeply through a forested mountainside that bristles with pine, fir, and aspen, terminating at sparkling blue Cabresto Lake. The lake is nestled in a breathtakingly beautiful setting, framed by mountain peaks and thickly forested banks of pine and fir that slope to the edge of the lake's calm waters. At the very edge of the lake is a small campground with picnic tables, grills, and pit toilets, with room for convenient parking next to the camp sites. Posted at a trailhead at the northern edge of the campground is a direction sign pointing the way to Heart Lake, a four-mile hike north.

Wildlife abounds here in this secluded and remote wonderland of the Carson National Forest. Deer, elk, grouse and numerous small game animals can be seen throughout the area, and this beautiful hideaway is especially scenic in the fall, when the aspens turn to russets and gold. It is advisable at this time of year to have warm clothing available, as the high altitude can cause evening temperatures to dip to freezing. During winter season, snowmobiling is permitted to the lake. Other trails beyond the lake permit cross-country skiing.

## Directions from Albuquerque

Take I-25 north through Santa Fe, to the junction of U.S. 84/285. Continue north to NM 68 to Taos, then take U.S. 64 north connecting with NM 522 to Questa. At Questa turn right on NM 518, then connect with FR 134. Go about five miles and turn left on FR 134A and up a winding, narrow, single-lane rough road about two miles to the lake. Four-wheel-drive, high-clearance vehicles are advised.

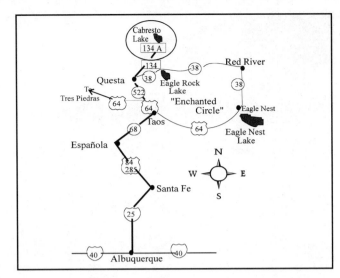

| | | |
|---|---|---|
| **Surface acres:** 15 | | **Distance from Albuquerque:** 158 miles |
| **Elevation:** 9,500 feet | | **Location:** 6 miles northeast of Questa |
| **Max. trailer size & fee:** No fee; no large RVs | | **Fish species:** Cutthroat, rainbow, and brook trout |
| **Mailing address:** None | | |
| **Police emergency tel. #:** 911 | | **Season:** May-October |
| **Medical emergency tel. #:** 911 | | |

## ACTIVITIES AND FACILITIES

| | NO | YES | Proximity to Lake in Miles | | NO | YES | Proximity to Lake in Miles |
|---|---|---|---|---|---|---|---|
| Bait and supplies | X | | *6 | Airplane runway | X | | |
| Boat gas | X | | | Bottled gas | X | | |
| Boat ramp | X | | | Café/snack bar | X | | *6 |
| Boat rental | X | | | Chemical toilets | X | | |
| Camping | | X | | Drinking water | X | | |
| Fire pits | | X | | Electrical hook-up | X | | |
| Fire places | | X | | Flush toilets | X | | |
| Firewood | X | | | Grocery store | X | | *6 |
| Fishing | | X | | Handicapped access | X | | |
| Golf | X | | | Ice | X | | *6 |
| Hiking | | X | | Laundry | X | | *6 |
| Marina | X | | | Lodgings | X | | *6 |
| Picnicking | | X | | Pit toilets | | X | |
| Riding | X | | | Playground | X | | |
| Scuba diving | X | | | Restaurant | X | | *6 |
| Stables | X | | | Trash cans | | X | |
| Swimming | X | | | Sewer hook-up | X | | |
| Skiing | | X | | Shelters | X | | |
| Tables | | X | | Shopping | X | | |
| Telephone | X | | | Showers | X | | |
| Tent sites | | X | | Trailer space | | X | |
| Winter sports | | X | | Water hook-up | X | | |

*Lodgings, food, bait and groceries in Questa, 6 miles, and in Red River.

**Special Rules and Regulations**
   **Fishing:** State fishing license required; Regulations apply
   **Catch limit:** 6 fish (1994-95) Proclamation); see current year Proclamation for current limits
   **Boating:** Small boats with electric motors
   **Other:** Snowmobiles up to lake only; cross-country skiing beyond lake permitted

*Red River State Hatchery Pond*

# RED RIVER STATE HATCHERY POND

Red River State Fish Hatchery is located five miles southwest of Questa and eighteen miles west of Red River. It lies at the bottom of a steep canyon and produces about 300,000 pounds of rainbow and brown trout annually. It is run by the New Mexico Department of Game and Fish, who stock the streams and lakes of New Mexico with the trout raised in its breeding tanks and ponds. A self-guided tour explains the trout rearing process. The hatchery was built in 1941 and was remodeled in 1974 and 1979. A complete reconstruction project was completed in 1985 at a cost of $2.7 million, funded by the 1983 State Legislature through severance tax bonds.

Located on the premises, in an attractive setting ringed by a forested landscape and a view of the mountains in the distance, is a fishing pond reserved for children under the age of twelve, for senior citizens, and for the handicapped. Along the Hatchery road, a no-fee picnicking and camping area equipped with trailer spaces and tent sites is available to the public. A trail from the hatchery parking lot permits campers to hike to the Rio Grande where they can enjoy some fine fishing along its banks for rainbows and browns. Other campgrounds with camping and picnicking facilities are located above nearby Questa in United States Forest Service sites in the Red River Canyon, and in the Bureau of Land Mangement's Wild Rivers Recreation Area west of Questa.

## Directions from Albuquerque

Take I-25 north through Santa Fe to the junction of U.S. 84/285. Continue north and take NM 68 to Taos, then take U.S. 64 north and take NM 522 about nineteen miles to junction of NM 515. Turn west on NM 515 and go two miles to Red River State Hatchery. Access is via paved roads all the way.

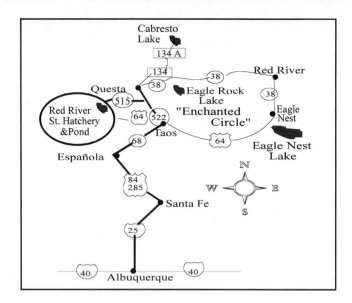

| | | | | | | | |
|---|---|---|---|---|---|---|---|
| **Surface acres:** 1 | | | | **Distance from Albuquerque:** 150 miles | | | |
| **Elevation:** 8,000 feet | | | | **Location:** 5 miles southwest of Questa; 18 miles | | | |
| **Max. trailer size & fee:** No limit, no fee | | | | southwest of Red River; 21 miles north of Taos | | | |
| **Time limit:** No limit | | | | **Fish species:** Rainbow trout | | | |
| **Mailing address:** Red River State Hatchery, | | | | **Season:** 1 April-31 October | | | |
| Box 410, Questa, NM 87556 | | | | **Camping:** Along hatchery road | | | |
| **Police emergency tel. #:** At hatchery | | | | **Medical emergency tel. #:** Small clinic in Questa | | | |

## ACTIVITIES AND FACILITIES

| | NO | YES | Proximity to Lake in Miles | | NO | YES | Proximity to Lake in Miles |
|---|---|---|---|---|---|---|---|
| Bait and supplies | X | | *5 | Airplane runway | X | | |
| Boat gas | X | | | Bottled gas | X | | |
| Boat ramp | X | | | Café/snack bar | X | | *5 |
| Boat rental | X | | | Chemical toilets | | X | |
| Camping | | X | | Drinking water | | X | |
| Fire pits | | X | | Electrical hook-up | X | | |
| Fire places | | X | | Flush toilets | X | | |
| Firewood | X | | | Grocery store | X | | *5 |
| Fishing | | X | | Handicapped access | | X | |
| Golf | X | | | Ice | X | | *5 |
| Hiking | | X | | Laundry | X | | *5 |
| Marina | X | | | Lodgings | X | | *5 |
| Picnicking | | X | | Pit toilets | X | | |
| Riding | X | | | Playground | X | | |
| Scuba diving | X | | | Restaurant | X | | *5 |
| Stables | X | | | Trash cans | | X | |
| Swimming | X | | | Sewer hook-up | X | | |
| Tables | | X | | Shelters | X | | |
| Telephone | | X | | Shopping | X | | |
| Tennis | X | | | Showers | X | | |
| Tent sites | | X | | Trailer space | | X | |
| Winter sports | X | | | Water hook-up | X | | |

*Stores and facilities in Questa, 5 miles southwest.

**Special Rules and Regulations**

 **Fishing:** Fishing reserved for children under 12, senior citizens 65 and older, and the handicapped

 **Catch limit:** 6 trout; state Regulations apply

 **Boating:** No boats or floating devices permitted

 **Other:** Check at hatchery office for latest rules and regulations

*Plaza de Arriba*
*(The Historical Center of Costilla)*
*Costilla, New Mexico*

# In the Vicinity of Costilla

## *Costilla/Amalia*

*There are several lakes in the vicinity of Costilla and Amalia. The following are covered in the next few pages: Costilla Diversion Dam, Latir Lakes, Shuree Ponds*

Costilla is a small town located twenty miles north of Questa. It is reached by NM 522 North and lies east of the junction with NM 196. Costilla was named after the Costilla River that flows through the town. It was founded in 1852, when a group of settlers led by Juan de Jesus Bernal purchased the land from Charles Beaubien, who was part-owner of the Maxwell Land Grant. When the Spanish came to the southwest, Costilla was one of the first settlements established. Most of the early settlers were Spaniards that came from Mexico and settled in the Colorado town of San Luis and Fort Garland, which was one of the first forts where the first cavalry originated to protect the settlements of San Luis, Costilla, and the surrounding area from Indian raids. Costilla is only a mile and a quarter from the state line of Colorado.

The settlement consisted of four large plazas that stretched beyond the Colorado border. One of the plazas served as a watch tower for guards to alert the villagers of impending raids by Ute and Apache Indians. The Plaza de Arriba is the historic center of Costilla. It has a shopping center and a service station. Another one is close by at the junction of NM 522 and NM 196. Picnic and fishing supplies are available in the shopping center for those entering Rio Costilla Park and the Latir Lakes

NM 196 is a good paved and scenic road that passes through rocky hills and parallels the fast-flowing Costilla River. The high Latir Peaks loom in the distance. The road leads to Amalia, five miles east, a small village and the gateway to the Valle Vidal and the Shuree Ponds—three small ponds where fishing on one of the ponds is reserved for children under twelve years of age. (On our visit to Shuree Ponds, a deteriorated and muddy road prevented our entry, so it is not detailed in this writing.) Amalia is also the gateway to the spectacular Latir Lakes, owned and managed by the Rio Costilla Cooperative Livestock Association. Amalia has a grocery store, a gas station, a bait and tackle shop, and a few residences. A colorful cemetery on the north side of the road serves as a landmark identifying the tiny village as you pass through it.

**Note:** The lake that bears the same name as the village of Costilla—Costilla Lake—cannot be accessed by way of Costilla (although many try to without success). This lake is located on the private resort property of Vermejo Park, a huge property famous for its great hunting, fishing, and accommodations. (Costilla Lake, in Vermejo Park, is accessed from Raton.)

*Costilla Diversion Dam*

# COSTILLA DIVERSION DAM

The Costilla Diversion Dam is located on the north side of NM 196, about a mile east of the town of Costilla. It is barely visible from the highway as you drive east toward Amalia. It is a diversion dam for irrigation of the farms in the area. The dam backs up a small pond where fishing is permitted. The water comes from the Costilla Reservoir located on the Vermejo Park property.

There are no picnic, camping, or toilet facilities here, nor is there handicapped access. Access is off the highway by a narrow, steep road, with limited parking at the spillway below. The pond contains rainbow trout.

## Directions from Albuquerque

Take I-25 north to Santa Fe and connect with U.S. 285/64 through Española. At Española continue northeast to Taos on NM 68. In Taos connect with NM 522 north to Costilla. Turn east on NM 196, and travel one mile to Costilla Diversion Dam. The dam is on the north side of NM 196, a mile east of Costilla.

| | |
|---|---|
| **Surface acres:** 1 | **Distance from Albuquerque:** 172 miles |
| **Elevation:** 7,700 feet | **Location:** 1 mile east of Costilla, off NM 196 |
| **Max. trailer size & fee:** No camping | **Fish species:** Rainbow trout |
| **Time limit:** No camping | **Season:** 1 April-31 October |
| **Mailing address:** RCCA, Box 111, Costilla, NM 87524 | |
| (505) 586-0542 | |
| **Police emergency tel. #:** 911 | |

## ACTIVITIES AND FACILITIES

| | NO | YES | Proximity to Lake in Miles | | NO | YES | Proximity to Lake in Miles |
|---|---|---|---|---|---|---|---|
| Bait and supplies | X | | * 1 | Airplane runway | X | | |
| Boat gas | X | | | Bottled gas | X | | |
| Boat ramp | X | | | Café/snack bar | X | | *1 |
| Boat rental | X | | | Chemical toilets | X | | |
| Camping | X | | | Drinking water | X | | |
| Fire pits | X | | | Electrical hook-up | X | | |
| Fire places | X | | | Flush toilets | X | | |
| Firewood | X | | | Grocery store | X | | * 1 |
| Fishing | | X | | Handicapped access | X | | |
| Golf | X | | | Ice | X | | |
| Hiking | X | | | Laundry | X | | |
| Marina | X | | | Lodgings | X | | *1 |
| Picnicking | X | | | Pit toilets | X | | |
| Riding | X | | | Playground | X | | |
| Scuba diving | X | | | Restaurant | X | | |
| Stables | X | | | Sanitary disposal | X | | |
| Swimming | X | | | Sewer hook-up | X | | |
| Tables | X | | | Shelters | X | | |
| Telephone | X | | | Shopping | X | | |
| Tennis | X | | | Showers | X | | |
| Tent sites | X | | | Trailer space | X | | |
| Winter sports | X | | | Water hook-up | X | | |

*Stores and services in Costilla, 1 mile.

**Special Rules and Regulations**

    **Fishing:** State fishing license and permit from Rio Costilla Livestock Association required

    **Catch limit:** 4 trout per day

    **Boating:** No boats

*Latir Lakes*

# LATIR LAKES

Latir Lakes are a series of nine lakes located within the 80,000-acre Rio Costilla Park, owned and operated by the Rio Costilla Cooperative Livestock Association. The lakes rise tier-like up the Latir Mountains of the Sangre de Cristo Range. The entrance to this magnificent recreational area, called Rio Costilla Park, is located just ten miles southeast of Amalia. The nine lakes, and all of the recreational activities, including camping, hunting, and fishing, are owned and managed by the Rio Costilla Cooperative Livestock Association (RCCA)—a cooperative formed in 1942 as a private entity. The Association takes great pride in its management program of preservation of its scenic natural wonders and recreational resources. The revenue from fees is used for taxes and to maintain the area for recreation. The entire area has been kept in its natural state and has not been disturbed by logging or pole cutting.

I was fortunate to be guided through part of the area by the Park Ranger, Joaquin Valdez. In his half-ton four-wheel-drive truck, we made our slow and tortuous ascent to Lake #3, on a forty-five-minute drive over precipitous switchbacks and steep grades, within earshot of the rush of the foamy white water of Latir Creek, spilling in sheets across dark gray ledges of stairs down into the canyon far below. Lake #3 is typical of the Latir Lakes and holds the state record catch of Rio Grande cutthroat caught in 1989. The RCCA stocks Rio Grande cutthroat trout exclusively. The area around Lake #3 excludes hunting privileges. It is preserved as a fisherman's dream; heavily forested in dog fir, blue spruce, aspen, cork bark, cedar, white pine, and Douglas fir. There is no trailer accessibility to these high alpine lakes, but camping in tents is permitted, and chemical toilets are provided at most of the lakes. A campground near the entrance to the park is equipped with electric and water hook-ups.

## Directions from Albuquerque

Take I-25 north to Santa Fe and connect with U.S. 285/64 through Española. At Española continue northeast to Taos on NM 68. In Taos connect with NM 522 North through Questa to Costilla

From Costilla: Turn right on NM 196 and go about fifteen miles southeast to the entrance of Rio Costilla Park and Latir Lakes. At the entrance is a Ranger Station and fee collection area. Regulations and fee schedule are posted at the entrance.

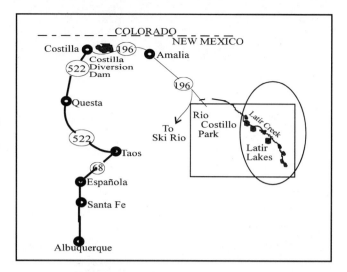

| | |
|---|---|
| **Surface acres:** 9 lakes, 1-10 acres in size | **Distance from Albuquerque:** 186 miles |
| **Elevation:** 9,000-12,000 feet | **Location:** 15 miles southeast of Costilla |
| **Max. trailer size & fee:** Sites at entrance | **Fish species:** Rio Grande cutthroat trout |
| **Time limit:** No limit | **Season:** 1 April-31 October |
| **Mailing address:** P.O. Box 111, Costilla, NM 87524, (505) 586-0542 | |
| **Police emergency tel. #:** 911 | |

## ACTIVITIES AND FACILITIES

| | NO | YES | Proximity to Lake in Miles | | NO | YES | Proximity to Lake in Miles |
|---|---|---|---|---|---|---|---|
| Bait and supplies | X | | | Airplane runway | X | | |
| Boat gas | X | | | Bottled gas | X | | |
| Boat ramp | X | | | Café/snack bar | X | | |
| Boat rental | X | | | Chemical toilets | | X | * |
| Camping | | X | * | Drinking water | | X | * |
| Fire pits | | X | | Electrical hook-up | | X | * |
| Fire places | X | | | Flush toilets | X | | |
| Firewood | X | | | Grocery store | X | | |
| Fishing | | X | | Handicapped access | X | | |
| Golf | X | | | Ice | X | | |
| Hiking | | X | | Laundry | X | | |
| Marina | X | | | Lodgings | X | | |
| Picnicking | | X | | Pit toilets | | X | |
| Riding | X | | | Playground | X | | |
| Scuba diving | X | | | Restaurant | X | | |
| Stables | X | | | Trash cans | | X | |
| Swimming | X | | | Sewer hook-up | X | | |
| Tables | X | | | Shelters | X | | |
| Telephone | X | | | Shopping | X | | |
| Tennis | X | | | Showers | X | | |
| Tent sites | | X | | Trailer space | | X | * |
| Winter sports | X | | | Water hook-up | | X | * |

*Tent camping only, at lakes. RVs and trailer camping near entrance.

**Special Rules and Regulations**

**Fishing:** No state license required; RCCA permit required

**Catch limit:** 4 fish per day at least 12 inches long; fish taken by flies, lures, barbless hooks

**Boating:** Car-top boats without motors permitted

**Other:** Camping and hook-ups available near entrance to park and parking area.; fee is $10.00 per day when available; other fees are posted at entrance

# In the Vicinity of Red River

## *Red River*

*There are six lakes in the vicinity of Red River. The asterisked lakes below are reached by trail only, so are not considered suitable for a day visit. Though Goose Lake is accessible by four-wheel-drive vehicles, the road is rough and inaccessible during inclement weather: *Lost Lake, *Middle Fork Lake, *Pioneer Lake, *Goose Lake, *Horse Lake, *Fawn Lakes.*

*Fawn Lakes are detailed on the next two pages.*

Red River is often billed as the *"year-round playground of the Southwest."* It is one of the "Enchanted Circle" resort towns, nestled high in the Sangre de Cristos at an elevation of 8,800 feet, catering to skiiers, fishermen, backpackers, campers, hunters, photographers, and artists. In spring and summer its sparkling alpine lakes, and miles of stocked streams that twist and cascade through the mountains and forests, bathed in the heady scent of pine and juniper, lure thousands of anglers, backpackers, campers, and picnickers. Thousands more nature lovers, photographers, and artists come to witness the blaze of color that autumn briskness brings to the aspens, which glow in gold, and to the scrub oak swathed in russets and red. Autumn aspencades and festivals draw thousands more, but Red River is best known for its skiing. In winter, Red River is transformed into a wonderland.

Both downhill and cross-country skiing is unsurpassed here, as miles of marked and unmarked trails criss-cross the Carson National Forest. Snowmobilers, Nordic skiiers, and downhillers track the wooded trails, even into the town itself. Red River is a fun town, created for, and devoted exclusively to, tourism and recreation—a winter fun town where skiiers can ski right to their front doors and are within walking distance from most lodges to the lifts. Full accommodations, restaurants, shops, and entertainment are in abundance in this town, whose resident population is far outnumbered by fun-seeking visitors.

Red River takes its name from the river that flows through the town. Its mineral content casts a reddish tint to the water and through the years its color has never changed. Red River was inhabited by Native Americans in the twelth century, long before Coronado passed through in 1540. In the early 1800s trappers were drawn by the abundance of fur-bearing animals. Later, gold strikes in the nearby area of Elizabethtown near Eagle Nest brought a rush of settlers in 1870. In 1894 the Mallette brothers, pioneers in the area, laid out the town. When the mines played out, the population of Red River—once over 3,000—decreased to near ghost town status, but the town was rediscovered by vacationers seeking respite from the desert heat, and it became a resort community in 1925. In 1958 the Red River Ski Area started construction and it has become a thriving and prosperous town.

*Fawn Lakes*

# FAWN LAKES

Fawn Lakes are two lakes totaling two acres, lying at an elevation of 8,500 feet. They are another of the many delightful surprises that one comes across in this spectacularly scenic part of the "Enchanted Circle" deep in the Carson National Forest. Fawn Lakes are located just three miles west of the town of Red River off NM Highway 38, in a lush, forested mountain setting, framed by spectacular rock formations called thermal pipes, that rise hundreds of feet above the landscape. Fawn Lakes are visible from the highway, well marked by a Forest Service sign, and conveniently located next to Fawn Lakes Campground. The campground is easily accessed off the highway and is equipped with toilets, tables, fireplaces with grills, and trailer and tent sites. The lakes are accessed by a foot bridge across Red River, which is also a fine trout fishing stream. The lakes are stocked with rainbow trout, and the streams are populated with rainbow, brook, and brown trout.

No camping is permitted at the lakes, but there are benches and pit toilets around them for the convenience of visitors. Several National Forest campgrounds and private campgrounds are nearby. Some provide water, electricity, sewer hook-ups, and even cable TV. It is advisable to stop at the Questa Ranger Station in Questa or the Red River Chamber of Commerce for information on the many other recreational opportunities in this area. In Questa, eight miles west and in Red River three miles east, there are full accommodations, including restaurants, and picnicking and fishing supplies.

## Directions from Albuquerque

(Via Eagle Nest and Red River) take I-25 north to Santa Fe and connect with U.S. 84/285. Go north through Española to the junction of NM 68. Continue northeast on NM 68 and swing right on U.S. 64 to Eagle Nest then on to NM 38 to Red River. Follow signs three miles to Fawn Lakes.  They are visible, well marked, and lie next to Fawn Lakes Campground on the right side of the highway. Fawn Lakes can also be reached by taking U.S. 64 through Taos and connecting with NM 522 north to Questa then turning right on NM 38, about eight miles to the lakes.

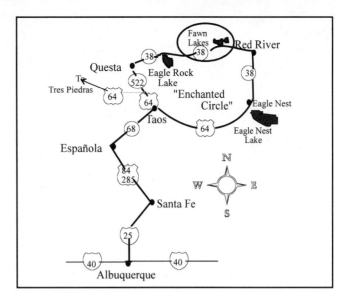

| | | |
|---|---|---|
| **Surface acres: 2** lakes, totaling 2 acres | | **Distance from Albuquerque:** 167 miles |
| **Elevation:** 8,500 feet | | **Location:** 3 miles downstream from town of Red |
| **Max. trailer size & fee:** 36 feet; $8.00 per night | | River on NM 38 (8 miles east of Questa) |
| **Time limit:** 14 days | | **Fish species:** Rainbow trout |
| **Police emergency tel. #:** At campground | | **Season: 15** May-15 October |
| **Medical emergency tel. #:** At campground | | |

## ACTIVITIES AND FACILITIES

| | NO | YES | Proximity to Lake in Miles | | NO | YES | Proximity to Lake in Miles |
|---|---|---|---|---|---|---|---|
| Bait and supplies | X | | 3 | Airplane runway | X | | 3 |
| Boat gas | X | | | Bottled gas | X | | 3 |
| Boat ramp | X | | | Café/snack bar | X | | 3 |
| Boat rental | X | | | Chemical toilets | | X | |
| Camping | | X | | Drinking water | | X | |
| Fire pits | | X | | Electrical hook-up | X | | 3 |
| Fire places | | X | | Flush toilets | X | | 3 |
| Firewood | | X | | Grocery store | X | | 3 |
| Fishing | | X | | Handicapped access | X | | |
| Golf | X | | 3 | Ice | | X | |
| Hiking | | X | | Laundry | X | | X |
| Marina | X | | | Lodgings | X | | X |
| Picnicking | | X | | Pit toilets | X | | |
| Riding | X | | | Playground | X | | 3 |
| Scuba diving | X | | | Restaurant | X | | 3 |
| Stables | X | | | Sanitary disposal | X | | 3 |
| Swimming | X | | | Sewer hook-up | X | | 3 |
| Tables | | X | | Shelters | X | | 3 |
| Telephone | X | | | Shopping | X | | 3 |
| Tennis | X | | 3 | Showers | X | | 3 |
| Tent sites | | X | | Trailer space | | X | |
| Winter sports | | X | | Water hook-up | X | | 3 |

*Food, stores, lodgings and complete facilities in Red River, 3 miles east.
**Special Rules and Regulations**
   **Fishing:** State fishing license required
   **Catch limit:** 6 trout; state catch limits apply, see Fishing Proclamation on page 343
   **Boating:** No boats or floating devices permitted
   **Other:** No camping at lake, but good camping and facilities in Fawn Lakes Campground next to lakes

# In the Vicinity of Eagle Nest

## *Eagle Nest*

*There are two lakes in the vicinity of Eagle Nest: Eagle Nest Lake, Gravel Pit Lakes*

The village of Eagle Nest lies at an elevation of 8,200 feet above sea level, on the north bank of Eagle Nest Lake, at the bottom of the Moreno Valley adjacent to the 1.6 million-acre Carson National Forest. It is backed by the high, majestic mountain peaks and forests of the Sangre de Cristo Range. The village was founded in 1920 after the Eagle Nest Dam was built in 1919 by Charles and Frank Springer. Its purpose was to store surplus waters of the Cimarron River for irrigation of part of the Maxwell Land Grant, where Charles Springer's C.S. Cattle Ranch was located. The village was originally called Therma, but later, in 1935, the name was changed by the residents to Eagle Nest after the golden eagles that nest and soar along the thermal updrafts on the windward sides of the surrounding mountains. (To take advantage of these thermal drafts, a high-altitude glider and soaring festival is held on Thanksgiving weekends, attracting many visitors to enjoy the colorful show.)

The lake and the scenic Sangre de Cristo range have drawn thousands of visitors to Eagle Nest, which has become a paradise for the nature lover, the camper, hiker, backpacker, fisherman, hunter, artist, and photographer. History buffs delight in the turn-of-the-century gold mining towns of Idlewild and Elizabethtown on the outskirts of Eagle Nest, and in the old wild west towns of Cimarron, Red River, and Taos, home of the famous frontier scout Kit Carson. These towns are all within an hour's drive from Eagle Nest and offer a pleasureable visit into the past. Eleven museums display memorabilia and chronicle the wild west days of the 1870s. Abandoned mines and their remains are still visible, and centuries-old historic Taos Pueblo represents the center of Indian culture in New Mexico for over 900 years.

Eagle Nest is now one of the most popular resort communities in the state, with motels, cabins, bait and tackle shops, grocery stores, service stations, and restaurants. Six miles south of Eagle Nest, rising in a bird-like profile on the hillside, is a chapel that was built by the Wesphall family as a memorial to their son and to other servicemen who were killed in Vietnam. The chapel is open to the public and is a must stop on the way to Eagle Nest. Just twelve miles south of the village is the four-seasons resort of Angel Fire, best known for its miles of downhill ski trails and its well-designed and maintained condominiums, golf course, and recreational opportunities.

*Eagle Nest Lake*

# EAGLE NEST LAKE

Eagle Nest Lake is a 2,000- to 2,500-acre lake enjoying the reputation of being one of the finest rainbow trout waters in the Southwest. The dam was built at the head of Cimarron Canyon in 1919 by Charles Springer, who owned the C.S. Cattle Ranch located on the Maxwell Land Grant. The dam backs up a lake five miles long and two miles wide, with a capacity of 78,800 acre-feet. Its purpose was to irrigate part of the Moreno Valley on which his ranch was located. Today, the water impounded in Eagle Nest Lake provides irrigation for a farming area fifty miles east of this point. Since the lake is under private ownership, fishing has been open to the public for only short periods in the past, but now it is open to public fishing through Department of Game and Fish leases with the Eagle Nest Reservoir Corporation, a subsidiary of the C.S. Cattle Company. The Department of Game and Fish stocks the lake and surrounding streams regularly with frys and three-inch fingerlings, and supervises its maintenance.

Eagle Nest Lake is famous for its excellent fishing for trophy rainbow trout, and cutthroat trout. A privately owned marina offers guided fishing tours, boat rental, a boat dock, and moorings. There is no camping at the lake, but camping is available in nearby private sites and in the adjacent Carson National Forest. In the Cimarron State Park, three miles east of the lake, there is a fully equipped campground, and just a few miles farther east and passing through some of the most spectacular scenery in the state is the Colin Neblett Wildlife Area, a hunters' and birdwatchers' favorite, where anglers fish the Cimarron for stocked rainbows and stream-bred browns. Campgrounds here are equipped with complete facilities.

## Directions from Albuquerque

Take I-25 north to the junction of U.S. 84/285 at Santa Fe. Continue on U.S. 84/285 north to the junction of NM 68. Continue northeast on NM 68 to the junction of U.S. 64, then take U.S. 64 east and follow signs to Eagle Nest.

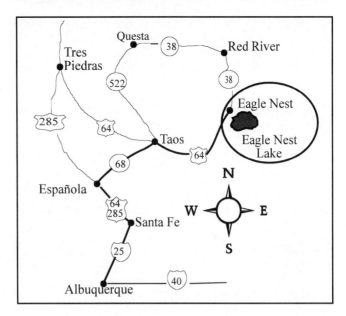

| | | |
|---|---|---|
| Surface acres: 2,000 to 2,500 | | Distance from Albuquerque: 164 miles |
| Elevation: 8,215 feet | | Location: 17 miles southeast of Red River; |
| Max. trailer size & fee: No camping | | 12 miles north of Angel Fire |
| Time limit: Day use only | | Fish species: Rainbow trout, cutthroat trout, and |
| Mailing address: Eagle Nest Chamber of Commerce, | | kokanee salmon |
| Box 322, Eagle Nest, NM 87718 (505) 377-6271 | | Season: 1 April-31 October (Kokanee 1 Oct-31 Dec) |
| Medical emergency tel. #: 911 | | Police emergency tel. #: 911 |

## ACTIVITIES AND FACILITIES

| | NO | YES | Proximity to Lake in Miles | | NO | YES | Proximity to Lake in Miles |
|---|---|---|---|---|---|---|---|
| Bait and supplies | | X | | Airplane runway | | X | |
| Boat gas | | X | | Bottled gas | X | | * |
| Boat ramp | | X | | Café/snack bar | | X | |
| Boat rental | | X | | Chemical toilets | | X | |
| Camping | X | | * | Drinking water | | X | |
| Fire pits | X | | * | Electrical hook-up | X | | * |
| Fire places | X | | * | Flush toilets | | X | |
| Firewood | X | | | Grocery store | | X | |
| Fishing | | X | | Handicapped access | | X | |
| Golf | X | | * | Ice | | X | |
| Hiking | X | | * | Laundry | X | | * |
| Marina | | X | | Lodgings | | X | |
| Picnicking | | X | | Pit toilets | | X | |
| Riding | X | | * | Playground | X | | * |
| Scuba diving | X | | * | Restaurant | | X | |
| Swimming | X | | * | Sanitary disposal | X | | * |
| Tables | X | | * | Sewer hook-up | X | | * |
| Telephone | | X | * | Shelters | X | | * |
| Tennis | X | | | Shopping | X | | * |
| Tent sites | X | | | Showers | X | | * |
| Water skiing | X | | | Trailer space | X | | * |
| Winter sports | X | | | Water hook-up | X | | * |

*Camping facilities in Cimarron State Park, 3 miles east in Carson National Forest.

**Special Rules and Regulations**
   **Fishing:** State fishing license required with trout stamp validation
   **Catch limit:** 10 trout per day, kokanee salmon, 12 per day; see Fishing Proclamation
   **Boating:** Boats available for rental at private marina or bring own boat
   **Other:** Day use only; no water-skiing

*Gravel Pit Lakes*

# GRAVEL PIT LAKES

Gravel Pit Lakes is the name given to a group of three lakes totaling about two to three acres. They were formed by flooding of abandoned gravel excavations, then developed for recreational use and stocked with rainbow trout by the New Mexico Department of Game and Fish. They are located in a picturesque setting at the Maverick Campground within Cimarron Canyon State Park on U.S. 64, just three miles east of Eagle Nest and twelve miles west of Cimarron. Maverick Campground has forty-eight camp sites with tables and grills, five water hydrants, and two modern restrooms (no showers). Nature has endowed this region with some of the most beautiful scenery in the west. Scenic highway U.S. 64 snakes through the deep canyons of the Sangre de Cristo Mountains, skirting their towering peaks and the spectacular cliffs of the Palisades Sill. These crenulated rock formations were formed millions of years ago by the uplift of these southern Rocky Mountains and the

Cimarron River, as it carved its way from the west. The Cimarron River and its streams provide sportsmen with superb fishing, boating, hunting, camping, and myriad other recreational opportunities. The Cimarron State Park is part of the Colin Neblett Wildlife Area, and special regulations are unique to this area. Since it is a State Wildlife Area, whose facilities were originally purchased and developed with fish and wildlife funds, certain license requirements are enforced. At least one member of each party must have a current New Mexico fishing license. Camping and vehicles are allowed in designated and developed areas only, and some specially designated quality fishing waters within the area are posted. The park has over a hundred developed sites. Most of the sites have a picnic table, a grill, and two paved parking spaces. There are no hook-ups, but the three major developed campgrounds all have modern restrooms, sinks, toilets, dump stations, and water hydrants.

## Directions from Albuquerque

Take I-25 north to the junction of U.S. 84/ 285 at Santa Fe. Continue north to the junction of NM 68. Take NM 68 to the junction of U.S. 64 at Taos. Go east on U.S. 64 through Eagle Nest and continue on U.S. 64, three miles east, to Cimarron Canyon State Park and follow signs to Gravel Pit Lakes within the Maverick Campgrounds, a unit within the state park.

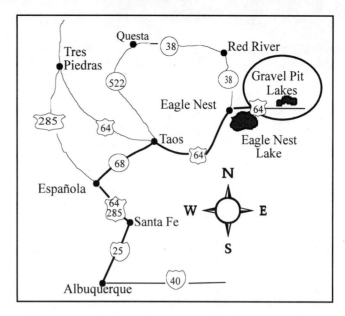

| | | |
|---|---|---|
| **Surface acres:** 2-3 | | **Distance from Albuquerque:** 168 miles |
| **Elevation:** 8,300 feet | | **Location:** In Maverick Campgrounds within the |
| **Max. trailer size:** 20-30 feet | | Cimarron Canyon State Park, three miles east of |
| **Time limit:** 14 days; fees are posted | | Eagle Nest, off U.S. 64 |
| **Mailing address:** Box 147, Ute Park, NM 87749 | | **Fish species:** Rainbow trout (brown trout in the |
| (505) 377-6271 | | river) |
| **Medical emergency tel. #:** 911 | | **Season:** 1 April-31 October |

## ACTIVITIES AND FACILITIES

| | NO | YES | Proximity to Lake in Miles | | NO | YES | Proximity to Lake in Miles |
|---|---|---|---|---|---|---|---|
| **Boat gas** | X | | | **Bottled gas** | X | | |
| **Boat ramp** | X | | | **Café/snack bar** | X | | |
| **Boat rental** | X | | | **Chemical toilets** | | X | |
| **Camping** | | X | | **Drinking water** | | X | |
| **Fire pits** | | X | | **Electrical hook-up** | X | | |
| **Fire places** | | X | | **Flush toilets** | | X | |
| **Firewood** | | X | | **Grocery store** | X | | 3 |
| **Fishing** | | X | | **Handicapped access** | | X | |
| **Golf** | X | | | **Ice** | X | | 3 |
| **Hiking** | | X | | **Laundry** | X | | 3 |
| **Marina** | X | | | **Lodgings** | X | | 3 |
| **Picnicking** | | X | | **Pit toilets** | | X | |
| **Riding** | | X | | **Playground** | X | | |
| **Scuba diving** | X | | | **Restaurant** | X | | |
| **Skiing (water)** | X | | | **Sanitary disposal** | X | | ** |
| **Swimming** | X | | | **Sewer hook-up** | X | | |
| **Tables** | | X | | **Shelters** | X | | ** |
| **Telephone** | | X | | **Shopping** | X | | 3 |
| **Tennis** | X | | | **Showers** | X | | |
| **Tent sites** | | X | | **Trailer space** | | X | |
| **Winter sports** | | X | | **Water hook-up** | | X | |

*Lodgings, food and stores in Eagle Nest, 3 miles west.
**Special Rules and Regulations**
    **Fishing:** See Fishing Proclamation for special rules in Colin Neblett Wildlife Area
    **Catch limit:** 6 trout per day; see Fishing Proclamation for Regulations
    **Boating:** No boats or floating devices permitted
    **Other:** Some waters in the Colin Neblett Wildlife Area are Quality Water; see Fishing Proclamation and observe posted rules

# In the Vicinity
# of Springer

## *Springer*

*There are three lakes in the vicinity of Springer:
Springer Lake, Charette Lakes, Miami Lake*

Springer has a population of about 1,700. It is
located at the junction of Highways I-25/85 and
U.S. 56. It lies in a picturesque and historical part
of northeastern New Mexico, where the high plains
meet the Rocky Mountain foothills, at an elevation
of 5,857 feet above sea level. Before the coming of
the railroad in 1879, the area in which Springer is
situated was a territory with a colorful and stormy
past reaching back to the days of the Maxwell Land
Grant, a huge tract of land owned by Lucien B.
Maxwell. It was a territory of roaming Ute and
Apache Indians, of outlaws and trappers,
prospectors, cattlemen, buffalo hunters, and traders,
lured by the prospect of fortunes to be made in this
thriving town in the rich grasslands.

In the days of the stagecoach and the wagon
train, it was a favorite watering stop on the old
Santa Fe Trail. With the coming of the railroad in
1879, the town became an important trading
station, serving the vast ranches and farms that
stretched for miles beyond the town. Hotels,
boarding houses, livery stables, stores, and saloons
sprang up, and the town was named Springer, in
honor of a Maxwell Land Grant lawyer, Frank

Springer, and his brother Charles, a noted rancher
near Cimarron. Springer became the county seat of
Colfax County but later lost its status to Raton,
another thriving city in the north. After almost two
years of bitter debate and arguments, the New
Mexico Supreme Court ruled that a legislative act
moving the courthouse to Raton was valid, and
Springer lost out as the county seat. The old Colfax
County Courthouse still stands in the heart of town
on Maxwell Street. Inside its old jail, many of the
west's most colorful and meanest outlaws were
incarcerated to await trial and punishment. It is now
a museum and a must stop for visitors. On display
in this over one-hundred-year-old building is a
fascinating collection of memorabilia of history,
romance, and drama, emphasizing the early days
when the Santa Fe Trail crossed the area. It exhibits
the life and times of the pioneers who built the
town. It honors the builders and the planners who
transformed this primitive watering stop into the
modern city of today.

There are many outdoor recreational
opportunities in and around Springer. Just four
miles north of Springer is Springer Lake, which
offers boating and fishing. Other recreational
opportunities are available, such as camping,
hunting, and skiing. Springer has full
accommodations, services, restaurants, stores, and
service stations.

*Springer Lake*

# SPRINGER LAKE

Springer Lake is a 450-acre lake lying in rolling grasslands four miles northwest of Springer, off I-25. The lake was created to supply irrigation waters to the surrounding farms and ranches. In 1968, Springer Ditch Company entered into an agreement with the State Game Commission to lease to the Department the rights to the surface and fishing on the lake for a period of five years. Under the agreement, the company would provide a minimum pool of 300 acre-feet, and the Department would make dam and recreation improvements.

The lake is stocked regularly with rainbow trout. It was first stocked with northern pike in 1963 and is noted for its fine northern catches. Record catches of thirty-pounders have been taken at Springer Lake, making it a favorite for anglers and spin casters. Bullheads, channel catfish, and perch are also taken. There is a primitive boat launching ramp at the southern end of the lake, and boats are limited to trolling speeds. There is a no-fee camping area offering primitive camping and picnicking facilities that include a few sanitary facilities. The lake is open year round. There is handicapped access from both the southern and northern shoreline, where a good gravel road on the dam links both ends of the lake. There are no stores at the lake, nor is there drinking water. Needed supplies for fishing or picnicking are available four miles southeast, in Springer.

## Directions from Albuquerque

Take I-25 to Springer. From Springer go to the Texaco service station north of town and take NM 468 west to Boys School. A dirt road goes west and two miles to the lake.

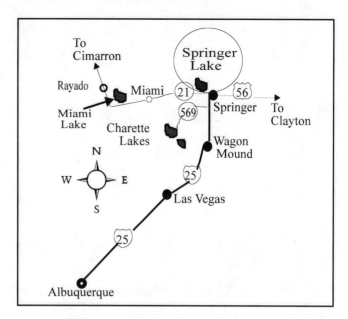

| | | | |
|---|---|---|---|
| **Surface acres**: 450 | | **Distance from Albuquerque:** 194 miles | |
| **Elevation**: 5,857 feet | | **Location:** 4 miles northwest of Springer off | |
| **Max. trailer size & fee:** No restrictions, no fee | | NM 468 | |
| **Time limit:** 10 days | | **Fish species:** Rainbow trout, northern pike, and | |
| **Mailing address:** None | | channel catfish | |
| **Police emergency tel. #:** 483-2884 | | **Season:** 1 April-31 March | |
| **Medical emergency tel. #:** 911 | | | |

## ACTIVITIES AND FACILITIES

| | NO | YES | Proximity to Lake in Miles | | NO | YES | Proximity to Lake in Miles |
|---|---|---|---|---|---|---|---|
| Bait and supplies | X | | | Airplane runway | X | | |
| Boat gas | X | | | Bottled gas | X | | |
| Boat ramp | | X | | Café/snack bar | X | | |
| Boat rental | X | | | Chemical toilets | X | | |
| Camping | X | | | Drinking water | X | | |
| Fire pits | X | | | Electrical hook-up | X | | |
| Fire places | X | | | Flush toilets | X | | |
| Firewood | X | | | Grocery store | X | | 4 |
| Fishing | | X | | Handicapped access | | X | |
| Golf | X | | 4 | Ice | X | | 4 |
| Hiking | X | | | Laundry | X | | 4 |
| Marina | X | | | Lodgings | X | | 4 |
| Picnicking | | X | | Pit toilets | | X | |
| Riding | X | | | Playground | X | | |
| Scuba diving | X | | | Restaurant | X | | 4 |
| Stables | X | | | Sanitary disposal | X | | 4 |
| Swimming | X | | | Sewer hook-up | X | | |
| Tables | | X | | Shelters | X | | |
| Telephone | X | | | Shopping | X | | 4 |
| Tennis | X | | | Showers | X | | 4 |
| Tent sites | | X | | Trailer space | | X | |
| Winter sports | X | | | Water hook-up | X | | 4 |

Accommodations, stores and services in Springer, 4 miles southeast.

**Special Rules and Regulations**

**Fishing:** State fishing license required
**Catch limit:** 6 trout, a 12 inch mimimum size keeper for black bass (1994-95 Proclamation)
**Boating:** Trolling speeds only, when water storage is under 1,000 feet; no ice fishing
**Other:** Camping permitted (no fee); no open fires

# CHARETTE LAKES

Charette Lakes are located twenty-three miles southwest of Springer and about thirteen miles northwest of Wagon Mound. They are reached off I-25, then west off NM 569. The lakes are a combination of two lakes formed by the diversion of water from Ocate Creek into natural depressions in the terrain that lies on a mesa top at an elevation of about 6,500 feet above sea level. To the west loom the towering peaks of the Sangre de Cristo Mountains, and to the east vast prairies of grama grass stretch far into the distant horizon. The lower lake is about three hundred acres in size; the upper lake is about a hundred acres.

The lower lake is a refuge that provides a haven for Canadian geese and other waterfowl. It was purchased in 1949 to be developed as a refuge for waterfowl and to provide improved opportunities for fishing and recreation. The lakes have become a favorite fishing spot for anglers and are considered two of the finer lakes for catching larger trout, some three to four pounds. The lower lake is stocked with sub-catchable and some catchable rainbows; the upper lake is stocked with sub-catchables. It is also stocked with yellow perch. Camping and picnicking are permitted around the lower lake. Good access is by way of a dirt/gravel road that circles the lake. The facilities include tents and trailer sites, water, tables, pit toilets, and fireplaces. There is a boat ramp for boats limited to trolling speed. There are no stores or services at the lake, but needed picnicking and fishing supplies are available in Springer.

## Directions from Albuquerque

Take I-25 through Wagon Mound. Connect with NM 569 west, and follow signs to Charette Lakes. Access is good, on an improved dirt/gravel road.

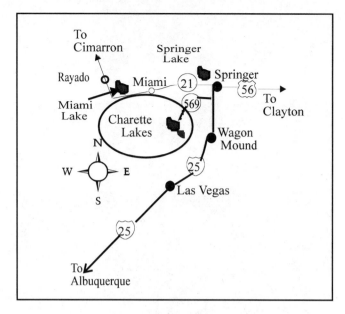

| | | |
|---|---|---|
| **Surface acres:** 2 lakes, totaling 400 acres | | |
| **Elevation:** 5,800 feet | | |
| **Max. trailer size & fee:** No fee; no size limit | | |
| **Time limit:** 10 days | | |
| **Mailing address:** None | | |
| **Police emergency tel. #:** 911 | | |
| **Medical emergency tel. #:** 911 | | |

**Distance from Albuquerque:** 170 miles

**Location:** 23 miles southwest of Springer; 13 miles northwest of Wagon Mound

**Fish species:** Rainbow trout, yellow perch

**Season:** 1 April-31 October

## ACTIVITIES AND FACILITIES

| | NO | YES | Proximity to Lake in Miles | | NO | YES | Proximity to Lake in Miles |
|---|---|---|---|---|---|---|---|
| **Bait and supplies** | X | | | **Airplane runway** | X | | |
| **Boat gas** | X | | | **Bottled gas** | X | | |
| **Boat ramp** | | X | | **Café/snack bar** | | X | |
| **Boat rental** | X | | | **Chemical toilets** | X | | |
| **Camping** | | X | | **Drinking water** | | X | |
| **Fire pits** | | X | | **Electrical hook-up** | X | | |
| **Fire places** | | X | | **Flush toilets** | X | | |
| **Firewood** | X | | | **Grocery store** | X | | |
| **Fishing** | | X | | **Handicapped access** | | X | |
| **Golf** | X | | | **Ice** | X | | |
| **Hiking** | X | | | **Laundry** | X | | |
| **Marina** | X | | | **Lodgings** | X | | |
| **Picnicking** | | X | | **Pit toilets** | | X | |
| **Riding** | X | | | **Playground** | X | | |
| **Scuba diving** | X | | | **Restaurant** | X | | |
| **Stables** | X | | | **Sanitary disposal** | X | | |
| **Swimming** | X | | | **Sewer hook-up** | X | | |
| **Tables** | | X | | **Shelters** | X | | |
| **Telephone** | X | | | **Shopping** | X | | |
| **Tennis** | X | | | **Showers** | X | | |
| **Tent sites** | | X | | **Trailer space** | | X | |
| **Winter sports** | X | | | **Water hook-up** | X | | |

Full services and stores in Springer
**Special Rules and Regulations**
   **Fishing:** New Mexico fishing license required
   **Catch limit:** 10 trout per day (1994 and 1995); see current year Fishing Proclamation
   **Boating:** Restricted to trolling speed and permitted during fishing season only
   **Other:** No open fires; no shooting

*Miami Lake*

# MIAMI LAKE

Miami Lake is a 190-acre artificial lake, eight miles west of the small town of Miami, and about eighteen miles west of Springer, off NM 21. On our approach to the lake the vista spread before us in startling beauty. A gauzy mist cloaked the dark shadow of the Rocky Mountain foothills along the horizon on the far side of the lake. Wildflowers bordered a fence with a posted "No Trespassing" sign at a secured entrance gate. Paintbrush, tiny bouquets of violet, lodge pole, and lupine poked through its wire strands. A gentle slope led down to the lake's edge.

The lake is on private land, owned and operated by the Miami Domestic Water Users Association. No public fishing is allowed on Miami Lake. It is restricted to use by Miami Water Users Association members only. We continued west on NM 21, which skirts the lake then heads north to the town of Rayado. Although it is private, it is well worth the time to visit this beautiful lake—to view its magnificence, or just to enjoy its solitude.

## Directions from Albuquerque

Take I-25 to Springer. Connect with NM 21 and turn west. Then go twenty-one miles to lake. NM 21 is a good paved road. Miami Lake is visible off NM 21.

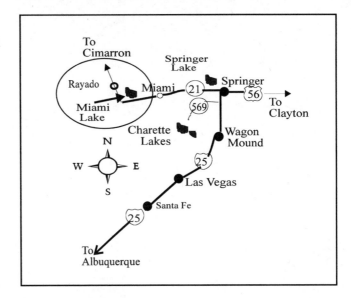

| | | |
|---|---|---|
| **Surface acres:** 190 | | **Distance from Albuquerque:** 206 miles |
| **Elevation:** 6,000 feet | | **Location:** 8 miles west of Miami, 18 miles west of |
| **Max. trailer size & fee:** Private, no camping | | Springer |
| **Time limit:** Private; no trespassing | | **Fish species:** Northern pike |
| **Mailing address:** None | | **Season:** Private; fishing restricted to use by |
| **Police emergency tel. #:** 911 | | Miami Water Users Members only; no public fishing |
| **Medical emergency tel. #:** 911 | | permitted |

## ACTIVITIES AND FACILITIES

| | NO | YES | Proximity to Lake in Miles | | NO | YES | Proximity to Lake in Miles |
|---|---|---|---|---|---|---|---|
| Bait and supplies | X | | | Airplane runway | X | | |
| Boat gas | X | | | Bottled gas | X | | |
| Boat ramp | X | | | Café/snack bar | X | | |
| Boat rental | X | | | Chemical toilets | X | | |
| Camping | X | | | Drinking water | X | | |
| Fire pits | X | | | Electrical hook-up | X | | |
| Fire places | X | | | Flush toilets | X | | |
| Firewood | X | | | Grocery store | X | | |
| Fishing | X | | | Handicapped access | X | | |
| Golf | X | | | Ice | X | | |
| Hiking | X | | | Laundry | X | | |
| Marina | X | | | Lodgings | X | | |
| Picnicking | X | | | Pit toilets | X | | |
| Riding | X | | | Playground | X | | |
| Scuba diving | X | | | Restaurant | X | | |
| Stables | X | | | Sanitary disposal | X | | |
| Swimming | X | | | Sewer hook-up | X | | |
| Tables | X | | | Shelters | X | | |
| Telephone | X | | | Shopping | X | | |
| Tennis | X | | | Showers | X | | |
| Tent sites | X | | | Trailer space | X | | |
| Winter sports | X | | | Water hook-up | X | | |

Stores, services and lodgings in Springer, 18 miles east.

**Special Rules and Regulations**

  **Fishing:** Not open to the public
  **Catch limit:** No fishing, except for members of Miami Water Users Association
  **Boating:** No boating
  **Other:** Private land; no camping or littering

# In the Vicinity of Maxwell

## *Maxwell*

*In the vicinity of Maxwell is the Maxwell National Wildlife Refuge. The refuge contains about two dozen small lakes, the largest is Maxwell Lake #13. Other lakes on the refuge are Maxwell Lake #14, Maxwell Lake #12. Only Lakes #13 and #14 permit fishing, the rest of the lakes are maintained as a bird refuge. Just outside the refuge is the largest of the lakes in the vicinity, Stubblefield Lake. Next to Stubblefield Lake, and connected by a canal, is Laguna Madre.*

The town of Maxwell is located thirteen miles north of Springer and twenty-five miles south of Raton, off I-25. It was founded in the late 1880s by the Maxwell Land and Irrigation Company, whose owner Lucien B. Maxwell, a hunter and trapper from Illinois, settled on land granted in 1841 by Governor Manuel Armijo to Charles Beaubien, a French trapper, and to Guadalupe Miranda of Taos. After the death of Beaubien in 1864, Maxwell, who had married Beaubien's daughter, inherited the property and bought out the shares of the remaining heirs, establishing it as the largest single landholding in the western hemisphere. It comprises an area of land three times the area of Rhode Island and became known as the Maxwell Land Grant. The town of Maxwell became the shipping center for the company and the farmers, cattle and sheep ranchers in the area.

Four miles northwest of Maxwell is the Maxwell Wildlife Refuge, a resting, nesting, and feeding sanctuary for migratory waterfowl. The several irrigation impoundments and numerous ponds and lakes on the refuge attract large concentrations of wild ducks and geese each spring, fall, and winter. More than 187 species of waterfowl have been recorded on the refuge. Picnicking, camping, and fishing are permitted on the refuge on a seasonal basis.

The town of Maxwell has adequate conveniences for visitors to the refuge. There are gas stations, restaurants, lodgings, and stores where picnic and fishing supplies are available.

*Maxwell Lakes*

# MAXWELL LAKES

Maxwell Lakes are located on the Maxwell National Wildlife Refuge four miles northwest of the town of Maxwell and sixteen miles north of Springer. The refuge was established in 1966 as a resting, nesting, and feeding sanctuary for migratory waterfowl and is used extensively by ducks and geese during fall and winter seasons. All of the Maxwell Lakes are owned and operated by the Vermejo Conservancy District for irrigation and water storage. The refuge is comprised of 2,800 acres of grassland and is situated in the heart of an agricultural area served by several irrigation impoundments. Each fall, winter, and spring thousands of ducks and geese are attracted to these impoundments. Maxwell Lake #13 is the largest of the impoundments and attracts the largest concentration of ducks and geese. The wildlife refuge has recorded 187 species of birds, including eagles, hawks, loons, pheasants, quail, and a numerous variety of smaller birds, such as swallows, owls, pigeons, larks, magpies, hummingbirds, kingfishers, and jays. Of interest to birdwatchers and photographers, the peak wildlife numbers occur in the fall and winter.

The three main lakes on the refuge are Maxwell Lake #12, #13, and #14. Only lakes #13 and #14 are open to fishing during state-regulated fishing seasons. Lake #12 is used as a wildlife sanctuary only and is not for public use. Boats are permitted on Lake #13 only. This is the largest of the lakes. Boats are not to exceed trolling speeds. Two other lakes—#11 and # 20—are located on private land with no public access or use. During certain seasons camping, picnicking and walking are permitted. The refuge manager can provide information on public use, access, and recreational activities allowed during these special seasons. Stores, lodgings, and services are available in Maxwell, four miles south, or in Springer, sixteen miles south.

## Directions from Albuquerque

Take I-25 north and follow the Interstate through Santa Fe, through Las Vegas, and continue north through the towns of Wagon Mound, Springer and Maxwell. Four miles northwest off I-25 is the Maxwell Wildlife Refuge. Access to the refuge and to the lakes is off I-25 at Maxwell via NM 505 West or via NM 445 North. The Wildlife Office will provide information on the activities permitted on the lakes. (Certain activities are permitted on a seasonal basis.)

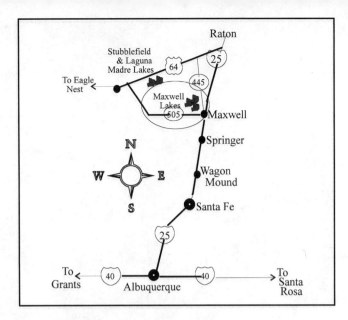

| | |
|---|---|
| **Surface acres:** Lake #13, 338 acres; | **Distance from Albuquerque:** 208 miles |
| Lake #14, 100 acres; Lake #12, 335 acres | **Location:** 4 miles northwest of Maxwell, 16 miles north of Springer |
| **Time limit:** 3 days | **Fish species:** Largemouth bass, channel catfish, walleye, white bass, stocked sub-catchable trout |
| **Mailing address:** Refuge Manager P.O. Box 276, Maxwell, New Mexico 87728 (505) 375-2331 | **Season:** 1 Mar-31 October (See or call Refuge for information on special seasons and regulations) |

## ACTIVITIES AND FACILITIES

| | NO | YES | Proximity to Lake in Miles | | NO | YES | Proximity to Lake in Miles |
|---|---|---|---|---|---|---|---|
| Bait and supplies | X | | | Airplane runway | X | | |
| Boat gas | X | | | Bottled gas | X | | |
| Boat ramp | X | | | Café/snack bar | X | | |
| Boat rental | X | | | Chemical toilets | X | | |
| Camping | | X | | Drinking water | X | | |
| Fire pits | X | | | Electrical hook-up | X | | |
| Fire places | X | | | Flush toilets | X | | |
| Firewood | X | | | Grocery store | X | | |
| Fishing | | X | | Handicapped access | | X | |
| Golf | X | | | Ice | X | | |
| Hiking | X | | | Laundry | X | | |
| Marina | X | | | Lodgings | X | | |
| Picnicking | | X | | Pit toilets | | X | |
| Riding | X | | | Playground | X | | |
| Scuba diving | X | | | Restaurant | X | | |
| Stables | X | | | Sanitary disposal | X | | |
| Swimming | X | | | Sewer hook-up | X | | |
| Tables | | X | | Shelters | X | | |
| Telephone | | X | | Shopping | X | | |
| Tennis | X | | | Showers | X | | |
| Tent sites | X | | | Trailer space | | X | |
| Winter sports | X | | | Water hook-up | X | | |

Stores & accommodations in Maxwell and Springer.

**Special Rules and Regulations**

**Fishing:** Permitted in Lakes #13 & #14 only. See Refuge Manager for special regulations.

**Catch limit:** 6 trout /day. See Fishing Proclamation or check with Refuge Manager.

**Boating:** Permitted on Lake #13 only. Boats with motors limited to trolling speed.

**Other:** Primitive camping, picnicking, and walking during special season prmitted on Lake #13

*Stubblefield and Laguna Lakes*

# STUBBLEFIELD AND LAGUNA MADRE LAKES

Stubblefield and Laguna Madre Lakes are located just outside of the Maxwell Wildlife Refuge, accessed from NM Highway 505 about five miles east of the refuge entrance. Stubblefield Lake is a 1,000-acre lake and is the largest of all the lakes in the area. Laguna Madre Lake is a 420-acre lake connected to Stubblefield Lake by a channel. These lakes are stocked regularly with rainbow trout, channel catfish, and fry-size walleye. The lakes may also contain perch, largemouth bass, and white bass.

Both Stubblefield and Laguna Madre Lakes are open for public use within the guidelines of the Vermejo Conservancy District and the New Mexico Department of Game and Fish. There are no restrictions on camping or picnicking at these lakes. There are a few pit toilets, but no other facilities are provided. It is recommended that visitors stock up on fishing or picnicking supplies in either Springer, sixteen miles south, or Maxwell, four miles southeast. The lakes are open from 1 March to 31 October.

## Directions from Albuquerque

Take I-25 north and follow the Interstate through Santa Fe, through Las Vegas, and continue north through the towns of Wagon Mound and Springer, then thirteen miles from Springer to Maxwell. Four miles northwest off I-25 is the Maxwell Wildlife Refuge. Turn west off I-25 on NM 505 and follow signs to the lakes.

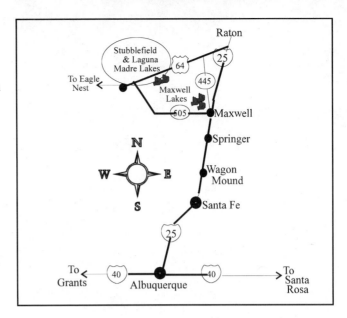

| | | |
|---|---|---|
| **Surface acres:** Stubblefield Lake, 1,000 ; | **Distance from Albuquerque:** 213 miles | |
| Laguna Madre Lake, 420 | **Location:** 9 miles northwest of Maxwell | |
| **Time limit:** 3 days | **Fish species:** Walleye, channel catfish, perch, | |
| **Mailing address:** U.S. Dept. of Interior; Fish | largemouth bass, white bass, and rainbow trout | |
| and Wildlife Service, Maxwell National Wildlife | **Season:** 1 March-31 October; consult Proclamation | |
| Refuge, P.O. Box 276, Maxwell, NM 87728 | **Camping:** Permitted but no facilities provided | |
| (505)375-2331 | | |

## ACTIVITIES AND FACILITIES

| | NO | YES | Proximity to Lake in Miles | | NO | YES | Proximity to Lake in Miles |
|---|---|---|---|---|---|---|---|
| **Bait and supplies** | X | | | **Airplane runway** | X | | |
| **Boat gas** | X | | | **Bottled gas** | X | | |
| **Boat ramp** | X | | | **Café/snack bar** | X | | |
| **Boat rental** | X | | | **Chemical toilets** | X | | |
| **Camping** | | X | | **Drinking water** | X | | |
| **Fire pits** | X | | | **Electrical hook-up** | X | | |
| **Fire places** | X | | | **Flush toilets** | X | | |
| **Firewood** | X | | | **Grocery store** | X | | |
| **Fishing** | | X | | **Handicapped access** | X | | |
| **Golf** | X | | | **Ice** | X | | |
| **Hiking** | X | | | **Laundry** | X | | |
| **Marina** | X | | | **Lodgings** | X | | |
| **Picnicking** | | X | | **Pit toilets** | | X | |
| **Riding** | X | | | **Playground** | X | | |
| **Scuba diving** | X | | | **Restaurant** | X | | |
| **Stables** | X | | | **Sanitary disposal** | X | | |
| **Swimming** | X | | | **Sewer hook-up** | X | | |
| **Tables** | X | | | **Shelters** | X | | |
| **Telephone** | X | | | **Shopping** | X | | |
| **Tennis** | X | | | **Showers** | X | | |
| **Tent sites** | X | | | **Trailer space** | X | | |
| **Winter sports** | X | | | **Water hook-up** | X | | |

**Special Rules and Regulations**
   **Fishing:** Public fishing under New Mexico Department of Game and Fish and Vermejo Conservancy regulations
   **Catch limit:** 6 trout per day; see Fishing Proclamation for detailed information
   **Boating:** Boating permitted at trolling speeds
   **Other:** No fishing within 150 feet of outlet; this area is posted

*Palace Hotel*
*Raton, New Mexico*
*(Built in 1896)*

# In the Vicinity of Raton

### Raton

*There are two lakes in the vicinity of Raton: Lake Maloya and Lake Alice.*

*Lake Alice was drained in 1993 for a new pipeline installation to be completed in 1994. Another lake, located close to Lake Maloya, is Lake Dorothy. Since Lake Dorothy lies over the state line in Colorado, it is not included in our descriptions.*

Raton is a small, progressive town of 9,400, lying at an elevation of 6,600 feet above sea level. It is located in the foothills of the Rockies, at the junction of I-25 and U.S. 87, eight and a half miles south of the Colorado state line. It is bordered by the high country of mesas, alpine meadows, and mountains, abundant in natural wonders and year-round recreational opportunities that include skiing, hunting, fishing, hiking, and camping.

Raton is the county seat of Colfax County. It was originally called Willow Springs and was a watering and resting place for travelers along the Santa Fe Trail. When the Atchison, Topeka, and Santa Fe Railroad came through, Raton became a railroad, mining, and ranching center for the northeastern part of New Mexico.

It is not only the gateway to an abundance of recreational opportunities, but it is also a fascinating town whose historical downtown section is a draw for thousands of visitors each year to see buildings dating to the town's beginnings. One such building, the Palace Hotel, is still in operation. It was built in 1896 by the Smith brothers, Scottish immigrant coal miners. Industrious and frugal, they acquired many holdings, including the Palace Hotel, which became one of the most popular meeting places in town. Its ambience of crystal chandeliers, stained glass, and luxurious carpets typifies the elegance of that period. A fire almost destroyed it in 1932. In 1973 it was purchased by the Tinnie Mercantile Company and is still in operation and as elegant as it was in the past.

Raton has all of the accommodations for the convenience of tourists: more than 600 rooms, twenty-four restaurants, grocery stores, shopping centers, and gas stations. Reservations are recommended during the busy summer season.

# LAKE MALOYA

Lake Maloya is a 150-acre reservoir twelve miles northeast of Raton. It is within Sugarite Canyon State Park. It is an eleven-mile drive from Raton on NM Highway 72, which connects with NM 526 and north to Lake Maloya, and is a good well-maintained paved highway. The road is heavily edged with wildflowers on either side as it goes through a green valley bordered by rolling hills and towering pines. Lake Maloya is on the north side of Sugarite Canyon State Park. This beautiful alpine lake is stocked with rainbow trout. Fishing from its banks is rewarding. Boats are restricted to oars or electric motors. The lake has handicapped access and facilities along the lake's shore, including a fishing dock, a boat ramp, conveniently placed vault toilets, trash barrels, fire grills, and picnic tables.

On the way to Lake Maloya, and about six miles from Raton, a sign shows the elevation of Lake Alice Spillway at 7,090 feet above sea level. At the time of our visit in August of 1993, the spillway and the lake were dry. The lake was drained to install a new pipeline. The project was completed in February 1995. The location of Lake Alice is about a mile and a quarter south of the visitor center in Sugarite Canyon State Park. It lies off NM 526 and directly opposite a campground and picnic area. According to the campground hosts, Dora May and Clyde, a husband and wife team, funds are being appropriated to improve this campground and install electric hook-ups, a dump station, and a modern restroom. This project was completed in February 1995. Lake Alice has a capacity of four-acres and when completed will be stocked with some fry and some catchable rainbow trout.

## Directions from Albuquerque

Take I-25 north and follow the signs to Raton. From Raton take a right on NM 72, connect with NM 526 north, and follow signs to the lake and Sugarite State Park. There are good paved roads all the way to the lake.

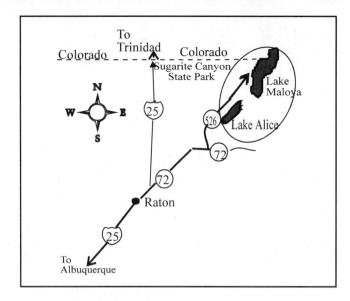

| | | |
|---|---|---|
| **Surface acres:** 150 | | **Distance from Albuquerque:** 235 miles |
| **Elevation:** 7,800 feet | | **Location:** 12 miles N.E. of Raton in Sugarite Canyon State Park |
| **\*Max. trailer size & fee:** No camping at lake; a developed | | **Fish species:** Rainbow trout |
| campground at Lake Alice and Soda Park | | **Season:** 1 April-31 March |
| Campgrounds close by (Park fees posted) | | **Police emergency tel. #:** 911 |
| **Mailing address:** Sugarite State Park, HCR 63, | | |
| Box 386, Raton NM 87740 (505) 445-5607 | | |
| **Medical emergency tel. #:** 911 | | |

## ACTIVITIES AND FACILITIES

| | NO | YES | Proximity to Lake in Miles | | NO | YES | Proximity to Lake in Miles |
|---|---|---|---|---|---|---|---|
| **Bait and supplies** | X | | | **Airplane runway** | X | | |
| **Boat gas** | X | | | **Bottled gas** | X | | |
| **Boat ramp** | | X | | **Café/snack bar** | X | | |
| **Boat rental** | X | | | **Chemical toilets** | | X | |
| **Camping** | X | | * | **Drinking water** | X | | * |
| **Fire pits** | X | | * | **Electrical hook-up** | X | | * |
| **Fire places** | | X | * | **Flush toilets** | X | | |
| **Firewood** | X | | | **Grocery store** | X | | |
| **Fishing** | | X | | **Handicapped access** | | X | |
| **Golf** | X | | | **Ice** | X | | |
| **Hiking** | | X | | **Laundry** | X | | |
| **Marina** | X | | | **Lodgings** | X | | |
| **Picnicking** | | X | | **Pit toilets** | | X | |
| **Riding** | | X | | **Playground** | X | | * |
| **Scuba diving** | X | | | **Restaurant** | X | | * |
| **Stables** | X | | | **Sanitary disposal** | X | | * |
| **Swimming** | X | | | **Sewer hook-up** | X | | * |
| **Tables** | | X | | **Shelters** | X | | * |
| **Telephone** | X | | * | **Shopping** | X | | |
| **Tennis** | X | | | **Showers** | X | | * |
| **Tent sites** | X | | * | **Trailer space** | X | | * |
| **Winter sports** | | X | | **Water hook-up** | X | | * |

*Developed camp areas in Sugarite Canyon State Park close by.

**Special Rules and Regulations**

   **Fishing:** New Mexico fishing license required

   **Catch limit:** 6 trout per day (1994 and 1995); see Fishing Proclamation for current year

   **Boating:** Restricted to oars or electric motors

   **Other:** *No camping around lake; developed campgrounds at Lake Alice and Soda Pocket Campgrounds; additional hook-ups and improvements completed February 1995

# In the Vicinity of Roy

## *Roy*

*In the vicinity of Roy there is one lake that is listed in publications as a lake containing trout and open to fishing: Chicosa Lake State Park. On a visit to this park, in May of 1993, the lake was completely dry!*

The small town of Roy, population about 400, lies at an elevation of 5,900 feet above sea level in the grasslands of eastern New Mexico, thirty-five miles east of Wagon Mound, and eighty-nine miles southwest of Clayton. It was established in 1901 by Frank and William Roy. Frank was its first postmaster. When homesteading opened these grasslands to settlement, Roy became the center of a farming and ranching area. Further growth was stimulated when the Dawson Railway was built in 1906, connecting Tucumcari to the Dawson Coal Fields west of Raton.

The area around Roy overlies the Bravo Dome carbon dioxide gas field. During the 1920s and 1930s, the mining of gas fields and the production of dry ice added to the town's prosperity. The highlight of the thirty-five-mile drive from Wagon Mound to Roy on NM 120 is Canadian River Canyon, about five miles west of Roy. At the canyon's rim, at an elevation of 5,400 feet, a sign warns truck drivers to reduce to lower gear. The road descends steeply for a mile and a half to its bottom, along sharp curves and switchbacks, with posted twenty-five miles per hour speed limits. At the bottom of this scenic and steep canyon, the Canadian River flows swiftly, and a warning sign cautions against swimming because of dangerous undercurrents. The climb out of the canyon to Roy, five miles east, is as spectacular as the descent, and at its top the terrain is dotted with pine, mesquite, scrub vegetation, and grassland.

Roy is a typical small quiet western town, some parts resembling a Western movie set. On its main street and at the entrance to the town there are a couple of grocery stores and gas stations and only a few accommodations for the tourist.

*Chicosa Lake*

# CHICOSA LAKE STATE PARK

Chicosa Lake was once a popular watering stop for cattlemen and their herds on the Goodnight-Loving Trail. It is eight miles northeast of Roy off NM 120 and lies at an elevation of 5,900 feet above sea level. NM 120, which leads to Chicosa Lake State Park, is a good paved road. At the turn-off to the park, a sign welcomes visitors. Here, you turn left on a hard-packed dirt road, and drive eight-tenths of a mile to the park. We visited Chicosa Lake State Park in May of 1993 and at that time the lake was a complete disappointment; what was once a forty-acre lake stocked with rainbow trout was now dry, and the complex was completely devoid of trees. The Park Manager, Levi Garcia,

explained that the lake is dependent on run-off from heavy rainfall, and although there was heavy precipitation during 1992 and in previous years, even during heavy rainfalls diversion channels were necessary to bring the waters in. He was not optimistic about a future fill. It would be advisable to call the Park Manager's Office—(505) 485-2424—before planning a fishing outing on this lake.

The park itself has good facilities. The main building has flush toilets, and there are hot showers in a solar-heated pavilion. There are camping and picnic sites with shelters with piped-in water, tables, and a children's playground. The camping sites are not equipped with hook-ups.

## Directions from Albuquerque

Take I-25 to Wagon Mound, then go east on NM 120 past Roy. Follow the signs to Chicosa Lake State Park.

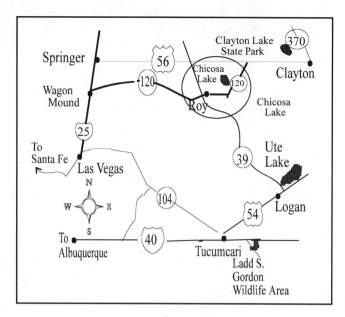

| | | |
|---|---|---|
| **Surface acres:** 40 acres (was dry in 1992, 1993, and 1994) | **Distance from Albuquerque:** 209 miles | |
| **Elevation:** 5,900 feet | **Location:** 9 miles northeast of Roy off NM 120; | |
| **Max. trailer size & fee:** 40 feet; fees posted | 55 miles southeast of Springer | |
| **Time limit:** 14 days | **Fish species:** Completely dry in 1992, 1993, and 1994 | |
| **Mailing address:** New Mexico State Parks; | **Season:** Park open all year | |
| P.O. Box 1147 Santa Fe, NM 87504 (505) 485-2424 | | |

## ACTIVITIES AND FACILITIES

| | NO | YES | Proximity to Lake in Miles | | NO | YES | Proximity to Lake in Miles |
|---|---|---|---|---|---|---|---|
| **Bait and supplies** | X | | 9 | **Airplane runway** | X | | |
| **Boat gas** | X | | | **Bottled gas** | X | | |
| **Boat ramp** | X | | | **Café/snack bar** | X | | 9 |
| **Boat rental** | X | | | **Chemical toilets** | | X | |
| **Camping** | | X | | **Drinking water** | | X | |
| **Fire pits** | X | | | **Electrical hook-up** | | X | |
| **Fire places** | | X | | **Flush toilets** | | X | |
| **Firewood** | | X | | **Grocery store** | X | | 9 |
| **Fishing** | X | | | **Handicapped access** | | X | |
| **Golf** | X | | | **Ice** | X | | 9 |
| **Hiking** | | X | | **Laundry** | X | | 9 |
| **Marina** | X | | | **Lodgings** | X | | 9 |
| **Picnicking** | | X | | **Pit toilets** | X | | |
| **Riding** | X | | | **Playground** | | X | |
| **Scuba diving** | X | | | **Restaurant** | X | | 9 |
| **Stables** | X | | | **Sanitary disposal** | X | | |
| **Swimming** | X | | | **Sewer hook-up** | X | | |
| **Tables** | | X | | **Shelters** | | X | |
| **Telephone** | | X | | **Shopping** | X | | 9 |
| **Tennis** | X | | | **Showers** | | X | |
| **Tent sites** | | X | | **Trailer space** | | X | |
| **Winter sports** | X | | | **Water hook-up** | | X | |

Closest services and stores in Roy, 9 miles.

**Special Rules and Regulations**

    **Fishing:** Was completely dry in 1992, 1993 and 1994; call (505) 485-2424 for current conditions

    **Catch limit:** Not applicable

    **Boating:** No

# In the Vicinity of Clayton

## *Clayton*

*There is one lake in the vicinity of Clayton: Clayton Lake State Park.*

Clayton is an attractive small town of paved, tree-lined streets. It is located in the northeast corner of New Mexico, just a few miles west of the Oklahoma and Texas borders. It lies at an elevation of 5,050 feet in the grasslands of the high plains that cover the east third of New Mexico and stretch eastward into the mid-continent. The site on which Clayton is now located was a resting and watering place used by early settlers traveling the Santa Fe Trail. It became a favorite campground for cattle drovers and herdsmen during the 1820s. The town was founded in 1888 with the coming of the Chicago and Southern Pacific Railroad and was named after the son of Steve Dorsey, a former senator from Arkansas, a participant in the railroad's beginning and local rancher and merchant. When the Denver and Fort Worth Railroad built a line through the town, it became an important shipping and supply station.

Several buildings built in downtown Clayton at the turn of the century still stand. Notable among these is the Eklund Hotel. This building and the ambience of its interior typify the elegance of the Victorian period. The west side of the building was built in 1892 by John C. Hill, Range Manager for Steve Dorsey. The first floor was used as a store, rooms for rent were available on the second floor. In 1894, Carl Eklund, a Swedish immigrant and successful entrepreneur, bought the building from Hill. He added a saloon and a bar that he purportedly won in a poker game. As the hotel dining room and saloon prospered, he added a third story and expanded the dining room

and kitchen on the east side of the building, The Eklund became a first-class establishment, attractively furbished with mirrored walls, paintings, and fine crystal chandeliers. During the years that followed, the enterprise suffered through neglect and recessions. After many transfers of ownership and attempts at restoration, the building was almost abandoned and destroyed, but to protect its historical heritage a group of concerned citizens banded together and formed the Eklund Association. They bought the hotel, restored it to its original "turn-of-the-century" state, and in March 1992 it was opened for business. Today it is prospering as it did in the 1890s.

Clayton has had its share of violence, as did most growing towns of the southwest. It was in nearby Folsum in 1901 that the notorious train robber, Thomas E. "Black Jack" Ketchum, attempted a single-handed train robbery. The attempt was unsuccessful. He was caught, convicted, and hanged in Clayton, the county seat. An improper adjustment of the noose caused his decapitation as he went through the trap. "Black Jack" Ketchum is buried in a cemetery just outside of town.

Downtown Clayton has all of the services and accommodations needed for the visitor. There are service stations, grocery stores, motels, medical facilities, and an airport. Clayton also provides easy access to interesting historical and geological sites and many recreational opportunities. Just fifteen miles north is Clayton Lake State Park, where there are great fishing and boating available. There are also traces of dinosaur presence in the area on the spillway. More than 500 footprints have been identified along the Clayton Lake spillway, and a sheltered gazebo and a boardwalk trackway provide information regarding the dinosaurs who traveled here long ago.

*Clayton Lake*

# CLAYTON LAKE STATE PARK

Clayton Lake is a 170-acre lake located twelve miles northwest of Clayton, off NM 370. It is an impressive lake that was created in 1955 by the New Mexico State Department of Game and Fish, when it built a dam across Seneca Creek for recreation and as a winter waterfowl resting area. More than one hundred million years ago, dinosaurs roamed the Clayton Lake area, leaving their tracks along the muddy shoreline of an ancient seaway that at one time stretched from the Gulf of Mexico to Canada. These fossilized footprints can be seen along the spillway at Clayton Lake State Park, where more than 500 dinosaur tracks have been preserved and identified. A boardwalk trail along a trackway provides information regarding the dinosaurs that traveled here in ages past. The irregularly shaped lake is set amid rolling hills with sandstone escarpments, and juniper bordering its shoreline. At one end of the lake there is a natural rock garden composed of large boulders, sculptured by the elements, forming an attractive natural garden of native plants.

The lake is stocked with rainbow trout, catfish, bass, and walleye. Boats restricted to trolling speeds are permitted. The lake is closed to fishing and boating after the regular fishing season ends in October. It then serves as a winter resting place for waterfowl. The facilities in the park include a couple of boat launching ramps, modern restrooms, drinking water, shelters, tables, fireplaces, and camping sites. According to the park manager, Charles Jordan, funds are being developed in Santa Fe for improvements and the installation of nine electric hook ups (four pull-throughs and five back-ins) and a dump station—all to be completed in early 1996.

## Directions from Albuquerque

**Northern Route:**

Take I-25 to Springer. Then go east on U.S. Highway 56 to Clayton, then north on NM 370 and follow the signs to the lake.

**Eastern Route:**

Go east on I-40 to Tucumcari. Then go on U.S. 54 to Logan, then north on NM 402 to Clayton, then north on NM 370 to the lake.

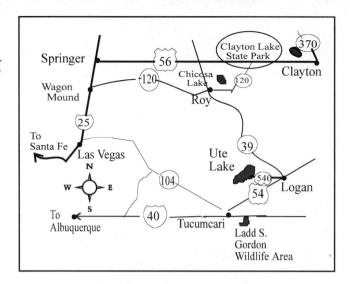

| | | | | | | |
|---|---|---|---|---|---|---|
| **Surface acres:** 170 | | | | **Distance from Albuquerque:** 288 miles | | |
| **Elevation:** 5,200 feet | | | | **Location:** 15 miles N.W. of Clayton off NM 370 | | |
| **Max. trailer size & fee:** 40 feet; park fees posted | | | | **Fish species:** Rainbow trout, walleye, crappie, | | |
| **Time limit:** 14 days | | | | bullheads channel catfish, and bass | | |
| **Mailing address:** Clayton Lake State Park; Rural Rte. Box 20, | | | | **Season:** 1 April-31 October; no boating or fishing after season | | |
| Seneca, NM 88437 (505) 374-8808 | | | | ends; then becomes waterfowl rest area | | |
| **Medical emergency tel. #:** 911 | | | | **Police emergency tel. #:** 911 | | |

## ACTIVITIES AND FACILITIES

| | NO | YES | Proximity to Lake in Miles | | NO | YES | Proximity to Lake in Miles |
|---|---|---|---|---|---|---|---|
| Bait and supplies | X | | | Airplane runway | X | | * |
| Boat gas | X | | | Bottled gas | X | | * |
| Boat ramp | | X | | Café/snack bar | X | | * |
| Boat rental | X | | | Chemical toilets | | X | |
| Camping | | X | | Drinking water | | X | |
| Fire pits | | X | | Electrical hook-up | | X | |
| Fire places | | X | | Flush toilets | | X | |
| Firewood | X | | | Grocery store | X | | * |
| Fishing | | X | | Handicapped access | | X | |
| Golf | X | | * | Ice | X | | * |
| Hiking | | X | | Laundry | X | | * |
| Marina | X | | | Lodgings | X | | * |
| Picnicking | | X | | Pit toilets | | X | |
| Riding | X | | | Playground | | X | |
| Scuba diving | | X | | Restaurant | X | | * |
| Stables | X | | | Sanitary disposal | | X | |
| Swimming | | X | | Sewer hook-up | | X | |
| Tables | | X | | Shelters | | X | |
| Telephone | | X | | Shopping | X | | * |
| Tennis | X | | * | Showers | | X | |
| Tent sites | | X | | Trailer space | | X | |
| Winter sports | X | | | Water hook-up | | X | |

*Lodgings and services in Clayton, 15 miles.

**Special Rules and Regulations**

**Fishing:** New Mexico fishing license required

**Catch limit:** 6 trout; 6 in possession; black bass, 14 inch minimum size; scuba diving for game fish permitted

**Boating:** Restricted to trolling speeds only

**Other:** Funds are being developed to install 9 electric hook-ups—4 pull-throughs, 5 back-ins—and a dump station to be completed in early 1996; check park for progress

# In the Vicinity of Santa Rosa

## *Santa Rosa*

*Nine miles north of the city of Santa Rosa is Santa Rosa Lake and State Park. Other lakes within the city and its vicinity open to public use are as follows: Power Dam Lake (South of I-40 in Zone 3), Perch Lake (South of I-40 in Zone 3), Park Lake (South of I-40 in Zone 3), Hidden Lake (South of I-40 in Zone 3), Tres Lagunas Lakes.*

Often referred to as *"The City of Lakes,"* Santa Rosa is a community of 3,000 people and lies at an elevation of 4,600 feet. It is located 114 miles east of Albuquerque at the crossroads of I-40 and U.S. 54 and U.S. 84. Native Americans drawn by its natural lakes first settled this area, followed later in the 1860s by Hispanics from the northern areas of New Mexico, who settled on land grants awarded them by the Mexican government. In 1879, an early settler, Don Celso Baca, built a small adobe chapel in honor of his mother and dedicated to the first canonized saint of the New World, Santa Rosa de Lima. Remnants of the old chapel, now in ruins, are located opposite the new church, St. Rose of Lima.

While still retaining its tri-cultural past and traditions, Santa Rosa is a progressive community, offering abundant services to the tourist. There are gas stations, grocery stores, lodgings, and restaurants. It offers a variety of recreational opportunities, and some of the best fishing and water sports can be found in this community of natural and man-made lakes.

One of Santa Rosa's main attractions is Blue Hole, a geological phenomenon. Blue Hole is a natural artesian spring. It measures an average of eighty feet across, expanding to about 130 feet across at the bottom, and it is eighty-one feet in depth. Its spring delivers 3,000 gallons of water per minute and maintains a constant temperature of sixty-four degrees Fahrenheit, permitting year-round diving. It is a beautiful bell-shaped pool, attracting scuba divers and photographers.

Other places of interest include the Original Guadalupe County Courthouse, built in the mid-1800s. Tourists are invited to visit this historic landmark located in Puerto de Luna, ten miles south on NM 91. Puerto de Luna itself is an historic village that follows the lush green valley along the Pecos River. Puerto de Luna displays classic examples of old adobe architecture.

*Santa Rosa Lake*

# SANTA ROSA LAKE

Santa Rosa Lake was built by the United States Army Corps of Engineers to control the flood waters of the Pecos River. The 1,500-acre warm-water fishing lake is stocked with fry-size walleye, and catchable and sub-catchable yellow perch. It also contains crappie, largemouth bass, bluegill, and channel catfish. Santa Rosa Lake is a recreational playland for fishermen, water-skiers, windsurfers, and campers.

The United States Army Corps of Engineers owns all the land comprising the Santa Rosa Project, but leases 550 acres to the New Mexico State Park Division. This acreage comprises two recreational facilities.

The main campground (Rocky Point), with fifty camp sites— most with tables, shelters, and grills— offers fifteen sites with electricity. Three sites are set aside for the handicapped. Picnic shelters with drinking water are also available, and there is one fully equipped comfort station with hot showers. There are lights for security, and all roads are paved.

A secondary campground (Juniper Park) is a day-use area with two group units of three tables each. It has twenty-five sites, but no electricity. The comfort station is identical to the Rocky Point facility, but no showers are available. There is also a double wide boat launching ramp at the lake. The United States Corps of Engineers office is located near the dam, where there is a visitors center displaying the lake's fish population. There is also a scenic nature trail designed for wheelchair access. Fishing and picnic supplies can be purchased in Santa Rosa.

## Directions from Albuquerque

Take I-40 east to Santa Rosa Exit 273. Take Exit 273 and follow 2nd St. north to Eddy Ave., then follow the signs north, seven miles to Santa Rosa Lake State Park. The road is a good, paved, double-laned highway.

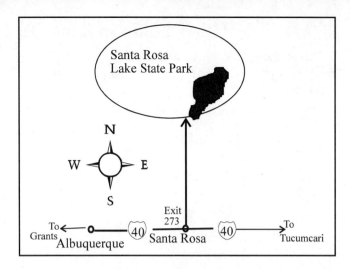

| | | |
|---|---|---|
| **Surface acres:** 1,500 | | |
| **Elevation:** 4,600 feet | | |
| **Max. trailer size & fee:** No limit; $7.00 per day; $11.00 with electricity | | |
| **Time limit:** 14 days | | |
| **Mailing address:** Manager, Santa Rosa Lake, Box 345, Santa Rosa, NM 88435 (505) 472-3110 | | |
| **Medical emergency tel. #:** 472-3417 | | |

**Distance from Albuquerque:** 121 miles

**Location:** 9 miles north of Santa Rosa off I-40, Exit 273

**Fish species:** Stocked walleye frys, sub- and catchable yellow perch; also contains crappie, largemouth bass, bluegill, and channel catfish

**Season:** 1 April-31 March

## ACTIVITIES AND FACILITIES

| | NO | YES | Proximity to Lake in Miles | | NO | YES | Proximity to Lake in Miles |
|---|:--:|:--:|:--:|---|:--:|:--:|:--:|
| Bait and supplies | X | | | Airplane runway | X | | |
| Boat gas | X | | | Bottled gas | X | | |
| Boat ramp | | X | | Café/snack bar | X | | |
| Boat rental | X | | | Chemical toilets | | X | |
| Camping | | X | | Drinking water | | X | |
| Fire pits | | X | | Electrical hook-up | | X | |
| Fire places | | X | | Flush toilets | | X | |
| Firewood | X | | | Grocery store | X | | |
| Fishing | | X | | Handicapped access | | X | |
| Golf | | | 9 | Ice | X | | |
| Hiking | | X | | Laundry | X | | |
| Marina | | X | | Lodgings | X | | |
| Picnicking | | X | | Pit toilets | X | | |
| Riding | | X | | Playground | | X | |
| Scuba diving | | X | | Restaurant | X | | |
| Stables | X | | | Sanitary disposal | | X | |
| Swimming | | X | | Sewer hook-up | | X | |
| Water skiing | | X | | Shelters | | X | |
| Tables | | X | | Shopping | X | | |
| Tennis | X | | | Showers | | X | |
| Tent sites | | X | | Trailer space | | X | |
| Winter sports | | X | | Water hook-up | | X | |

Full facilities in Santa Rosa, 9 miles south.

### Special Rules and Regulations

**Fishing:** State Regulations apply; see Fishing Proclamation

**Catch limit:** 6 trout; black bass, minimum size 14 inches; see Proclamation for details

**Boating:** An all-purpose recreational lake; no restrictions except general state boating and and safety rules are enforced; see page 344, Boating Regulations

**Other:** Swimming at own risk

# Other Lakes in Santa Rosa and Vicinity

Power Dam Lake, Perch Lake, Park Lake, Hidden Lake, Tres Lagunas Lakes. Photographs and a brief description of these lakes appear on pages 181–182. The map below is a city map of Santa Rosa showing the location of these lakes.

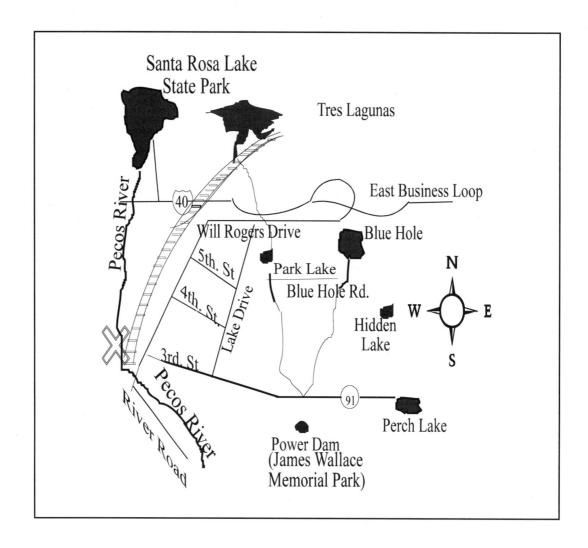

## Power Dam

James Wallace Memorial Park is the location of Power Dam. It is a beautiful fifteen-acre spring-fed lake, operated by the New Mexico Game and Fish Department, one mile southeast of Santa Rosa off NM 91. It provides some of the best fishing in the area, with no-fee fishing, and is stocked with trout, catfish, and bass. A state fishing license is required here. It is a no-fee, day-use area with no facilities except trash cans for the convenience of picnickers and campers. No boats or floating devices are allowed.

*Power Dam*

*Perch Lake*

## Perch Lake

Perch Lake is near the Rodeo Grounds, one and a half miles past Power Dam on NM 91. Submerged, fifty-five feet deep, is a twin-engine plane, which is used primarily for advanced scuba diving training. The lake is stocked with channel catfish and bass. There are no facilities provided, but chemical toilets are available for the convenience of users of the lake.

## Park Lake

Park Lake is a two-acre lake, located in a city-maintained park at the end of Main Street, one block east of Blue Hole, midway between Blue Hole and downtown Santa Rosa. It is a spring-fed lake and billed as the "largest free swimming pool in the world." Among the free recreational activities available in this facility are tennis, baseball, and softball fields, a basketball court, a large playground, a picnic area, and a hiking trail. Swimming hours are from 10 A.M.–8 P.M. No fishing is allowed in the swimming area. Nor are boats or other floating devices permitted.

*Park Lake*

*Hidden Lake*

# Hidden Lake

Hidden Lake, as the title implies, is truly a secluded and hidden "jewel" and a favorite for photographers, fishermen, and those interested in Indian pictographs, which are sketched on some of the rock formations in the area around the lake. It is a seven-acre, spring-fed lake, obscured from entry roads, due to the hilly and rocky terrain of the area. It is located a quarter-mile east of the cemetery and seven miles east of Santa Rosa. To reach Hidden Lake, turn left at the southwest corner of the cemetery and veer right toward a large rock outcropping. It is just to the left of the largest of the outcroppings and not visible until you are almost upon it.

Hidden Lake is on private land. As on all private lands, permission should be obtained from the owner before attempting to fish on this no-facility lake. The lake contains bass and catfish.

# Tres Lagunas

Tres Lagunas are situated north of I-40 near Santa Rosa. There are two lakes totaling about thirty acres when full. To reach Tres Lagunas, take Exit 273 off I-40, go through the town for approximately five miles and turn left around the Texaco service station. Continue on this road until you see a dirt road that goes under the railroad overpass. Drive under the overpass and turn left on the second dirt road; this road parallels the railroad and the lakes are about a mile ahead.

Tres Lagunas are on private land, but they are open to the public. They are stocked with bluegill, crappie, and bass. There are no facilties at Tres Lagunas. It is a no-fee area, and a New Mexico fishing license is required.

*Tres Lagunas*

*La Familia de Sagrada
(Church of the Holy Family)
Newkirk, New Mexico*

# In the Vicinity
of Newkirk

## *Newkirk*

*Twenty-four miles north of Newkirk, off I-40 from
Exit 300 there is one lake: Conchas Lake*

Heading east from Albuquerque, the closest
access town to Conchas Lake is Newkirk. Exit 300
off I-40 puts you on NM 129 and takes you through
Newkirk, a tiny village with a population of ten. It
is located between the Pecos and Canadian Rivers.
Newkirk was originally set up as a trading post in
1901 when the railroad came through. At that time
it was known as Conant, named for an early
rancher, James P. Conant. Later, a settler from
Oklahoma, changed its name to Newkirk, after
himself.

The area was once inhabited by nomadic Plains
Indians of the Apache, Kiowa, and Comanche
Tribes. They used the Canadian River as a trade
route and later, in the 1800s, settled north, where
white caliche limestone caps the landscape of
shales and sandstones deposited by an inland sea
that covered much of New Mexico and the western
United States more than 200 million years ago.

Newkirk has a post office and a gas station/
grocery store where fishing and picnic supplies are
available. There are no other accommodations in
this tiny town. The old church, La Familia de
Sagrada (Church of the Holy Family), no longer in
use, still stands at the entrance to the village. The
villagers attend services in Santa Rosa, twenty-
seven miles west, or in the next large town,
Tucumcari, thirty-three miles east. Both towns offer
complete accommodations and services for tourists.

From Tucumcari, Conchas Lake can be reached
thirty-two miles to the northwest by NM 104.

*Conchas Lake*

# CONCHAS LAKE

Conchas Lake State Park is one of the most popular and most developed state parks in New Mexico. The dam is an irrigation and flood control project on the Canadian River, and is one of the largest man-made lakes in New Mexico. It is a United States Corps of Engineers project, authorized by Congress in 1935 under the Emergency Relief Act and completed in 1939. With over fifty miles of shoreline, the dam is 1,250 feet long, and rises 200 feet above the floor of the Canadian River.

The lake has become a major recreation area, attracting fishermen, boaters, and water sportsmen from New Mexico and Texas. The lake is stocked by the New Mexico Department of Game and Fish with fry-size walleye, and it contains black bass, crappie, bluegill, channel catfish. It is open year round. It caters to the larger pleasure boats, to water-skiers, and windsurfers. There are restaurant and lounge facilities at both the north and south sides plus a nine-hole golf course, a motel, a paved airstrip, two marinas, eight boat ramps, stores, and a bait and tackle shop. There are over 150 camping sites. Many with full hook-ups, water and electricity, tables, grills, and restrooms, some with flush toilets. There are many with no hook-up sites. Other facilities include a grocery store, a public telephone, and an RV dump station.

The area surrounding Conchas Lake was part of the historic Pablo Montoya Mexican Land Grant of 1824. It comprises over 1,023 sections or more than 655,000 acres. Since the original land grant to Pablo Montoya, then the mayor of Santa Fe, many ownership transfers ensued. In 1872, it became Bell Ranch, and later much of the property was sold and divided into several ranches, which border the northern part of the lake.

## Directions from Albuquerque

Take I-40 east to Newkirk. Turn off on Exit 300. Go west on NM 129. Follow signs to lake (about twenty-five miles north). Conchas Lake can also be reached from Tucumcari by NM 104. Then follow signs thirty-two miles northwest to the lake. Both highways to the lake are paved. Road access to lake is good and well maintained.

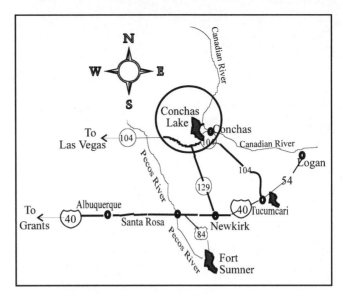

| | | |
|---|---|---|
| **Surface acres:** 16,000 | | **Distance from Albuquerque:** 142 miles |
| **Elevation:** 4,200 feet | | **Location:** 25 miles north of Newkirk; 76 miles east of Las Vegas; |
| **Max. trailer size & fee:** State park rules and fees | | 32 miles west of Tucumcari |
| **Time limit:** 14 days | | **Fish species:** Walleye, black bass, crappie, bluegill, and |
| **Mailing address:** New Mexico State Park and Recreation | | channel catfish |
| Division, P.O. Box 35, Conchas Dam , NM 88416 | | **Season:** Year round |
| **Medical emergency tel. #:** 868-2770 | | **Police emergency tel. #:** 461-3330 |

## ACTIVITIES AND FACILITIES

| | NO | YES | Proximity to Lake in Miles | | NO | YES | Proximity to Lake in Miles |
|---|---|---|---|---|---|---|---|
| Bait and supplies | | X | | Airplane runway | | X | |
| Boat gas | | X | | Bottled gas | | X | |
| Boat ramp | | X | | Café/snack bar | | X | |
| Boat rental | | X | | Chemical toilets | | X | |
| Camping | | X | | Drinking water | | X | |
| Fire pits | | X | | Electrical hook-up | | X | |
| Fire places | | X | | Flush toilets | | X | |
| Firewood | | X | | Grocery store | | X | |
| Fishing | | X | | Handicapped access | | X | |
| Golf | | X | | Ice | | X | |
| Hiking | | X | | Laundry | | X | |
| Marina | | X | | Lodgings | | X | |
| Picnicking | | X | | Pit toilets | | X | |
| Riding | X | | | Playground | | X | |
| Scuba diving | | X | | Restaurant | | X | |
| Stables | X | | | Sanitary disposal | | X | |
| Swimming | | X | | Sewer hook-up | | X | |
| Tables | | X | | Shelters | | X | |
| Telephone | | X | | Shopping | | X | |
| Tennis | | X | | Showers | | X | |
| Tent sites | | X | | Trailer space | | X | |
| Winter sports | | X | | Water hook-up | | X | |

### Special Rules and Regulations

**Fishing:** State Regulations and fees apply; see Fishing Proclamation

**Catch limit:** 5 per day, black bass minimum keeper size, 14 inches; see page 344, Warm Water Fishing Regulations, for other species bag limits

**Boating:** Observe all state park and Corps of Engineer Rules

**Other:** Swimming and snorkeling at own risk

# In the Vicinity of Tucumcari

## *Tucumcari*

*There are three lakes in the vicinity of Tucumcari: Tucumcari Lake (in the Ladd S. Gordon Wildlife Preserve), Conchas Lake (see Newkirk vicinity, pages 183–85), Ute Lake (see Logan Vicinity, pages 191–93)*

Tucumcari had its beginnings in 1901 when the Rock Island Railroad came through. A lake on the east side of Tucumcari was the watering place for prehistoric animals, Spanish conquistadors, outlaws, pioneers, and riders of the Goodnight, Chisholm, and Comanchero trails that crossed this area. Tucumcari lies at an elevation of 4,000 feet above sea level, with a growing population of 8,200, and is located 168 miles east of Albuquerque and 100 miles west of Amarillo, Texas. It is a transportation crossroads for four major highways and a railroad. Tucumcari abounds with excellent tourist facilities: motels, restaurants, department stores, grocery stores, a nine-hole golf course, and two airstrips. One 7,100-feet runway accommodates business jets and private aircraft. Another runway is 5,175 feet long. Both airstrips are equipped with night lights.

The name Tucumcari, is at the center of a legend handed down through generations of Indian tribes. The story goes that an Apache Indian chief, Wautonomah, aging and troubled over who would succeed him on his passing, offered his daughter Kari in marriage to one of his two finest braves—Tocom and Tonopah—who were enemies and deadly rivals for the hand of Kari. He arranged for them to meet in deadly combat, the survivor winning the hand of Kari. During the hand-to-hand mortal combat, Kari watched from hiding. When Tonopah's knife found its mark in the heart of Tocom, whom Kari loved, she rushed from her hiding place, plunged her knife into the heart of Tonopah, and stabbed herself in grief. Wautonomah was taken to the scene and in a fit of emotion seized Kari's knife and plunged it into his own heart crying out *"Tocom-Kari!"* The name lives on with its slight spelling change to *Tucumcari*.

Tucumcari has the enviable distinction of lying midway between two large lakes: Conchas Lake twenty-seven miles to the northwest, and Ute Lake twenty-two miles to the northeast. There is also a natural lake off U.S. highway 54, on the eastern edge of Tucumcari in the Ladd S. Gordon Wildlife Preserve. This is Tucumcari Lake. The preserve encompasses 770 acres. It is a wildlife laboratory that attracts more migratory birds each year than any of the other New Mexico lakes. Ducks and geese number in the thousands on their winter migratory flights to the warmer climate of the south. Bald and golden eagles also stop here. The lake permits sport fishing and small hand-powered boats. It contains bullheads and bass. There are several camping facilities in Tucumcari to accommodate the tourist. A must stop for the visitor, historian, or antique buff is the Tucumcari Historical Museum operated by the Tucumcari Historical Research Institute, whose purpose it is to preserve the relics and history of the southwest. Thousands of items are on display in this museum, including the early Tucumcari Sheriff's Office, Indian artifacts dating back to 12,000 B.C., gems, minerals, a barbedwire collection, and a vintage 1900 windmill.

*Tucumcari Lake*

# TUCUMCARI LAKE
## (Ladd S. Gordon Wildlife Area)

Tucumcari Lake is a 430-acre natural lake within the 770 acre Ladd S. Gordon Wildlife Preserve. The preserve is a wildlife laboratory, which during winter months attracts ducks and geese by the thousands. The preserve is bordered by U.S. 66 on the south, U.S. 54 on the west, and the Chicago Rock Island and Pacific Railroad right of way on the north. The preserve was recently acquired by the New Mexico Department of Game and Fish. Prior to the acquisition, uncontrolled recreational use and overgrazing by livestock resulted in a degraded shoreline habitat, devoid of vegetation in some places, and invaded by unfriendly vegetative species in others. The Department of Game and Fish fenced the boundaries. It was commissioned to study bird life and assist in recovery of the area for recreational use. Proposals are under way for actions to be considered, such as the construction of a nature trail, the installation of waterfowl nesting structures, of camping and picnic sites and shelters, of toilet facilities, and the rehabilitation of two existing parking lots.

At present, due to shallow water, limited fishing opportunities occur for bullhead catfish, carp, bass, and sunfish. Fishing is permitted from the shoreline and from hand-powered or electric motor-powered boats. There are a parking lot on the north side of the lake, pit toilets, and a concrete boat ramp. Another parking lot is located on the northwest corner of the property.

## Directions from Albuquerque

Take I-40 east to Tucumcari. In Tucumcari take Old Historic Route U.S. 66 (Tucumcari Blvd.) on the east side of Tucumcari. Going east, look for a barn-like metal building; a sign directs you left to Ladd S. Gordon Wildlife Area. Follow signs to lake by way of a gravel road.

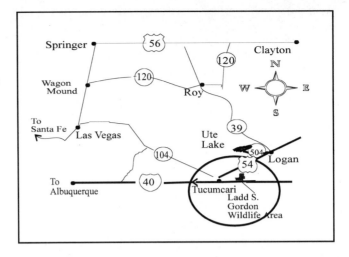

| | | |
|---|---|---|
| **Surface acres:** 430 | | **Distance from Albuquerque:** 174 miles |
| **Elevation:** 4,085 feet | | **Location:** 1 mile east of Tucumcari |
| **Max. trailer size & fee:** Plans to develop and improve campgrounds and facilities under study | | **Fish species:** Bullhead, bass, carp, sunfish |
| | | **Season:** All year |
| **Mailing address:** Department of Game and Fish; Box 25112 Santa Fe, NM 87504 (505) 827-7911 | | **Police emergency tel. #:** 461-3300 |
| **Medical emergency tel. #:** 911 | | |

## ACTIVITIES AND FACILITIES

| | NO | YES | Proximity to Lake in Miles | | NO | YES | Proximity to Lake in Miles |
|---|---|---|---|---|---|---|---|
| Bait and supplies | X | | *1 | Airplane runway | X | | |
| Boat gas | X | | * | Bottled gas | X | | * |
| Boat ramp | | X | | Café/snack bar | X | | * |
| Boat rental | X | | | Chemical toilets | X | | |
| Camping | | X | | Drinking water | X | | |
| Fire pits | | X | | Electrical hook-up | X | | |
| Fire places | X | | | Flush toilets | X | | |
| Firewood | X | | | Grocery store | X | | * |
| Fishing | | X | | Handicapped access | | X | |
| Golf | X | | * | Ice | X | | |
| Hiking | X | | | Laundry | X | | * |
| Marina | X | | | Lodgings | X | | * |
| Picnicking | | X | | Pit toilets | | X | |
| Riding | X | | | Playground | X | | |
| Scuba diving | X | | | Restaurant | X | | |
| Skiing (water) | X | | | Sanitary disposal | X | | |
| Swimming | X | | | Sewer hook-up | X | | |
| Tables | | X | | Shelters | X | | |
| Telephone | X | | * | Shopping | X | | * |
| Tennis | X | | | Showers | X | | |
| Tent sites | | X | | Trailer space | | X | |
| Winter sports | X | | | Water hook-up | X | | |

*Full facilities, stores, services in Tucumcari, 1 mile west.
**Special Rules and Regulations**
  **Fishing:** State fishing license required
  **Catch limit:** See Warm Water Fishing Regulations page 344
  **Boating:** Hand-powered or electric motor-powered boats permitted
  **Other:** Plans under study for extensive improvement and development of camp and picnic grounds, and installation of nature trails and sanitary facilities

# In the Vicinity of Logan

## *Logan*

*In the vicinity of Logan there is one lake: Ute Lake*

Logan is a prosperous ranching, farming, and recreation community located along the Canadian River, at the junctions of U.S. Highway 54 and NM 469 and NM 540. It is twenty-four miles northeast of Tucumcari and eighty miles north of Clovis. Logan was named after a former United States Marshal and Texas Ranger, Captain Logan, who settled the site and ranched in the area. In 1901, when the Chicago, Rock Island and Pacific Railroad built a bridge over the Canadian River, a "tent town" was erected at its banks to house the construction workers. Deep irrigation wells were dug, and Logan became noted for its irrigated crops and cattle-feeding operations. As the railroad moved westward, Logan remained to become the center of a prosperous ranching, farming, business, and recreation community.

In 1963, an irrigation dam was built across the Canadian River creating Ute Lake, now tied with Caballo Lake as the fourth-largest lake in New Mexico (source: New Mexico Department of Game and Fish Operational Plan). A two-mile drive along Main Street in the town of Logan leads directly to Ute Lake and Ute Lake State Park, now a favorite fishing and water recreation lake, which draws thousands of visitors from eastern New Mexico and west Texas. Logan has many facilities for boaters and water sportsmen. There are grocery stores, medical facilities, bait and tackle shops, marine service centers with factory-trained mechanics, gas stations, and motels.

*Ute Lake*

# UTE LAKE

Ute Lake is an 8,200-acre lake located on the Canadian River at the town of Logan, New Mexico, twenty-four miles northwest of Tucumcari at the junctions of U.S. 54 and NM 469 and NM 540. The lake was created by an irrigation dam built across the Canadian River. The dam was completed in 1963 and is owned by the New Mexico Interstate Stream Commission.

A two-mile drive west on Main Street through the town of Logan, leads directly to Ute Lake, which has become a favorite fishing, water-skiing, and boating spot for thousands of Eastern New Mexicans and West Texans. Ute Lake State Park is easily accessible by paved roads and is open seven days a week. The state operates and maintains three camping facilities. These facilities include developed and undeveloped camping areas with picnic areas, tables, shelters and grills, RV facilities, modern restrooms, hot showers, sanitary stations, boat docks, ramps, two marinas, nature trails and an airstrip requiring no landing fees. The Visitors Center also has hot showers and modern restrooms with flush toilets. The lake is stocked with fry-size walleye and contains channel catfish, crappie, bluegill, largemouth bass, smallmouth bass, and white bass.

The town of Logan has bait and tackle shops, restaurants, motels, grocery stores, RV parks, and vacation home rentals.

## Directions from Albuquerque

Take I-40 to Tucumcari. Connect with U.S. 54 East and continue twenty-four miles to Logan.  Follow signs to lake, about two miles. There is good access by paved roads all the way to the lake.

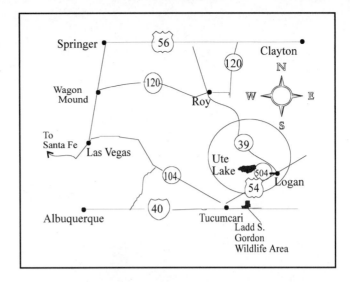

| | |
|---|---|
| **Surface acres:** 8,200 | **Distance from Albuquerque:** 197 miles |
| **Elevation:** 3,900 feet | **Location:** In Logan; 24 miles northwest of Tucumcari off U.S. 54 |
| **Max. trailer size & fee:** 40 feet; state park fees | **Fish species:** Channel catfish, crappie, northern |
| **Time limit:** 14 days | pike, walleye, black bass, bluegill, largemouth bass, and |
| **Mailing address:** P.O. Box 1147, 408 Gallisteo, | smallmouth bass |
| Santa Fe, N.M. 87504 (505) 487-2284 | **Season:** All year |
| **Medical emergency tel. #:** 911 | |

## ACTIVITIES AND FACILITIES

| | NO | YES | Proximity to Lake in Miles | | NO | YES | Proximity to Lake in Miles |
|---|---|---|---|---|---|---|---|
| Bait and supplies | X | | * | Airplane runway | X | | |
| Boat gas | X | | * | Bottled gas | X | | * |
| Boat ramp | | X | | Café/snack bar | X | | * |
| Boat rental | X | | | Chemical toilets | | X | |
| Camping | | X | | Drinking water | | X | |
| Fire pits | | X | | Electrical hook-up | | X | |
| Fire places | | X | | Flush toilets | | X | |
| Firewood | X | | * | Grocery store | X | | * |
| Fishing | | X | | Handicapped access | | X | |
| Golf | X | | | Ice | X | | * |
| Hiking | X | | | Laundry | X | | * |
| Marina | | X | | Lodgings | X | | * |
| Picnicking | | X | | Pit toilets | | X | |
| Riding | X | | | Playground | | X | |
| Scuba diving | | X | | Restaurant | X | | * |
| Skiing (water) | | X | | Sanitary disposal | | X | |
| Swimming | | X | | Sewer hook-up | | X | |
| Tables | | X | | Shelters | | X | |
| Telephone | | X | | Shopping | X | | * |
| Tennis | X | | | Showers | | X | |
| Tent sites | | X | | Trailer space | | X | |
| Winter sports | X | | | Water hook-up | | X | |

*Full accommodations and services in Logan, 1 mile.
**Special Rules and Regulations**
   **Fishing:** State fishing license required
   **Catch limit:** No black bass less than 14 inches in possession; see page 344 for other limits
   **Boating:** Any size and power; windsurfing permitted; Boating Regulations apply
   **Other:** Three developed campgrounds

# ZONE 3

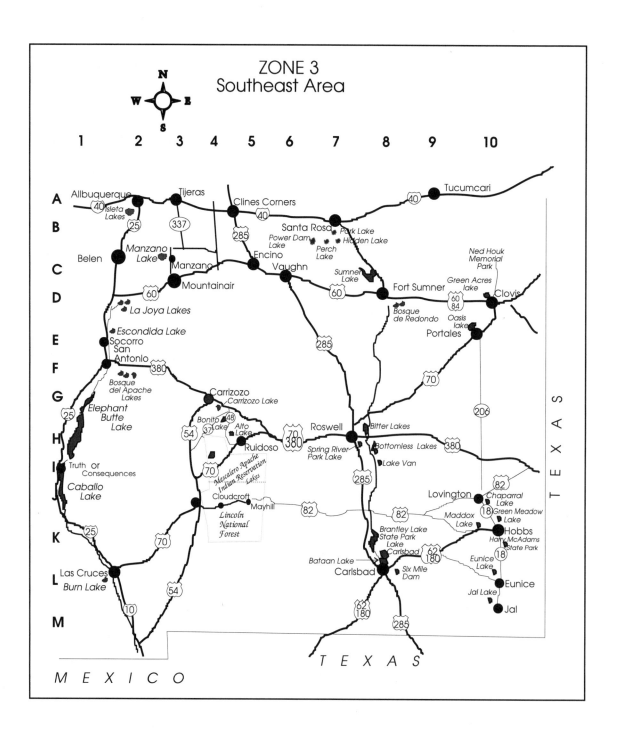

ZONE 3
Southeast Area

# ZONE 3

AREA EAST OF I-25 AND I-10, AND SOUTH OF I-40 TO THE TEXAS BORDER

## Table of Distances
(Miles to vicinity)

| VICINITY (lake access from nearest town) | Map Key | Albuquerque | Farmington | Las Cruces | Clayton | Hobbs |
|---|---|---|---|---|---|---|
| **Manzano** | C3 | 57 | 272 | 223 | 262 | 266 |
| Manzano Lake, p. 200 | | | | | | |
| **Belen** | C2 | 34 | 216 | 189 | 307 | 322 |
| La Joya Lakes, p. 204 | | | | | | |
| **Socorro** | E2 | 77 | 259 | 146 | 339 | 281 |
| Escondida Lake, p. 208 | | | | | | |
| **San Antonio** | F2 | 86 | 268 | 137 | 348 | 272 |
| Bosque del Apache, p. 212 | | | | | | |
| **Truth or Consequences** | I1 | 149 | 331 | 75 | 411 | 324 |
| Elephant Butte Lake, p. 216; Caballo Lake, p. 218 | | | | | | |
| **Carrizozo** | G4 | 149 | 331 | 126 | 288 | 205 |
| Carrizozo Lake, p. 224 | | | | | | |
| **Ruidoso** | H5 | 191 | 373 | 114 | 330 | 187 |
| Bonito Lake, p. 228; Alto Lake, p. 230; Mescalero Apache Lakes, p. 232; Eagle Lake, p. 227; Silver Lake, p. 227 | | | | | | |
| **Roswell** | H7 | 199 | 381 | 185 | 271 | 116 |
| Spring River Park Lake, p. 236; Van Lake, p. 238; Bitter Lakes, p. 240; Bottomless Lakes, p. 242 | | | | | | |
| **Carlsbad** | L8 | 275 | 457 | 208 | 346 | 69 |
| Bataan Lake, p. 246; Carlsbad Lake (Municipal Lake), p. 248; Six Mile Dam Lake, p. 250; Brantley Reservoir, p. 252 | | | | | | |

## Table of Distances
(Miles to vicinity)

| VICINITY (lake access from nearest town) | Map Key | Albuquerque | Farmington | Las Cruces | Clayton | Hobbs |
|---|---|---|---|---|---|---|
| **Lovington** | J10 | 293 | 475 | 414 | 274 | 22 |
| Chaparral Lake, p. 256 | | | | | | |
| **Hobbs** | K10 | 315 | 497 | 255 | 296 | -- |
| Green Meadow Lake, p. 260; Lea County Park Lake (Harry McAdams State Park), p. 262; Maddox Lake, p. 264 | | | | | | |
| **Eunice** | L10 | 328 | 510 | 268 | 309 | 13 |
| Eunice Lake, p. 268 | | | | | | |
| **Jal** | M10 | 337 | 519 | 277 | 318 | 22 |
| Jal Lake, p. 272 | | | | | | |
| **Fort Sumner** | D8 | 159 | 341 | 263 | 193 | 177 |
| Lake Sumner, p. 276; Bosque Redondo Lakes, p. 278 | | | | | | |
| **Clovis** | D10 | 219 | 401 | 295 | 168 | 128 |
| Green Acres Lake, p. 282; Ned Houk Memorial Park, p. 284 | | | | | | |
| **Portales** | E10 | 227 | 409 | 276 | 187 | 109 |
| Oasis Lake, p. 288 | | | | | | |
| **Santa Rosa Lake** | B7 | 114 | 296 | 244 | 170 | 222 |
| Power Dam Lake, p. 181; Perch Lake, p. 181; Park Lake, p. 181; Hidden Lake (Private), p. 182 | | | | | | |

# In the Vicinity of Manzano

## *Manzano*

*There is one lake in the vicinity of Manzano:*
*Manzano Lake*

The small, quiet town of Manzano was founded in 1829. It is cradled in a beautiful wooded valley at the foot of the 10,600 feet Manzano Mountains, fifty-six miles south of Albuquerque and twelve miles north of Mountainair. The town and the mountains are named after the Spanish word for apples. It was thought that during the seventeenth century, apple trees were planted here by Franciscan friars, but recent examination of the rings of those trees still in existence dates them to the early 1800s. It is thought that two of the old trees that still stand and blossom are the oldest apple trees in the state. They are located just past the church at the southern edge of town near the turn-off to Manzano State Park, three miles southwest of the village. (The park is detailed on the next page.) Manzano Lake is one-eighth of a mile off the highway at the southern edge of town just past Our Lady of Sorrows Church, which was built in 1829.

Capilla Peak Camp and Picnic Ground is at the top of the Manzano Mountains at an elevation of 9,600 feet. From the Capilla Peak look-out tower above the campgrounds, you can enjoy a 360-degree view of the surrounding country—the Sandia Mountains to the north, Mt. Taylor to the west, Magdalena and the Ladron Mountains to the southwest, and Gallinas, Jicarilla, and Capitan Mountains to the southeast. Toilets, tables, grills, and shelters are available at the campground and picnic area. The campground is reached by Forest

Road 245, located just opposite Our Lady of Sorrows Catholic church. The gravel road up the mountain is steep, and large motor homes or vehicles pulling large trailers are discouraged. Each spring and fall, hawk watching is a favorite activity here, as thousands of hawks, eagles, and falcons migrate between their nesting areas in the north and wintering grounds to the south. It is a spectacular sight, as these raptors glide along the windward side of the steep mountainside seeking strong updrafts along mountain ridges, where the winds are deflected upward, creating a source of lift to speed them along on their long journey. The Manzano Hawk Watch Look-out is located about a half-mile west of the Capilla Peak Fire Tower and Campground. A trail leads to the lookout at the top of a ridge.

Located in the nearby region of Manzano, the most complete regional complex of seventeenth-century ruins is preserved within Salinas National Monument, which includes the ruins of three Indian pueblos: Abo, Quarai, and Gran Quivira. The massive walls of the structures still standing are four to six feet thick and worth visiting while in the area. The town of Mountainair, only twelve miles south of Manzano, provides an audio-visual program and museum display to acquaint visitors with the three sites.

Even though there are no restaurants or other facilities in the town of Manzano, Mountainair has the necessary accommodations to make a tour of this area enjoyable. The Shaffer Hotel draws many visitors to enjoy a lunch or a dinner or to browse through the gift shop and the "Wooden Zoo," a collection of creations by Clem "Pop" Shaffer, original owner of the Shaffer Hotel.

*Manzano Lake*

# MANZANO LAKE

Manzano Lake is a six-acre lake in the town of Manzano, about an eighth of a mile off NM 55, which runs through the center of town. It is five miles south of Torreon and twelve miles north of Mountainair. Although it is located on private land, the lake is open to public use through an agreement with the New Mexico Department of Game and Fish and the owners. Under the agreement, the Department of Game and Fish stocks the lake with rainbow trout in return for permission to allow public fishing. A state fishing license is required and all state fishing Regulations apply. The lake is fed by a swift-flowing spring called the *Ojo de Gigante ("eye of the giant")*. It is rimmed with large cottonwoods, marsh grasses, reeds and cattails, providing a pleasant screen that secludes it from the buildings and farms of the residents close to the lake. There is a pit toilet at the lake, but no other facilities are available. The nearest store where fishing or food supplies can be purchased is located about one mile north of the lake. More complete facilities are located twelve miles south, in the town of Mountainair, where stores, gas stations, restaurants, and lodgings are available.

Just three miles south of the lake on Forest Road 253 is Manzano State Park, lying in the foothills of the 10,600 feet Manzano Mountain Range. This full-facilitied and heavily forested park contains a mile-and-a-half-long nature trail bordered with ponderosa pine, miniature alligator juniper, wildflowers, and other flora identified by placards along the trail. There are forty-eight picnic/camping sites. Six have electric hook-ups, and one is equipped for handicapped use. There are modern restrooms, a group shelter, a dump station, tables, grills, a playground with a slide and swings, a volleyball court, a basketball court, and horseshoe courts. (The park provides the balls and horseshoes.) There is also a gate that allows entry for horseback riders to ride the surrounding Forest Service trails. The convenient location of Manzano State Park makes Manzano Lake a popular lake for the camper and fisherman.

## Directions from Albuquerque

Go east on I-40 to Exit 175 at Tijeras, then south on NM 337. Continue south on 337 to the junction of NM 337 and NM 55. Turn right on NM 55 and go through the small villages of Tajique and Torreon. Five miles farther south is the small village of Manzano. Just past the Church of Our Lady of Sorrows on the right is a Manzano Lake sign. Take this road past the sign. It curves around (about an eighth of a mile to the lake). This is private land, open to the public. The road may be muddy in heavy rain or thawing snow, but it is negotiable. Food and groceries are in Tajique, nine miles north.

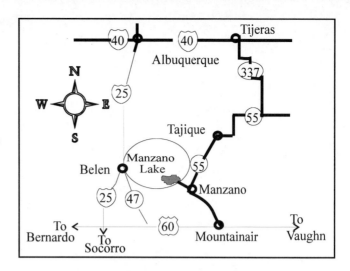

| | |
|---|---|
| **Surface acres:** 6 | **Distance from Albuquerque:** 56 miles |
| **Elevation:** 6,800 feet | **Location:** In town of Manzano, 12 miles north of Mountainair, |
| **Max. trailer size:** No camping | 5 miles south of Torreon |
| **Time limit:** Day use only | **Fish species:.** Rainbow trout |
| **Mailing address:** None | **Season:** 1 April-31 March |
| **Police emergency tel. #:** 911 | **Camping:** In Manzano State Park, 3 miles southwest of lake; |
| **Medical emergency tel. #:** 911 | accessed by good gravel road |

## ACTIVITIES AND FACILITIES

| | NO | YES | Proximity to Lake in Miles | | NO | YES | Proximity to Lake in Miles |
|---|---|---|---|---|---|---|---|
| **Bait and supplies** | X | | 9 | **Airplane runway** | X | | |
| **Boat gas** | X | | | **Bottled gas** | X | | |
| **Boat ramp** | X | | | **Café/snack bar** | X | | 9 |
| **Boat rental** | X | | | **Chemical toilets** | X | | 3 |
| **Camping** | X | | 3 | **Drinking water** | X | | 3 |
| **Fire pits** | X | | 3 | **Electrical hook-up** | X | | 3 |
| **Fire places** | X | | 3 | **Flush toilets** | X | | |
| **Firewood** | X | | | **Grocery store** | X | | 9 |
| **Fishing** | | X | | **Handicapped access** | X | | |
| **Golf** | X | | | **Ice** | X | | 9 |
| **Hiking** | X | | | **Laundry** | X | | |
| **Marina** | X | | | **Lodgings** | X | | 12 |
| **Picnicking** | | X | | **Pit toilets** | | X | |
| **Riding** | X | | 3 | **Playground** | X | | 3 |
| **Scuba diving** | X | | | **Restaurant** | X | | 12 |
| **Stables** | X | | | **Sanitary disposal** | X | | 3 |
| **Swimming** | X | | | **Sewer hook-up** | X | | 3 |
| **Tables** | X | | 3 | **Shelters** | X | | 3 |
| **Telephone** | X | | 3 | **Shopping** | X | | 12 |
| **Tennis** | X | | | **Showers** | X | | |
| **Tent sites** | X | | 3 | **Trailer space** | X | | 3 |
| **Winter sports** | X | | | **Water hook-up** | X | | 3 |

Full camping facilities in Manzano Mts. State Park, 3 miles southwest.

**Special Rules and Regulations**

    **Fishing:** State license required

    **Catch limit:** 6 trout; 6 in possession

    **Camping:** A full-facilitied park, located 3 miles south in Manzano State Park; trailer and tent space; electric and water hook-ups; drinking water and toilets

    **Boating:** No boats or floating devices permitted

# In the Vicinity of Belen

## *Belen*

*In the vicinity of Belen, within the La Joya State Game Refuge, there is a group of lakes: La Joya Lakes*

Belen is a progressive town with a population of 11,000. It lies in the heart of the Middle Rio Grande Valley, thirty-four miles south of Albuquerque off south I-25, at an elevation of 4,800 feet above sea level. It was founded in 1741 when two Spaniards, Diego Torres and Antonio Salazar, petitioned the governor of New Mexico in Santa Fe for a land grant. The request was granted and was known as Nuestra Señora de Belen ("Our Lady of Belen"). Belen is Spanish for Bethlehem.

Twenty-four families settled on the land grant and farmed the fertile soil of the rich river-bottom lands of the valley. When the railroad came, in the mid-1880s, it became the commercial center. Later, when the Santa Fe Railroad opened, the cut-off established Belen as its "hub city." Because of its central location in the state, Belen became a railroad center and an important shipping point for the agricultural products of the Rio Grande Valley. Dairying is now its growing industry, and Belen has continued to grow. Vacationers and health seekers are attracted by its ideal climate, and sportsmen, too, find it a convenient place to stop to hunt in the Manzano Mountains and to fish the irrigation ditches, which are stocked by the New Mexico Department of Game and Fish. Also inviting to visitors are the six small lakes in the La Joya State Game Refuge, twenty-one miles south. This wildlife refuge offers fishing and is a favorite spot for birdwatchers and photographers.

Today, Belen is a thriving city that has retained its country atmosphere. It has full accommodations and services for the visitor: restaurants, stores, hotels, a hospital, a library, schools, and a newspaper. Since no camping is permitted in the La Joya Lakes preserve, nor are stores available, it is advisable to acquire necessary refreshments, bait supplies, or lodgings in Belen.

# LA JOYA LAKES

La Joya Lakes are a series of six lakes totaling 480 acres, owned by the Department of Game and Fish. They are located on the Rio Grande, seven miles south of Bernardo on the east side of I-25 South (Bernardo is fifteen miles south of Belen). The lakes are located on the La Joya State Game Refuge that was established in 1973, when the Nature Conservancy purchased much of the old Sevilleta Grant and turned it over to the United States Fish and Wildlife Service.

Driving south from Albuquerque on I-25 and leaving at Exit 169 provides good access to the lakes on paved roads. Since the La Joya State Game Refuge is on the flypath of birds migrating from their breeding grounds in the north, thousands of snow geese, cranes, ducks, and other species stop to rest and feed here on their journey to the warmer climate in the south. Cattails, bulrushes, and other sedges and marsh plants line the canals and ditches that connect the lakes, which contain bass and catfish. The lakes permit public fishing. Fishing licenses are required and all state Fishing Regulations apply. Boats are permitted but are restricted to those without motors.

There are no camping, picnicking, or other facilities at the lakes. Lodging accommodations and services, groceries, bait supplies, and service stations are available in Belen.

## Directions from Albuquerque

Take I-25 south. Go fifty-four miles to Exit 169, south of Bernardo. Follow direction signs east for about seven miles to the refuge and the lakes.

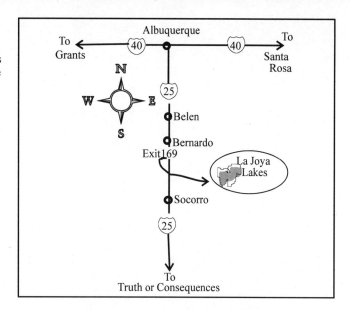

| | | | | | | | |
|---|---|---|---|---|---|---|---|
| **Surface acres:** 6 lakes, total 480 acres | | | | **Distance from Albuquerque:** Sixty miles | | | |
| **Elevation:** 4,900 feet | | | | **Location:** 7 miles south of Bernardo off South I-25 | | | |
| **Max. trailer size & fee:** No camping | | | | **Fish species:** Bass, and channel catfish | | | |
| **Time limit:** Day use only | | | | **Season:** May–September | | | |
| **Mailing address:** U.S. Fish & Wildlife Service, | | | | **Police emergency tel. #:** 911 | | | |
| P.O. Box 1306, Albuquerque, NM 87103 | | | | | | | |
| **Medical emergency tel. #:** 911 | | | | | | | |

### ACTIVITIES AND FACILITIES

| | NO | YES | Proximity to Lake in Miles | | NO | YES | Proximity to Lake in Miles |
|---|---|---|---|---|---|---|---|
| **Bait and supplies** | X | | | **Airplane runway** | X | | |
| **Boat gas** | X | | | **Bottled gas** | X | | |
| **Boat ramp** | X | | | **Café/snack bar** | X | | |
| **Boat rental** | X | | | **Chemical toilets** | X | | |
| **Camping** | X | | | **Drinking water** | X | | |
| **Fire pits** | X | | | **Electrical hook-up** | X | | |
| **Fire places** | X | | | **Flush toilets** | X | | |
| **Firewood** | X | | | **Grocery store** | X | | |
| **Fishing** | | X | | **Handicapped access** | X | | |
| **Golf** | X | | | **Ice** | X | | |
| **Hiking** | X | | | **Laundry** | X | | |
| **Marina** | X | | | **Lodgings** | X | | |
| **Picnicking** | X | | | **Pit toilets** | X | | |
| **Riding** | X | | | **Playground** | X | | |
| **Scuba diving** | X | | | **Restaurant** | X | | |
| **Stables** | X | | | **Sanitary disposal** | X | | |
| **Swimming** | X | | | **Sewer hook-up** | X | | |
| **Tables** | X | | | **Shelters** | X | | |
| **Telephone** | X | | | **Shopping** | X | | |
| **Tennis** | X | | | **Showers** | X | | |
| **Tent sites** | X | | | **Trailer space** | X | | |
| **Winter sports** | X | | | **Water hook-up** | X | | |

Accommodations, food, and supplies in Belen, 21 miles north.

**Special Rules and Regulations**

**Fishing:** State Fishing Regulations apply; see Fishing Proclamation

**Catch limit:** See page 344 for possession limits

**Boating:** Boats without motors permitted

**Other:** No camping; day use only; full facilities in Belen, 21 miles north off I-25

*Old San Miguel Mission
Socorro, New Mexico
(Completed in 1821)*

# In the Vicinity of Socorro

## *Socorro*

*There is one lake in the vicinity of Socorro:
Escondida Lake*

Socorro is a thriving town seventy-seven miles south of Albuquerque off I-25 South, situated in a wide fertile valley between the Rio Grande and the Magdalena Mountains to the west. A large spring at the base of the mountains provides Socorro with ample water for drinking and irrigation. Socorro, at an elevation of 4,700 feet above sea level, has a growing population of 8,159. Steeped in history, it is one of the oldest towns in New Mexico. Before the Juan de Oñate Expedition in 1598, the Piro Indians of the centuries-old Pueblo of Pilabó inhabited the area. When Oñate's expedition arrived from the south, through the dangerous and forbidding desert known as *La Jornada del Muerto* ("journey of the dead man"), the weary travelers camped on the east bank of the Rio Grande and were given much needed food, grain, and other supplies by the friendly Piro Indians. Accompanying Oñate on the expedition were two Franciscan priests who remained to do missionary work among the Indians. One of the priests, Father Alfonso Benavidez, named the village *Nuestra Señora Perpetuo Socorro* ("Our Lady of Perpetual Help"), in gratitude and recognition of the help they had received from the Indians. As the years passed, the name was shortened to Socorro.

In 1615, the two priests, with the help of the Indians, began to build a church that they called the San Miguel Mission, completing it in 1626. It was burned down during the Pueblo Revolt in 1680. The revolt caused an exodus to El Paso. The Apaches controlled the area until 1816 when the Spanish Crown awarded twenty-one families a land grant. By 1821 the San Miguel Mission was rebuilt on its original site. It features large carved vigas and supporting corbelled arches.

The discovery of rich mineral deposits and silver in the Magdalena Mountains west of Socorro set in motion the town's boom in 1866. Smelters were built. Then gold, lead, and other minerals were discovered, establishing Socorro as the mining capital of the New Mexico Territory. With the coming of the Atcheson, Topeka, and Santa Fe Railroad, businessmen, speculators, and entrepreneurs flocked to the town and its surrounding area by the thousands. Today, Socorro is a bustling city with a mixture of old and modern. A gallery of buildings representing outstanding examples of the early Spanish period is in the area around the old San Miguel Mission located in the oldest part of town. The Chamber of Commerce offers a printed self-guided walking or driving tour of the major historic sites in this part of town, which is a mecca for those interested in early Spanish architecture. There are modern accommodations for the visitor and tourists. There is an eighteen-hole golf course, a hospital, restaurants, an airport, and all of the modern facilities that one may find in a progressive town.

*Escondida Lake*

# ESCONDIDA LAKE

Escondida Lake is a four-acre lake five miles north of Socorro. It is one of those pleasant discoveries that we made on our drive south on I-25 toward Socorro. We turned off the Escondida exit on Exit 162 and accessed this remote lake by good paved roads. We were pleasantly surprised at its appealing serenity. The lake is situated in Escondida Park and is edged with cottonwoods, tamarisks, and cattails, as it dog-legs around part of a large well-maintained picnic ground with tables, fire pits, grills, and pit toilets. Although our visit was during a mid-summer day, there were only three fishermen at this quiet lake, which permitted a vehicle to be driven and parked at its edge, allowing convenient access for the handicapped. It is a pleasant place to spend the day picnicking and fishing for the catfish, bass, and winter trout, that are stocked by the Department of Game and Fish.

No camping is permitted at the lake or on the picnic grounds. Escondida Park is open from dawn to 10 P.M. It prohibits the use of alcoholic beverages, firearms, fireworks, and littering. Fires are permitted in designated areas only.

## Directions from Albuquerque

Drive south on I-25 to Escondida cut-off Exit 152. Bear left under freeway overpass to intersection. Go two miles on paved road to first intersection. Turn right and go across rairoad tracks two-tenths of a mile to lake. The lake is one mile from the town of Escondida.

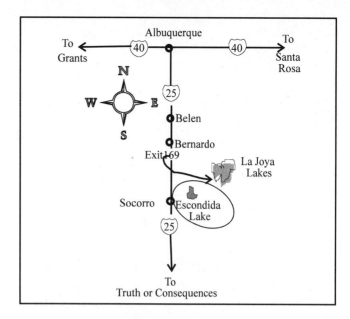

| | |
|---|---|
| **Surface acres:** 4 | **Distance from Albuquerque:** 76 miles |
| **Elevation:** 4,500 feet | **Location:** 5 miles north of Socorro |
| **Max. trailer size & fee:** No camping | |
| **Time limit:** No overnight | **Fish species:** Bass, and channel catfish, stocked with |
| **Mailing address:** None | trout in winter |
| **Police emergency tel. #:** 835-0741 | **Season:** All year, from dawn to 10 P.M. |
| **Medical emergency tel. #:** 911 | |

## ACTIVITIES AND FACILITIES

| | NO | YES | Proximity to Lake in Miles | | NO | YES | Proximity to Lake in Miles |
|---|---|---|---|---|---|---|---|
| Bait and supplies | X | | | Airplane runway | X | | |
| Boat gas | X | | | Bottled gas | X | | |
| Boat ramp | X | | | Café/snack bar | X | | |
| Boat rental | X | | | Chemical toilets | X | | |
| Camping | X | | | Drinking water | | X | |
| Fire pits | | X | | Electrical hook-up | X | | |
| Fire places | | X | | Flush toilets | X | | |
| Firewood | X | | | Grocery store | X | | |
| Fishing | | X | | Handicapped access | | X | |
| Golf | X | | | Ice | X | | |
| Hiking | X | | | Laundry | X | | |
| Marina | X | | | Lodgings | X | | |
| Picnicking | | X | | Pit toilets | | X | |
| Riding | X | | | Playground | | X | |
| Scuba diving | X | | | Restaurant | X | | |
| Stables | X | | | Sanitary disposal | X | | |
| Swimming | X | | | Sewer hook-up | X | | |
| Tables | | X | | Shelters | X | | |
| Telephone | X | | | Shopping | X | | |
| Tennis | X | | | Showers | X | | |
| Tent sites | X | | | Trailer space | X | | |
| Winter sports | X | | | Water hook-up | X | | |

Store for food, picnic, and fishing supplies in Escondida, 1 mile.

**Special Rules and Regulations**

**Fishing:** State fishing license required; state Fishing Regulations apply

**Catch limit:** 6 trout, see page 344 for warm-water catch limits and regulations

**Boating:** No boating

**Other:** No alcoholic beverages, no fireworks, no littering; open from dawn to 10 P.M.

# In the Vicinity of San Antonio

## *San Antonio*

*There is one fishing lake in the vicinity of San Antonio: Bosque del Apache*

San Antonio is a small town nine miles southeast of Socorro off I-25 south. During its settlement in the early 1800s, it was a farming community. Crops of onions, beans, grain, chile, and grapes thrived in the soil of this fertile area, watered by the ample waterflow from the Magdalena Mountains to the west. The town flourished during the 1860s, when Socorro to the north became the mining capital of the New Mexico Territory, after minerals and the precious metals of silver and gold were discovered in the Magdalena Mountains. In the early 1800s, San Antonio became a favorite stopover for travelers between Santa Fe and Chihuahua, Mexico. A mercantile store was built by Estanislado Montoya a former distinguished general in the Civil War. His son opened coal mines west of the town and built coke ovens to process the coal. During this period, another store was built by Augustus Hilton, father of Conrad Hilton. Gus Hilton became known as the "Merchant King of San Antonio." From his large general store, he traded with the miners and trappers and operated a stage line to White Oaks, seventy-eight miles to the east, north of Carrizozo, connecting the towns of Magdalena, west of Socorro, and Nogal, just north of Ruidoso. During a depression in 1907, Gus Hilton converted part of the store into hotel rooms.

Years later, his son Conrad took his lead and successfully established his famous Conrad Hilton Hotel empire, building hotels in major cities internationally. San Antonio is best known as the birthplace of Conrad Hilton. San Antonio is also famous as the home of the well-known and popular Owl Bar. Thousands of tourists traveling the major highways running north, east, south, and west, detour from their main destinations to stop at the Owl Bar to enjoy what is billed as *"the best green chile hamburger in the world."* The bar itself, in the main dining area, is on the State Historical and Cultural Properties List and is reputed to have come from the Crystal Bar, no longer in operation but still standing on south Main Street near the Owl Bar. The Owl Bar is a must stop on the way to the Bosque del Apache National Wildlife Refuge about nine miles southeast. San Antonio also has several souvenir shops, convenience stores, and a service station.

*Bosque del Apache*

# BOSQUE DEL APACHE

Bosque del Apache National Wildlife Refuge is located eight miles south of San Antonio. It is part of the 1845 Bosque del Apache Land Grant awarded by Mexico to Antonio Sandoval for his military services. In 1936 the land grant was purchased by the United States Government. Three years later, in 1939, the refuge was established to protect the whooping crane, then threatened with extinction. The refuge was allotted 57,190 acres of the land purchased as a wintering area for over 30,000 snow geese, 12,000 sandhill cranes, 20,000 ducks, and the endangered whooping crane. It also provides habitat for almost 300 different bird species, and over 400 different mammals, reptiles, and amphibians. Water is diverted from irrigation canals or pumped from underground wells to provide temporary ponds or marshes, where birds may rest and feed during winter months. During the summer, most of these temporary ponds are drained, and the water is used for agricultural purposes on the refuge and the surrounding area. Local farmers participate in a cooperative farming effort, by farming 1,500 acres of the refuge on a share-crop arrangement. They provide the seed, the equipment, and the labor, leaving one-third of their crops in the field for wildlife.

Walking trails are available, and a fifteen-mile self-guided auto tour is available year round from one hour before sunrise to one hour after sunset. In the evenings, from October through January, it is a birdwatchers' paradise. Fishing is allowed in designated areas from the Memorial Day weekend until 30 September and it is subject to state and federal regulations. Camping is allowed on the north boundary only, but adequate overnight accommodations and services are available in San Antonio and Socorro.

## Directions from Albuquerque:

Take I-25 South to Exit 139 at San Antonio. Then drive eight miles south on NM 1 and follow signs to Refuge. From the south, take Exit 139, connect with NM 1, and follow signs to Refuge.

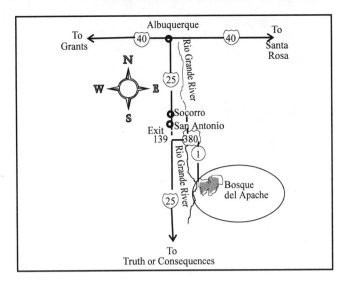

| | | |
|---|---|---|
| **Surface acres:** 1-2 | | **Distance from Albuquerque:** 93 miles |
| **Elevation:** 4,600 feet | | **Location:** 10 miles southeast of San Antonio |
| **Max. trailer size:** No camping | | **Fish species:** Catfish, bass, and winter trout |
| **Time limit:** Day use only | | **Season:** Memorial Day weekend-30 September |
| **Mailing address:** Bosque del Apache, Wildlife Refuge, | | |
| Box 1246, Socorro, NM 87801 (505)835-1828 | | |

## ACTIVITIES AND FACILITIES

| | NO | YES | Proximity to Lake in Miles | | NO | YES | Proximity to Lake in Miles |
|---|---|---|---|---|---|---|---|
| Bait and supplies | X | | | Airplane runway | X | | |
| Boat gas | X | | | Bottled gas | X | | |
| Boat ramp | X | | | Café/snack bar | X | | |
| Boat rental | X | | | Chemical toilets | X | | |
| Camping | X | | | Drinking water | X | | |
| Fire pits | X | | | Electrical hook-up | X | | |
| Fire places | X | | | Flush toilets | X | | |
| Firewood | X | | | Grocery store | X | | |
| Fishing | | X | | Handicapped access | X | | |
| Golf | X | | | Ice | X | | |
| Hiking | | X | | Laundry | X | | |
| Marina | X | | | Lodgings | X | | |
| Picnicking | X | | | Pit toilets | X | | |
| Riding | X | | | Playground | X | | |
| Scuba diving | X | | | Restaurant | X | | |
| Stables | X | | | Sanitary disposal | X | | |
| Swimming | X | | | Sewer hook-up | X | | |
| Tables | X | | | Shelters | X | | |
| Telephone | | X | | Shopping | X | | |
| Tennis | X | | | Showers | X | | |
| Tent sites | X | | | Trailer space | X | | |
| Winter sports | X | | | Water hook-up | X | | |

Lodgings, supplies, and restaurants available in Socorro, 10 miles north.

**Special Rules and Regulations**

**Fishing:** New Mexico fishing license required; see Fishing Proclamation

**Catch limit:** New Mexico Regulations on possession limits apply; see page 344

**Boating:** No boating permitted

**Other:** Restrooms are in visitors center, open daily; closed weekends in summer; open October-March on weekends only

# In the Vicinity of Truth or Consequences

## *Truth or Consequences*

*There are three lakes in the vicinity of Truth or Consequences: Elephant Butte Lake (east of I-25 South on the Rio Grande), Caballo Lake (east of I-25 South, on the Rio Grande), Percha Dam Lake (west of I-25 South, on the Rio Grande in Zone 4)*

Truth or Consequences is the county seat of Sierra County. The city was originally called *Hot Springs,* because of the hot mineral waters bubbling to the surface in the many springs in the area, which resulted from the tremendous upheavals of the earth milleniums ago, draining the sea that covered the Rio Grande Valley. Truth or Consequences is located 149 miles south of Albuquerque and is 4,269 feet above sea level. It is a friendly town of 6,000 people who enjoy its small-town atmosphere, moderate climate, and year-round recreational and social activities. Thousands flock to Truth or Consequences in any season to enjoy the pollution-free air, the sunny dry climate, and the recreational opportunities offered at the two large lakes nearby: Elephant Butte and Caballo. These advantages make Truth or Consequences an ideal retirement spot, where people can enjoy year-round golf, tennis, fishing, boating, good restaurants, and western-style nightlife. Visitors are also attracted to the many special events such as the Easter Weekend Hot Air

Balloon Rally, the Hillsboro Apple Festival during the Labor Day Weekend, and the New Mexico State Old Time Fiddlers Contest in the fall. The Truth or Consequences Fiesta in early May, featuring TV personality Ralph Edwards, has become a major annual event. Truth or Consequences became its legal name in 1950, when the top-rated night-time radio show *Truth or Consequences,* hosted by Ralph Edwards, offered free publicity in the form of an annual Fiesta to any town or city in the United States, willing to change its name to Truth or Consequences. The small resort town of Hot Springs showed the most interest, and the residents voting for the name change won out over their opponents. From that point on, Ralph Edwards and his wife Barbara and other television and motion picture friends came each year to the promised Annual Fiesta Celebration. Ralph Edwards has also donated many of his memorabilia to the popular Geronimo Springs Museum on Main Street. The Museum displays artifacts, and arts and crafts indigenous to the area, where visitors can become acquainted with the history of the surrounding area.

There are excellent accommodations for the tourist or visitor in Truth or Consequences. Many health seekers come from miles around to drink or bathe in the hot therapeutic mineral waters offered in the many bath houses in the town. Stores, gas stations, and medical facilities are also available to serve visitors.

*Elephant Butte Lake*

# ELEPHANT BUTTE LAKE

Elephant Butte Lake is located five miles northeast of Truth or Consequences and is the largest lake in New Mexico. Construction was begun by the Bureau of Reclamation on the Rio Grande in 1911 and completed in 1916. At that time it was the largest man-made dam in the world. Its primary purpose was for irrigation of the areas around Hatch, Las Cruces, El Paso, and Juarez, Mexico. The structure is 306 feet high and 1,674 feet long, creating a lake forty-five miles long with 200 miles of shoreline. The original capacity of the lake was 2,500,000 acre-feet of water at an elevation of 4,407 feet above sea level. It is fringed by mountains and lies amid a spectacular geologic setting of volcanic necks and sandy beaches. The name *"Elephant Butte"* comes from the volcanic neck of an eroded core of a volcano, which emerges from the lake and resembles the head of an elephant. The lake and state park in which it lies are a haven for thousands of vacationers, water sportsmen, fishermen, water skiers, sail and motorboaters, windsurfers, parasailers, campers, and hikers who frequent the lake year round. The best fishing is in late April through August. Fishing is also good in March, September, and October. Elephant Butte Lake is the only lake in New Mexico that contains striped bass. These trophy-size striped bass can weigh fifty pounds.

The park is divided into two sections: New Hot Springs Landing and the Elephant Butte Damsite. The main entrance is at New Hot Springs Landing, where users pay their fees, and boats are inspected for safety. The campgrounds below the office are fully developed; with comfort stations, shelters, picnic tables and grills, a playground, drinking water, two electric hook-up areas, and two dump stations. There is also a marina with a gas dock and a concrete boat launching ramp, a restaurant, a store, and a bar. Boat rentals are available. There is also a boat ramp and marina at Rock Canyon, with a marine toilet pump-out, fishing and bait supplies, and groceries. The Damsite area is located at the southern end of the lake, where there is a lodge with a restaurant, a lounge, cabin rentals, and a trailer park with full hook-ups.

## Directions from Albuquerque

Take I-25 south to Exit 83. Exit on 83 and connect with NM 195. Continue on 195 following signs to the Park Office and Visitors Center, where you can pay fees, and get maps and complete information on the lake and park facilities. Access is via paved roads.

## Distances to Truth or Consequences

Farmington: 331 miles
Las Cruces: 75 miles
Clayton: 411 miles
Hobbs: 324 miles
El Paso: 118 miles

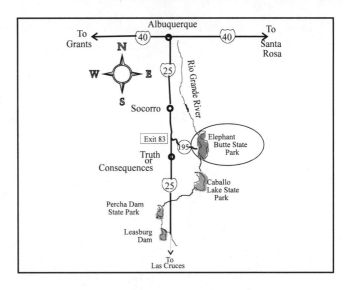

| | |
|---|---|
| **Surface acres:** 40,000 | **Distance from Albuquerque:** 145 miles |
| **Elevation:** 4,407 feet | **Location:** 5 miles northeast of Truth or Consequences on the |
| **Max. trailer size & fee:** 40 feet | Rio Grande |
| **Time limit:** 14 days | **Fish species:** Striped bass, largemouth bass, white bass, |
| **Mailing address:** Elephant Butte Lake State Park, P.O. Box 13 | walleye, catfish, and crappie |
| Elephant Butte, NM 87935 (505)744-5421 | **Season:** All year |
| **Police emergency tel. #:** (505) 894-6617 | **Medical emergency tel. #:** (505) 894-2111 |

## ACTIVITIES AND FACILITIES

| | NO | YES | Proximity to Lake in Miles | | NO | YES | Proximity to Lake in Miles |
|---|---|---|---|---|---|---|---|
| Bait and supplies | | X | | Airplane runway | X | | |
| Boat gas | | X | | Bottled gas | | X | |
| Boat ramp | | X | | Café/snack bar | | X | |
| Boat rental | | X | | Chemical toilets | | X | |
| Camping | | X | | Drinking water | | X | |
| Fire pits | | X | | Electrical hook-up | | X | |
| Fire places | | X | | Flush toilets | | X | |
| Firewood | | X | | Grocery store | | X | |
| Fishing | | X | | Handicapped access | | X | |
| Golf | X | | 5 | Ice | | X | |
| Hiking | | X | | Laundry | | X | |
| Marina | | X | | Lodgings | | X | |
| Picnicking | | X | | Pit toilets | | X | |
| Riding | | X | | Playground | | X | |
| Scuba diving | | X | | Restaurant | | X | |
| Stables | | X | | Sanitary disposal | | X | |
| Swimming | | X | | Sewer hook-up | | X | |
| Tables | | X | | Shelters | | X | |
| Telephone | | X | | Shopping | | X | |
| Tennis | | X | | Showers | | X | |
| Tent sites | | X | | Trailer space | | X | |
| Winter sports | X | | | Water hook-up | | X | |

Full facilities and accommodations in Truth or Consequences, 5 miles south.

**Special Rules and Regulations**

**Fishing:** New Mexico State Regulations apply, see page 344

**Catch limit:** Minimum size for black bass, 14 inches; see page 344 for other catch limits

**Boating:** No size restrictions; park rules apply and are available at park office; see pages 342, 343 for park and boating regulations

**Other:** Excellent camping and RV facilities

*Caballo Lake*

# CABALLO LAKE

Caballo Lake is an 11,000-acre lake within Caballo Lake State Park, twenty miles south of Truth or Consequences on the Rio Grande River, south of Elephant Butte Lake. Its construction was started in 1936 to provide supplementary water storage for irrigation of the Rio Grande Valley south of Elephant Butte. Rising sharply from the eastern edge of the lake is the rugged escarpment of the Caballos Mountains, which the early Spanish called "*Horse Mountains.*" (*Caballo* in Spanish means "*horse*"), and refers to the horse head shape of the mountains. The lake is visible from I-25 as it stretches along the highway for about eighteen miles, with over seventy miles of shoreline. It is over one mile wide. Near the southern tip of the lake, a portion of the west shore was set aside as Caballo Lake State Park in 1964. It is a full-facilitied recreation area, offering year-round fishing, camping, picnicking, water sports, and boating. In the two separate areas—one lakeside, and one riverside—there are 100 sites (twenty-five with electric hook-ups), flush toilets, tables, showers, drinking water, and a grocery store. The lake facilities also include a boat ramp, a marina with boat rentals, and fishing supplies.

Access to the eastern side of the Caballos is by way of NM 52 from Truth or Consequences at the northern end of the Caballos Mountains. Caballo Lake is a major attraction for vacationers and retirees. The lake contains white bass, largemouth bass, crappie, catfish, and walleye. (Minimum keeper size for black bass is 14 inches.) In the nearby small community of Caballo there is a post office, a church, stores, and a KOA campground.

## Directions from Albuquerque

Take I-25 south to Exit 59 at Truth or Consequences. Follow signs about fifteen miles south of Truth or Consequences to Caballo Lake State Park.

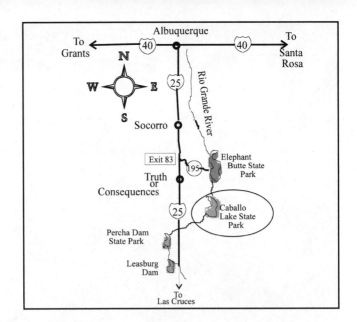

| | | |
|---|---|---|
| Surface acres: 11,000 | | Distance from Albuquerque: 160 miles |
| Elevation: 4,182 feet | | Location: 15 miles south of Elephant Butte |
| Max. trailer size & fee: 40 feet | | Fish species: Largemouth bass, white bass, catfish, and |
| Time limit: 14 days | | walleye |
| Mailing address: Box 1147, Santa Fe, NM 87504 | | Season: All year |
| (505) 743-3942 | | Police emergency tel. #: 911 |
| Medical emergency tel. #: 911 | | |

## ACTIVITIES AND FACILITIES

| | NO | YES | Proximity to Lake in Miles | | NO | YES | Proximity to Lake in Miles |
|---|---|---|---|---|---|---|---|
| Bait and supplies | | X | | Airplane runway | X | | *15 |
| Boat gas | | X | | Bottled gas | X | | *15 |
| Boat ramp | | X | | Café/snack bar | | X | |
| Boat rental | | X | | Chemical toilets | | X | |
| Camping | | X | | Drinking water | | X | |
| Fire pits | | X | | Electrical hook-up | | X | |
| Fire places | | X | | Flush toilets | | X | |
| Firewood | | X | | Grocery store | | X | |
| Fishing | | X | | Handicapped access | | X | |
| Golf | X | | *15 | Ice | | X | |
| Hiking | | X | | Laundry | X | | *15 |
| Marina | | X | | Lodgings | X | | *15 |
| Picnicking | | X | | Pit toilets | | X | |
| Riding | X | | | Playground | | X | |
| Scuba diving | | X | | Restaurant | | X | |
| Skiing (water) | X | | | Sanitary disposal | | X | |
| Swimming | | X | | Sewer hook-up | | X | |
| Tables | | X | | Shelters | | X | |
| Telephone | | X | | Shopping | X | | *15 |
| Tennis | X | | | Showers | | X | |
| Tent sites | | X | | Trailer space | | X | |
| Winter sports | X | | | Water hook-up | | X | |

*Full facilities in Truth or Consequences, 15 miles north.

**Special Rules & Regulations**

**Fishing:** State Regulations apply; see Fishing Proclamation

**Catch limit:** Black bass, minimum keeper size, 14 inches; see page 344 for limits on other species

**Boating:** NM State Boating Regulations apply; see page 342

**Other:** Excellent camping facilities

*Percha Dam Lake*

# PERCHA DAM LAKE

Percha Dam State Park is fourteen miles southwest of Truth or Consequences off I-25 on the Rio Grande and a short distance from Caballo Dam. Access to the lake and campgrounds after exiting I-25 is by good graded gravel roads. It is a small dam constructed in 1917 for water storage and irrigation of farms in the lower valley. It is set in the remnants of the Bosque (Spanish for *"woods,"* referring to the thick stands of cottonwood trees that grew along the Rio Grande). The huge cottonwoods provide shade for the camp and picnic sites. Percha Dam State Park is a small but well maintained and attractively engineered park with large expanses of well-kept lawns that slope down to the river's bank. This park was created in 1970 and is a pleasant place to spend a day or a week away from the thousands of visitors to the nearby parks of Elephant Butte and Caballo Lakes to the northeast. On each of my many visits to Percha Dam State Park, the fishing pressure and

camp site occupancy was much lighter than at the crowded lakes of Elephant Butte and Caballo. The grounds have a playground, clean and well-maintained flush toilets and showers, shelters with tables, grills, hiking trails, and drinking water.

North of the dam, and spillway to the south, is a scenic little warm-water lake of approximately six acres, which is populated with bass, catfish, crappie, and walleye. It is a quiet and remote lake surrounded with towering cottonwoods and reached through a gate and elevated walkway. Standard New Mexico state park user fees and fishing licensing apply. At this writing, the fees were three dollars for day use, six dollars for camping, seven dollars for sheltered sites, and eleven dollars for electric hook-ups. The fees and regulations are posted at the entrance to the park. Since fees fluctuate each year, it is advisable to check current fees and regulations with the State Parks and Recreation Department.

## Directions from Albuquerque

Take I-25 south, then go twenty-two miles south of Truth or Consequences following signs to Percha Dam State Park.

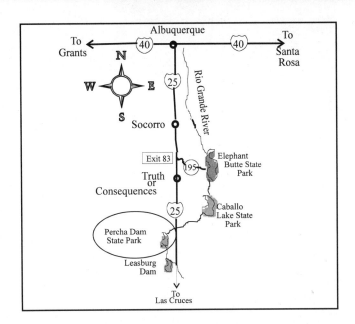

| | |
|---|---|
| **Surface acres:** 6 | **Distance from Albuquerque:** 171 miles |
| **Elevation:** 4,180 feet | **Location:** 22 miles south of Truth or Consequences |
| **Max. trailer size & fee:** 40 feet | **Fish species:** Bass, catfish, crappie, and walleye |
| **Time limit:** 14 days | **Season:** All year |
| **Mailing address:** Percha Dam, Box 1147, Santa Fe, NM 87504 (505) 743-3942 | **Police emergency tel. #:** 894-7118 |
| **Medical emergency tel. #:** 911 | |

## ACTIVITIES AND FACILITIES

| | NO | YES | Proximity to Lake in Miles | | NO | YES | Proximity to Lake in Miles |
|---|---|---|---|---|---|---|---|
| Bait and supplies | X | | | Airplane runway | X | | |
| Boat gas | X | | | Bottled gas | X | | |
| Boat ramp | X | | | Café/snack bar | X | | |
| Boat rental | X | | | Chemical toilets | | X | |
| Camping | | X | | Drinking water | | X | |
| Fire pits | | X | | Electrical hook-up | | X | |
| Fire places | | X | | Flush toilets | | X | |
| Firewood | X | | | Grocery store | X | | |
| Fishing | | X | | Handicapped access | X | | |
| Golf | X | | | Ice | X | | |
| Hiking | | X | | Laundry | X | | |
| Marina | X | | | Lodgings | X | | |
| Picnicking | | X | | Pit toilets | X | | |
| Riding | X | | | Playground | | X | |
| Scuba diving | X | | | Restaurant | X | | |
| Skiing (water) | X | | | Sanitary disposal | X | | |
| Swimming | X | | | Sewer hook-up | X | | |
| Tables | | X | | Shelters | | X | |
| Telephone | | X | | Shopping | X | | |
| Tennis | X | | | Showers | | X | |
| Tent sites | | X | | Trailer space | | X | |
| Winter sports | X | | | Water hook-up | | X | |

Full facilities, stores and services in Truth or Consequences.
**Special Rules and Regulations**
  **Fishing:** State Regulations apply; see Fishing Proclamation
  **Catch limit:** See Fishing Proclamation or page 344 for warm water fish catch limits
  **Boating:** No floating devices permitted
  **Other:** Excellent camping facilities

# In the Vicinity of Carrizozo

## *Carrizozo*

*There is one lake in the vicinity of Carrizozo:*
*Carrizozo Lake*

Carrizozo is a small town with a population of 1,225, lying at an elevation of 5,438 feet above sea level in the foothills of the Sacramento Mountains. It is on the main line of the Southern Pacific Railroad, at the intersection of U.S. Highways 54 and 380. The name Carrizozo is derived from the Spanish word *carrizo,* which means and describes a reed-type grass, which grows plentifully in this area and is an excellent livestock feed. The abundance of these grasslands makes cattle ranching big business here. It was not until later years that the name was changed from Carrizo to Carrizozo. A ranch foreman, Jim Allcook, added an extra *"zo"* to the word, alluding to the abundance of the grasses in the area.

The town was founded in 1899, when the El Paso and Northeastern Railroad bypassed White Oaks, which at that time was a prosperous gold mining town twelve miles north of Carrizozo. This led to the development of Carrizozo as a shipping point and supply and trade center, and it became the county seat of Lincoln County. Names like Pat Garrett and Governor Lew Wallace figured prominently in the history of the area, but it is best known as "Billy the Kid Country." It was in Lincoln that Billy the Kid made his last escape. Each year in August, thousands of visitors are drawn to the town of Lincoln, about thirty-five miles east of Carrizozo, to watch the re-enactment of Billy the Kid's escape and killing of two deputies. Visitors are also drawn to many other historical and scenic attractions in the area, all within thirty or forty minutes from Carrizozo. Nearby, at White Sands, is Trinity Site where the first atomic bomb was detonated in July of 1945. Other places of interest like the Valley of Fires State Park lava flow attract visitors. This lava flow is also known as the Malpais (Spanish for "badlands") and is reputedly the most recent lava flow in the continental United States. Carrizozo also has an airport with a 4,900-feet paved runway. Just a mile east of town is a recreation park with a lake, a Little League baseball park, and a nine-hole golf course. The town has ample facilities for the visitor's convenience: restaurants, grocery stores, motels, gas stations, and RV parks. Its proximity to the recreation areas of Ruidoso, only forty-two miles south, makes this a pleasant and convenient sightseeing stop for the traveler.

223

*Carrizozo Lake*

# CARRIZOZO LAKE

Carrizozo is a two-acre lake located one mile east of Carrizozo, in the Carrizozo Recreation Park. It is adjacent to a nine-hole, seventy-two par golf course that has a pro-shop and boasts its greens, tee-boxes, and fairways as the finest in the southwest. I was particularly impressed with the location and the recreational opportunities offered in this tidy little park. It was well maintained and conveniently located, with excellent access by a paved entrance right off the highway. A New Mexico state fishing license is required to fish the lake, which contains bass, and catfish, and is stocked with winter trout. The park, the lake, and the golf course are open year round, and the picnic area is equipped with a playground, tables, and toilets.

It is a day-use lake and park. No camping is permitted, but full overnight camping facilities for trailers, RVs and tents are available just five miles west of town in the Valley of Fires Campgrounds. Stores for picnic and fishing supplies, service stations, motels, and restaurants are available in the town of Carrizozo one mile west of Carrizozo Recreation Park.

## Directions from Albuquerque

Take I-25 south to San Antonio exit and connect with Highway 380 east. Go sixty-four miles east to Carrizozo, then one mile east of town to Carrizozo Lake and Recreation Park. The lake is next to the Golf Course, and it has excellent accessibility via paved highway.

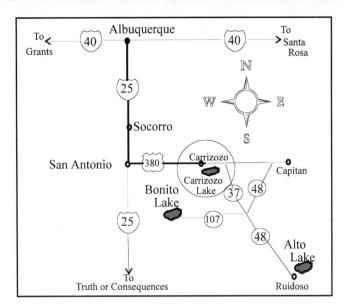

| | |
|---|---|
| **Surface acres:** 2 | **Distance from Albuquerque:** 150 miles |
| **Elevation:** 5,438 feet | **Location:** On U.S. Highway 380, 64 miles |
| **Max. trailer size & fee:** No camping | east of San Antonio; 1 mile east of Carrizozo |
| **Time limit:** No overnight | **Fish species:** Bass, catfish, and winter trout |
| **Mailing address:** Chamber of Commerce, | **Season:** All year; full camping facilities 5 miles |
| P.O. Box 567, Carrizozo, NM 88301 | west, in Valley of Fires Campgrounds |
| **Medical emergency tel. #:** At golf course | **Police emergency tel. #:** At golf course |

## ACTIVITIES AND FACILITIES

| | NO | YES | Proximity to Lake in Miles | | NO | YES | Proximity to Lake in Miles |
|---|---|---|---|---|---|---|---|
| Bait and supplies | X | | | Airplane runway | X | | *1 |
| Boat gas | X | | | Bottled gas | X | | *1 |
| Boat ramp | X | | | Café/snack bar | X | | *1 |
| Boat rental | X | | | Chemical toilets | X | | |
| Camping | X | | *5 | Drinking water | | X | |
| Fire pits | | X | | Electrical hook-up | X | | *5 |
| Fire places | | X | | Flush toilets | X | | |
| Firewood | X | | | Grocery store | X | | *1 |
| Fishing | | X | | Handicapped access | | X | |
| Golf | | X | | Ice | X | | |
| Hiking | | X | | Laundry | X | | |
| Marina | X | | | Lodgings | X | | *1 |
| Picnicking | | X | | Pit toilets | | X | |
| Riding | X | | | Playground | | X | |
| Scuba diving | X | | | Restaurant | X | | *1 |
| Stables | X | | | Sanitary disposal | X | | *5 |
| Swimming | X | | | Sewer hook-up | X | | *5 |
| Tables | | X | | Shelters | X | | *5 |
| Telephone | | X | | Shopping | X | | |
| Tennis | X | | | Showers | X | | |
| Tent sites | X | | *5 | Trailer space | X | | *5 |
| Winter sports | X | | | Water hook-up | X | | *5 |

*Food and lodgings, 1 mile west in town. Camping, 5 miles west of town.

**Special Rules and Regulations**

    **Fishing:** New Mexico license required; Fishing Regulations apply; no fee

    **Catch limit:** New Mexico state possession limits apply; see page 344 for catch limits

    **Boating:** No boating permitted

    **Other:** Full camping facilities at Valley of Fires Campgrounds, 5 miles west of town

# In the Vicinity
# of Ruidoso

## *Ruidoso*

*There are two lakes in the vicinity of Ruidoso:
Bonito Lake, Alto Lake.*

*There are also several lakes on the Mescalero
Apache Indian Reservation, three miles and a few
minutes south of Ruidoso: Mescalero Lake, Eagle
Lakes, Silver Lakes*

Ruidoso is located in the southeast corner of
Lincoln County at the foot of Old Baldy Peak,
forty-one miles southeast of Carrizozo. It is a year-
round resort town 6,911 feet above sea level, with a
population of about 9,000 and is billed as the
"playground of the southwest." Ruidoso is also
home of the All American Futurity Quarter Horse
Race, offering a $1,035,900 purse, and held
annually on Labor Day. Ruidoso means *"noisy"*
taking its name from the swiftrunning stream that
runs through the town. It was here in the 1880s
that the stream powered a grist mill known as
Dowlin's Mill. Dowlin's Mill was the original
name of the town.

If getting close to nature is your whim, then
Ruidoso is the place to visit and enjoy any time of
the year. Each year, thousands of visitors are
attracted to the Ruidoso area, which abounds in
recreational opportunities. You can ski, fish, hike,
or camp in the several sites scattered through this
scenic mountain town. There are snow-clad
mountains in the winter and changing colors of
aspens that swath the surrounding forests in red,
yellow, and gold in the fall.

Sixteen miles from Ruidoso, by way of a good
paved road, is the Sierra Blanca Ski Area. It is on
the Mescalero Apache Indian Reservation and is
equipped with full facilities, including a restaurant
and tavern, a warming lodge, and an equipment
rental shop. The town of Ruidoso has full facilities
and accommodations for overnighters. There are
more than seventy hotels and lodges, including
supper clubs, restaurants, swimming pools, tennis
courts, golf courses, riding stables, playgrounds,
antique shops, and gift shops. The many camping,
hunting, and cold- and clear-fishing streams and
lakes are within a five- to ten-minute drive from
town, making Ruidoso a sportsman's paradise. Just
three miles south of Ruidoso, in a spectacular
forested setting at an elevation of 7,200 feet, is the
luxurious resort hotel, *Inn of the Mountain Gods,*
owned, operated, and located on the Mescalero
Apache Indian Reservation. This beautifully
designed and appointed complex offers the ultimate
in modern and attractive facilities, a restaurant, gift
shops, and many recreational packages for guests.
It overlooks Lake Mescalero. This beautiful
hundred-acre fishing and boating lake is detailed on
pages 232 and 233.

*Bonito Lake*

# BONITO LAKE

Bonito Lake is a sixty-acre lake located fourteen miles northwest of Ruidoso and 177 miles southwest of Albuquerque. It was formed by damming Bonito Creek to serve as a water supply for the city of Alamogordo, located eighty miles south. Bonito Lake is a beautiful mountain lake situated at an elevation of 7,370 feet above sea level, amid 1,700 acres owned by the city of Alamogordo. In 1986 it was leased from the city of Alamogordo by the New Mexcio Game Commission for public fishing. The city of Alamogordo and the Lincoln National Forest Service operate the camping and picnic facilities located near the lake.

Bonito Lake's proximity to the town of Ruidoso, which attracts thousands of sportsmen each year, has made Bonito Lake a favorite spot for fishermen and campers, and records one of the highest uses in the state. Bonito Lake is regularly stocked with rainbow trout by the Department of Game and Fish.

It is also populated with wild brook trout. A Wildlife Habitat Improvement stamp and a state fishing license are required to fish Bonito Lake. Camping is not permitted on the lakeshore, but the lake is adjacent to, and accessed by, paved roads to the Forest Service-operated South Fork Campground. A fee is charged at this campground, which contains sixty-one camp sites and is equipped with flush toilets, water, electric hook-ups, fire places, fire rings, and room for twenty-feet trailers. From the trailhead at the parking area, the well-maintained and scenic South Fork Trail enters the White Mountain Wilderness, offering opportunities to view wildlife and enjoy some of the most beautiful scenery in the Lincoln National Forest.

On the approach to the lake on NM 107—about a mile and a half before you reach the lake—is a grocery store where needed fishing and picnic supplies can be purchased. There are no other stores around the Bonito Lake area.

## Directions from Albuquerque

Take I-25 south to the San Antonio exit and connect with U.S. Highway 380 East. Continue past Carrizozo to junction of NM 37 and turn south (right). Continue and merge on NM 48 to NM 107 turn-off. Follow signs to Bonito Lake about five miles west.

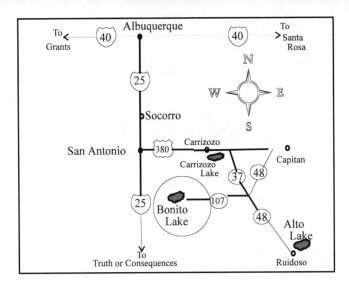

| | | |
|---|---|---|
| **Surface acres:** 60 | | **Distance from Albuquerque:** 107 miles |
| **Elevation:** 7,370 feet | | **Location:** 14 miles northwest of Ruidoso |
| **Max. trailer size & fee:** No camping at lake | | **Fish species:** Brook trout, rainbow, and cutthroat |
| **Time limit:** 14 days | | **Season:** 1 April-30 November; 5 A.M.-10 P.M. |
| **Mailing address:** Box 25112, Santa Fe, NM 87504 | | **Medical emergency tel. #:** 911 |
| **Police emergency tel. #:** 257-9111 | | |

## ACTIVITIES AND FACILITIES

| | NO | YES | Proximity to Lake in Miles | | NO | YES | Proximity to Lake in Miles |
|---|---|---|---|---|---|---|---|
| **Bait and supplies** | X | | | **Airplane runway** | X | | 14 |
| **Boat gas** | X | | | **Bottled gas** | X | | |
| **Boat ramp** | X | | | **Café/snack bar** | X | | 1.5 |
| **Boat rental** | X | | | **Chemical toilets** | X | | 1 |
| **Camping** | | X | | **Drinking water** | X | | 1 |
| **Fire pits** | | X | | **Electrical hook-up** | X | | 1 |
| **Fire places** | | X | | **Flush toilets** | X | | 1 |
| **Firewood** | | X | | **Grocery store** | X | | 1.5 |
| **Fishing** | | X | | **Handicapped access** | X | | 1 |
| **Golf** | X | | 14 | **Ice** | X | | 1.5 |
| **Hiking** | | X | | **Laundry** | X | | |
| **Marina** | X | | | **Lodgings** | X | | |
| **Picnicking** | X | | 1 | **Pit toilets** | | X | |
| **Riding** | | X | | **Playground** | X | | |
| **Skiing (water)** | X | | | **Restaurant** | X | | 14 |
| **Skiing** | X | | 15 | **Sanitary disposal** | X | | 1 |
| **Swimming** | X | | | **Sewer hook-up** | X | | 1 |
| **Tables** | X | | | **Shelters** | X | | 1 |
| **Telephone** | X | | 1.5 | **Shopping** | X | | 14 |
| **Tennis** | X | | 14 | **Showers** | X | | |
| **Tent sites** | X | | 1 | **Trailer space** | X | | 1 |
| **Winter sports** | X | | 14 | **Water hook-up** | X | | 1 |

Full facilities and services, 14 miles in Ruidoso. Camping, 1 mile from lake.

**Special Rules and Regulations**

**Fishing:** Fishing license and Wildlife Habitat stamp required; see Fishing Proclamation

**Catch limit:** 10 trout per day; 10 in possession; hours, 5 A.M. to 10 P.M.

**Boating:** No boats or floating devices permitted

**Other:** Full camping facilities 1 mile from lake by way of paved roads

# ALTO LAKE

Alto Lake is a twenty-acre lake on Eagle Creek in the small community of Alto, off NM 37, just two and a half miles north of Ruidoso. A sign posted at its entrance proclaims its use as a municipal water supply and states its restrictions and regulations. Public fishing is permitted year round between the hours of 6 A.M. to 8 P.M. No overnight camping, wading, swimming, boating, or hunting is allowed. No fishing is permitted within 600 feet of the east end of the lake, and cleaning and washing of fish in the lake is prohibited.

Alto Lake is stocked in the summer with catchable-size rainbow trout by the New Mexico Department of Game and Fish. Eagle Creek to the west along Forest Road 127 also offers fine fishing for some brook trout, cutthroat, and browns, as well as rainbows, and is open year round. Good access by paved road to the lake is off NM 37 and parking is available off the lakeshore. Information on catch limits, licenses, and regulations is available at the Ruidoso Valley Chamber of Commerce and sporting goods stores. There are some stores, gas stations, and accommodations in Alto. However, full facilities are available in Ruidoso, just a few minutes' drive south.

## Directions from Albuquerque

Follow the same directions as for the route to Ruidoso. Take I-25 south to the San Antonio exit. Go east on U.S. 380 past Carrizozo to junction of NM 37. Turn right (or south) on NM 37 and follow the signs to Ruidoso. Alto Lake is two and a half miles north of Ruidoso.

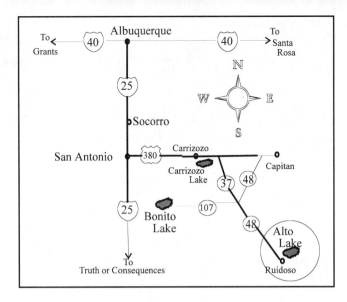

| | |
|---|---|
| **Surface acres:** 20 | **Distance from Albuquerque:** 189 miles |
| **Elevation:** 6,950 feet | **Location:** 2 1/2 miles north of Ruidoso |
| **Max. trailer size & fee:** No camping | **Fish species:** Rainbow trout, brook trout, brown, |
| **Time limit:** Day use only | and cutthroat |
| **Mailing address:** None | **Season:** 1 April-31 March |
| **Police emergency tel. #:** 257-9111 | |
| **Medical emergency tel. #:** 911 | |

## ACTIVITIES AND FACILITIES

| | NO | YES | Proximity to Lake in Miles | | NO | YES | Proximity to Lake in Miles |
|---|---|---|---|---|---|---|---|
| **Bait and supplies** | X | | * | **Airplane runway** | X | | * |
| **Boat gas** | X | | * | **Bottled gas** | X | | * |
| **Boat ramp** | X | | * | **Café/snack bar** | X | | * |
| **Boat rental** | X | | * | **Chemical toilets** | X | | * |
| **Camping** | X | | * | **Drinking water** | X | | * |
| **Fire pits** | X | | * | **Electrical hook-up** | X | | * |
| **Fire places** | X | | * | **Flush toilets** | X | | * |
| **Firewood** | X | | * | **Grocery store** | X | | * |
| **Fishing** | | X | * | **Handicapped access** | X | | |
| **Golf** | X | | 2½ | **Ice** | X | | * |
| **Hiking** | X | | * | **Laundry** | X | | * |
| **Marina** | X | | * | **Lodgings** | X | | * |
| **Picnicking** | | X | | **Pit toilets** | X | | * |
| **Riding** | X | | * | **Playground** | X | | * |
| **Scuba diving** | X | | * | **Restaurant** | X | | * |
| **Stables** | X | | * | **Sanitary disposal** | X | | * |
| **Swimming** | X | | * | **Sewer hook-up** | X | | * |
| **Tables** | X | | * | **Shelters** | X | | * |
| **Telephone** | X | | * | **Shopping** | X | | * |
| **Tennis** | X | | * | **Showers** | X | | * |
| **Tent sites** | X | | * | **Trailer space** | X | | * |
| **Winter sports** | X | | * | **Water hook-up** | X | | * |

*Full facilities and services in Ruidoso, 2½ miles south.

**Special Rules and Regulations**
   **Fishing:** Fishing permitted 6 A.M. to 8 P.M.; license required; posted portion near outlet closed to fishing
   **Catch limit:** 6 per day; 6 in possession; see Fishing Proclamation
   **Boating:** No boats or floating devices permitted
   **Other:** Full services and accommodations in Ruidoso 2 1/2 miles south

*Mescalero Lake*

# MESCALERO LAKE

Mescalero Lake is a one-hundred acre lake on the Mescalero Apache Indian Reservation, three miles south of Ruidoso, on U.S.70. Overlooking the lake is the luxurious mountain resort *Inn of the Mountain Gods* owned and operated by the Mescalero Tribe and located in a beautiful, secluded, and spectacular setting of the scenic and heavily forested 460,000-acre Mescalero Apache Indian Reservation. This beautiful resort complex is situated at 7,200 feet in the Sacramento Mountains. The Inn offers full conveniences for guests and visitors; a restaurant, gift shop, and a variety of recreational packages of tennis, golf, horseback riding, archery, and trap and skeet shooting. The lake is open to the public and guests for fishing. There is a boat dock with a complete bait and tackle shop where canoes, row boats, and pedal boats are available for rent. Users are advised to bring their own electric trolling motors. Lake Mescalero is stocked by the Mescalero Fish

Hatchery with rainbow and cutthroat trout. No New Mexico License is required, but a Mescalero fishing permit is necessary. These permits are available in the hotel lobby or at the boat dock. Fishing hours are from sun-up to sun-down. No picnicking or camping is permitted at the lake, which is open year round.

Camping is permitted at the Eagle Creek and Silver Springs areas, where the Upper and Lower Eagle Lakes and Silver Lake are located. Permits can be obtained at the guard house near the upper lake. The Eagle Lakes are one to two acres. Silver Lake is a six-acre lake. Both campgrounds of these areas are equipped with RV hook-ups, water, electric, and sewers, and have good handicapped access. Eagle Lake is accessed from NM 532 about a mile off Ski Apache Highway. Silver Lake is located off SR 24 between Ruidoso and Cloudcroft. No boats or floating devices are permitted at these lakes.

## Directions from Albuquerque

Follow directions to Ruidoso. To review, take I-25 south from Albuquerque to San Antonio exit. Take U.S. 380 east past Carrizozo to junction of NM 37, turn south on NM 37 merging with NM 48 and follow signs to Mescalero Lake. Eagle Lakes are accessed from NM 532 about a mile off Ski Apache Highway. Silver Lake is located off NM 24 between Ruidoso and Cloudcroft.

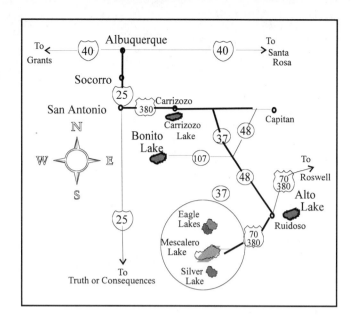

| | | |
|---|---|---|
| **Surface acres:** 100 | **Distance from Albuquerque:** 202 miles |
| **Elevation:** 7,200 | **Location:** Three miles southwest of Ruidoso |
| **Max. trailer size & fee:** No camping | **Fish species:** Rainbow, and cutthroat trout |
| **Time limit:** *No overnight | **Season:** Mid-May–Mid-September |
| **Mailing address:** Box 269, Mescalero, NM 88340 | |
| 1-800-545-9011 or (505) 257-5141 | |
| **Police emergency tel. #:** At office | **Medical emergency tel. #:** 911 |

## ACTIVITIES AND FACILITIES

| | NO | YES | Proximity to Lake in Miles | | NO | YES | Proximity to Lake in Miles |
|---|---|---|---|---|---|---|---|
| Bait and supplies | | X | | Airplane runway | X | | 3 |
| Boat gas | X | | | Bottled gas | X | | |
| Boat ramp | X | | | Café/snack bar | X | | At Inn |
| Boat rental | | X | | Chemical toilets | | X | * |
| Camping | X | | * | Drinking water | | X | * |
| Fire pits | X | | * | Electrical hook-up | X | | * |
| Fire places | X | | * | Flush toilets | | X | * |
| Firewood | X | | | Grocery store | X | | 3 |
| Fishing | | X | | Handicapped access | | X | |
| Golf | | X | | Ice | X | | * |
| Hiking | | X | | Laundry | X | | 3 |
| Marina | X | | * | Lodgings | | X | At Inn |
| Picnicking | X | | * | Pit toilets | X | | * |
| Riding | X | | | Playground | X | | * |
| Scuba diving | X | | | Restaurant | | X | At Inn |
| Stables | X | | | Sanitary disposal | X | | * |
| Swimming | X | | | Sewer hook-up | X | | * |
| Tables | X | | * | Shelters | X | | |
| Telephone | | X | At Inn | Shopping | X | | At Inn |
| Tennis | | X | | Showers | X | | |
| Tent sites | X | | * | Trailer space | X | | * |
| Winter sports | X | | * | Water hook-up | X | | * |

*Camping in Eagle Creek and Silver Springs Area.
**Special Rules and Regulations**
  **Fishing:** No state license required; Mescalero permit necessary—available at inn
  **Catch limit:** Check regulations when permit is granted
  **Boating:** Canoes, row boats, pedal boats available for rent
  **Other:** Camping at Eagle Creek and Silver Springs areas; full facilities available; no camping around Mescalero Lake nor fishing from golf course shores

# In the Vicinity of Roswell

## *Roswell*

*There are four public-use lakes in the vicinity of Roswell: Spring River Park Lake, Lake Van, Bitter Lakes, Bottomless Lakes State Park*

Roswell is located in the fertile Pecos River Valley in southeastern New Mexico at the major intersections of U.S. 285, 70, and 380. It lies at an elevation of 3,560 feet and has a population of almost 50,000. It is a modern city whose diversified and prosperous economy is based on agriculture and livestock, with more than 100,000 acres of irrigated farmland.

During the "Long Drive" of cattle along the Goodnight-Loving Trail in the 1860s, it was a favorite resting place and camp site for drovers and herdsmen. As the site became popular, other cattlemen and settlers followed; a primitive hotel, houses, and cattle pens were built, and the site grew into a town. Today, Roswell is the financial and commercial center of southeastern New Mexico, serving the towns of Vaughn and Clovis to the north, and Artesia, Carlsbad, and Hobbs to the south.

Worth seeing in Roswell is the downtown Historical District, where stately homes—some dating back to the turn of the century—are shaded by towering elms, willows, and cottonwoods. Notable of these buildings is the Chaves County Historical Museum, a two-story mansion turned museum, built in 1910. A visit to the museum provides an introduction to the history of Roswell, with many artifacts and displays of photographs depicting frontier life in the early 1900s. In 1978 the National Municipal League selected Roswell as the All-American City, and during a visit by Will Rogers in the 1930s, he referred to Roswell as "the prettiest little town in the West."

The abundance of accommodations, services, cultural activities, and restaurants in Roswell makes the town an ideal place for visitors who frequent the recreational opportunities offered at the many lakes in its vicinity.

*Spring River Park Lake*

# SPRING RIVER PARK LAKE

Spring River Park Lake is a one-acre lake located in Roswell. Fishing is reserved for children under fifteen years of age. It is a deep, attractive, quiet lake bordered with shade trees. The bank slopes gently down to the water's edge, where ducks and geese at home on the lake add charm to the idyllic setting. Facilities at the lake include picnic tables, grills, trash cans, and a modern building with flush toilets and drinking water. Also next to the lake is a zoo, an antique carousel, and a miniature railroad. No swimming, wading, or boating is permitted on the lake. It contains catfish and is stocked with winter trout. A New Mexico fishing license and trout validation stamp are required to fish the lake.

The entrance to Spring River Park Lake is off Atkinson Road. The park, lake, and zoo are open from 10:00 A.M. to 6:30 P.M.

## Directions from Albuquerque

Take I-40 to Clines Corners. Turn south on U.S. 285 to Roswell. Take U.S. 380 ( 2nd St.) The park is located three blocks off U.S. 380 on Atkinson Road. (Driving east on U.S. 380, turn left on Atkinson Rd. Driving West on U.S. 380, turn right on Atkinson and go three blocks.)

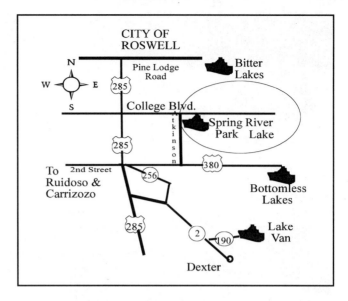

| | | |
|---|---|---|
| Surface acres: 1 | | Distance from Albuquerque: 199 miles |
| Elevation: 3,560 feet | | Location: 3 blocks off U.S. 380, on Atkinson Road |
| Max. trailer size & fee: No camping | | Fish species: Catfish, and winter trout |
| Time limit: Day use (10 A.M.-6:30 P.M.) | | Season: (For winter trout, 1 November-31 March); |
| Mailing address: Spring River Park & Zoo, | | for other species, all year; the pond is reserved |
| Box 1838, Roswell, NM 88201 (505) 624-6760 | | for children under 15 |
| Police emergency tel. #: 622-7200 | | |

## ACTIVITIES AND FACILITIES

| | NO | YES | Proximity to Lake in Miles | | NO | YES | Proximity to Lake in Miles |
|---|---|---|---|---|---|---|---|
| Bait and supplies | X | | | Airplane runway | X | | |
| Boat gas | X | | | Bottled gas | X | | |
| Boat ramp | X | | | Café/ snack bar | X | | |
| Boat rental | X | | | Chemical toilets | X | | |
| Camping | X | | | Drinking water | | X | |
| Fire pits | X | | | Electrical hook-up | X | | |
| Fire places | | X | | Flush toilets | | X | |
| Firewood | X | | | Grocery store | X | | |
| Fishing | | X | | Handicapped access | | X | |
| Golf | X | | | Ice | X | | |
| Hiking | X | | | Laundry | X | | |
| Marina | X | | | Lodgings | X | | |
| Picnicking | | X | | Pit toilets | X | | |
| Riding | X | | | Playground | | X | |
| Scuba diving | X | | | Restaurant | X | | |
| Stables | X | | | Sanitary disposal | X | | |
| Swimming | X | | | Sewer hook-up | X | | |
| Tables | | X | | Shelters | X | | |
| Telephone | X | | | Shopping | X | | |
| Tennis | X | | | Showers | X | | |
| Tent sites | X | | | Trailer space | X | | |
| Winter sports | X | | | Water hook-up | X | | |

*Roswell has complete facilities and services.

**Special Rules and Regulations**
    **Fishing:** Reserved for children under 15; trout stamp not required
    **Catch limit:** 6 fish
    **Boating:** No boating or floating devices permitted

*Lake Van*

# LAKE VAN

Lake Van is a twelve-acre lake located sixteen miles south of Roswell and a half-mile east of Dexter off NM 190. It is stocked with channel catfish, fourteen to sixteen inches long and one and a quarter pounds on average. The lake also contains bass, bluegill, and is stocked with winter trout. Paved roads allow easy access to the lake, where a host of recreational facilities greet visitors. The lake is attractively bordered by trees, and a paved road encircles the entire lake, making all sides accessible to the diversity of activities offered here. Water-skiing, in a counter-clockwise direction only, is permitted.

Facilities at Lake Van include fishing piers, boat docks, launching ramps, group shelters, sheltered picnic tables and fire grills, trash cans, and pit toilets. There are a playground, a swimming pool with a lifeguard on duty, and a developed campground with electric and water hook-ups. A small café at the edge of the lake, and conveniently located off the parking area, offers a complete breakfast, luncheon, and dinner menu. Foods are prepared "to go" or to dine inside its comfortable interior with a view of the lake. Lake Van is well worth the short drive while in the area of Roswell.

## Directions from Albuquerque

Take I-40 east to Clines Corners then south on U.S. 285 to Roswell. From Roswell take U.S. 380 east to Atkinson Rd. and turn south on NM 256 to junction of NM 2, which goes to Dexter. NM 2 swings left and crosses railroad tracks and connects with NM 190. Continue on NM 190 and look for a sign that points to Lake Van turnoff to the lake. (Good access to lake by paved roads).

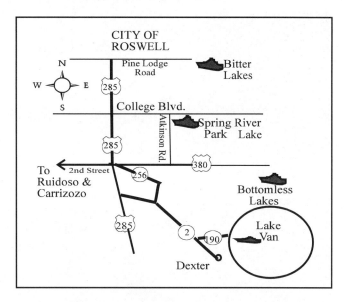

| | | | | | | |
|---|---|---|---|---|---|---|
| **Surface acres:** 12 | | | **Distance from Albuquerque:** 175 miles | | | |
| **Elevation:** 5,000 feet | | | **Location:** 17 miles south of Roswell; 1/2 mile east of Dexter | | | |
| **Max. trailer size & fee:** 40 feet; with electricity, $10.00 per day; without electricity, $6.00 per day; other fees posted | | | **Fish species:** Channel catfish, bass, bluegill, and stocked winter trout | | | |
| **Mailing address:** None | | | **Season:** All year for warm-water fish; winter trout, 1 November-31 March; boating, April-September | | | |
| **Police emergency tel. #:** 911 | | | | | | |
| **Medical emergency tel. #:** 911 | | | | | | |

## ACTIVITIES AND FACILITIES

| | NO | YES | Proximity to Lake in Miles | | NO | YES | Proximity to Lake in Miles |
|---|---|---|---|---|---|---|---|
| **Bait and supplies** | | X | | **Airplane runway** | X | | |
| **Boat gas** | | X | | **Bottled gas** | X | | |
| **Boat ramp** | | X | | **Café/snack bar** | | X | |
| **Boat rental** | X | | | **Chemical toilets** | | X | |
| **Camping** | | X | | **Drinking water** | | X | |
| **Fire pits** | | X | | **Electrical hook-up** | | X | |
| **Fire places** | | X | | **Flush toilets** | | X | |
| **Firewood** | X | | | **Grocery store** | X | | |
| **Fishing** | | X | | **Handicapped access** | | X | |
| **Golf** | X | | | **Ice** | X | | |
| **Hiking** | X | | | **Laundry** | X | | |
| **Marina** | X | | | **Lodgings** | X | | |
| **Picnicking** | | X | | **Pit toilets** | | X | |
| **Riding** | X | | | **Playground** | | X | |
| **Scuba diving** | | X | | **Restaurant** | | X | |
| **Skiing (water)** | | X | | **Trash cans** | | X | |
| **Swimming** | | X | | **Sewer hook-up** | X | | |
| **Tables** | | X | | **Shelters** | | X | |
| **Telephone** | | X | | **Shopping** | X | | |
| **Tennis** | X | | | **Showers** | X | | |
| **Tent sites** | | X | | **Trailer space** | | X | |
| **Winter sports** | X | | | **Water hook-up** | | X | |

Stores and services in Dexter, 1/2 mile.

**Special Rules and Regulations**

**Fishing:** New Mexico fishing license and trout stamp required during trout season
**Catch limit:** 6 trout; 6 in possession; stocked with channel catfish 14-16 inches long, average 1 1/4 pounds; bag limit, 2 per day (part of the Big Cat Program); for other species, consult page 344
**Boating:** Permitted April-September only
**Other:** Swimming pool, adults, $1.50; children $1.00; pool open 1 P.M.-6 P.M. Tuesday-Sunday

*Bitter Lakes*

# BITTER LAKES

Bitter Lakes is a series of lakes totaling 100 acres, located about nine miles northeast of Roswell, within the Bitter Lakes National Wildlife Refuge. These are man-made impoundments formed within the ancient river beds of the Pecos River. These impoundments receive no water from the Pecos River. They rely solely on springs that flow during high water levels. At high water levels they may store about 750 acres. The high salt content of the water does not allow for fish survival. At one time an attempt to introduce catfish in the lakes met with no success. The fish did not survive, and fishing was discontinued.

The refuge provides a resting place for migratory waterfowl. Some thirty species of waterfowl have been recorded on the refuge.

Canada geese also populate the refuge during the winter, as well as ducks of various species. Commonly seen are mallards, pintails, wigeons, and ruddy ducks. Other wildlife include quail, pheasant, cottontail and black-tailed jackrabbits, mule deer, bobcats, and badgers. Both prairie and western diamondback rattlesnakes are also residents, so caution should be taken while hiking around the ponds. Hiking and picnicking are permitted in designated areas only. Some sites overlook the lake. Facilities include shelters with tables and fire grills. Camping is not permitted, neither is boating, or swimming. The refuge is open year-round and from the headquarters, visitors may drive the self-guided road around some of the lakes or hike some of the trails.

## Directions from Albuquerque

Take I-40 to Clines Corners, then go south on U.S. 85 to Roswell. In Roswell go north on Main St. to Pine Lodge Rd. Turn right on Pine Lodge Rd. (east), then go nine miles to the Refuge. Access is good via a narrow paved road.

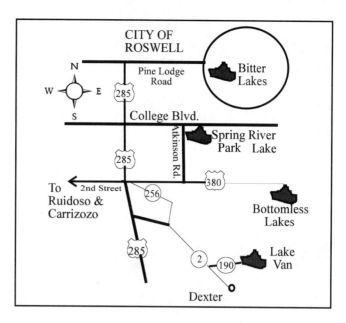

| | | |
|---|---|---|
| Surface acres: 100 | Distance from Albuquerque: 190 miles |
| Elevation: 3,500 feet | Location: 9 miles north of Roswell off U.S. 70 |
| Max. trailer size & fee: No camping | Fish species: No fish due to high salt content. |
| Time limit: Day use only | Season: All year; day use only, sunrise to sunset; |
| Mailing address: Bitter Lakes Wildlife Refuge, | great bird watching. |
| P.O. Box 7, Roswell, NM 88201 (505) 672-6755 | Police emergency tel. #: 622-7200 |
| Medical emergency tel. #: 911 | |

## ACTIVITIES AND FACILITIES

| | NO | YES | Proximity to Lake in Miles | | NO | YES | Proximity to Lake in Miles |
|---|---|---|---|---|---|---|---|
| Bait and supplies | X | | | Airplane runway | X | | |
| Boat gas | X | | | Bottled gas | X | | |
| Boat ramp | X | | | Café/snack bar | X | | |
| Boat rental | X | | | Chemical toilets | | X | |
| Camping | X | | | Drinking water | X | | |
| Fire pits | X | | | Electrical hook-up | X | | |
| Fire places | | X | | Flush toilets | X | | |
| Firewood | X | | | Grocery store | X | | |
| Fishing | X | | | Handicapped access | | X | |
| Golf | X | | | Ice | X | | |
| Hiking | | X | | Laundry | X | | |
| Marina | X | | | Lodgings | X | | |
| Picnicking | | X | | Pit toilets | | X | |
| Riding | X | | | Playground | X | | |
| Scuba diving | X | | | Restaurant | X | | |
| Stables | X | | | Sanitary disposal | X | | |
| Swimming | X | | | Sewer hook-up | X | | |
| Tables | | X | | Shelters | | X | |
| Telephone | | X | | Shopping | X | | |
| Tennis | X | | | Showers | X | | |
| Tent sites | X | | | Trailer space | X | | |
| Winter sports | X | | | Water hook-up | X | | |

## Special Rules and Regulations

**Fishing:** Closed to fishing; no longer stocked due to high salt content
**Boating:** No boating permitted
**Other:** Bow hunting for carp during special seasons permitted

# BOTTOMLESS LAKES STATE PARK

Bottomless Lakes State Park is located twelve miles east of Roswell off U.S. 380 and three miles south off NM 409. It was established in 1933, the first state park created in New Mexico. The park is situated in an attractive setting at the foot of red sandstone bluffs. Within the park are six lakes formed by underground water currents that dissolved and eroded the gypsum beds in the underlying rock formations resulting in the formation of huge subterrranean caverns. When the roofs of these caverns caved in under their own weight, sinkholes were formed and filled with water. The lakes were a favorite watering hole and camp site for drovers herding cattle along the Goodnight-Loving Trail in the 1800s. The name "Bottomless" is credited to the drovers who tried to determine the depth of the lakes with lariats tied together. Unbeknownst to them, the strong undercurrents prevented the lariats from touching bottom, giving the impression that the lakes were bottomless. The lakes range from seventeen to ninety feet in depth.

Due to the high salt content in some of the lakes, only Cottonwood, Mirror, Devil's Inkwell, and Pasture Lakes are suitable for stocking and fish survival. Not stocked is Lazy Lagoon, where visitors are cautioned to avoid walking or driving too closely, as a deceptive thin crust covers a deep mud flat. The other lake, Lea Lake (pictured above), is the deepest and largest of the lakes (fifteen acres and ninety feet deep). It is the only lake that permits swimming and is the center of most of the activity. At the lake's edge is a fully developed campground with electric and water hookups, paved and level pull-through sites with gravelled accesses, a dump station, and picnic facilities that include shelters with tables, fire grills, and trash cans. A modern building houses flush toilets and showers. This building faces the lake and swimming area; complete with a sandy beach, a boat dock, and styrofoam-padded slips for the boats available for rent. Private boats are not permitted.

## Directions from Albuquerque

Take I-40 east to Clines Corners, then go south on U.S. 285 to Roswell and junction of U.S. 285 and 380. Take U.S. 380, in Roswell (2nd St.), and go east ten miles to NM 409. Turn south on NM 409 and go six miles to Bottomless Lake State Park.

**Note:** The only stocked Bottomless Lakes are Cottonwood, Devil's Inkwell, Mirror Lake, and Pasture Lakes.

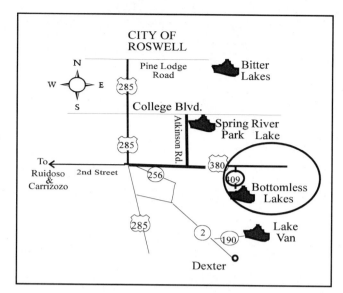

| | | |
|---|---|---|
| **Surface acres:** 15 | | **Distance from Albuquerque:** 215 miles |
| **Elevation:** 3,458 feet | | **Location:** 10 miles east of Roswell then 6 miles |
| **Max. trailer size & fee:** 40 feet; $7.00 per day no hook-up; | | south to park via NM 409 |
| $11.00 with hook-ups; $2.00, sewer; $4.00 per car, day use | | **Fish species:** Channel catfish and winter trout |
| **Time limit:** 14 days | | **Season:** Trout, 1 November-31 October; other, all year |
| **Mailing address:** Bottomless Lakes State Park, | | **Medical emergency tel. #:** 911 |
| Auto Rte. E, Box 1200, Roswell, NM 88201 | | **Police emergency tel. #:** 622-7200 |

## ACTIVITIES AND FACILITIES

| | NO | YES | Proximity to Lake in Miles | | NO | YES | Proximity to Lake in Miles |
|---|---|---|---|---|---|---|---|
| **Bait and supplies** | X | | * 16 | **Airplane runway** | X | | |
| **Boat gas** | X | | * 16 | **Bottled gas** | X | | |
| **Boat ramp** | | X | | **Café/snack bar** | | X | |
| **Boat rental** | | X | | **Chemical toilets** | | X | |
| **Camping** | | X | | **Drinking water** | | X | |
| **Fire pits** | | X | | **Electrical hook-up** | | X | |
| **Fire places** | | X | | **Flush toilets** | | X | |
| **Firewood** | | X | | **Grocery store** | | X | |
| **Fishing** | | X | | **Handicapped access** | | X | |
| **Golf** | X | | * 16 | **Ice** | | X | |
| **Hiking** | | X | | **Laundry** | X | | * 16 |
| **Marina** | X | | | **Lodgings** | X | | * 16 |
| **Picnicking** | | X | | **Pit toilets** | | X | |
| **Riding** | | X | | **Playground** | | X | |
| **Scuba diving** | | X | | **Restaurant** | | X | |
| **Stables** | | X | | **Sanitary disposal** | | X | |
| **Swimming** | | X | | **Sewer hook-up** | | X | |
| **Tables** | | X | | **Shelters** | | X | |
| **Telephone** | | X | | **Shopping** | X | | * 16 |
| **Tennis** | X | | * 16 | **Showers** | | X | |
| **Tent sites** | | X | | **Trailer space** | | X | |
| **Winter sports** | X | | | **Water hook-up** | | X | |

*Lodgings and services in Roswell, 16 miles west.
**Special Rules and Regulations**
　**Fishing:** New Mexico fishing license. (trout stamp required 1 November-31 October)
　**Catch limit:** 6 trout per day; 6 in possession; see page 344 for other species and limits
　**Boating:** No motors; no private boats permitted; rentals only
　**Other:** Lea Lake, the largest, permits paddle boating, swimming, and has a restaurant

# In the Vicinity of Carlsbad

## *Carlsbad*

*There are five lakes open to public use in the vicinity of Carlsbad: \*Bataan Lake, Lake Carlsbad, Avalon Lake (not detailed), \*Six Mile Dam Lake, \*Brantley Lake.*

    *Asterisked lakes are detailed in the following pages.*

Carlsbad is an attractive, modern, and progressive city, located at the junction of U.S. Highways 285 and 180 in southeast New Mexico. It lies at an elevation of 3,110 feet, extending gleaming and immaculate along the banks of the Pecos River in the Pecos River Valley. It is a smiling, sunny city, offering first-class hotel accommodations and social and aquatic sports facilities. It has deservedly earned a reputation for having more parks and recreational facilities than any other city in the state. These activities are centered on the Pecos River that flows through town and where an expansive network of aquatic activities and recreational facilities have been developed on both sides of the river to provide water-skiing, boating, sailing, fishing, swimming, and an abundance of picnicking and camping.

A popular attraction along the east bank of the river is President's Park, an amusement area with shops, a restaurant, and a miniature narrow-guage railroad on which rides can be taken on its Abe Lincoln Train. Rides are also offered on a small, authentic paddle-wheel boat powered by an 1858 steam engine. Another favorite attraction in President's Park is a large antique carousel. Its carved wood replicas of ostriches, horses, and pigs have been restored, and it is in operation.

Tourism shares honors with potash mining as the town's most important industries. Aside from the host of recreation attractions, there is Carlsbad National Park, one of the largest and most spectacular cave systems in the world. The Caverns draw thousands of visitors annually. The city of Carlsbad has an abundance of accommodations, stores, shopping centers, fine restaurants, and services for the visitor.

# BATAAN LAKE

Bataan Lake is a forty-two-acre lake on the Pecos River that flows through the city of Carlsbad. It contains largemouth bass and catfish and is stocked with winter trout. The Pecos River has been dammed here, forming both Bataan Lake and Lake Carlsbad Recreational Area farther up the river. Both lakes and their well-designed recreational facilities are the center of activity in Carlsbad for both residents and visitors.

Bataan is located off Greene Street. To reach the lake from the south, take U.S. 285 to Greene Street, turn right on Greene Street, cross the railroad tracks, and turn left just before Bataan Bridge. The lake is off the main street and is easily accessible. There is a modern restroom with flush toilets, picnic tables, fire grills, and drinking water. Shade trees line both banks of the lake. No camping is permitted at Bataan Lake, but camping facilities are available within walking distance farther up the river in the Lake Carlsbad Recreational Area. Lake Carlsbad and Bataan Lake are joined to form a large recreational complex with boat rentals, concessions, and docks for fishing, boating, and water sport activities.

## Directions from Albuquerque

Take I-40 to Clines Corners, then go south on U.S. 285 to Carlsbad. Turn left on Greene St., cross the railroad tracks, then turn left just before Bataan Bridge on Park Drive.

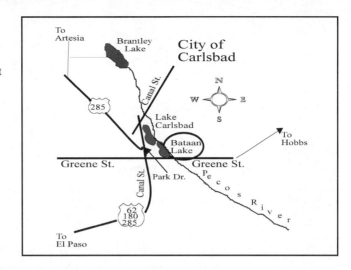

| | |
|---|---|
| Surface acres: 42 | Distance from Albuquerque: 275 miles |
| Elevation: 3,110 feet | Location: In Carlsbad on Pecos River, on Park Dr. |
| Max. trailer size & fee: *40 feet; $4.00 per night | and Greene St. |
| Time limit: *5 days | Fish species: Largemouth bass, catfish, crappie, and |
| Mailing address: Carlsbad Chamber of Commerce, | winter trout |
| Box 910, Carlsbad, NM 88221 (505) 887-2576 | Season: Trout, 1 November-31 March; other, all year |
| Police emergency tel. #: 885-3137 | Medical emergency tel. #: 911 |

## ACTIVITIES AND FACILITIES

| | NO | YES | Proximity to Lake in Miles | | NO | YES | Proximity to Lake in Miles |
|---|---|---|---|---|---|---|---|
| Bait and supplies | | X | | Airplane runway | X | | |
| Boat gas | | X | | Bottled gas | X | | |
| Boat ramp | | X | | Café/snack bar | | X | |
| Boat rental | X | | | Chemical toilets | X | | |
| Camping | | *X | * | Drinking water | | X | |
| Fire pits | X | | | Electrical hook-up | | *X | |
| Fire places | | X | | Flush toilets | | X | |
| Firewood | X | | | Grocery store | X | | |
| Fishing | | X | | Handicapped access | | X | |
| Golf | X | | | Ice | X | | |
| Hiking | | X | | Laundry | X | | |
| Marina | X | | | Lodgings | X | | |
| Picnicking | | X | | Pit toilets | X | | |
| Riding | X | | | Playground | | X | |
| Scuba diving | | X | | Restaurant | | X | |
| Skiing (water) | | X | | Sanitary disposal | | X | |
| Swimming | | X | | Sewer hook-up | X | | |
| Tables | | X | | Shelters | | X | |
| Telephone | | X | | Shopping | X | | |
| Tennis | X | | | Showers | | *X | |
| Tent sites | | *X | * | Trailer space | | *X | * |
| Winter sports | X | | | Water hook-up | | *X | * |

*Campground upriver in Carlsbad Recreational Area.

**Special Rules and Regulations**

Fishing: New Mexico fishing license required

Catch limit: 6 trout, 1 November-31 March; see Fishing Regulations page 344 for limits on others

Boating: Boating permitted; park rules are posted

Other: *Developed campgrounds located upriver in Lake Carlsbad Recreation Area

*Lake Carlsbad*

# LAKE CARLSBAD

Lake Carlsbad, also called Municipal Lake, is a ninety-five-acre lake formed by a dam across the Pecos River in Carlsbad. It is an expansive recreational complex that was created in the late 1800s by James Hagerman as a water holding tank for distribution to irrigation canals. The use of spillways maintains this portion of the Pecos River at a constant level, providing one of the finest intra-city recreational complexes in the state for family outings and acquatic activities. Facilities include large picnic areas with tables, fire grills, and a playground. There are modern restrooms with flush toilets and a bandstand for concerts. Water-skiing and swimming are permitted, and there is a bath house for changing clothes and a boat ramp with posted regulations for the aquatic activities. Lake Carlsbad Campground is a developed fee campground. The fee is $4.00 per night with a five-day limit.

The amusement area in President's Park, located across the river, contains a restaurant, gift shops, and a narrow-guage railroad. Next to the park is an eighteen-hole municipal golf course and pro-shop. The lake contains largemouth bass, crappie, and channel catfish, and is stocked with winter trout. To fish this lake, a New Mexico fishing license and trout validation stamp are required.

## Directions from Albuquerque

Take I-40 East to Clines Corners, then go south on U.S. 285 to Carlsbad. In Carlsbad turn left on Greene St., cross the railroad tracks, then turn left just before the Bataan Bridge. The lake is off Church St. on Park Dr.

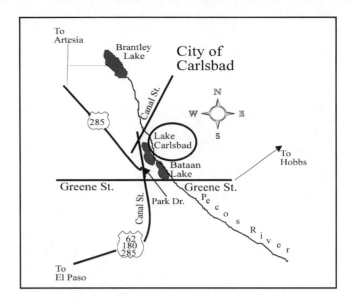

| | |
|---|---|
| Surface acres: 95 | Distance from Albuquerque: 175 miles |
| Elevation: 3,110 feet | Location: In Carlsbad at Church St. and Park Dr. |
| Max. trailer size & fee: 40 feet, $4.00 per night | Fish species: Largemouth bass, channel catfish, |
| Time limit: 5 days | crappie, and winter trout |
| Mailing address: Carlsbad Chamber of Commerce, | Season: Trout, 1 November-31 March; other, see page 344 |
| Box 910, Carlsbad, NM 88221 (505) 887-6516 | |
| Police emergency tel. #: 885-3137 | Medical emergency tel. # 911 |

## ACTIVITIES AND FACILITIES

| | NO | YES | Proximity to Lake in Miles | | NO | YES | Proximity to Lake in Miles |
|---|---|---|---|---|---|---|---|
| Bait and supplies | | X | | Airplane runway | X | | |
| Boat gas | | X | | Bottled gas | X | | |
| Boat ramp | | X | | Café/snack bar | | X | |
| Boat rental | X | | | Chemical toilets | X | | |
| Camping | | X | | Drinking water | | | |
| Fire pits | X | | | Electrical hook-up | | X | |
| Fire places | | X | | Flush toilets | | X | |
| Firewood | X | | | Grocery store | X | | |
| Fishing | | X | | Handicapped access | | X | |
| Golf | | X | | Ice | X | | |
| Hiking | | X | | Laundry | X | | |
| Marina | X | | | Lodgings | X | | |
| Picnicking | | X | | Pit toilets | X | | |
| Riding | X | | | Playground | | X | |
| Scuba diving | | X | | Restaurant | | X | |
| Skiing (water) | | X | | Sanitary disposal | | X | |
| Swimming | | X | | Sewer hook-up | X | | |
| Tables | | X | | Shelters | | X | |
| Telephone | | X | | Shopping | X | | |
| Tennis | X | | | Showers | | X | |
| Tent sites | | X | | Trailer space | | X | |
| Winter sports | X | | | Water hook-up | | X | |

Campground adjacent to lake, fully developed.
**Special Rules and Regulations**
 **Fishing:** New Mexico fishing license required; see Fishing Proclamation on page 343
 **Catch limit:** 6 fish, see Regulations (page 344) for detailed information on other species
 **Boating:** Restricted to 35 mph; muffler required; registration required
 **Other:** Restaurant in President's Park opposite bank of lake

*Six Mile Dam*

# SIX MILE DAM LAKE

Six Mile Dam Lake is a 125-acre lake on the Pecos River, six miles southeast of Carlsbad. It is populated with catfish, bass and bluegill. Six Mile Dam Lake is less frequented than other lakes in the area of Carlsbad due to its remote location and limited publicity. However, it is popular with residents who are aware of its advantage of being a low-pressured lake with good catches of bass, bluegill, and catfish from its banks and spillway. The lake has no facilities for camping or picnicking.

To reach Six Mile Dam from Carlsbad, take U.S. 285 past the junction that leads to Loving. A mile past this junction is a Phillips 66 station on the right, and on the opposite side of the highway is a tin-roofed building (Walter Sheid Trucking and Farms Inc.). Turn left on the road just past this building (Smedley Road), continue on Smedley to Grandi, and turn left on Grandi to Forni, then right on Forni. Watch for the Six Mile Dam direction sign, and turn right. This road is County Road 727, a hard-packed gravel road. Go about one and a half miles until the road dead-ends at the spillway. A New Mexico Fishing license is required to fish this lake.

## Directions from Albuquerque

Take I-40 to Clines Corners. Turn south on U.S. 285 to Carlsbad. Continue south on U.S. 285 to Smedley. (Look for the Walter Sheid Trucking and Farm Building, it is just before Smedley.) Turn left on Smedley to Grandi, turn left on Grandi to Forni, then go right on Forni, and watch for a small *Six Mile Dam* sign. Turn right at the sign on to County Road 727 to Six Mile Dam. Access is by a good gravel road that dead-ends at the spillway.

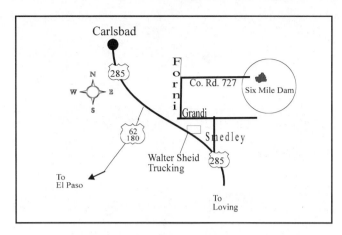

| | | |
|---|---|---|
| **Surface acres:** 125 | | **Distance from Albuquerque:** 285 miles |
| **Elevation:** 3,200 feet | | **Location:** 6 miles southeast of Carlsbad, off County |
| **Max. trailer size & fee:** Primitive area; no restictions | | Road 727 |
| or facilities | | **Fish species:** Bass, catfish, and bluegill |
| **Time limit:** None | | **Season:** All year |
| **Mailing address:** None | | |
| **Police emergency tel. #:** 885-3137 | | |
| **Medical emergency tel. #:** 911 | | |

## ACTIVITIES AND FACILITIES

| | NO | YES | Proximity to Lake in Miles | | NO | YES | Proximity to Lake in Miles |
|---|---|---|---|---|---|---|---|
| Bait and supplies | X | | | Airplane runway | X | | |
| Boat gas | X | | | Bottled gas | X | | |
| Boat ramp | X | | | Café/snack bar | X | | |
| Boat rental | X | | | Chemical toilets | X | | |
| Camping | X | | | Drinking water | X | | |
| Fire pits | X | | | Electrical hook-up | X | | |
| Fire places | X | | | Flush toilets | X | | |
| Firewood | X | | | Grocery store | X | | |
| Fishing | | X | | Handicapped access | X | | |
| Golf | X | | | Ice | X | | |
| Hiking | X | | | Laundry | X | | |
| Marina | X | | | Lodgings | X | | |
| Picnicking | X | | | Pit toilets | X | | |
| Riding | X | | | Playground | X | | |
| Scuba diving | X | | | Restaurant | X | | |
| Stables | X | | | Sanitary disposal | X | | |
| Swimming | X | | | Sewer hook-up | X | | |
| Tables | X | | | Shelters | X | | |
| Telephone | X | | | Shopping | X | | |
| Tennis | X | | | Showers | X | | |
| Tent sites | X | | | Trailer space | X | | |
| Winter sports | X | | | Water hook-up | X | | |

Isolated area, no facilities.
**Special Rules and Regulations**
   **Fishing:** New Mexico fishing license required
   **Catch limit:** See Fishing Regulations, page 344, for warm-water fish bag limits
   **Boating:** No boating
   **Other:** No facilities; Six Mile Dam is in a remote area

*Brantley Lake*

# BRANTLEY LAKE

Brantley Lake State Park, the newest of the New Mexico state parks, is located about fifteen miles north of Carlsbad and twenty-five miles south of Artesia, off U.S. Highway 285. If heading north from Carlsbad on U.S. 285, turn east at the direction sign to Brantley Lake and go about four and a half miles on a good paved road to the state park. At the entrance to the east-side parking area, there is a visitors center that has restrooms, a pay telephone, and a reception and information desk.

The park has full facilities for camping, boating, and recreation. The lake contains largemouth bass, white bass, walleye pike, catfish, crappie, and pan fish. Black bass minimum keeper size is 14 inches. There are two paved boat ramps with paved parking areas and docks: one at the Seven Rivers day-use area on the west side, and one on the east side.

The Seven Rivers Area entrance is about a mile north of the east entrance. This portion of the park is visible from U.S. 285, and its facilities include sheltered sites with tables and grills, a group shelter, and restroom with flush toilets. Other facilities include a volleyball court, horseshoe pits, and a fully developed campground. Limestone Campground on the east side of the lake has forty-nine sites with water and electric hook-ups, and paved pads. Two of them are pull-throughs. The sites are easily accessed by a loop road centered by a comfort station with flush toilets, hot showers, and a playground. Sites for the handicapped are also available. The lake permits boating and all forms of water sports. New Mexico state park fees apply.

## Directions from Albuquerque

Take I-40 East to Clines Corners, then U.S. 285 South to Artesia. Continue about twenty-five miles south to the Brantley Lake State Park sign. Turn east at the sign and go four and a half miles to the park. Access is by good roads all the way to lake.

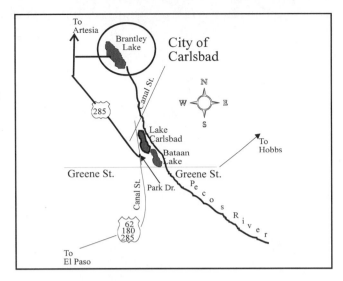

| | |
|---|---|
| **Surface acres:** 3,072 | **Distance from Albuquerque:** 265 miles |
| **Elevation:** 3,275 feet | **Location:** 25 miles south of Artesia; 15 miles |
| **Max. trailer size & fee:** 40 feet; see state park fees | north of Carlsbad off U.S. 285 |
| and regulations, page 342 | **Fish species:** Largemouth bass, walleye pike, |
| **Time limit:** 14 days | white bass, catfish, crappie, and pan fish |
| **Mailing address:** Brantley Lake State Park, | **Season:** All year |
| Box 2288, Carlsbad, NM 88221 (505) 457-2384 | **Police emergency tel. #:** 911 |

## ACTIVITIES AND FACILITIES

| | NO | YES | Proximity to Lake in Miles | | NO | YES | Proximity to Lake in Miles |
|---|---|---|---|---|---|---|---|
| Bait and supplies | X | | *15 | Airplane runway | X | | *15 |
| Boat gas | X | | *15 | Bottled gas | X | | *15 |
| Boat ramp | | X | | Café/snack bar | X | | *15 |
| Boat rental | X | | | Chemical toilets | | X | |
| Camping | | X | | Drinking water | | X | |
| Fire pits | | X | | Electrical hook-up | | X | |
| Fire places | | X | | Flush toilets | | X | |
| Firewood | X | | | Grocery store | X | | *15 |
| Fishing | | X | | Handicapped access | | X | |
| Golf | X | | *15 | Ice | | | |
| Hiking | | X | | Laundry | X | | *15 |
| Marina | X | | | Lodgings | X | | *15 |
| Picnicking | | X | | Pit toilets | X | | *15 |
| Riding | X | | | Playground | | X | |
| Scuba diving | | X | | Restaurant | X | | *15 |
| Skiiing (water) | | X | | Sanitary disposal | | X | |
| Swimming | | X | | Sewer hook-up | X | | *15 |
| Tables | | X | | Shelters | | X | |
| Telephone | | X | | Shopping | X | | 815 |
| Tennis | X | | *15 | Showers | | X | |
| Tent sites | | X | | Trailer space | | X | |
| Winter sports | X | | | Water hook-up | | X | |

*Full services, stores and accommodations in Carlsbad, 15 miles.
**Special Rules and Regulations**
    **Fishing:** New Mexico license required; see Fishing Regulations, page 343
    **Catch limit:** Black bass, minimum keeper size, 14 inches; see page 344 for other species limits
    **Boating:** Not restricted to size or power; boating regulations apply; see page 344
    **Other:** Fully developed campground in park; see campground fees, page 342

# In the Vicinity of Lovington

## *Lovington*

*There is one lake in the vicinity of Lovington: Chaparral Lake*

Lovington is the county seat of Lea County. It is located twenty-two miles northwest of Hobbs, lying at an elevation of 3,974 feet above sea level, with a population of over 9,300. Lovington is a friendly, attractive city, named after Robert F. Love who homesteaded the land in 1903. In 1908, the first store, "Jim B. Love Grocery Store," was built by J.B. Love, brother of the founder. The store also housed the first post office. Ranching, irrigated farming, and cattle and sheep raising were the original industries in Lovington. In the 1930s, oil strikes changed Lovington's future significantly, and in 1950 when the Denton Pool was discovered just nine miles northeast of Lovington it set Lovington on a steady growth in population that has continued to the present day.

Lovington is now a progressive city boasting five elementary schools, one middle school, one high school, a junior and a four-year fully accredited college, three banks, a hospital, motels, restaurants, stores, and service stations. Its recreational activities include a golf course, ten tennis courts, an eighty-acre park containing ten-acre Chaparral Lake and facilities for fishing. The park is also equipped with a playground, volleyball and basketball courts, and a softball field.

*Chaparral Lake*

# CHAPARRAL LAKE

Chaparral Lake is a ten-acre lake on the east side of Lovington, lying within a beautiful eighty-acre park. If you have a free day while in Lovington and like peace and relaxation in a quiet setting, Chaparral Lake will meet all your needs. It is charmingly laid out, divided into two segments by a foot bridge that leads to a grassy knoll that extends to the opposite side of the lake. On one side of the lake is a lagoon with an animated population of ducks. There is a large parking area close to all the facilities. The lake is bordered with trees that provide shade to the tables, benches, and fire grills set on manicured grass that slopes down to the lake's edge.

A well-maintained modern building of slump rock construction houses restrooms with flush toilets and water. Other facilities in the park include a badminton court with nets, areas equipped for softball and basketball, and a playground with slides and swings. The lake contains bass, catfish, and bluegill, and is stocked with winter trout. A New Mexico fishing license and trout validation stamp are required during the period between 1 November and 31 March. No boats or floating devices are permitted. Neither does the lake permit trotlines or throwlines. Other restrictions are posted in the park.

## Directions from Albuquerque

Take I-40 to Clines Corners. Go south on U.S. 285 to Roswell, then west on U.S. 380 to Tatum. Then go south on NM 206 to Lovington and west on U.S. 82. Turn left on NM 83 then right on U.S. 82 West to truck by-pass and follow signs to Chaparral Recreation Park.

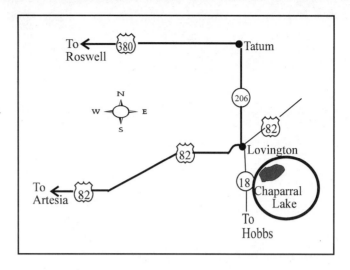

| | |
|---|---|
| **Surface acres:** 10 | **Distance from Albuquerque:** 293 miles |
| **Elevation:** 3,900 feet | **Location:** In Lovington |
| **Max. trailer size & fee:** No camping | |
| **Time limit:** No camping | **Fish species:** Bass, bluegill, catfish, and winter trout |
| **Mailing address:** Lovington Chamber of Commerce, | **Season:** *For winter trout, 1 November-31 March; |
| P.O. Box 1347, Lovington, NM 88260 | all year for other species |
| **Medical emergency tel. #:** 911 | **Police emergency tel. #:** 396-2811 |

## ACTIVITIES AND FACILITIES

| | NO | YES | Proximity to Lake in Miles | | NO | YES | Proximity to Lake in Miles |
|---|---|---|---|---|---|---|---|
| Bait and supplies | X | | * | Airplane runway | X | | |
| Boat gas | X | | | Bottled gas | X | | |
| Boat ramp | X | | | Café/snack bar | X | | * |
| Boat rental | X | | | Chemical toilets | X | | |
| Camping | X | | | Drinking water | | X | |
| Fire pits | X | | | Electrical hook-up | X | | |
| Fire places | | X | | Flush toilets | | X | |
| Firewood | X | | | Grocery store | X | | * |
| Fishing | | X | | Handicapped access | | X | |
| Golf | X | | * | Ice | X | | * |
| Hiking | X | | | Laundry | X | | * |
| Marina | X | | | Lodgings | X | | * |
| Picnicking | | X | | Pit toilets | X | | |
| Riding | X | | | Playground | | X | |
| Scuba diving | X | | | Restaurant | X | | * |
| Stables | X | | | Trash cans | | X | |
| Swimming | X | | | Sewer hook-up | X | | |
| Tables | | X | | Shelters | | X | |
| Telephone | X | | | Shopping | X | | * |
| Tennis | | X | | Showers | X | | |
| Tent sites | X | | | Trailer space | X | | |
| Winter sports | X | | | Water hook-up | X | | |

*Full services in Lovington.

**Special Rules and Regulations**

**Fishing:** New Mexico fishing license and trout validation stamp required

**Catch limit:** 6 trout; 6 in possession; no minnows for bait permitted; see page 343

**Boating:** No boats or floating devices permitted

# In the Vicinity of Hobbs

## *Hobbs*

*There are three lakes in the vicinity of Hobbs: Green Meadow Lake, Harry McAdams State Park, Maddox Lake*

Hobbs is located twenty-two miles south of Lovington in the flat plains and prairie lands of the southeastern corner of Lea County, New Mexico. It lies at an elevation of 3,625 feet above sea level. It is a progressive and growing city of almost 32,000, the largest of the five towns of Lea County that were originally settled as ranching and farming communities.

The early history of this area tells of Comanche Indians who roamed the area and of the conquistadors in search of gold, bringing with them the horse and the sheep. Then in the 1860s and 1870s came the Texas Longhorn cattle drives, bringing in settlers and homesteaders. In 1907, James Hobbs, a Texan, became the first homesteader. After he built his primitive home on the site where Hobbs now stands, a school, a store, and a post office followed. The town grew slowly until everything changed in 1928, when the Midwest Oil Company struck oil in one of the richest oil pools in the Southwest. A tent city

sprang up, and by 1930 the population of tiny Hobbs swelled to over 12,000. The town flourished, and oil strikes occurring in other regions of Lea County made the county the largest oil producer in the United States.

After World War II began, Hobbs became the site for an Army Air Corps training base for pilots to fly the B-17 and B-24 bombers. In 1948, the base was purchased by the city and renamed Hobbs Industrial Center and Recreational Park. It is now home to the National Headquarters of the Soaring Society of America and to the Confederate Air Force Museum, which houses authentic World War II planes and memorabilia. Hobbs is now the commercial center for the southeastern corner of New Mexico and West Texas.

Located just a short distance from the city limits of Hobbs is Harry McAdams State Park, one of the most attractive and well maintained state parks of New Mexico. It is located on the site of the old Hobbs Airfield and was created in the early 1980s, to provide recreational resources in addition to the city's park system and the state Conservation Division's fishing lakes. This park is detailed on pages 262 and 263. Hobbs has an abundance of lodging accommodations, grocery stores, shopping centers, restaurants, gas stations, and two eighteen-hole golf courses.

*Green Meadow Lake*

# GREEN MEADOW LAKE

Green Meadow Lake is a quiet, pretty fourteen acre lake located three miles north of Hobbs, off NM 18. It is owned and stocked with winter trout by the New Mexico Department of Game and Fish. This charming little lake also contains bluegill, catfish, and largemouth bass. It is part of the Big Cat Program, a program of stocking fourteen- to sixteen-inch channel catfish to provide enhanced opportunity for anglers. At this writing, Green Meadow Lake is one of seven lakes in New Mexico that is part of this program, which was started in 1993 by the New Mexico Department of Game and Fish.

To reach Green Meadow Lake from Hobbs, proceed on NM 18 north about three miles and watch for a Honda dealer on the right. Turn right on Lakeview Drive (the first street before the Honda dealer), and continue for about one block, then make a right turn to the lake.

There is a large parking area at the lake with some facilities and a walk-through gate to the lake. The lake has limited facilities but there are two vault toilets, some trash cans, and a fishing platform. Two peninsulas were created on the lake to allow fishing access. Green Meadow Lake is a popular lake with residents and visitors to the area, who can spend a quiet day fishing or picnicking. A large population of ducks on Green Meadow Lake enhances its charm and tranquility.

## Directions from Albuquerque

Take I-40 to Clines Corners. Turn south on U.S. 285. Go to junction of U.S. 380 at Roswell, then take U.S. 380 East to Tatum. Then go south on NM 206 to Lovington and connect with NM 18 to Hobbs. Just before reaching the city limits of Hobbs, look for a Honda dealer on the left side of the highway. Take the first street past the Honda dealer (Lakeview Dr.). Go one block on Lakeview Dr., and turn right to the lake.

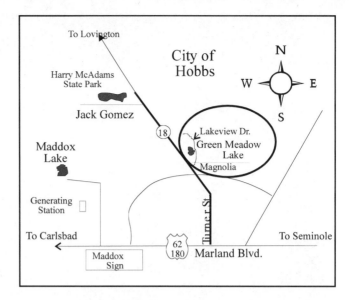

| | | |
|---|---|---|
| Surface acres: 14 | Distance from Albuquerque: 312 miles | |
| Elevation: 3,600 feet | Location: 3 miles north of Hobbs, off NM 18 | |
| Max. trailer size & fee: *Camping on roadside parking area next to lake; limited facilities | Fish species: Catfish, largemouth bass, bluegill, and winter trout | |
| Mailing address: Hobbs Chamber of Commerce, 400 N. Marland, Hobbs, NM 88240 (505) 397-320 | Season: Trout, 1 November-31 March; other, all year; see page 344 for warm-water fish bag limits | |
| Police emergency tel. #: 392-5588 | Medical emergency tel. #: 911 | |

## ACTIVITIES AND FACILITIES

| | NO | YES | Proximity to Lake in Miles | | NO | YES | Proximity to Lake in Miles |
|---|---|---|---|---|---|---|---|
| Bait and supplies | X | | | Airplane runway | X | | |
| Boat gas | X | | | Bottled gas | X | | |
| Boat ramp | | X | | Café/snack bar | X | | |
| Boat rental | X | | | Chemical toilets | X | | |
| Camping | | *X | | Drinking water | X | | |
| Fire pits | X | | | Electrical hook-up | X | | |
| Fire places | X | | | Flush toilets | X | | |
| Firewood | X | | | Grocery store | X | | |
| Fishing | | X | | Handicapped access | | X | |
| Golf | X | | | Ice | X | | |
| Hiking | X | | | Laundry | X | | |
| Marina | X | | | Lodgings | X | | |
| Picnicking | | X | | Pit toilets | | X | |
| Riding | X | | | Playground | X | | |
| Scuba diving | X | | | Restaurant | X | | |
| Stables | X | | | Sanitary disposal | | X | |
| Swimming | X | | | Sewer hook-up | X | | |
| Tables | X | | | Shelters | X | | |
| Telephone | X | | | Shopping | X | | |
| Tennis | X | | | Showers | X | | |
| Tent sites | X | | | Trailer space | | *X | |
| Winter sports | X | | | Water hook-up | X | | |

*Roadside camping with limited facilities.

**Special Rules and Regulations**

    **Fishing:** New Mexico fishing license required, and trout stamp for winter trout

    **Catch limit:** 6 trout; catfish, 2 per day; see regulations page 344 for warm water species limits

    **Boating:** Boats restricted to oars or electric motors

    **Other:** Camping available at roadside parking area at lake entrance

*Harry McAdams State Park*

# HARRY McADAMS STATE PARK

Harry McAdams State Park is a day-use park located four miles northwest of Hobbs via NM 18. It is one of the most attractive and well maintained of the New Mexico state parks. Its forty acres is beautifully landscaped and contains two fishing ponds for children under twelve years of age, seniors over sixty-five, and the handicapped. The ponds are stocked with winter trout on 1 November and every two weeks thereafter through March. A New Mexico fishing license and trout validation stamp are required to fish the ponds. The park closes at 8 P.M. A camping area is adjacent to, and is part of, the park. Throughout the park are tables, shelters, fire grills, and modern restrooms with flush toilets. The park is open year round.

The park site is the old Hobbs Airfield, where World War II pilots received their combat training in B-17 and B-24 bombers used in the European/African/Middle East theaters of operation. There is a museum at the visitors and information center that provides a history of the park and of Harry McAdams for whom the park is named. Harry McAdams was a member of the crew manning "Dirty Gertie" when the aircraft was shot down over the Straits of Messina in 1943. Following his military career in 1946, he took residence in Hobbs. In 1970, he was nominated and elected State Senator. In 1977, he spearheaded a drive in the legislature to develop Lea County State Park. At the time of its dedication in June of 1982, Harry McAdams was re-elected to the State Senate.

Aside from the many recreational facilities at the park, there is a regulation eighteen-hole golf course for public use, located opposite the park and within walking distance of the ponds.

## Directions from Hobbs

Go north on NM 18, and turn left (west) on Jack Gomez Boulevard to Harry McAdams State Park. Access is good via a paved road.

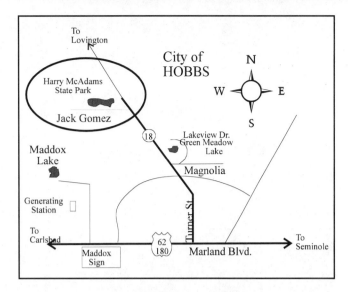

**Surface acres:** 1

**Elevation:** 3,700 feet

**Max. trailer size & fee:** 40 feet; $7.00 per day; $4.00, electricity

**Time limit:** 14 days

**Mailing address:** NM State Parks, Box 1147, Santa Fe, NM 87504 (505) 392-5845

**Police emergency tel. #:** 392-5588

**Distance from Albuquerque:** 311 miles

**Location:** 4 miles north of Hobbs via NM 18

**Fish species:** Winter trout, stocked every two weeks during season

**Season:** Winter trout, 1 November-31 March

### ACTIVITIES AND FACILITIES

| | NO | YES | Proximity to Lake in Miles | | NO | YES | Proximity to Lake in Miles |
|---|---|---|---|---|---|---|---|
| Bait and supplies | X | | *4 | Airplane runway | X | | * |
| Boat gas | X | | | Bottled gas | X | | * |
| Boat ramp | X | | | Café/snack bar | X | | * |
| Boat rental | X | | | Chemical toilets | X | | |
| Camping | | X | | Drinking water | | X | |
| Fire pits | X | | | Electrical hook-up | | X | |
| Fire places | | X | | Flush toilets | | X | |
| Firewood | X | | | Grocery store | X | | * |
| Fishing | | X | | Handicapped access | | X | |
| Golf | | X | | Ice | X | | * |
| Hiking | | X | | Laundry | X | | * |
| Marina | X | | | Lodgings | X | | * |
| Picnicking | | X | | Pit toilets | X | | |
| Riding | X | | | Playground | | X | |
| Scuba diving | X | | | Restaurant | X | | * |
| Stables | X | | | Sanitary disposal | | X | |
| Swimming | X | | | Sewer hook-up | | X | |
| Tables | | X | | Shelters | | X | |
| Telephone | | X | | Shopping | X | | * |
| Tennis | X | | | Showers | | X | |
| Tent sites | | X | | Trailer space | | X | |
| Winter sports | X | | | Water hook-up | | X | |

*Full facilities in Hobbs, four miles south.

**Special Rules and Regulations**

    **Fishing:** New Mexico fishing license required; fishing reserved for children under 12 and seniors 65+

    **Catch limit:** 6 trout per day; 6 in possession

    **Boating:** No boats or floating devices permitted

    **Other:** Developed campgounds in designated area adjacent to park

*Maddox Lake*

# MADDOX LAKE

Maddox Lake is a twenty-acre warm-water fishing lake located ten miles west of Hobbs behind the Southwest Public Service Electric Generating Station. It is a dumping pond for the cooling waters that come from the generating plant. The access to Maddox Lake is by way of a good gravel road to a locked entrance gate to the lake. A sign at the gate bars vehicles from entry, but there is a walk-through passage on each side of the gate that allows walk-in entry to the lake located about 400 yards in. At the lake, a posted sign contains the lake's regulations; it reads: *"No guns, shooting or hunting. Use hours, 1/2 hour before sunrise, and 1/2 hour after sunset. No camping, no swimming, no open fires. No gas powered motors, no vehicles."*

The only facilities provided are a pit toilet and a trash can located near the sign, where the lake is almost obscured by heavy growths of cattails and reeds that line the bank. In my opinion, the trek to this lake is for only those who want to get away from it all. The more attractive and conveniently located lakes are Green Meadow Lake and the ponds in Harry McAdams State Park. Maddox Lake contains bass and channel catfish. Winter trout cannot survive in its warm waters.

## Directions from Hobbs

Go eight miles west on U.S. 180, and turn at the direction sign to Maddox Lake, located about half a mile from the Generating Station, ten miles west of Hobbs off U.S. Highway 180.

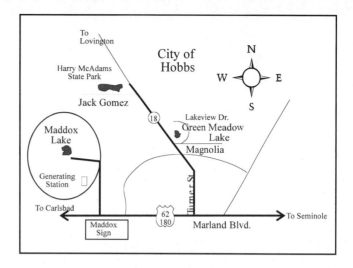

| | |
|---|---|
| **Surface acres:** 20 | **Distance from Albuquerque:** 305 miles |
| **Elevation:** 4,000 feet | **Location:** 10 miles west of Hobbs off U.S. 180 |
| **Max. trailer size & fee:** No camping, no fee | **Fish species:** Channel catfish, and bass |
| **Time limit:** Day use only | **Season:** All year; open 1/2 hour before sunrise |
| **Mailing address:** NM Dept. of Game and Fish, | until 1/2 hour after sunset |
| Box 25112, Santa Fe, NM, 87504  (505) 827-7882 | |
| **Police emergency tel. #:** 392-5588 | |

## ACTIVITIES AND FACILITIES

| | NO | YES | Proximity to Lake in Miles | | NO | YES | Proximity to Lake in Miles |
|---|---|---|---|---|---|---|---|
| Bait and supplies | X | | | Airplane runway | X | | |
| Boat gas | X | | | Bottled gas | X | | |
| Boat ramp | X | | | Café/ snack bar | X | | |
| Boat rental | X | | | Chemical toilets | X | | |
| Camping | X | | | Drinking water | X | | |
| Fire pits | X | | | Electrical hook-up | X | | |
| Fire places | X | | | Flush toilets | X | | |
| Firewood | X | | | Grocery store | X | | |
| Fishing | | X | | Handicapped access | X | | |
| Golf | X | | | Ice | X | | |
| Hiking | X | | | Laundry | X | | |
| Marina | X | | | Lodgings | X | | |
| Picnicking | X | | * | Pit toilets | | X | |
| Riding | X | | | Playground | X | | |
| Scuba diving | X | | | Restaurant | X | | |
| Stables | X | | | Sanitary disposal | X | | |
| Swimming | X | | | Sewer hook-up | X | | |
| Tables | X | | | Shelters | X | | |
| Telephone | X | | | Shopping | X | | |
| Tennis | X | | | Showers | X | | |
| Tent sites | X | | | Trailer space | X | | |
| Winter sports | X | | | Water hook-up | X | | |

*No picnic or camping facilities.

**Special Rules and Regulations**

    **Fishing:** New Mexico fishing license required; warm-water fish; no trout
    **Catch limit:** See Fishing Regulations, page 344, for warm-water species
    **Boating:** Boats powered by electric motors or oars only; a long walk to lake
    **Other:** No camping or picnicking facilities available

# In the Vicinity of Eunice

## *Eunice*

*There is one lake in the vicinity of Eunice: Eunice Lake*

Eunice is one of the five towns in Lea County in the southeastern corner of New Mexico that shares the wealth of the oil country in which they are located. Scores of working pumpjacks dot the landscape. Eunice was established in 1908, when John Carson homesteaded 320 acres. His application for a post office was approved after compliance with the rule that a name should be given the town and mail delivery performed without charge for three months. The town was named Eunice after his daughter.

Eunice is known for its weekly musical gatherings started by the Carson family, featuring Eunice at the piano. People come from miles around to the fiddling contest held annually during August. As in Lovington, one of the biggest celebrations in Eunice is the Fourth of July when everyone turns out to watch the parade and share barbecues. The huge natatorium is a popular place for both young and old in Eunice to swim year round. Like the other five cities in Lea County, Eunice enjoys 360 days of sunshine, with warm summers and mild winters. One of the more popular recreational spots for visitors and residents is Eunice Lake just three miles south, in Stephens Recreation Park. Eunice has overnight accommodations, stores, and services for visitors.

*Eunice Lake*

# EUNICE LAKE

Eunice Lake is a four-acre lake located three miles west of Eunice. It is reached by NM 8, off U.S. 180, west of Hobbs. NM 8 goes directly south to Eunice. About three miles before reaching Eunice on NM 8, there is a rest stop equipped with tables and shelters. Turn east on the road adjacent to this rest area. A sign identifies the area as Stephens Recreation Area. The road is a good, hard-packed gravel road that goes to the lake and its large gravelled parking area. A road from the parking area winds around the tree-shaded perimeter of this attractive lake. The recreational facilities at the lake include tables, shelters, trash cans, drinking water, and a unisex restroom with a flush toilet and sink. In an area close to the lake there is a basketball court, a softball field, a playground, and a campground with a three-day stay limit. It offers sites for trailers, campers, recreational vehicles, and tents.

A New Mexico fishing license is required to fish at Eunice Lake, which is stocked with winter trout and channel catfish, and contains a bass and bluegill population. Eunice Lake is one of the seven lakes in the State of New Mexico that is part of the Big Cat Program (see page 344, Warm-Water Fish Regulations for details of this program). The lake does not permit swimming, wading, boats, or floating devices.

## Directions from Lovington

Take NM 18 south to Hobbs, then take U.S. 180, west to NM 8. Go south on NM 8 toward Eunice. Three miles west of Eunice take the road past the rest stop and entrance to Stephens Recreation Park. Follow the gravel road to the lake.

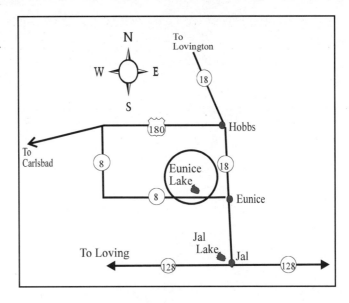

| | | |
|---|---|---|
| Surface acres: 4 | | Distance from Albuquerque: 329 miles |
| Elevation: 3,569 feet | | Location: 3 miles west of Eunice |
| Max. trailer size & fee: 40 feet | | |
| Time limit: 3 days | | Fish species: Bass, catfish, bluegill, and winter |
| Mailing address: None | | trout |
| Police emergency tel. #: 911 | | Season: Winter trout, 1 November-31 March; |
| Medical emergency tel. #: 911 | | for warm-water species, all year |

## ACTIVITIES AND FACILITIES

| | NO | YES | Proximity to Lake in Miles | | NO | YES | Proximity to Lake in Miles |
|---|---|---|---|---|---|---|---|
| Bait and supplies | X | | *3 | Airplane runway | X | | |
| Boat gas | X | | | Bottled gas | X | | *3 |
| Boat ramp | X | | | Café/snack bar | X | | *3 |
| Boat rental | X | | | Chemical toilets | X | | |
| Camping | | X | | Drinking water | | X | |
| Fire pits | | X | | Electrical hook-up | X | | |
| Fire places | | X | | Flush toilets | | X | |
| Firewood | X | | | Grocery store | X | | *3 |
| Fishing | | X | | Handicapped access | | X | |
| Golf | X | | | Ice | X | | *3 |
| Hiking | X | | | Laundry | X | | *3 |
| Marina | X | | | Lodgings | X | | *3 |
| Picnicking | | X | | Pit toilets | | X | |
| Riding | X | | | Playground | | X | |
| Scuba diving | X | | | Restaurant | X | | *3 |
| Stables | X | | | Sanitary disposal | X | | *3 |
| Swimming | X | | | Sewer hook-up | X | | |
| Tables | | X | | Shelters | | X | |
| Telephone | X | | *3 | Shopping | X | | *3 |
| Tennis | X | | | Showers | X | | |
| Tent sites | | X | | Trailer space | | X | |
| Winter sports | X | | | Water hook-up | X | | |

*Stores and services in Eunice, 3 miles.

**Special Rules and Regulations**

**Fishing:** New Mexico fishing license and trout validation stamp required

**Catch limit:** 6 trout daily; 6 in possession; catfish 2 per day; see page 344 for other species

**Boating:** No boats or floating devices permitted

**Other:** Camping facilities with a 3-day stay limit located near the lake

# In the Vicinity of Jal

## *Jal*

*There is one lake in the vicinity of Jal: Jal Lake*

Jal is a small farming and oil-producing town in the southeastern corner of Lea County, New Mexico, just seven miles west and nine miles north of the Texas border. It is located at the intersection of two state highways: NM 18 and NM 128.

Jal had its beginnings in the late 1880s when the Cowden Land and Cattle Co. purchased a huge herd of cattle from the John A. Lynch Ranch in East Texas. They set up their headquarters at Monument Draw, the only water hole in the area, located six miles east of the present site of Jal. The cattle bore the "JAL" brand (initials of the John A. Lynch Ranch). It became one of the largest ranches in southeastern New Mexico, and this area, upon which thousands of head of cattle roamed, was referred to by settlers and cowboys as Jal, after the JAL brand. After a nearby town developed and a post office was established in 1910, the town was named Jal. The distinctive JAL brand stands out all over town. It is seen on restaurant menus, building signs, and business logos. Its most unusual evidence is in the city's main park that contains a man-made ten-acre lake designed and built in the configuration of the JAL brand. The brand is the letter "A" without the cross-bar. It was a large brand that seared the animal from shoulder to hip. The bar in the "A" was omitted to avoid injury to the animal, but it did include extensions to the legs of the "A" to form the initials "JAL."

Along with ranching and farming, Jal owes its prosperity to the discovery of oil and gas in the mid-1920s. Although it is a small town with a population of about 2,800 it offers a broad range of accommodations, services, and recreational facilities for tourists and residents. These include the city park with its ten-acre stocked lake, tennis courts, softball fields, and free camping spaces. The town also boasts an airport with a 6,285 feet runway that is lighted and certified.

*Jal Lake*

# JAL LAKE

Jal Lake is a ten-acre man-made lake within Jal Lake Park. It is located within the city, just a few blocks south of the Chamber of Commerce building. Jal Lake and its surrounding park were constructed in 1973. The lake was designed and built in the shape of the JAL brand, a letter "A" with extensions on each leg to form the initials of John A. Lynch, a Texas rancher, who in the 1880s sold a huge herd of cattle to the Cowden Land and Cattle Co. based in Monument Draw, six miles east of the present site of Jal.

An island, attractively landscaped in shade trees and grass, forms the bar inside the letter "A" dividing the lake into two sections. A footbridge to the island allows access to both portions of the lake. Both sections of the lake have a playground and restrooms with flush toilets, a sink, and water. Other facilities include shelters with tables and fire grills, trash cans, a basketball court, and a lighted

tennis courts with nets. Adjacent to the tennis courts is a no-fee camping area with limited spaces for RVs and trailers. The facilities are easily accessed by gravel roads that go directly to the lake, where a short but adequate paved ramp allows for boat launching. A docking facility is provided next to the ramp. The lake is limited to hand-powered boats. On the east side of the lake there is a large group shelter with covered, smoker-type grills and trash cans.

Jal Lake is stocked by the New Mexico Game and Fish Department with winter trout, largemouth bass, and channel catfish. It is one of the seven lakes in New Mexico included in the Big Cat Program (see page 344, Warm-Water Regulations, for details of this program). Jal Lake also contains bluegill. Jal Lake is popular with Jal residents, visitors, and the many geese, ducks, and transient waterfowl that swim its waters.

## Directions from Albuquerque

Take I-40 to Clines Corners, then go south on U.S. 285 to Roswell and connect with U.S. 380 East to Tatum. Turn south on NM 206 to Lovington, then continue south on NM 18 to Jal. A couple of blocks past the Jal Chamber of Commerce is a direction sign to Jal Lake Park. Turn west across the railroad tracks. Go about one block to the lake and the park.

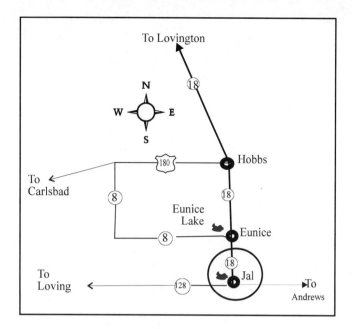

| | | |
|---|---|---|
| **Surface acres:** 10 | | **Distance from Albuquerque:** 350 miles |
| **Elevation:** 3,615 feet | | **Location:** In Jal, 7 miles west of Texas border |
| **Max. trailer size & fee:** Day use, unless engaged in camping | | **Fish species:** Trout |
| | | **Season:** All year, 6 A.M.-6 P.M.; trout season, |
| **Mailing address:** Box 1205, Jal, NM 88252 | | 1 November-31 March |
| **Police emergency tel. #:** 911 | | **Medical emergency tel. #:** 911 |

## ACTIVITIES AND FACILITIES

| | NO | YES | Proximity to Lake in Miles | | NO | YES | Proximity to Lake in Miles |
|---|---|---|---|---|---|---|---|
| Bait and supplies | X | | | Airplane runway | X | | |
| Boat gas | X | | | Bottled gas | X | | |
| Boat ramp | | X | | Café/snack bar | X | | |
| Boat rental | X | | | Chemical toilets | X | | |
| Camping | | X | | Drinking water | | X | |
| Fire pits | X | | | Electrical hook-up | X | | |
| Fire places | | X | | Flush toilets | | X | |
| Firewood | X | | | Grocery store | X | | |
| Fishing | | X | | Handicapped access | | X | |
| Golf | X | | | Ice | X | | |
| Hiking | | X | | Laundry | X | | |
| Marina | X | | | Lodgings | X | | |
| Picnicking | | X | | Pit toilets | X | | |
| Riding | X | | | Playground | | X | |
| Scuba diving | X | | | Restaurant | X | | |
| Stables | X | | | Sanitary disposal | X | | |
| Swimming | X | | | Sewer hook-up | X | | |
| Tables | | X | | Shelters | | X | |
| Telephone | X | | | Shopping | X | | |
| Tennis | | X | | Showers | X | | |
| Tent sites | | X | | Trailer space | | X | |
| Winter sports | X | | | Water hook-up | X | | |

Stores and facilities in town of Jal.
**Special Rules and Regulations**
   **Fishing:** New Mexico fishing license required
   **Catch limit:** 2 catfish; 6 trout or catch-and-release all day; see page 344 for other bag limits
   **Boating:** No motorized craft permitted

# In the Vicinity
# of Fort Sumner

## *Fort Sumner*

*The following lakes are in the vicinity of Fort Sumner: Lake Sumner, Bosque Redondo Lakes*

Fort Sumner is the county seat of DeBaca County; it is located at the intersection of U.S. Routes 60 and 84 and NM Highway 20, in the fertile valley of the Pecos River. It began in 1862 as a military experiment—part of a new reservation for the relocation of the Mescalero Apaches and Navajos. The relocation of these Indians from their homelands to Fort Sumner under the supervision of Colonel Kit Carson is known as *"The Long Walk."* The reservation, plagued by disease and the shortage of food and fuel, was considered a failure and finally closed in 1868, when General William T. Sherman inspected the fort and decided to send the Indians back to their original homes. The site is now Fort Sumner State Monument with a visitors center and a museum. After the Army withdrew, the fort buildings were sold to an early settler, Lucien B. Maxwell, one of the West's wealthiest men. The town of Fort Sumner grew out of settlements clustering around the Maxwell family properties. It moved to its present site with the construction of the Belen cut-off of the Santa Fe Railroad around 1907.

The town became famous as a hangout for the notorious young outlaw Billy the Kid, also known as Kid Antrim, William H. Bonney, and El Chivo.

During the famous Lincoln County war, Billy the Kid sided with the Tunstall faction (one of the newcomers to the Territory), while the Governor and local law officers were pitted on the other side of a busines conflict. During the bloody violence that followed, Billy became the most hunted man in the Territory and fled to his friends in Fort Sumner. It was at the home of Lucien Maxwell that he was cornered and shot dead by Sheriff Pat Garrett on 14 July, 1881. Billy the Kid was twenty-one years old when killed and was credited with killing twenty-one men. Billy the Kid is buried in the old government cemetery behind the Fort Sumner Museum with his Lincoln County war pals, Charlie Bowdie, Tom O'Folliard, Lucien B. Maxwell, and Maxwell's son Pete. There is no charge to visit Billy's grave. The original tombstone of Billy the Kid was stolen and later found in California. New Mexico Governor Bruce King had it returned and iron-shackled to the grave site to avoid another theft.

Water sports are popular in the Fort Sumner area, with the nearby lakes of Bosque Redondo near the Fort Museum and Lake Sumner State Park just eighteen miles northwest. The Pecos River nearby also offers good fishing for the angler. Restaurants, motels, gas stations, stores, and campgrounds are available in Fort Sumner, and since Lake Sumner is the closest large lake to Clovis and Portales, it has become a popular recreation area for Eastern New Mexicans and Texans.

*Lake Sumner*

# LAKE SUMNER

Lake Sumner is a 4,650-acre lake eighteen miles northwest of Fort Sumner, within a more than 11,000-acre state park of which almost 1,800 acres have been developed as campgrounds or cabin sites. Most of the land surrounding the lake is privately owned. The cabin area on the west side of the lake is a popular weekend retreat and retirement community with tennis courts, a playground, and a nature trail.

Lake Sumner was originally called Alamagordo Reservoir, since the dam backs up the water of Alamogordo Creek at its junction with the Pecos River sixteen miles north of Fort Sumner. In 1974 the name was changed to Lake Sumner to avoid confusion with the fast-growing city of Alamogordo, 200 miles to the southwest. The dam was built by the Federal Bureau of Reclamation in 1936 to impound the waters of the Pecos River for the Carlsbad Irrigation District. The Dam is 164 feet high and 3,084 feet long. At its crest, the dam backs up a maximum of 110,655 acre-feet of water.

It is one of the largest lakes in New Mexico.

Lake Sumner is stocked by the New Mexico Department of Game and Fish with largemouth bass (usually two-inch fingerlings), and (once a year) with seven- to ten-inch-long channel catfish. It is also stocked with fry-size walleye. In addition, the lake contains bluegill, crappie, and white bass. During the cold winter months, the Stilling Basin and a short stretch of the Pecos River below the lake are stocked with rainbow trout. Dirt roads at both the east and west ends of the dam lead down to the river. At the southern end of the lake there are four boat ramps. Boats—both large and small, motor and sail—are accommodated. The campground along the western shore above the dam and overlooking the lake is well maintained, easily accessible, and is a full-facility complex with sheltered picnic tables, grills, a heated and lighted restroom with hot showers, a large group shelter, electric hook-ups, a dump station, and playgrounds. A bar, store, and cafe are located close to the dam.

## Directions from Albuquerque

Drive east on I-40 to Santa Rosa. Take Exit 277, connecting with U.S. 84 at east end of Santa Rosa. Drive south to junction of NM 203 and U.S. 84. Turn west on NM 203 and go six miles to Sumner Lake. The distance from Santa Rosa to the lake is forty-two miles. The road is excellent all the way to the lake. At the entrance to the park and campground, there is a general store where picnic, bait and tackle supplies. and ice are available. There is also a lounge and a restaurant.The town of Fort Sumner is ten miles south of the junction of NM 203 and U.S. 84.

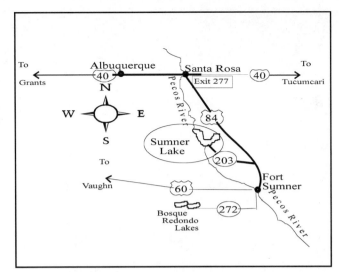

| Surface acres: 4,650 | Distance from Albuquerque: 158 miles |
|---|---|
| Elevation: 4,030 feet | Location: 16 miles northwest of Fort Sumner; |
| Max. trailer size & fee: State park rules and fees | 42 miles southeast of Santa Rosa |
| Time limit: 14 days; see park rules, page 342 | Fish species: Walleye, whitemouth and smallmouth bass, |
| Mailing address: Sumner Lake State Park, | crappie, bluegill, and catfish |
| Fort Sumner, NM 88119 | Season: All year; winter trout fishing below dam at |
| Police emergency tel. #: 345-2405 | Stilling basin, November-March |

## ACTIVITIES AND FACILITIES

| | NO | YES | Proximity to Lake in Miles | | NO | YES | Proximity to Lake in Miles |
|---|---|---|---|---|---|---|---|
| Bait and supplies | | X | | Airplane runway | X | | 16 |
| Boat gas | | X | | Bottled gas | X | | 16 |
| Boat ramp | | X | | Café/snack bar | | X | |
| Boat rental | X | | | Chemical toilets | | X | |
| Camping | | X | | Drinking water | | X | |
| Fire pits | | X | | Electrical hook-up | | X | |
| Fire places | | X | | Flush toilets | | X | |
| Firewood | X | | | Grocery store | | X | |
| Fishing | | X | | Handicapped access | | X | |
| Golf | X | | | Ice | | X | |
| Hiking | | X | | Laundry | X | | |
| Marina | X | | | Lodgings | X | | |
| Picnicking | | X | | Pit toilets | | X | |
| Riding | X | | | Playground | | X | |
| Scuba diving | | X | | Restaurant | | X | |
| Stables | X | | | Sanitary disposal | | X | |
| Swimming | | X | | Sewer hook-up | X | | |
| Tables | | X | | Shelters | | X | |
| Tennis | | X | | Shopping | X | | |
| Tent sites | | X | | Showers | | X | |
| Water skiing | | X | | Trailer space | | X | |
| Winter sports | X | | | Water hook-up | | X | |

Full accommodations and services in Fort Sumner, 16 miles southeast.
### Special Rules and Regulations
**Fishing:** New Mexico Department of Game and Fish Regulations apply; see Fishing Proclamation
**Catch limit:** Trout, 6 per day; Black bass, 14 inches minimum; see page 344 for warm-water bag limits
**Boating:** No restrictions as to size or type; park safety rules must be observed
**Other:** Park maintains full-facility campgrounds

*Bosque Redondo Lakes*

# BOSQUE REDONDO LAKES

Bosque Redondo Lakes is a series of lakes totaling about fifteen acres and stocked by the New Mexico Department of Game and Fish with winter trout. The lakes also contain bass, bluegill, and catfish. They are located five miles south of Fort Sumner and are adjacent to the Pecos River. Bosque Redondo Lakes are open all year, and access to the lakes is excellent. Vehicles can enter the park off the main road that passes the lakes. Cars can drive the entire circumference of the main lake, where fishing or picnicking can be enjoyed off the bank. Swimming is not permitted, neither are boats or other floating devices allowed. Camping is not permitted, but trash cans, shelters, tables, chemical toilets, and a playground are provided.

Though the lakes are off the main road leading to the lakes, there is a charming seclusion to the area. The park is well maintained and it is a pleasant place to spend the day fishing or picnicking.

## Directions from Albuquerque

Follow the same directions as those on the previous page for route to Fort Sumner. Go through Fort Sumner and turn right on NM 272. This is also Billy the Kid Road, the same road that goes to Billy the Kid's grave. Follow the signs to Redondo Lakes.

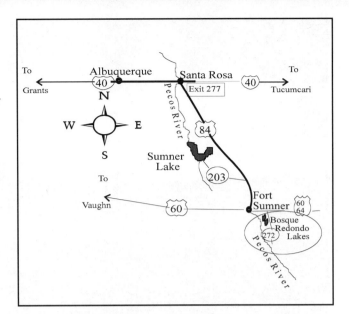

| | |
|---|---|
| **Surface acres:** 15 | **Distance from Albuquerque:** 165 miles |
| **Elevation:** 4,000 feet | **Location:** 5 miles south of Fort Sumner |
| **Max. trailer size & fee:** No camping, no fee | **Fish species:** Bass, bluegill, catfish, and winter rainbow trout |
| **Time limit:** No camping | |
| **Mailing address:** DeBaca Chamber of Commerce, P.O. Box 28, Ft. Sumner, NM 88119, (505) 355-7705 | **Season:** All year for warm-water species; for winter trout, 1 November-31 March |

## ACTIVITIES AND FACILITIES

| | NO | YES | Proximity to Lake in Miles | | NO | YES | Proximity to Lake in Miles |
|---|---|---|---|---|---|---|---|
| Bait and supplies | X | | | Airplane runway | X | | |
| Boat gas | X | | | Bottled gas | X | | |
| Boat ramp | X | | | Café/snack bar | X | | |
| Boat rental | X | | | Chemical toilets | | X | |
| Camping | X | | | Drinking water | X | | |
| Fire pits | | X | | Electrical hook-up | X | | |
| Fire places | X | | | Flush toilets | X | | |
| Firewood | X | | | Grocery store | X | | |
| Fishing | | X | | Handicapped access | | X | |
| Golf | X | | 5 | Ice | X | | |
| Hiking | X | | | Laundry | X | | |
| Marina | X | | | Lodgings | X | | |
| Picnicking | | X | | Pit toilets | X | | |
| Riding | X | | | Playground | | X | |
| Scuba diving | X | | | Restaurant | X | | |
| Stables | X | | | Sanitary disposal | X | | |
| Swimming | X | | | Sewer hook-up | X | | |
| Tables | | X | | Shelters | | X | |
| Telephone | X | | | Shopping | X | | |
| Tennis | X | | | Showers | X | | |
| Tent sites | X | | | Trailer space | X | | |
| Winter sports | X | | | Water hook-up | X | | |

Full facilities and services in Ft. Sumner, 5 miles north.

**Special Rules and Regulations**

**Fishing:** New Mexico Department of Game and Fish Regulations apply; see Fishing Proclamation

**Catch limit:** 6 trout, see Fishing Regulations for warm water species limits, page 344

**Boating:** No boats or floating devices permitted

# In the Vicinity
# of Clovis

## *Clovis*

*There are two lakes in the vicinity of Clovis: Green Acres Lake, Ned Houk Memorial Park (also known as Running Water Draw State Park)*

Clovis is an agricultural and farming community located on the high plains of the southeast corner of Curry County, just nine miles from the Texas border. It lies at an elevation of 4,280 feet above sea level, with a population of about 35,000. When the Santa Fe Railroad looked for a location to establish the Belen cut-off that would intersect the Pecos Valley Line, the company selected a site called Riley's Switch, a siding with a few shacks. A railroad official's daughter, who was studying French history at the time, was given the honor of naming the town. She chose Clovis, after the first French Christian King, Clovis 1, King of the Franks.

Clovis soon grew from a remote railroad siding and a few shacks to a fast-growing city. Deep wells were dug to provide irrigation to the surrounding grass and farmlands, which became one of the most productive areas in New Mexico. It became the largest wheat producer west of Kansas and has the largest storage capacity in the state. On the approach to Clovis, as far as the eye can see from horizon to horizon in any direction, are farms, livestock-raising ranches, and grasslands.

Clovis has a stable economy based on its military base (Cannon Air Force Base), its livestock and agricultural industry, and the railroad. Visitors from the outlying communities are attracted each September to the largest county fair in the state. They can also enjoy picnicking and fishing at Green Acres Lake located in the city, or at beautiful Ned Houk Memorial Park just six and a half miles north of Clovis. Many visitors are attracted to the Hillcrest Park and Zoo, which contains more than 200 species of birds and animals. Its facilities include picnic tables, sunken gardens, a swimming pool, a children's amusement park, and a children's fishing pond. The Hillcrest Park Zoo is located on twenty-two acres and houses 500 animals. Most of these animals are exhibited in their natural habitat. The zoo was located in downtown Clovis when it was started in 1931. It was later moved to where it is today, at 10th and Sycamore Streets. In Clovis, the largest town in the area, ample lodgings, service stations, restaurants, and grocery stores are available.

*Green Acres Lake*

# GREEN ACRES LAKE

Green Acres Lake is an eight-acre lake in the city of Clovis, located at 21st and Main Streets. Its easy access and convenient location make this a popular spot for locals to picnic and to fish. It is a no-fee lake, but a New Mexico fishing license is required to fish for the bass, catfish, and winter trout that is stocked by the Department of Game and Fish. The complex is well maintained and offers picnic tables and toilet facilities.

## Directions from Albuquerque

Take I-40 east through Santa Rosa, then take Exit 277, connecting with U.S. 84 at east end of Santa Rosa. Continue east on U.S. 84 through Fort Sumner then go east on U.S. 60/84 to Clovis. Green Acres Lake is located in the City of Clovis, at 21st and Main Streets

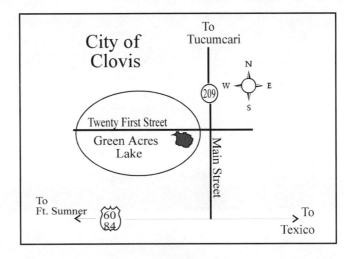

| | | |
|---|---|---|
| Surface acres: 8 | | Distance from Albuquerque: 219 miles |
| Elevation: 4,270 feet | | Location: In Clovis at 21st and Main Streets |
| Max. trailer size & fee: No camping, no fee | | Time limit: No camping |
| Mailing address: None | | Fish species: Bass, catfish, and winter trout |
| Police emergency tel. #: (505) 763-3426 | | Season: All year; for winter trout, 1 November-31 March |
| Medical emergency tel. #: 911 | | |

## ACTIVITIES AND FACILITIES

| | NO | YES | Proximity to Lake in Miles | | NO | YES | Proximity to Lake in Miles |
|---|---|---|---|---|---|---|---|
| Bait and supplies | X | | * | Airplane runway | X | | |
| Boat gas | X | | | Bottled gas | X | | |
| Boat ramp | X | | | Café/snack bar | X | | |
| Boat rental | X | | | Chemical toilets | | X | |
| Camping | X | | | Drinking water | | X | |
| Fire pits | X | | | Electrical hook-up | X | | |
| Fire places | | X | | Flush toilets | | X | |
| Firewood | X | | | Grocery store | X | | |
| Fishing | | X | | Handicapped access | | X | |
| Golf | X | | | Ice | X | | * |
| Hiking | X | | | Laundry | X | | * |
| Marina | X | | | Lodgings | X | | * |
| Picnicking | | X | | Pit toilets | X | | |
| Riding | X | | | Playground | X | | |
| Scuba diving | X | | | Restaurant | X | | * |
| Skiing (water) | X | | | Trash cans | | X | |
| Swimming | X | | | Sewer hook-up | X | | |
| Tables | | X | | Shelters | | X | |
| Telephone | X | | | Shopping | X | | * |
| Tennis | X | | | Showers | X | | |
| Tent sites | X | | | Trailer space | X | | |
| Winter sports | X | | | Water hook-up | X | | |

*Stores and services in neighborhood.

**Special Rules and Regulations**

**Fishing:** New Mexico State fishing license required

**Catch limit:** 6 trout; see Fishing Regulations, page 344, for warm-water species limits

**Boating:** No boating permitted

# NED HOUK MEMORIAL PARK

Considering that this part of the Southeast Area of the New Mexico State Park System is a land of black lava fields and white sand dunes, where mountains slope down to the semi-arid Chihuahuan Desert zone, to me, few parks that I have visited have been more impressive at first sight than Running Water Draw State Park, better known as Ned Houk Memorial Park. It was named in honor of Ned Houk, Mayor of Clovis in the 1950s. The park was developed and maintained by the City of Clovis. It is located six and a half miles north of Clovis on NM 209, a beautiful park of 3,320 acres of rolling terrain on both sides of Running Water Draw. Some 400 acres of this park are in shade trees and mowed and irrigated grass, embracing four fish ponds stocked with catfish and winter trout. Three of the ponds are one acre each in size and the other is two and a half acres. The park lies in sharp and beautiful contrast to the flat terrain of the surrounding region that stretches out beyond the park's undulating landscape. It is a most impressive and well maintained park, offering a variety of recreational opportunities. There are picnic grounds with tables, shelters, drinking water, and fireplaces. There are two permanent restrooms and several conveniently placed portable ones. Visitors can enjoy concerts in a band shell and use the volleyball courts, the softball field, or the archery range. There are hiking trails, a model airplane track, and a motorcycle dirt track. There is a playground, and in the Draw itself there is a low-level flood control dam, which when full creates a 320-acre lake. Located in the park is Old Homestead Museum, created by and dedicated to H.A. "Pappy" Thornton, a former city employee. The museum exhibits a wide variety of farming equipment pre-dating 1926, including a Model T Ford truck. Ned Houk Memorial Park has become a favorite recreational spot for West Texans and Eastern New Mexicans.

## Directions from Albuquerque

Take I-40 east through Santa Rosa, then take Exit 277 connecting with U.S. 84 at east end of Santa Rosa. Continue through Fort Sumner then go east on U.S. 60/84 to Clovis. From Clovis take Prince St. (NM 209), and go north six and a half miles to Ned Houk Memorial Park (at top of hill).

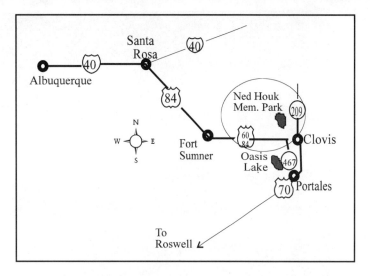

| | |
|---|---|
| **Surface acres:** 4 ponds, totaling 5 1/2 acres | **Distance from Albuquerque:** 229 miles |
| **Elevation:** 4,400 feet | **Location:** 6 1/2 miles north of Clovis |
| **Max. trailer size & fee:** No camping | **Fish species:** Catfish, and stocked winter trout |
| **Time limit:** Day use only | **Season:** All year; trout 1 November-31 March |
| **Mailing address:** Chamber of Commerce, 215 Main St., Clovis, NM 88101 (505) 763-3435 | **Police emergency tel. #:** (505) 763-3426 |
| **Medical emergency tel. #:** 911 | |

## ACTIVITIES AND FACILITIES

| | NO | YES | Proximity to Lake in Miles | | NO | YES | Proximity to Lake in Miles |
|---|---|---|---|---|---|---|---|
| Bait and supplies | X | | * 6 | Airplane runway | X | | *6 |
| Boat gas | X | | | Bottled gas | X | | |
| Boat ramp | X | | | Café/snack bar | X | | * |
| Boat rental | X | | | Chemical toilets | | X | |
| Camping | X | | | Drinking water | | X | |
| Fire pits | X | | | Electrical hook-up | X | | |
| Fire places | | X | | Flush toilets | | X | |
| Firewood | X | | | Grocery store | X | | * |
| Fishing | | X | | Handicapped access | | X | |
| Golf | X | | * | Ice | X | | * |
| Hiking | X | | | Laundry | X | | * |
| Marina | X | | | Lodgings | X | | * |
| Picnicking | | X | | Pit toilets | | X | |
| Riding | X | | | Playground | | X | |
| Scuba diving | X | | | Restaurant | X | | * |
| Skiing (water) | X | | | Sanitary disposal | X | | * |
| Swimming | X | | * | Sewer hook-up | X | | * |
| Tables | | X | | Shelters | | X | |
| Telephone | | X | | Shopping | X | | * |
| Tennis | X | | * | Showers | X | | * |
| Tent sites | X | | | Trailer space | X | | * |
| Winter sports | X | | | Water hook-up | X | | * |

*Full services, stores, lodgings in Clovis, 6 miles.
**Special Rules and Regulations**
  **Fishing:** New Mexico fishing license required
  **Catch limit:** 6 winter trout; see Fishing Regulations, page 344 for other species limits
  **Boating:** No boats or floating devices permitted
  **Other:** A day-use park; closes 11 P.M.

# In the Vicinity of Portales

## *Portales*

*In the vicinity of Portales there is one lake: Oasis Lake State Park*

Portales is located on the plains of northeastern Roosevelt County, about twenty-two miles west of the Texas border and nineteen miles southwest of Clovis. It lies at an elevation of 4,000 feet above sea level and has an estimated population of 11,000. Portales had its beginnings on a site called Portales Springs, six miles south of the present city. Portales Springs was a cowboy camp site, where spring waters flowed from a series of cave openings whose formations resembled porches of an adobe styled house. *Portales,* in Spanish, means "porches," and the name refers to these formations. Before the railroad came to Portales, a man known as "Uncle" Josh Morrison started a small store in a frame building at Portales Springs. After the Pecos Valley and Northern Railroad came through,

"Uncle" Josh pulled his store on skids from Portales Springs to where the railroad workers had set up a construction camp. It became the first store in Portales. The town grew up around it and was named Portales after Portales Springs. Today, Portales is a university town, boasting the third largest university in New Mexico, Eastern New Mexico University. In cooperation with the city, it sponsors an annual Peanut Valley Festival, attracting hundreds of visitors each year during the first weekend of October. Deep wells here provide irrigation to some of the best farmland in New Mexico, making agriculture the major industry and Portales famous for its peanut cultivation.

Portales has adequate facilities for tourists. There are motels, service stations, restaurants, and grocery stores. The 196-acre Oasis Lake State Park, seven miles north of town, is a welcome recreation, fishing, and picnicking respite from the desert heat of the surrounding countryside.

*Oasis Lake State Park*

# OASIS LAKE STATE PARK

At Oasis Lake State Park is a two-acre lake lying at an elevation of 4,010 feet above sea level. It is an appropriately named 196-acre park ensconced in a desert setting of shifting sand dunes. Its main attraction is the lake, which is shaded by towering cottonwoods, locusts, cedar, and chinaberry trees, planted there in 1902 by Will Taylor, a homesteader. It was once a natural artesian lake, but heavy demands for irrigation lowered its water table. Its water is now supplied by a well, and it serves as a stopover for migratory waterfowl, mostly ducks. It is a favorite place for nearby villagers to picnic and to fish for the catfish, perch, and winter trout stocked by the New Mexico Department of Game and Fish.

The park facilities include thirty-six camping, picnic, and RV sites, ten with electric hook-ups and a dump station. There are tables with shelters, grills, and modern restrooms with flush toilets and hot showers. There is access for the handicapped. As are all state parks, it is a fee area for day and overnight use. Grocery stores, fishing supplies, restaurants, lodgings, and service stations are in Portales, seven miles south.

## Directions from Albuquerque

Take I-40 east through Santa Rosa to Exit 277, and connect with U.S. 84 at east end of Santa Rosa. Go south through Fort Sumner, then east on U.S. 60/84 to junction of NM 467. Turn south on NM 467 and follow signs to lake. Lake is two miles west, off NM 467 and accessible by a paved road.

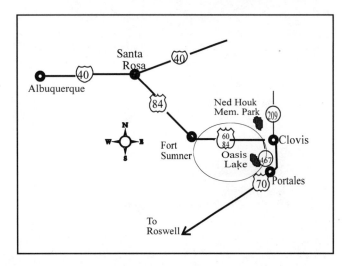

| | | |
|---|---|---|
| **Surface acres:** 2 | | **Distance from Albuquerque:** 220 miles |
| **Elevation:** 4,010 feet | | **Location:** 7 miles north of Portales |
| **Max. trailer size & fee:** 40 feet; state park fee | | **Fish species:** Catfish, perch, and winter trout |
| **Time limit:** 14 days | | **Season:** All year; trout 1 November-31 March |
| **Mailing address:** P.O. Box 1147, Santa Fe, NM 87504 | | **Medical emergency tel. #:** 911 |
| (505) 356-5331 | | |
| **Police emergency tel. #:** 911 | | |

## ACTIVITIES AND FACILITIES

| | NO | YES | Proximity to Lake in Miles | | NO | YES | Proximity to Lake in Miles |
|---|---|---|---|---|---|---|---|
| Bait and supplies | X | | * 7 | Airplane runway | X | | * |
| Boat gas | X | | | Bottled gas | X | | * |
| Boat ramp | X | | | Café/snack bar | X | | * |
| Boat rental | X | | | Chemical toilets | | X | |
| Camping | | X | | Drinking water | | X | |
| Fire pits | X | | | Electrical hook-up | | X | |
| Fire places | | X | | Flush toilets | | X | |
| Firewood | X | | | Grocery store | X | | * |
| Fishing | | X | | Handicapped access | | X | |
| Golf | X | | * | Ice | X | | * |
| Hiking | | X | | Laundry | X | | * |
| Marina | X | | | Lodgings | X | | * |
| Picnicking | | X | | Pit toilets | | X | |
| Riding | X | | | Playground | | X | |
| Scuba diving | X | | | Restaurant | X | | * |
| Skiing (water) | X | | | Sanitary disposal | | X | |
| Swimming | X | | * | Sewer hook-up | | X | |
| Tables | | X | | Shelters | | X | |
| Telephone | X | | * | Shopping | X | | * |
| Tennis | X | | * | Showers | | X | |
| Tent sites | | X | | Trailer space | | X | |
| Winter sports | X | | | Water hook-up | | X | |

*Full services, stores and lodgings in Portales, 7 miles south.
**Special Rules and Regulations**
   **Fishing:** New Mexico fishing license required
   **Catch limit:** 6 winter trout; catfish 2 per day; see page 344 for other limits on warm-water fish
   **Boating:** No boats permitted

# ZONE 4

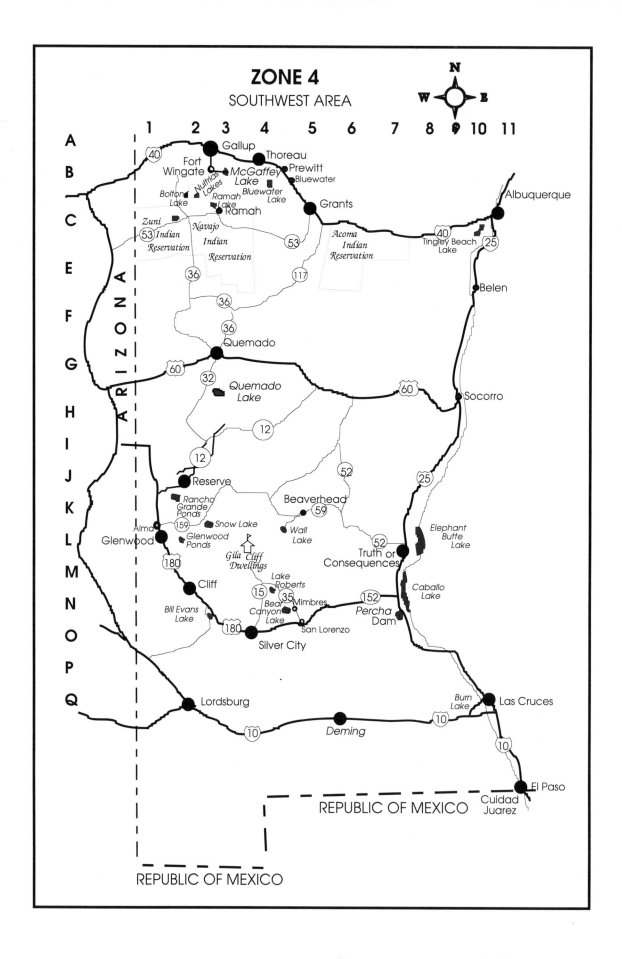

# ZONE 4

AREA WEST OF I-25 TO THE ARIZONA BORDER AND SOUTH OF I-40
TO THE TEXAS AND MEXICO BORDERS

## Table of Distances (Miles to vicinity)

| VICINITY (lake access from nearest town) | Map Key | Albuquerque | Farmington | Las Cruces | Clayton | Hobbs |
|---|---|---|---|---|---|---|
| **Albuquerque** | C11 | -- | 182 | 223 | 273 | 315 |

Tingley Beach, p. 6

| **Truth or Consequences** | L8 | 149 | 331 | 75 | 411 | 324 |
|---|---|---|---|---|---|---|

Percha Dam Reservoir, p. 220

| **Grants** | C5 | 78 | 182 | 405 | 351 | 393 |
|---|---|---|---|---|---|---|

Bluewater Lake, p. 296

| **Gallup** | A3 | 138 | 122 | 339 | 411 | 463 |
|---|---|---|---|---|---|---|

McGaffey Lake, p. 300

| **Ramah** *Asterisks denote Zuni Lakes | C3 | 133 | 155 | 284 | 406 | 448 |
|---|---|---|---|---|---|---|

Ramah Lake, p. 304
*Nutria Lakes, p. 306
Stop at tribal office in Zuni for information and permits for the following lakes on the Zuni reservation
*Bolton Lake
*Black Lake
*Galisteno Lake
*Eustace Lake
*Ojo Lake

| **Quemado** | G3 | 181 | 250 | 250 | 444 | 386 |
|---|---|---|---|---|---|---|

Quemado Lake, p. 310

| **Reserve** | J2 | 206 | 381 | 211 | 468 | 410 |
|---|---|---|---|---|---|---|

Rancho Grande Ponds, p. 314
Snow Lake, p. 316

| **Beaverhead** | K4 | 232 | 410 | 168 | 494 | 417 |
|---|---|---|---|---|---|---|

Wall Lake, p. 320

| **Glenwood** | L2 | 234 | 406 | 186 | 493 | 385 |
|---|---|---|---|---|---|---|

Glenwood Ponds, p. 324

## Table of Distances (Miles to vicinity)

| VICINITY (lake access from nearest town) | Map Key | Albuquerque | Farmington | Las Cruces | Clayton | Hobbs |
|---|---|---|---|---|---|---|
| **Silver City** | O4 | 238 | 378 | 112 | 500 | 367 |

Bill Evans Lake, p. 325
Bear Canyon Reservoir, p. 330
Lake Roberts, p. 332

| **Las Cruces** | Q11 | 223 | 405 | -- | 414 | 255 |
|---|---|---|---|---|---|---|

Burn Lake, p. 336
Leasburg Dam, p. 338

# In the Vicinity of Grants

## *Grants*

*There are three lakes in the vicinity of Grants: Bluewater Lake, \*Paquate Reservoir (on the Paquate Reservation), \*Acomita Lake (on the Ácoma Reservation). Bluewater lake is detailed on the next two pages.*

Grants is located on I-40, seventy-eight miles west of Albuquerque, at an elevation of 6,460 feet above sea level. It lies in the heart of Indian Country, offering tourists a scenic assortment of majestic geological formations, colorful sandstone mesas and bluffs, extinct volcanoes, ice caves, and archaeological wonders. The area surrounding Grants was settled more than 2,000 years ago by the ancient Anasazi Indians. The entire area is marked by ancient trails and the ruins of pueblos and cliff dwellings in which they lived centuries ago. Just east of Grants are the Ácoma (Sky City) and Laguna Pueblos. At Ácoma there is a visitors center with a snack bar and gift shop, and a museum. A shuttle service and guide are offered on a fee basis to take visitors to the top of Sky City, which for over a thousand years was the mesa-top home for the Ácomas. On the reservation is Acomita Lake, which was dry for a couple of years, but at the time of our visit was being reconstructed for future public use. The Paquate Reservoir on the Laguna Reservation is open for fishing. Both pueblos require permits to fish their lakes.

Before two brothers from Canada, the Grant brothers, settled in the area and started a railroad in 1881, the town was known as Los Alamitos (Spanish for "little cottonwoods"). Later it was referred to as Grants Camp. In 1935 Grants became its official name. It took an oddly shaped piece of yellow rock found by Paddy Martinez, a Navajo sheepherder, to start Grants on the path to fame. Paddy Martinez showed the yellow rock to the authorities. They identified it as uranium, and the whole course of Grant's history was to change. From being a small "railroad stop," it became the "uranium capital of the world." The Anaconda Mining Company opened up the Jackpile Mine, and in the 1970s its production of uranium oxide was the source of more than half of all the uranium oxide mined in the United States. Since those boom years, Grants has weathered cycles of prosperity and depression. The New Mexico Museum of Mining, located on the site of the oldest uranium mine, at 100 Iron Street in Grants, displays mining equipment and local artifacts, and gives the history of the boom and bust years of the uranium industry. Museum tour guides who are ex-miners guide visitors around the mine. They descend the main shaft by an elevator that takes them to passages between levels, where through cool tunnels called drifts the guide points out the many inner workings of the mine. The guide explains the authenticity of the relics on display as he points out the old ore carts, drilling machine, blasting wires, and dynamite hanging from the walls.

Grants is a convenient place to overnight between visits or tours to the many fascinating historical and recreational sites just short drives away from town. There are well-equipped campgrounds for travel trailers and RVs. These campgrounds have complete hook-ups, showers, and picnicking facilities with tables, grills, shelters, and toilets. There are many motels, restaurants, grocery stores, gas stations, and most fast-food franchises.

*Bluewater Lake*

# BLUEWATER LAKE

Bluewater Lake is a 2,350-acre lake located just east of the Continental Divide, seven miles southwest of Prewitt and I-40, and twenty miles northwest of Grants. It sits at an elevation of 7,400 feet above sea level and is cradled in Bluewater Lake State Park, one of the most popular and best equipped parks in the state for camping, fishing, boating, and water sports. More than 200 million years ago, this region was submerged in a great sea. Eventually the waters receded, leaving only Bluewater Creek to cut its way through barrancas, which later became an irrigation source for the settlers, who in the 1880s moved into the Bluewater area near Prewitt. They built earthen dams on the creek to irrigate their farms, but the dams washed away. In 1925 the Bluewater-Toltec Irrigation District was established to build a permanent concrete arch dam that backs up the lake seven miles long and a mile across at its widest point. At its highest point, the eighty-feet-high dam

has an elevation of 7,402 feet above sea level and impounds 38,500 acre-feet of water. The water below 7,365 feet elevation is owned by the New Mexico Department of Game and Fish. It is maintained at or above this level and is stocked with fingerling rainbow trout by the department. The lake also contains catfish. It became a state park in 1955 and is one of the most beautiful of the state park lakes, surrounded by 2,100 acres of pine- and fir-forested land.

Bluewater Lake State Park provides all of the necessities for recreational activities at the lake. There is power- and sail-boating. There is water-skiing in the summer, and ice fishing in the winter. The campground is equipped with modern restrooms, hot showers, a dump station, electrical and water hook-ups, a boat service dock, a launching ramp, boat rentals, and a store with camping, fishing, and picnic supplies.

## Directions from Albuquerque

Go west on I-40 through Grants and continue about nineteen miles to Prewitt/Bluewater State Park exit. Turn left at first intersection on to paved NM 412. Go over the overpass and follow signs seven miles to Bluewater State Park. There is good access to many fishing, camping, and picnic areas by car or foot.

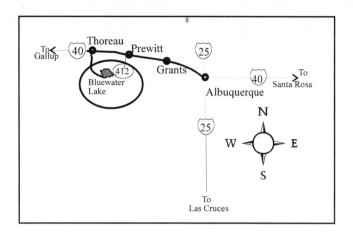

| | | |
|---|---|---|
| **Surface acres:** 2,350 | **Distance from Albuquerque:** 106 miles | |
| **Elevation:** 7,402 feet | **Location:** 28 miles west of Grants via I-40 and NM | |
| **Max. trailer size & fee:** 40 feet; fees posted | 412; 7 miles south of Prewitt | |
| **Time limit:** 14 days | **Fish species:** Rainbow trout, and channel catfish | |
| **Mailing address:** N.M. State Parks and Recreation | **Season:** All year, weather permitting | |
| Villagra Bldg. P.O. Box 1147, Santa Fe, NM | | |
| 87504 (505) 876-2391 | | |

## ACTIVITIES AND FACILITIES

| | NO | YES | Proximity to Lake in Miles | | NO | YES | Proximity to Lake in Miles |
|---|---|---|---|---|---|---|---|
| Bait and supplies | | X | | Airplane runway | X | | |
| Boat gas | | X | | Bottled gas | | X | |
| Boat ramp | | X | | Café/snack bar | | X | |
| Boat rental | | X | | Chemical toilets | | X | |
| Camping | | X | | Drinking water | | X | |
| Fire pits | | X | | Electrical hook-up | | X | |
| Fire places | | X | | Flush toilets | | X | |
| Firewood | X | | | Grocery store | | X | |
| Fishing | | X | | Handicapped access | | X | |
| Golf | X | | | Ice | | X | |
| Hiking | | X | | Laundry | X | | |
| Marina | X | | | Lodgings | X | | |
| Picnicking | | X | | Pit toilets | | X | |
| Riding | X | | | Playground | | X | |
| Scuba diving | | X | | Restaurant | X | | |
| Skiing (water) | | X | | Sanitary disposal | | X | |
| Swimming | | X | | Sewer hook-up | | X | |
| Tables | | X | | Shelters | | X | |
| Telephone | | X | | Shopping | X | | |
| Tennis | X | | | Showers | | X | |
| Tent sites | | X | | Trailer space | | X | |
| Winter sports | | X | | Water hook-up | | X | |

## Special Rules & Regulations

**Fishing:** New Mexico Department of Game and Fish Regulations apply; see latest Fishing Proclamation
**Catch limit:** 10 trout per day; minimum keeper size, 10 inches; see page 344 for warm-water limits
**Boating:** Power boats and sailboats permitted in posted areas
**Other:** Observe all state park and New Mexico Game and Fish Department Regulations

# In the Vicinity of Gallup

## *Gallup*

*There is one lake open to public use in the vicinity of Gallup: McGaffey Lake*

Gallup is located off I-40, 138 miles west of Albuquerque and twenty-two miles east of the Arizona border. It has a population of about 21,000 and lies at an elevation of 6,510 feet amid a spectacular setting of red sandstone formations and high bluffs. It is a fascinating city, often billed as the "Gateway to Indian Country," and applicably described, as is evident in the colorfully advertised trading posts that line the streets displaying their Indian crafts and wares.

Gallup had its beginnings in the late 1880s. The entire town at that time consisted of a saloon and a stagecoach stop. When rich coal deposits were discovered north of the site, it drew hundreds of miners from eastern Europe and shopkeepers and merchants from the East. Shops, stores, and saloons flourished, and as the town expanded the population grew. Added impetus to the town's expansion occurred in 1881, when the Atlantic and Pacific Railroad established a railroad stop about twenty-one miles west, on a site that is now on the border of Arizona. Gallup was officially founded ten years later in 1891 and named for the popular railroad paymaster.

The period following World War II saw a decline in the mining industry as the need for coal was replaced by one for oil. Tourism, which had shared the honors with mining as the major industry up to that time, now became the dominant industry. Gallup's location near the large Navajo Reservation to the east and west, and the Zunis to the south, facilitated Gallup's development as an Indian trade center. Trading posts offering Indian jewelry, rugs, crafts, and Indian ceremonials, are a must stopover for travelers along the East/West Old Historic Route 66, the main highway through town. A highlight for visitors is the Annual Inter-Tribal Ceremonial held in mid-August. It is famous the world over, atttracting thousands of tourists each year. It is a four-day inter-tribal celebration that starts with a huge parade through downtown Gallup with Indian performers from the Navajo Nation and others from New Mexico and other regions of the United States and Canada. Traditional dances are performed in the Ceremonial Grounds at Red Rock State Park, ten miles east, in a spectacular setting of red rock formations that form a natural amphi-theater. The park has full facilities for visitors who come in droves, quickly filling the camping sites that provide electric and water hook-ups. The park's facilities also include a dump station, shelters with tables and grills, trash cans, and modern restrooms with showers and flush toilets.

Gallup has full accommodations along I-40. There are gas stations, hotels, motels, restaurants with fine dining rooms, major chain fast-food restaurants, gift shops, and shopping centers. During the ceremonials, reservations for lodgings are recommended.

*McGaffey Lake*

# McGAFFEY LAKE

McGaffey Lake is a fourteen-acre lake located south of Fort Wingate off NM 400. It is reached by taking the Fort Wingate exit off I-40, about 120 miles west of Albuquerque and fifteen miles east of Gallup. The road is paved to within a mile of the lake and then accessed by a good gravel road. This rainbow trout mountain lake is set in a ponderosa pine forest at an elevation of 7,600 feet above sea level. The United States Forest Service and the New Mexico Department of Game and Fish cooperate in a joint effort to improve the quality of fishing at McGaffey Lake. One of their efforts is the introduction of the grass carp, a species of fish to reduce weed growth. They have also installed an aeration diffusion system across the lake to improve the oxygen level in the water for a better trout habitat. The Forest Service manages the land, and the Department of Game and Fish is charged with the management of the fish and wildlife population. McGaffey Lake was constructed prior to the 1930s and expanded in 1954. There are two fishing platforms for the handicapped: one on either side of the lake. These platforms are also available for use by the general public, but providing adequate space on the platforms for the handicapped is a priority. No camping is permitted at the lake and there are no tables or grills, but the lake's limited facilities do include vault toilets and trash cans. There are two well-maintained fee campgrounds near the lake. Closest to the lake is McGaffey Campgrounds. It is divided into two sections for picnicking and camping. The picnic area contains four group picnic areas and several tables. The camping area provides restrooms and water. Picnicking is free, but there is a fee for camping. Another campground, Quaking Aspen, is located within a mile of the lake. It is equipped with tables, grills, camping sites, and a restroom.

## Directions from Albuquerque

Go 120 miles west on I-40 to Fort Wingate exit. Turn left (south) on NM 400, go past Fort Wingate about eight miles to sign and cut-off to lake, then go about one mile on a gravel road to the lake.

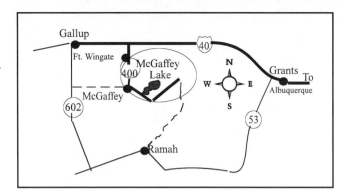

| | | | | |
|---|---|---|---|---|
| **Surface acres:** 14 | | **Distance from Albuquerque:** 134 miles | | |
| **Elevation:** 7,600 feet | | **Location:** 22 miles east of Gallup, 10 miles south of Fort Wingate | | |
| **Max. trailer size & fee:** 40 feet; fees posted | | **Fish species:** Rainbow trout | | |
| **Time limit:** 14 days | | **Season:** 1 April-31 October | | |
| **Mailing address:** NM Department of Game and Fish, Box 25112, Santa Fe, NM 87504 (505) 827-7917 | | **Police emergency tel. #:** 863-9353 | | |
| **Medical emergency tel. #:** 911 | | | | |

## ACTIVITIES AND FACILITIES

| | NO | YES | Proximity to Lake in Miles | | NO | YES | Proximity to Lake in Miles |
|---|---|---|---|---|---|---|---|
| Bait and supplies | X | | | Airplane runway | X | | |
| Boat gas | X | | | Bottled gas | X | | |
| Boat ramp | | X | | Café/snack bar | X | | *8 |
| Boat rental | X | | | Chemical toilets | X | | |
| Camping | | X | *1 mile | Drinking water | | X | |
| Fire pits | | X | | Electrical hook-up | X | | |
| Fire places | | X | | Flush toilets | X | | |
| Firewood | | X | | Grocery store | X | | 8 |
| Fishing | | X | | Handicapped access | | X | |
| Golf | X | | | Ice | X | | |
| Hiking | | X | | Laundry | X | | |
| Marina | X | | | Lodgings | X | | |
| Picnicking | | X | | Pit toilets | | X | |
| Riding | X | | | Playground | X | | |
| Scuba diving | X | | | Restaurant | X | | |
| Stables | X | | | Sanitary disposal | X | | |
| Swimming | X | | | Sewer hook-up | X | | |
| Tables | | X | *1 mile | Shelters | | X | *1 mile |
| Telephone | X | | | Shopping | X | | |
| Tennis | X | | | Showers | X | | |
| Tent sites | | X | | Trailer space | | X | *1mile |
| Winter sports | X | | | Water hook-up | X | | |

*Camping and picnic grounds within 1 mile of lake.
**Special Rules and Regulations**
   **Fishing:** New Mexico fishing license required
   **Catch limit:** 6 trout (1994 and 1995); see Fishing Proclamation for current regulations
   **Boating:** Boats without motors permitted
   **Other:** Camping within 1 mile of lake at McGaffey and Quaking Aspen from May to September

# In the Vicinity of Ramah

## *Ramah*

*There are two lakes in the vicinity of Ramah: Ramah Lake, Nutria Lakes*

Ramah is the access town to Ramah Lake. It is a small town about fifty-three miles southwest of Grants, New Mexico. Ramah has a large population of Navajos, who live away from the main reservation of Ramah but maintain their traditional and religious customs and cultural ties with those tribal members living on the reservation. The town of Ramah is not to be confused with the Ramah Navajo Reservation. Ramah was settled by Mormons in the 1880s by permission of the Navajos. The Mormons established a large mission and named the town after a religious figure in the Book of Mormon.

The approach to Ramah on NM 53 South is steeped in history. It offers visitors several opportunities to explore the historical sites and the lives and customs of Native Americans or collect fine native jewelry and Indian arts and crafts. NM 53 is a scenic highway. After the cut-off from I-40 at Grants, traveling south on NM 53, the terrain changes to hills and interesting rock formations. Wildflowers dot the landscape on both sides of the road with huge splashes of goldenrod and lupine. Soon, you enter the Malpais National Monument and the Malpais Conservation Area of cinder hills and lava rock—evidence of volcanic eruptions that occurred milleniums ago. Two miles farther, NM 53 leads to the Ice Caves, where underground air flows maintain a perpetual mass of ice at the rear of the cave. Nearby is Bandera Crater, an extinct volcanic cone. Pathways lead to its rim; offering a spectacular view of the volcano's interior and of the El Malpais craters and lava tubes, its forests, and sandstone bluffs.

Proceeding farther, and about eleven miles east of Ramah, is El Morro National Monument (Inscription Rock). Until it was bypassed by the railroad in 1880, El Morro's water hole was an important stop for travelers in the Acoma/Zuni region. Numerous inscriptions carved in the sandstone date from the pre-historic Spanish, Mexican, and territorial periods of New Mexico's history. The rock bears Oñate's inscription carved in 1605. There is a visitors center at the monument with restrooms, and access paths lead to a fee camping area operated by the government. The fee is $5.00 per night. The sites are attractively tucked among trees that provide a sense of privacy. The facilities include trash cans, water faucets, and handicapped sites. There are no toilet facilities at the sites, but these facilities are provided at the visitors center, and a couple of private campgrounds nearby offer full hook-ups. The visitors center is eleven miles east of Ramah.

*Ramah Lake*

# RAMAH LAKE

Ramah Lake is a 100- to 300-acre lake stocked with rainbow trout. The lake also contains a population of largemouth bass, catfish, and bluegill. It was leased in January 1988 by the New Mexico Game Commission from the Ramah Land and Irrigation Co. Some of the shoreline is private and not included in the lease. Ramah Lake is located a mile from the northeast section of town by way of Bloomfield Avenue. The last half-mile from town to the lake was by a badly deteriorated and deeply rutted winding dirt road, and high-clearance vehicles were recommended during wet weather, but in June of 1994, the road was graded and improved, and the lower parking lot was expanded. It is a scenic lake set between sandstone formations. It is bordered by heavy growths of Russian olive trees, tamarisks, and oak, on one end, and interesting sandstone rock formations, on the other. A heavy growth of weeds at one end of the lake inhibits bank fishing, but a couple of good concrete boat ramps provide access for boat fishing. Installation of these boat ramps was funded by the New Mexico Department of Game and Fish. Boating is restricted to trolling speeds. Fires are prohibited, and the facilities at the lake are limited to three vault toilets and some trash cans. No camping is permitted at the lake, but a sign near the entrance advertises a nearby campground with a $5.00 per night fee.

## Directions from Albuquerque

Go west on I-40 to Grants. Take Exit 81 south on NM 53 through El Malpais, past the Ice Caves to El Morro National Monument (Inscription Rock) to Ramah. In Ramah, turn off Bond St. on to Bloomfield Ave. (Bond St. is also NM 53.) Continue on Bloomfield Ave and watch for the direction sign to Ramah Lake. Turn right at the sign. The road is a deteriorated dirt road, deeply rutted the last quarter-mile.

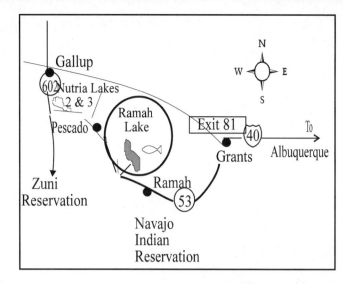

| | | |
|---|---|---|
| **Surface acres:** 100-300 | **Distance from Albuquerque:** 134 miles | |
| **Elevation:** 8,000 feet | **Location:** 1 mile northeast of Ramah off NM 53 | |
| **Max. trailer size & fee:** No camping; no fee | **Fish species:.** Rainbow trout, catfish, bluegill, and bass | |
| **Time limit:** Day use only | **Season:** All year | |
| **Mailing address:** NM Department of Game and Fish, | | |
| Box 25112, Santa Fe, NM 87504 (505) 827-7882 | | |
| **Police emergency tel. #:** 911 | | |

## ACTIVITIES AND FACILITIES

| | NO | YES | Proximity to Lake in Miles | | NO | YES | Proximity to Lake in Miles |
|---|---|---|---|---|---|---|---|
| **Bait and supplies** | X | | *1 | **Airplane runway** | X | | |
| **Boat gas** | X | | *1 | **Bottled gas** | X | | |
| **Boat ramp** | | X | | **Café/snack bar** | X | | |
| **Boat rental** | X | | | **Chemical toilets** | X | | |
| **Camping** | X | | | **Drinking water** | X | | |
| **Fire pits** | X | | | **Electrical hook-up** | X | | |
| **Fire places** | X | | | **Flush toilets** | X | | |
| **Firewood** | X | | | **Grocery store** | X | | *1 |
| **Fishing** | | X | | **Handicapped access** | X | | |
| **Golf** | X | | | **Ice** | X | | *1 |
| **Hiking** | X | | | **Laundry** | X | | |
| **Marina** | X | | | **Lodgings** | X | | |
| **Picnicking** | | X | | **Vault toilets** | | X | |
| **Riding** | X | | | **Playground** | X | | |
| **Scuba diving** | X | | | **Restaurant** | X | | |
| **Stables** | X | | | **Sanitary disposal** | X | | |
| **Swimming** | X | | | **Sewer hook-up** | X | | |
| **Tables** | X | | | **Shelters** | X | | |
| **Telephone** | X | | | **Shopping** | X | | |
| **Tennis** | X | | | **Showers** | X | | |
| **Tent sites** | X | | | **Trailer space** | X | | |
| **Winter sports** | X | | | **Water hook-up** | X | | |

*Stores and services in Ramah, 1 mile.

**Special Rules and Regulations**

   **Fishing:** New Mexico fishing license required

   **Catch limit:** 6 trout; for other species, see Fishing Regulations, page 344

   **Boating:** A "no-wake" lake; boats limited to trolling speeds only

   **Other:** Parking in designated areas only; no fires; no hunting; no camping

*Nutria Lakes*

# NUTRIA LAKES

Nutria Lakes comprises two lakes called Lake #2 and Lake #3. They are located on the Zuni Indian Reservation in southwest New Mexico, twenty-four miles south of Gallup, four miles west of Ramah, and about eleven miles north of the tiny village of Pescado. To reach the lakes, go about five miles past Pescado on NM 53. At this point watch for a Nutria Lakes direction sign; follow the road to another sign directing you to the lakes. Turn left on a gravel road. About a mile in on this road, deep ruts show evidence of muddy conditions during wet weather. Follow this road as it curves around a bend and watch for a spillway on the right side of the road. Turn right at the spillway on a

narrow access road up a steep grade, then bear right, and turn left to the top of a hill to the lakes. The first lake is Lake #2. The main road to the left continues around the lake to an area that is equipped with shelters, tables, fireplaces, and a primitive campground. Lake #3 is reached by this road, which separates both lakes.

On our visit during late August, we encountered just a few fishermen and picnickers at the lakes. They are pretty, with some piñon, juniper, and scrub oak. A Zuni permit is required to fish and to use the lakes' facilities. Boating is permitted, but it is limited to oars or electric motors. Both lakes are stocked with rainbow trout.

## Directions from Albuquerque

Take I-40 to Grants. Turn south at Exit 81 and take NM 53 through town of Ramah. Then go four miles through Pescado. Continue about five miles past Pescado and watch for direction sign on right side of road. Follow signs about seven miles to Nutria Lakes 2 and 3. Access is by a dirt/gravel road to the lakes.

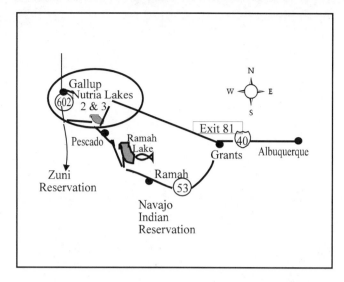

| | | |
|---|---|---|
| **Surface acres:** 15 | | **Distance from Albuquerque:** 150 miles |
| **Elevation:** 6,829 feet | | **Location:** 4 miles west of Ramah; 11 miles north of Pescado |
| **Max. trailer size & fee:** Tribal permit required | | **Fish species:** Rainbow trout |
| **Time limit:** Get regulations from Zuni Pueblo; | | **Season:** All Year |
| permit for use required | | **Police emergency tel. #:** 911 |
| **Mailing address:** Zuni Pueblo, 615 1st. St. N.W. | | |
| Albuquerque, N.M. 87125 (505) 782-4481 | | |

## ACTIVITIES AND FACILITIES

| | NO | YES | Proximity to Lake in Miles | | NO | YES | Proximity to Lake in Miles |
|---|---|---|---|---|---|---|---|
| Bait and supplies | X | | | Airplane runway | X | | |
| Boat gas | X | | | Bottled gas | X | | |
| Boat ramp | X | | | Café/snack bar | X | | |
| Boat rental | X | | | Chemical toilets | X | | |
| Camping | | X | | Drinking water | X | | |
| Fire pits | | X | | Electrical hook-up | X | | |
| Fire places | | X | | Flush toilets | X | | |
| Firewood | X | | | Grocery store | X | | |
| Fishing | | X | | Handicapped access | | X | |
| Golf | X | | | Ice | X | | |
| Hiking | X | | | Laundry | X | | |
| Marina | X | | | Lodgings | X | | |
| Picnicking | | X | | Pit toilets | | X | |
| Riding | X | | | Playground | X | | |
| Scuba diving | X | | | Restaurant | X | | |
| Stables | X | | | Sanitary disposal | X | | |
| Swimming | X | | | Sewer hook-up | X | | |
| Tables | | X | | Shelters | X | | |
| Telephone | X | | | Shopping | X | | |
| Tennis | X | | | Showers | X | | |
| Tent sites | | X | | Trailer space | | X | |
| Winter sports | X | | | Water hook-up | X | | |

**Special Rules and Regulations**

**Fishing:** Zuni permit required; no New Mexico license required
**Catch limit:** Check with Zuni Tribal Headquarters for fishing regulations
**Boating:** Boats restricted to electric motors at trolling speeds or oars
**Other:** Camping by Zuni Permit obtained in Zuni about 7 miles north of lakes

# In the Vicinity of Quemado

## *Quemado*

*There is one lake in the vicinity of Quemado: Quemado Lake*

Quemado is a small mountain town located in an extinct volcanic area. It sits at an elevation of 6,890 feet at the junction of U.S. Highway 60 and NM 36. U.S. Highway 60 is Quemado's main street. Its history as a hub and trade center of the area is evident in many of its original buildings still standing on either side of the highway. Quemado began as a settlement in 1880, when a sheep rancher from Belen, New Mexico, Jose Antonio Padilla, homesteaded with his family and introduced his stock to the area. Years before, a nearby spring was used as a watering stop for early travelers and Apache bands. These travelers burned the grass and brush on both sides of the spring to clear the area so that look-outs could sight threatened attacks by Apaches. The site was referred to as Rito Quemado, Spanish for *"burned creek."*

Quemado is a busy town of 1,028 inhabitants. Its main attraction is to the thousands of sportsmen and wildlife enthusiasts who hunt and fish the forests of the Gila Wilderness to the south. Game animals such as black bear, deer, elk, antelope and turkey thrive in this habitat. During our visit to Quemado in late September, the cafés—full of patrons—posted notices on regulations and hunting tips. Breakfasters were being briefed with outspread maps by their guides and outfitters, planning the morning hunt. Quemado has limited but adequate services and accommodations for the tourist. There are gas stations, three motels, a few good restaurants, cafés, and stores stocked with groceries, bait and tackle, and sporting goods.

Quemado Lake is located twenty miles south of Quemado in the Apache National Forest. It is reached by way of NM 32, a good paved highway.

*Quemado Lake*

# QUEMADO LAKE

Quemado Lake is a 130-acre lake, located twenty miles south of the small town of Quemado, in the Apache National Forest. The New Mexico Department of Game and Fish and the Apache National Forest Service began construction in 1970 and completed it in 1971. This gorgeous lake was formed by a dam across Largo Creek in beautiful Largo Canyon. It is cradled at 7,600 feet in a mountain setting, heavily wooded with ponderosa, piñon, and juniper trees. Funding for its construction was made possible by fishing licenses and the Sport Fish Restoration Act. About five miles south of the city limits of Quemado, NM 32 enters the Apache National Forest. It is a scenic drive with a winding descent through a pine forest. Well-placed signs give directions to the lake. At the junction of NM 103, a left turn takes you four miles to the lake.

About a mile before reaching the lake there is a restaurant, Snuffy's Steakhouse. It is a convenient stop with gas pumps and a combination gift shop and grocery store stocked with bait and tackle supplies. Rental services for boats and electric motors, and a campground with hook-ups are also available. From this point, the lake is about a mile farther. It is reached by a good gravel and partly paved road. There is a large parking area at the entrance to the lake to accommodate cars, RVs, and trailers. A modern building at the entrance to this parking area houses separate toilet facilities for men and women. Campgrounds with fourteen-day stay limits are located in designated areas. There are boat launching ramps for boats restricted to electric motors or oars. Extensive plans were under way to develop areas around the lake for electric and water hook-ups. At the time of our visit in the fall of 1993, phase one of this development stage was complete. Completion date for the project was May of 1994. The lake is stocked with mostly three-inch fingerling rainbow trout and some catchables.

## Directions from Albuquerque

Go west on I-40 to the junction of NM 117. Go south on NM 117 and connect with NM 36 south to Quemado. Continue south on NM 32 to the junction of NM 103, then go east on NM 103 and four miles to Quemado Lake.

**Note:** One mile before reaching the lake is Snuffy's Steakhouse, where gasoline, groceries, bait, and tackle and a restaurant are available. Quemado Lake is also reached via I-25 south to Socorro, then west on U.S. 60 through Datil to Quemado.

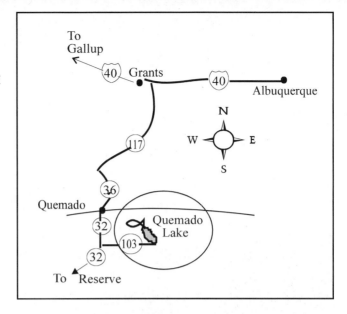

| | | |
|---|---|---|
| **Surface acres:** 130 | | **Distance from Albuquerque:** 201 miles |
| **Elevation:** 6,890 feet | | **Location:** 20 miles south of Quemado |
| **Max. trailer size & fee:** 40 feet; no fee | | **Fish species:** Stocked with mostly 3 inch fingerling rainbow |
| **Time limit:** 14 days | | trout and some catchables |
| **Mailing address:** New Mexico Department of Game and Fish, Box 25112, Santa Fe, NM 87504 (505) 827-7882 | | **Season:** 1 April-31 March |
| **Police emergency tel. #:** 911 | | |

## ACTIVITIES AND FACILITIES

| | NO | YES | Proximity to Lake in Miles | | NO | YES | Proximity to Lake in Miles |
|---|---|---|---|---|---|---|---|
| **Bait and supplies** | X | | * 1 | **Airplane runway** | X | | |
| **Boat gas** | X | | | **Bottled gas** | X | | |
| **Boat ramp** | | X | | **Café/snack bar** | X | | |
| **Boat rental** | X | | * 1 | **Chemical toilets** | | X | |
| **Camping** | | X | | **Drinking water** | | X | |
| **Fire pits** | | X | | **Electrical hook-up** | | X | |
| **Fire places** | | X | | **Flush toilets** | X | | |
| **Firewood** | X | | | **Grocery store** | X | | * 1 |
| **Fishing** | | X | | **Handicapped access** | | X | |
| **Golf** | X | | | **Ice** | X | | * 1 |
| **Hiking** | | X | | **Laundry** | X | | |
| **Marina** | X | | | **Lodgings** | X | | * 1 |
| **Picnicking** | | X | | **Vault toilets** | | X | |
| **Riding** | | X | | **Playground** | X | | |
| **Scuba diving** | | X | | **Restaurant** | X | | * 1 |
| **Water skiing** | X | | | **Sanitary disposal** | | X | |
| **Swimming** | | X | | **Sewer hook-up** | X | | |
| **Tables** | | X | | **Shelters** | | X | |
| **Telephone** | X | | | **Shopping** | X | | |
| **Tennis** | X | | | **Showers** | X | | |
| **Tent sites** | | X | | **Trailer space** | | X | |
| **Winter sports** | | X | | **Water hook-up** | X | | |

*Lodgings, store and restaurant, one mile.

**Special Rules and Regulations**

    **Fishing:** New Mexico fishing license required

    **Catch limit:** Special limit for trout, 10 per day; see page 343, Fishing Regulations

    **Boating:** Boats restricted to oars or electric motors

    **Other:** Expansion of the facilities including installation of water and electric hook-ups were undertaken in 1993; the project is now complete

# In the Vicinity of Reserve

## *Reserve*

*There are two lakes in the vicinity of Reserve:*
*Rancho Grande Ponds, Snow Lake*

Reserve is a small mountain town of 600 inhabitants, lying at an elevation of 5,765 feet in the San Francisco Valley of the Gila Wilderness. The settlement was founded by Mormon cattlemen in the 1860s. Spanish settlers followed, settling in three areas that became the communities of Upper San Francisco Plaza, Middle San Francisco Plaza, and Lower San Francisco Plaza. Of the three, only Upper San Francisco Plaza remained as the town of Reserve, named for the "reserves" in the area established by the Forest Service.

In 1884 the Middle Plaza was the scene of a gun battle between Elfego Baca, a deputy sheriff from Socorro, and drunken cowboys out to avenge a friend's arrest by Elfego Baca. During the gunfight, Baca was cornered in an old shack for two days and single-handedly fought off his attackers. After the fight he emerged unscathed, and three of his attackers lay dead with several others wounded. He returned to Socorro as a local folk hero, continuing his reputation as a fearless and tough lawman. He became Mayor, a district attorney, and later a practicing attorney in Albuquerque, where he died at the age of eighty in his law office. His story, *The Nine Lives of Elfego Baca,* was portrayed in a motion picture produced by Walt Disney.

Reserve is the gateway to an abundance of fishing, hunting, recreational, and sightseeing opportunities in the surrounding Apache and Gila National Forest. It is within a short drive of the finest fishing streams and game hunting areas in the state. A must see, and just a short distance south of Reserve, is the famous "Catwalk" National Recreational Trail near Glenwood and the fabled gold mining ghost town of Mogollon. Reserve offers adequate accommodations for tourists who wish to explore this fascinating part of New Mexico. There are service stations, motels, grocery stores, and a Ranger Station where maps and information about the area are available.

*Rancho Grande Ponds*

# RANCHO GRANDE PONDS

Rancho Grande Ponds are located on the west side of Reserve. They total two acres and are stocked with rainbow trout. There are no facilities at these ponds, but their convenient location offers a pleasant, quiet place for residents or visitors to cast a line or enjoy a picnic. There are no trash cans, but carry-in, carry-out picnics are permitted.

To get to Rancho Grande Ponds, take the main highway NM 12 west. Go past the Whispering Pines sign located in front of a restaurant on the left side of the highway. Take the first road to the left. It is a good dirt road, which curves left and skirts the fenced-in ponds. Continue around the ponds to an opening in the fence that allows access. The first pond has a small fishing platform. A New Mexico fishing license is required.

## Directions from Reserve

Go west on NM 12, past Whispering Pines sign in front of a large restaurant. Take the first road on the left. A good dirt road encircles a fenced-in pond. Continue around the fence to an opening that allows entrance to the ponds.

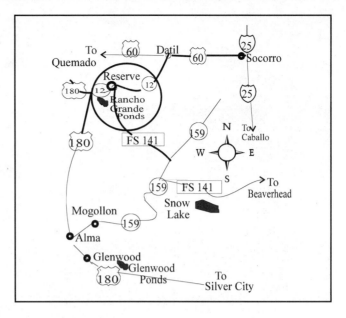

| | | |
|---|---|---|
| **Surface acres:** 2 | | **Distance from Albuquerque:** 206 miles |
| **Elevation:** 5,765 feet | | **Location:** 6 miles west of Reserve |
| **Max. trailer size & fee:** No camping | | |
| **Time limit:** Day use only | | **Fish species:** Stocked winter trout, and sunfish |
| **Mailing address:** None | | **Season:** All year |
| **Police emergency tel. #:**911 | | **Medical emergency tel. #:** 911 |

## ACTIVITIES AND FACILITIES

| | NO | YES | Proximity to Lake in Miles | | NO | YES | Proximity to Lake in Miles |
|---|---|---|---|---|---|---|---|
| Bait and supplies | X | | | Airplane runway | X | | |
| Boat gas | X | | | Bottled gas | X | | |
| Boat ramp | X | | | Café/snack bar | X | | |
| Boat rental | X | | | Chemical toilets | X | | |
| Camping | X | | | Drinking water | X | | |
| Fire pits | X | | | Electrical hook-up | X | | |
| Fire places | X | | | Flush toilets | X | | |
| Firewood | X | | | Grocery store | X | | |
| Fishing | | X | | Handicapped access | X | | |
| Golf | X | | | Ice | X | | |
| Hiking | X | | | Laundry | X | | |
| Marina | X | | | Lodgings | X | | |
| Picnicking | | X | | Pit toilets | X | | |
| Riding | X | | | Playground | X | | |
| Scuba diving | X | | | Restaurant | X | | |
| Stables | X | | | Sanitary disposal | X | | |
| Swimming | X | | | Sewer hook-up | X | | |
| Tables | X | | | Shelters | X | | |
| Telephone | X | | | Shopping | X | | |
| Tennis | X | | | Showers | X | | |
| Tent sites | X | | | Trailer space | X | | |

### Special Rules and Regulations
**Fishing:** New Mexico fishing license required
**Catch limit:** 6 trout; 6 in possession
**Boating:** No boats permitted
**Other:** Carry-in and carry-out; no facilities

*Snow Lake*

# SNOW LAKE

Snow Lake is a 100-acre lake, owned and managed by the New Mexico Department of Game and Fish. It is located in the rugged primitive area of the Gila National Forest, forty miles southeast of Reserve and thirty-nine miles east of Glenwood. It lies at an elevation of 7,400 feet in a remote setting surrounded by a woodland of juniper, ponderosa, and piñon pine. The lake is stocked by the Department of Game and Fish with three-inch fingerlings and some catchable rainbow trout. A spectacular view of this gorgeous lake is offered from the higher terrain above the lake, where a developed campground and picnic area are located. They are accessed by a good gravel road, and their facilities include tables, fire grills, trash cans, and some well-maintained vault toilets

The recommended access to Snow Lake is from Reserve on Forest Road 141, which is a maintained gravel road. There are alternate routes for those approaching from the east, but the last thirty miles to the lake from this direction are by way of rough unimproved roads that require high-clearance or four-wheel-drive vehicles. Fill up your fuel tank before starting a trip to this area, as there are no services available along the way. It is also recommended that you stop at a Ranger Station or Forest Service Office before entering the wilderness area. These offices can provide maps, and information on road conditions and recreational vehicle accessibility to the area.

## Directions from Albuquerque

Take I-25 to Socorro, then go west on U.S. 60 to Datil then southwest on NM 12 to Reserve to Forest Road 141, and follow signs to Snow Lake. FR 141 is a better maintained road than other routes from the east or the south. From the south from Mogollon, the Snow Lake portion of NM 78 is closed from first snowfall to spring. It is advisable to check road conditions before use.

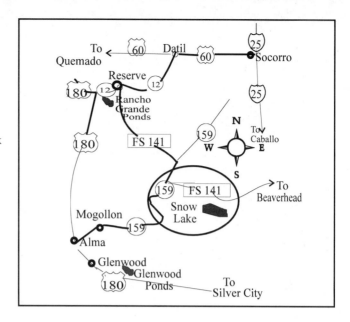

| | | | | | | |
|---|---|---|---|---|---|---|
| **Surface acres:** 100 | | | **Distance from Albuquerque:** 246 miles | | | |
| **Elevation:** 7,400 feet | | | **Location:** 40 miles southeast of Reserve | | | |
| **Max. trailer size:** Large trailers not advised | | | **Fish species:** Rainbow trout | | | |
| **Time limit:** 30-day stay limit, $5.00 per day | | | **Season:** 1 April-November 30 | | | |
| **Mailing address:** New Mexico Department of Game and Fish, | | | **Medical emergency tel. #:** 911 | | | |
| Box 25112, Santa Fe, NM 87504 (505) 827-7911 | | | **Police emergency tel. #:** 911 | | | |
| or Glenwood Ranger District (505) 539-2481 | | | | | | |

## ACTIVITIES AND FACILITIES

| | NO | YES | Proximity to Lake in Miles | | NO | YES | Proximity to Lake in Miles |
|---|---|---|---|---|---|---|---|
| Bait and supplies | X | | | Airplane runway | X | | |
| Boat gas | X | | | Bottled gas | X | | |
| Boat ramp | | X | | Café/snack bar | X | | |
| Boat rental | X | | | Chemical toilets | X | | |
| Camping | | X | | Drinking water | | X | |
| Fire pits | | X | | Electrical hook-up | X | | |
| Fire places | | X | | Flush toilets | X | | |
| Firewood | | X | | Grocery store | X | | |
| Fishing | | X | | Handicapped access | | X | |
| Golf | X | | | Ice | X | | |
| Hiking | | X | | Laundry | X | | |
| Marina | X | | | Lodgings | X | | |
| Picnicking | | X | | Pit toilets | | X | |
| Riding | | X | | Playground | X | | |
| Scuba diving | X | | | Restaurant | X | | |
| Stables | X | | | Sanitary disposal | X | | |
| Swimming | X | | | Sewer hook-up | X | | |
| Tables | | X | | Shelters | | X | |
| Telephone | X | | | Shopping | X | | |
| Tennis | X | | | Showers | X | | |
| Tent sites | | X | | Trailer space | | X | |
| Winter sports | X | | | Water hook-up | X | | |

Closest gas station and stores in Reserve, 40 miles.
**Special Rules and Regulations**
  **Fishing:** New Mexico fishing license required
  **Catch limit:** 6 trout; 6 in possession
  **Boating:** Restricted to oars or electric motors
  **Other:** No-fee camping in unimproved area at south end of lake

# In the Vicinity
# of Beaverhead

## *Beaverhead*

*There is one lake in the vicinity of Beaverhead:*
*Wall Lake*

Beaverhead is located about seventy-five miles west of Elephant Butte. It is reached by taking Exit 89 off I-25 South, then driving northwest on NM 52, through the towns of Cuchillo, Chloride, and Winston, to connect with NM 59 to Beaverhead. There is nothing of significance in Beaverhead except a Ranger Station. A sign on the highway identifies it as the *Beaverhead Work Center, Gila National Forest.* A few buildings, partially obscured by a heavy growth of pine and piñons, are visible on the left side of the road. Beaverhead is located in the rugged high country of the Gila National Forest, noted for its excellent hunting, its miles of trout-populated fishing streams, and its superb scenery. Heavily wooded forests of piñon,

spruce, and ponderosa pine line both sides of the highway as it winds, rising and descending in steep grades as it passes the Continental Divide at an elevation of 7,670 feet above sea level.

Wall Lake is located about fifteen miles south of Beaverhead off Forest Road 150. About eight miles before reaching Wall Lake, a sign indicates its distance and direction. There is a one-lane gravel road to the lake. There are alternate routes to Wall Lake. One interesting route is the drive north from San Lorenzo and the small village of Mimbres on Forest Road 150. However, this road is not recommended for trailers. It is rough, and during wet weather only high-clearance or four-wheel-drive vehicles are advised, as some of the creeks wash over the road. It is also recommended that information on road conditions be obtained from a Forest Service Office or Ranger Station before attempting access to Wall Lake from this southern route.

*Wall Lake*

# WALL LAKE

Wall Lake is a fifteen-acre lake, managed by the New Mexico Department of Game and Fish. It is cradled in a scenic canyon in the Gila National Forest fifteen miles south of Beaverhead. The lake is stocked with rainbow trout; boats are permitted, but power is limited to oars or electic motors. The approach to the lake south of the Beaverhead turn-off is by way of a gravel road that winds and twists along steep rises and descents. Thickly wooded forests of ponderosa pine line both sides of the road, which occasionally opens to vistas of green valleys then narrows to hug steep canyon walls. A sheer sandstone rock formation towers above one edge of the lake, where an overhang at its base served as a primitive shelter for early hunters in the area. Traces of their camp fires still remain on the smoke-smudged surface of the wall beneath the overhang.

Wall Lake and a 100-feet perimeter of land around it were leased by the State Game Commission from a private party in 1948. A ten-acre tract included in the lease was developed as a campground and picnic area. The facilities include sites for tents and trailers, tables, pit toilets, and fire places. No hook-ups are provided, nor is there drinking water. Other campgrounds are located south of the lake along Forest Road 150, but these may become inaccessible due to bad road conditions during inclement weather. There are no service stations along the routes to Wall Lake, so it is advisable to start the trip with a full tank of fuel and knowledge of current road conditions.

## Directions from Albuquerque

Take I-25 South to the Cuchillo Exit 89 (near Elephant Butte). Take NM 52 west past Cuchillo, Chloride, and Winston to the junction of NM 59 west to Beaverhead. Continue on NM 59. Watch for signs south (on Forest Road 150) about five miles to Wall Lake. It is advisable to check road conditions before use of FR 150. It is deeply rutted and hazardous in wet weather. Four-wheel-drive and high-clearance vehicles is recommended.

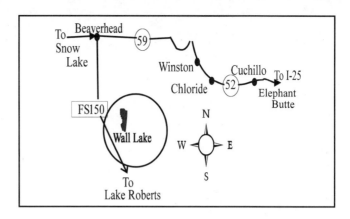

| | |
|---|---|
| Surface acres: 10 | Distance from Albuquerque: 100 miles |
| Elevation: 7,500 feet | Location: 15 miles south of Beaverhead in the |
| Max. trailer size & fee: No fee; due to rough | Gila National Forest |
| road, large campers or trailers are not advised | Fish species: Rainbow trout |
| Mailing address: New Mexico Department of Game and Fish, | |
| Box 25112, Santa Fe, NM 87504  (505) 827-7882 | Season: 1 April-31 March, weather permitting |
| Police emergency tel. #: 911 | |

## ACTIVITIES AND FACILITIES

| | NO | YES | Proximity to Lake in Miles | | NO | YES | Proximity to Lake in Miles |
|---|---|---|---|---|---|---|---|
| Bait and supplies | X | | | Airplane runway | X | | |
| Boat gas | X | | | Bottled gas | X | | |
| Boat ramp | | X | | Café/ snack bar | X | | |
| Boat rental | X | | | Chemical toilets | X | | |
| Camping | | X | | Drinking water | X | | |
| Fire pits | | X | | Electrical hook-up | X | | |
| Fire places | X | | | Flush toilets | X | | |
| Firewood | | X | | Grocery store | X | | |
| Fishing | | X | | Handicapped access | X | | |
| Golf | X | | | Ice | X | | |
| Hiking | | X | | Laundry | X | | |
| Marina | X | | | Lodgings | X | | |
| Picnicking | | X | | Pit toilets | | X | |
| Riding | X | | | Playground | X | | |
| Scuba diving | X | | | Restaurant | X | | |
| Stables | X | | | Sanitary disposal | X | | |
| Swimming | X | | | Sewer hook-up | X | | |
| Tables | | X | | Shelters | X | | |
| Telephone | X | | | Shopping | X | | |
| Tennis | X | | | Showers | X | | |
| Tent sites | | X | | Trailer space | | X | |
| Winter sports | X | | | Water hook-up | X | | |

## Special Rules and Regulations

**Fishing:** New Mexico fishing license required
**Catch limit:** 6 trout, 6 in possession
**Boating:** Boats restricted to oars or electric motors only
**Other:** Campgrounds are undeveloped, with limited facilities

# In the Vicinity of Glenwood

## *Glenwood*

*There is one lake in the vicinity of Glenwood:
Glenwood Ponds*

Glenwood is a small picturesque village located on the National Scenic Route U.S. 180, at the junction of Whitewater Creek and the San Francisco River. It had its beginnings after the discoveries of gold and silver in the Mogollon Mountains above Whitewater Canyon, in the late 1870s. These discoveries drew miners who set up mining camps and were then followed by cattlemen and homesteaders who settled the area. Glenwood was originally called Glenwood Springs, but in 1901 the name was changed to Glenwood. Located in the heart of the Gila National Forest, Glenwood has become the gateway to the scenic and awesome beauty of the forest's recreational areas. Scenic drives through majestic mountains, hundreds of miles of swift-flowing trout streams, and the availability of numerous camp and picnic grounds have established Glenwood as a base for thousands of hunters, fishermen, campers, hikers, and sightseers each year.

One of the main scenic attractions is the historic Catwalk. It is set in a beautiful box canyon at the edge of the wilderness just east of Glenwood. The Catwalk is a steel causeway that follows two pipelines, which supplied water power to the old town of Graham, where gold and silver were milled from nearby mines in the late 1890s. The causeway clings to the sides of the sheer walls of the box canyon above the swift-flowing Whitewater Creek on the canyon's floor. Workmen who had to risk the hazardous walk to repair leaks along the pipeline called it the "Catwalk." The present metal Catwalk was constructed in the 1970s by the Forest Service, and was designated as a National Recreation Trail on 18 December, 1978. The Catwalk is accessible by a foot trail from the Whitewater Picnic Ground at the Catwalk's entrance and parking area. The picnic ground is equipped with shelters, tables, fire grills, and restrooms, and each year thousands of nature lovers and hikers come to enjoy the picnicking facilities and take the exciting walk along the colorful canyon on the Catwalk that in some places rises more than twenty feet above the canyon floor. The United States Forest Service and the businesses of Glenwood work together to maintain this beautiful, historic spot.

Glenwood is also the home of the Glenwood Trout Hatchery, which supplies most of the trout in the streams and lakes of the southwestern quadrant of the state. Glenwood has lodgings, service stations, and stores, where food and picnic supplies are available. For those adventurers who plan trips into the wilderness, the Gila Wilderness Ranger Station in Glenwood can supply information on road conditions and maps of the loop tours and places of interest.

*Glenwood Ponds*

# GLENWOOD PONDS

Glenwood Ponds is a one-acre lake, located on the Glenwood Trout Hatchery, about a half-mile west of Glenwood, off U.S. Highway 180. The pond is supplied from the Whitewater Creek and water wells. It is stocked with rainbow trout by the New Mexico Department of Game and Fish. The pond is open to public fishing during daylight hours only. Within the hatchery grounds a gravel road allows easy access to a handicapped parking area. There are no facilities at the pond, but picnicking facilities and restrooms are on the hatchery grounds within walking distance, also reached by a good gravel road. The facilities include a playground with swings and a seesaw, four tables with grills, two pit toilets, and a shelter with tables, benches, and trash cans. It is an attractive picnic ground with huge cottonwoods that provide shade to the well-maintained grassed picnic area.

New Mexico Game and Fish regulations apply. A trout water license and trout stamp are required to fish the pond. There are no stores at the hatchery, but picnic supplies are available in Glenwood.

## Directions from Glenwood

Go half a mile east on U.S. 180 past mile marker 50 and follow signs to Glenwood Trout Hatchery. The ponds are on the hatchery grounds. There is good access on paved roads, and good gravel roads on the hatchery grounds allows easy access to the ponds and picnic area.

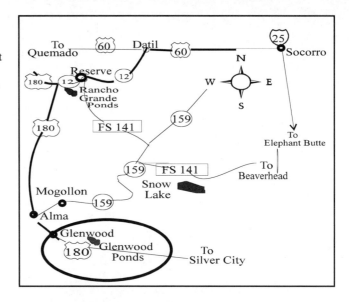

| | |
|---|---|
| **Surface acres:** 1 | **Distance From Albuquerque:** 181 miles |
| **Elevation:** 5,500 feet | **Location:** At the Glenwood Trout Hatchery |
| **Max. trailer size & fee:** No camping, no fee | one-half mile east of Glenwood |
| **Time limit (days):** Day use only | **Fish species:.** Rainbow trout |
| **Mailing address:** New Mexico Department of Game and Fish, | **Season:** Ap.1-Mar.31 Daylight hours only |
| Box 25112 Santa Fe, NM 87504 (505) 827-7911 | **Medical emergency tel. #:** 911 |
| Glenwood Ranger District, (505)539-2461 | **Police emergency tel. #:** 911 |

## ACTIVITIES AND FACILITIES

| | NO | YES | Proximity to Lake in Miles | | NO | YES | Proximity to Lake in Miles |
|---|---|---|---|---|---|---|---|
| Bait and supplies | X | | *1/2 | Airplane runway | X | | |
| Boat gas | X | | | Bottled gas | X | | |
| Boat ramp | X | | | Café/snack bar | X | | * 1/2 |
| Boat rental | X | | | Chemical toilets | X | | |
| Camping | X | | | Drinking water | | X | |
| Fire Pits | X | | | Electrical hook-up | X | | |
| Fire places | | X | | Flush toilets | X | | |
| Firewood | X | | | Grocery store | X | | * 1/2 |
| Fishing | | X | | Handicapped access | | X | |
| Golf | X | | | Ice | X | | |
| Hiking | X | | | Laundry | X | | |
| Marina | X | | | Lodgings | X | | * 1/2 |
| Picnicking | | X | | Pit toilets | | X | |
| Riding | | | | Playground | | X | |
| Scuba diving | X | | | Restaurant | X | | *1/2 |
| Stables | X | | | Sanitary disposal | X | | |
| Swimming | X | | | Sewer hook-up | X | | |
| Tables | X | | | Shelters | | X | |
| Telephone | X | | | Shopping | X | | |
| Tennis | X | | | Showers | X | | |
| Tent sites | X | | | Trailer space | X | | |
| Winter sports | X | | | Water hook-up | X | | |

*Lodgings, services and stores in Glenwood, 1/2 mile.
**Special Rules and Regulations**
   **Fishing:** NM State fishing license and trout stamp required
   **Catch limit:** 6 trout
   **Boating:** No boats or floating devices permitted
   **Other:** Picnic area is within walking distance of pond

# In the Vicinity of Silver City

## *Silver City*

*There are three lakes in the vicinity of Silver City:*
*Bill Evans Lake, Bear Canyon Reservoir,*
*Lake Roberts*

Silver City is located in Southwestern New Mexico on U.S. Highway 180. It was established as a mining town in 1870 after the discovery of silver deposits in the nearby hills. It is located in one of the Southwest's richest mineralized areas. Even before the discovery of silver in the area, turquoise was mined by Indians, and copper was mined by Spanish settlers east of a marsh called La Cienega de Vicente, the original name of the present Silver City.

In 1895 a series of floods washed out the main street, destroying homes and businesses, leaving a fifty-five-feet deep chasm through the heart of town. In later years the chasm, dubbed the "big ditch," was developed as a community park. Two foot bridges span the width of the "ditch" connecting the two parts of the town with paths and shaded picnic areas along its banks. It is still called main street and is an attractive point of interest for visitors to the city.

Another attraction for visitors is the Silver City Museum located at 312 West Broadway, in the Historic District. The Historic District has been preserved as an old western town. The Museum was originally a Victorian-style mansion. It was built in 1881 by H.B. Allman, who arrived penniless in Silver City, then made a fortune in mining. The mansion-turned-museum, features furnishings from early businesses and homes. It also displays a fine collection of Southwestern artifacts and examples of Mimbres Indian pottery, famous for its finely painted geometric designs.

Silver City is steeped in history. It is the boyhood home of Billy the Kid and the burial place of his mother, Catherine Antrim. Her grave can be found in the Memory Lane Cemetery on the western edge of the city off U.S. 180. Silver City also experienced the turbulence of Apache Indian raids by militant Indians like Cochise, Geronimo, and Victorio. Today, Silver City is the largest city in the four counties of Southwestern New Mexico and is billed as the *"Gateway to the Gila Wilderness,"* where unlimited recreational opportunities draw thousands of visitors throughout the year. Its scenic drives through fabled gold mining towns like Mogollon to its lakes and hundreds of miles of fishing streams and its abundance of wild game for the hunter make Gila country a recreational paradise.

Today, tourism, and copper mining and processing are the main sources of income for Silver City. It is a modern city now, with a full array of dining, shopping, and lodging conveniences, and it serves as a base for tourists, campers, hunters, sightseers, hikers, fishermen, and photographers.

*Bill Evans Lake*

# BILL EVANS LAKE

Bill Evans Lake is a sixty-two-acre lake located twenty-nine miles northwest of Silver City and nine miles southeast of Cliff. It is reached by way of U.S. 180 West, connecting with Forest Road 809, then driving south four miles to the lake. Forest Road 809 is a good paved road that runs parallel to the Gila River, which fills the lake that lies 300 feet above the river. The lake was created by pumping water from the river up the high mesa, where it was impounded and kept at a constant level. It was constructed by the Phelps Dodge Corporation in 1969 to provide a source of water for its mining and metallurgical operations near Tyrone, New Mexico. The New Mexico Department of Game and Fish tested the water's suitability to sustain trout and warm-water fish species. Satisfied with the results of the test, they entered into an agreement with Phelps Dodge Corporation for use

of the lake in perpetuity. Though the lake is lacking in shade trees, it is a pretty lake that offers a nice view of the surrounding mountains.

Facilities at the lake are limited to five clean and serviced vault toilets. There is a parking area at each end of the lake accessed by a good gravel road. The lake has no electric or water facilities. Camping is permitted with a ten-day stay limit on undeveloped grounds. Boats are permitted, but are restricted to oars or electric motors. The lake is stocked with rainbow trout and is also populated with channel catfish, bluegill, crappie, and largemouth bass. Several state record catches of largemouth bass have been pulled from Bill Evans Lake. These largemouth bass are Florida strain and Florida hybrids, which grow larger than the more common northern strain.

## Directions from Albuquerque

Take I-25 south to the junction of NM 152 at Caballo and go west. Connect with U.S. 180 West to Silver City. Go twenty-four miles to Forest Service Road 809, and go south four and a half miles to lake. From Cliff, go five miles east on U.S. 180 to FR 809. Turn south and drive four and a half miles to the lake.

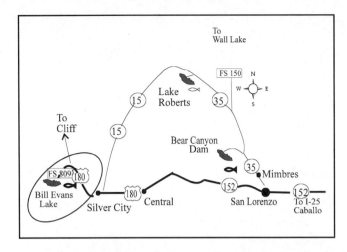

| | | |
|---|---|---|
| Surface acres: 62 | | Distance from Albuquerque: 269 miles |
| Elevation: 4,700 feet | | Location: 29 miles northwest of Silver City; |
| Max. trailer size & fee: No size limit, no fee | | 9 miles southeast of Cliff |
| Time limit: 10 days | | Fish species: Largemouth bass, channel catfish, |
| Mailing address: New Mexico Department of Game and Fish, | | crappie, bluegill, rainbow trout |
| Box 25112, Santa Fe, NM 87504 (505) 827-7882 | | Season: All year |
| Medical emergency tel. #: 911 | | Police emergency tel. #: 388-1542 |

## ACTIVITIES AND FACILITIES

| | NO | YES | Proximity to Lake in Miles | | NO | YES | Proximity to Lake in Miles |
|---|---|---|---|---|---|---|---|
| Bait and supplies | X | | * 29 | Airplane runway | X | | |
| Boat gas | X | | | Bottled gas | X | | |
| Boat ramp | X | | | Café/ snack bar | X | * | |
| Boat rental | X | | | Chemical toilets | X | | |
| Camping | | X | | Drinking water | X | | |
| Fire pits | | X | | Electrical hook-up | X | | |
| Fire places | X | | | Flush toilets | X | | |
| Firewood | X | | | Grocery store | X | * | |
| Fishing | | X | | Handicapped access | | X | |
| Golf | X | | * | Ice | X | | |
| Hiking | X | | | Laundry | X | * | |
| Marina | X | | | Lodgings | X | * | |
| Picnicking | | X | | Vault toilets | | X | |
| Riding | X | | | Playground | X | | |
| Scuba diving | X | | | Restaurant | X | * | |
| Stables | X | | | Sanitary disposal | X | | |
| Swimming | X | | | Sewer hook-up | X | | |
| Tables | X | | | Shelters | X | | |
| Telephone | X | | | Shopping | X | | |
| Tennis | X | | | Showers | X | | |
| Tent sites | | X | | Trailer space | | X | |
| Winter sports | X | | | Water hook-up | X* | | |

*Lodgings, services, stores in Silver City, 29 miles.
**Special Rules and Regulations**
  **Fishing:** State license required
  **Catch limit:** Black bass under 12 inches or over 16 inches; see page 344, Warm-Water Fish Regulations
  **Boating:** Boats restricted to oars or electric motors
  **Other:** Campgrounds, undeveloped

*Bear Canyon Reservoir*

# BEAR CANYON RESERVOIR

Bear Canyon Reservoir is a twenty-five-acre lake located two miles north of the small village of Mimbres, off NM 35, and fifteen miles southeast of Lake Roberts. It is cradled in a beautiful canyon setting of ponderosa, piñon, juniper, and scrub oak at an elevation of 6,000 feet above sea level. It was built by the Works Progress Administration in 1936–1937. It has a boat ramp and permits boats powered by oars or electric motors limited to trolling speeds. The lake is populated with catfish, crappie, bass, and sunfish and is stocked regularly with rainbow trout by the New Mexico Department of Game and Fish.

The highway from the south, leading to Bear Canyon Reservoir, is a good paved road just seven miles from the junction of NM 152 and NM 35. At this point, a direction sign points the way to the lake. A grocery store is off the road just before reaching this sign. The road to the lake is a narrow, hard-packed dirt and gravel road, which twists and turns uphill 2.1 miles to its top, where the road curves to the right, offering an excellent view of the lake. It is a crystal-clear lake with parking areas along its banks. A pit toilet is located on each end of the parking area. There are no camping facilities at the lake, but there is an area for camping and picnicking ground with tables, fire rings, and pit toilets, located at the top of the hill adjacent to the spillway that overlooks the lake. This road is not recommended for large RVs or trailers. A mile from the Bear Canyon Reservoir, on the way to Lake Roberts, is a trading post, food, lodgings, and a country and deli store where picnic and fishing supplies are available. Maps and information can be obtained from the Mimbres Ranger Station located here.

## Directions from Albuquerque

Take I-25 south to the junction of NM 152 near Caballo. Turn west on NM 152 to junction of NM 35, then at San Lorenzo go north through Mimbres and two miles to the lake.

## From Silver City

Drive east on U.S. 180, connect with NM 152 to San Lorenzo, then go north on NM 35 through Mimbres and follow the signs as mentioned above.

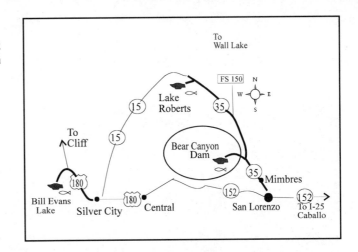

| | | |
|---|---|---|
| **Surface acres:** 25 | | **Distance from Albuquerque:** 224 miles |
| **Elevation:** 6,000 feet | | **Location:** 2 miles north of Mimbres; 15 miles |
| **Max. trailer size & fee:** 17 feet; no fee | | south of Lake Roberts |
| **Time limit:** 10 days | | **Fish species:** Rainbow trout, catfish, and crappie |
| **Mailing address:** New Mexico Department of Game and Fish, | | **Season:** All year |
| Box 25112, Santa Fe, NM 87504  (505) 827-7882 | | **Police emergency tel. #:** 911 |
| **Medical emergency tel. #:** 911 | | |

## ACTIVITIES AND FACILITIES

| | NO | YES | Proximity to Lake in Miles | | NO | YES | Proximity to Lake in Miles |
|---|---|---|---|---|---|---|---|
| Bait and supplies | X | | *3 | Airplane runway | X | | |
| Boat gas | X | | | Bottled gas | X | | |
| Boat ramp | | X | | Café/ snack bar | X | | *3 |
| Boat rental | X | | | Chemical toilets | X | | |
| Camping | | X | | Drinking water | X | | |
| Fire pits | | X | | Electrical hook-up | X | | |
| Fire places | | X | | Flush toilets | X | | |
| Firewood | | X | | Grocery store | X | | *3 |
| Fishing | | X | | Handicapped access | | X | |
| Golf | X | | | Ice | X | | |
| Hiking | | X | | Laundry | X | | |
| Marina | X | | | Lodgings | X | | *3 |
| Picnicking | | X | | Pit toilets | | X | |
| Riding | X | | | Playground | X | | |
| Scuba diving | X | | | Restaurant | X | | *3 |
| Stables | X | | | Sanitary disposal | X | | |
| Swimming | X | | | Sewer hook-up | X | | |
| Tables | | X | | Shelters | X | | |
| Telephone | X | | | Shopping | X | | |
| Tennis | X | | | Showers | X | | |
| Tent sites | | X | | Trailer space | | X | |
| Winter sports | X | | | Water hook-up | X | | |

*Lodging, cafe, stores, 1 mile from turnoff to Bear Canyon Lake.

**Special Rules and Regulations**

**Fishing:** New Mexico fishing license required

**Catch limit:** 6 trout; 6 in possession;  consult Fishing Regulations, page 344, for other species

**Boating:** Restricted to oars or electric motors

**Other:** Camping area is located next to spillway at one end of lake

*Lake Roberts*

# LAKE ROBERTS

Lake Roberts is located twenty-five miles northeast of Silver City and seventeen miles north of Mimbres, off NM 35. It is a seventy-two-acre man-made lake on Sapillo Creek, lying at an elevation of 6,000 feet, and cradled in a pristine setting of ponderosa and piñon within the Gila National Forest. The lake was constructed by the New Mexico Department of Game and Fish and completed in 1962, drawing its waters from Sapillo Creek. It was named in memory of Austin A. Roberts, a Department of Game and Fish pilot, who died in an airplane crash while in the line of duty in 1960. The drive north to the lake on NM 35 from Mimbres is a scenic drive that passes weathered sandstone formations interspersed with thick stands of ponderosa and piñon pines that line the roadside. From the lake's entrance, a gravel road leads to a boat launching and docking ramp. Parking is not permitted at the ramp. Fishing is permitted from the ramp when it is not in use for boat launching. Boats are restricted to hand power and electric motors. There are two vault toilets outside of the lake's entrance and two inside. The only other facilities at the lake are trash cans and drinking water. Since cleaning fish in the lake is prohibited, convenient fish-cleaning tables with water faucets are provided.

Lake Roberts Campground is located within walking distance of the lake. On our visit to this lake in the fall of 1993, plans were under way to add more toilets and other facilities. Dirt was being transferred from the lake to the campground to be used to level sites for RVs and trailers. Water, fire grills, tables, toilets, and a nature trail are presently available. The completion date for this project was set for May 1994, and the renovation was completed on schedule. On the upper section of the lake is Mesa Campground, a beautifully maintained complex that overlooks the lake. It has pull-through camper sites, trash cans, fire grills, tables, shelters, water, and a modern building with flush toilets.

## Directions from Albuquerque

Take I-25 south to the junction of NM 152 near Caballo. Go west on NM 152 to San Lorenzo. Go north on NM 35 then drive eleven miles north of Mimbres and follow signs to the lake. There is good access via paved roads.

## From Silver City

Go east on U.S. 180 to the junction of NM 15. Go north to junction of NM 35, continue east, and follow signs to the lake.

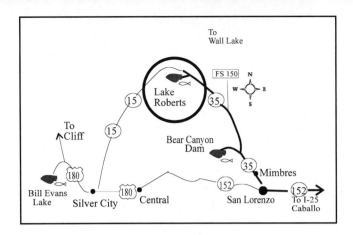

| | | |
|---|---|---|
| **Surface acres:** 72 | | |
| **Elevation:** 7,000 feet | | |
| **Max. trailer size & fee:** No size limit; fee, $5.00 | | |
| **Time limit:** 7 days | | |
| **Mailing address:** New Mexico Department of Game and Fish, Box 25112, Santa Fe, NM 87504 (505) 827-7882 | | |
| **Medical emergency tel. #:** 911 | | |

**Distance from Albuquerque:** 239 miles

**Location:** 17 miles north of Mimbres, 25 miles northeast of Silver City

**Fish species:** Rainbow trout, catfish, bluegill, bass, crappie, and sunfish

**Season:** All year

## ACTIVITIES AND FACILITIES

| | NO | YES | Proximity to Lake in Miles | | NO | YES | Proximity to Lake in Miles |
|---|---|---|---|---|---|---|---|
| **Bait and supplies** | | X | * | **Airplane runway** | X | | |
| **Boat gas** | X | | | **Bottled gas** | X | | |
| **Boat ramp** | | X | | **Café/ snack bar** | X | | |
| **Boat rental** | | X | | **Chemical toilets** | | X | |
| **Camping** | | X | | **Drinking water** | | X | |
| **Fire pits** | | X | | **Electrical hook-up** | X | | |
| **Fire places** | | X | | **Flush toilets** | | X | |
| **Firewood** | X | | | **Grocery store** | X | | |
| **Fishing** | | X | | **Handicapped access** | | X | |
| **Golf** | X | | | **Ice** | X | | * |
| **Hiking** | | X | | **Laundry** | X | | * |
| **Marina** | X | | | **Lodgings** | X | | * |
| **Picnicking** | | X | | **Vault toilets** | | X | |
| **Riding** | X | | | **Playground** | X | | |
| **Scuba diving** | X | | | **Restaurant** | X | | * |
| **Stables** | X | | | **Sanitary disposal** | X | | |
| **Swimming** | X | | | **Sewer hook-up** | X | | |
| **Tables** | | X | | **Shelters** | | X | |
| **Telephone** | X | | | **Shopping** | X | | |
| **Tennis** | X | | | **Showers** | X | | |
| **Tent sites** | | X | | **Trailer space** | | X | |
| **Winter sports** | X | | | **Water hook-up** | X | | |

*Accommodations and services in village of Lake Roberts.

**Special Rules and Regulations**

**Fishing:** New Mexico fishing license required

**Catch limit:** 6 trout; 6 in possession; see page 344 for other limits

**Boating:** Restricted to oars or electric motors

**Other:** Camping in Lake Roberts Campground, within walking distance of the lake

Amador Hotel
*(Now a Museum)*
*Las Cruces, New Mexico*

# In the Vicinity of Las Cruces

## *Las Cruces*

*There are two lakes in the vicinity of Las Cruces: Burn Lake, Leasburg Dam State Park*

For those outdoors enthusiasts who wish to pause from their recreational activities and enjoy a variety of other vacation pleasures; to sightsee or to stroll on old plazas or along streets where legendary wild-west heroes and outlaws walked—characters like Billy the Kid and Sheriff Pat Garrett—for those whose passions lean towards picturesque villages and thick-walled adobe buildings that once protected settlers from Apache attacks, Las Cruces is the place to visit. Here one can imagine life as it might have been years ago.

Las Cruces lies in the heart of the fertile Mesilla Valley and has retained the charm and old-west flavor, as evident in the village of La Mesilla, two miles south of town and a state monument, where colorful ristras of red chile, symbols of Southwestern hospitality, decorate homes and businesses in the town. It was in Mesilla that Billy the Kid received the death penalty at the county courthouse. He escaped from jail and later was tracked down and killed by Sheriff Pat Garrett. The Las Cruces Masonic Cemetery, downtown Las Cruces, bears the remains of Pat Garrett who was ambushed and killed in 1908 in the nearby Organ Mountains.

Las Cruces is a thriving and growing city of 60,000, lying at an elevation of 3,900 feet above sea level. It was established as a city in 1907 and is bordered by the jagged Organ Mountains on the east and the Rio Grande on the west. For centuries, the Las Cruces site has been a stopping place for traveling parties. In 1598, Don Juan de Oñate led colonists along El Camino Real ("The King's Highway"). The journey started from the city of Chihuahua, Mexico, passed through Las Cruces, and continued to Santa Fe. It was along this route, a few miles north of the present site of Las Cruces, that Apaches attacked and killed a party of travelers from Taos, New Mexico. Subsequent travelers, who found their bodies, erected crosses to mark their graves. Other travelers who followed referred to the site as La Placita de Las Cruces ("The Place of the Crosses"). The name was later shortened to Las Cruces.

Today, Las Cruces lies in an area surrounded by farms of chile, fields of cotton, groves of pecan trees, and acres of vineyards. It is only fifty miles south to the colorful shops and markets of Juarez, Mexico, and only an hour's drive north to the major recreation spots of Elephant Butte Lake, Caballo Lake, and Percha Dam State Parks. Las Cruces is just fifteen miles south of Leasburg Dam State Park. It offers the finest in dining, nightlife, and entertainment. There is a complete variety of fare—from an international menu to take-out picnic lunches, from Country and Western music to Symphony—and of course, there is a full array of accommodations, conveniences, facilities, stores, and service stations.

*Burn Lake*

# BURN LAKE

Burn lake is a seven-acre lake located in Las Cruces, on West Amador Avenue and I-10. It is easily accessed by paved roads. It is stocked by the New Mexico Department of Game and Fish with winter trout and channel catfish. It also contains largemouth bass and bluegill. Burn Lake is included in the Big Cat Program, started by the Department of Game and Fish in 1993 to provide improved fishing opportunities during the spring and summer months (see page 344, Warm-Water Fishing Regulations). Because of its convenient location, Burn Lake is popular among the locals and is an enjoyable stop for tourists who wish to "cast a line" in its stocked waters as a diversion from the many attractions in and around Las Cruces. Attractions like golf, tennis, sightseeing, horseback riding, camping in the nearby Organ Mountains, and shopping the colorful shops in La Mesilla lure many visitors. La Mesilla is a quaint colorful village just two miles south of town.

Burn Lake is open from 6 A.M.–11 P.M. daily. It is a well-maintained complex, equipped with picnic tables, shelters, flush toilets, a café/snack bar, and drinking water. During the period of mid-August through mid-May, no swimming, boating, or other water activities are allowed unless authorized by permit. Swimming and other water activities are allowed during swim season—mid-May through mid-August—from 1 P.M. to 7 P.M. daily, while a lifeguard is on duty or by authorized permit. Fishing, with handicapped access, is allowed during the hours of operation according to New Mexico Game and Fish Regulations.

## Directions from Albuquerque

Take I-25 south to Las Cruces exit. Go west on Lohman Ave. and connect with West Amador Ave. and follow signs to Burn Lake. Burn Lake is off I-10.

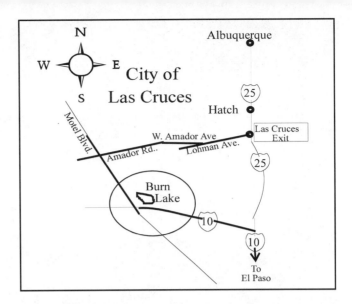

| | NO | YES | Proximity to Lake in Miles |
|---|---|---|---|
| Surface acres: 7 | | | |

| | | |
|---|---|---|
| Surface acres: 7 | Distance from Albuquerque: 223 miles | |
| Elevation: 3,900 feet | Location: In Las Cruces, off West Amador Ave. | |
| Max. trailer size & fee: No trailers | and I-10 | |
| Time limit: Day use only | Fish species: Bass, channel catfish, bluegill, and | |
| Telephone #: (505) 526-0668 | winter trout | |
| Police emergency tel. #: 524-6111 | Season: All year, winter trout, 1 November-31 March | |
| Medical emergency tel. #: 911 | | |

## ACTIVITIES AND FACILITIES

| | NO | YES | Proximity to Lake in Miles | | NO | YES | Proximity to Lake in Miles |
|---|---|---|---|---|---|---|---|
| Bait and supplies | X | | | Airplane runway | X | | |
| Boat gas | X | | | Bottled gas | X | | |
| Boat ramp | X | | | Café/snack bar | | X | |
| Boat rental | X | | | Chemical toilets | X | | |
| Camping | X | | | Drinking water | | X | |
| Fire pits | X | | | Electrical hook-up | X | | |
| Fire places | X | | | Flush toilets | | X | |
| Firewood | X | | | Grocery store | X | | |
| Fishing | | X | | Handicapped access | | X | |
| Golf | X | | | Ice | X | | |
| Hiking | X | | | Laundry | X | | |
| Marina | X | | | Lodgings | X | | |
| Picnicking | | X | | Pit toilets | X | | |
| Riding | X | | | Playground | X | | |
| Scuba diving | X | | | Restaurant | X | | |
| Stables | X | | | Sanitary disposal | X | | |
| Swimming | | X | | Sewer hook-up | | | |
| Tables | | X | | Shelters | | X | |
| Telephone | | X | | Shopping | X | | |
| Tennis | X | | | Showers | X | | |
| Tent sites | X | | | Trailer space | X | | |
| Winter sports | X | | | Water hook-up | X | | |

Full accommodations, stores, and services in city, within 1 mile.

**Special Rules and Regulations**

**Fishing:** New Mexico Department of Game and Fish regulations apply; see Fishing Proclamation

**Catch limit:** 6 trout; or 6 in possession; 2 catfish per day; see page 344 for other warm-water species limits

**Boating:** Allowed by special permit mid-August–mid-May

**Other:** Swimming between 1 P.M.- 7 P.M., while lifeguard on duty, and in season

*Leasburg Dam*

# LEASBURG DAM STATE PARK

Leasburg Dam forms a small lake in Leasburg Dam State Park. The lake is formed by the low-level Leasburg Dam that diverts water from the Rio Grande to irrigate the immense farming area of the upper Mesilla Valley. Its diversion channels provide irrigation to farms as far south as Las Cruces. The dam was built in 1908 and is operated by the Bureau of Reclamation for the Middle Rio Grande Conservancy District. It lies at an elevation of 4,000 feet above sea level and is located twenty miles south of Hatch, off I-25, and fifteen miles north of Las Cruces by way of U.S. Highway 85.

Leasburg Dam State Park was established in 1971. It totals 140 acres and occupies both sides of the Rio Grande, providing a pleasurable diversion and overnight camping spot for visitors to attractions in the area, including the nearby ruins of Fort Selden, a state monument. This now-abandoned United States military outpost was established in 1865 to protect settlers during the Indian Wars. The lake is stocked with winter trout and is populated with channel catfish, bass, bluegill, and perch. Fishing, swimming, and small motorless boats are permitted on the lake. A well-equipped fee campground and picnic area includes RV spaces with electric and water hook-ups, a dump station, twenty-two shelters with piped-in water, a large group shelter overlooking the river below the dam, and a modern well-maintained comfort station with flush toilets and hot showers. A miniature replica of Fort Selden and its adobe buildings serves as a children's playground. There are no stores or other services in the park, but needed picnic supplies are available at a grocery store in the nearby town of Fort Selden.

## Directions from Albuquerque

Take I-25 south, continue past Hatch to Radium Springs, Exit 19. Go one mile west on NM 157 to marker, and follow signs to Leasburg Dam State Park. The park is located twenty miles south of Hatch and fifteen miles north of Las Cruces. Stores for fishing and picnic supplies are available in nearby Fort Selden about half a mile.

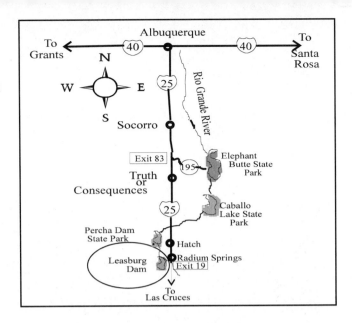

| | |
|---|---|
| **Elevation:** 4,000 feet | **Distance from Albuquerque:** 206 miles |
| **Max. trailer size & fee:** 40 feet; fee posted | **Location:** 20 miles south of Hatch off I-25; |
| **Time limit:** 14 days | 15 miles north of Las Cruces, via U.S. 85 |
| **Mailing address:** Leasburg Dam, P.O. Box 16, | **Fish species:** Channel catfish, bass, perch, |
| Radium Springs, NM 88054 (505) 524-5068 | and stocked winter trout |
| **Police emergency tel. #:** 911 | **Season:** All year; winter trout 1 November-31 March |
| **Medical emergency tel. #:** 911 | **Camping:** Full facilities and RV spaces |

## ACTIVITIES AND FACILITIES

| | NO | YES | Proximity to Lake in Miles | | NO | YES | Proximity to Lake in Miles |
|---|---|---|---|---|---|---|---|
| Bait and supplies | X | | *1/2 | Drinking water | | X | |
| Boat gas | X | | | Bottled gas | X | | |
| Boat ramp | X | | | Café/snack bar | X | | |
| Boat rental | X | | | Chemical toilets | | X | |
| Camping | | X | | Electrical hook-up | | X | |
| Fire pits | | X | | Flush toilets | | X | |
| Fire places | | X | | Grocery store | X | | |
| Firewood | X | | | Handicapped access | | X | |
| Fishing | | X | | Ice | X | | |
| Hiking | | X | | Laundry | X | | |
| Marina | X | | | Lodgings | X | | |
| Picnicking | | X | | Pit toilets | X | | |
| Riding | X | | | Playground | | X | |
| Scuba diving | X | | | Restaurant | X | | |
| Stables | X | | | Sanitary disposal | | X | |
| Swimming | | X | | Sewer hook-up | | X | |
| Tables | | X | | Shelters | | X | |
| Telephone | | X | | Shopping | X | | |
| Tennis | X | | | Showers | | X | |
| Tent sites | | X | | Trailer space | | X | |
| Winter sports | X | | | Water hook-up | | X | |

Accommodations in Las Cruces, 15 miles. Stores in Ft. Selden, nearby (1/2 mile).

**Special Rules and Regulations**

**Fishing:** New Mexico Department of Game and Fish Regulations apply; see Fishing Proclamation

**Catch limit:** 6 trout; 6 in possession; see page 344 for warm-water fish species limits

**Boating:** No boating

**Other:** No time limit for camping 1 November-31 March

# APPENDICES

# New Mexico State Park Regulations

The state park system in New Mexico was established in the 1930s to preserve and protect some of the state's finest recreational resources, natural scenic wonders, and historic sites. Its forty state parks are located throughout the state, and New Mexico can proudly boast of having six of the seven life zones, from the Chihuahuan Desert lowlands of 2,800 feet — with their wide range of flora and fauna — to the lush mountain forests and lakes of more than 13,000 feet.

New Mexico's state parks offer a full range of recreational opportunities, whether one's interest is in fishing, hiking, camping, boating, or learning about New Mexico's culture and rich heritage through the state park system's interpretive centers. The general regulations and fees for park use, effective in 1994 are as follows:

Fees are posted at the park entrances. Fees for state park use are generally the same at all parks. (There are some exceptions, and these are also posted at entrances.)

Fees shall be paid upon entrance to the park. Failure to obtain the permit results in a field collection of the required fee, plus an administrative surcharge of $10.00 in addition to the required fee.

Stay limit is 14 days unless otherwise noted.

Annual entrance fees and camping permits are issued by the calendar year and may be purchased at any state park or from the New Mexico State Park Division Office in Santa Fe, New Mexico.

## FEE SCHEDULE

**Daily Entrance Fees**
  Day-use (per vehicle): ................................$3.00
  Walk-in/bicycle: ...........................................Free
**Overnight Camping (per day)**
  Primitive site: ............................................$6.00
  Developed site: ..........................................$7.00
  Electrical hook-up: .....................................$4.00
  Sewage hook-up: ........................................$2.00
**Annual Entrance Permit:** ..........................$36.00
  Age 62 and over: ......................................$21.00
  Handicapped/disabled: ............................$21.00
**Annual Camping Permit:** ..........................$89.00
  Age 62 and over: ......................................$52.00
  Handicapped/disabled: ............................$52.00
  Extra vehicle: ............................................$5.00

Complete information on park regulations, etiquette, boating rules, boat safety and equipment requirements is available at local park headquarters or from New Mexico State Park and Recreation Division, P.O. Box 1147, Santa Fe, NM 87504-1147; (505) 827-7465.

# New Mexico Fishing License Requirements

A current New Mexico fishing license is required for all persons twelve years of age or older. The fishing license year is April 1–March 31 of each year.

Resident License Requirements are as follows:
1. Must be a United States citizen residing in New Mexico for at least ninety days immediately before purchasing the license
2. Can be a non-United States citizen, but must be legally in the U.S. and residing in New Mexico for at least ninety days immediately before purchasing the license
3. Some students in New Mexico educational institutions and United States Armed Forces members permanently stationed in New Mexico may purchase resident licenses if they submiit a verification document at time of purchase

Fishing licenses can be purchased by mail through the Santa Fe office of the New Mexico Department of Game and Fish, P.O. Box 25112, Santa Fe, NM 87504, or through vendors such as sporting goods stores or bait and tackle shops located throughout the state.

**Note:** Since fees and regulations are subject to change, please consult a current New Mexico Fishing Proclamation for current fees and regulations. No New Mexico fishing license is required to fish on Indian reservations. Permission must be obtained from the tribal government to fish on their property. Tribal rules are enforced, with the exception of Cochiti Lake, where a New Mexico fishing license is required. See below and page 344 for more detailed trout-water and warm-water fishing regulations.

# Trout-Water Fishing Regulations

The following information is true for the period 1 April, 1995–31 March, 1998. After that time, consult a current Fishing Proclamation. Unless otherwise noted, most trout lakes are stocked with catchable trout. Those stocked with sub-catchables or fry-size and fingerlings are noted in the text or in tables.

**Bag limits, possession limits, size limits:** 6 fish per day or 6 fish in possession; no more than two can be cutthroat or lake trout (mackinaw).

**Exceptions:** The following lakes allow a bag or possession limit of 10 fish per day—Abiquiu Lake, Charette Lake, Eagle Nest Lake, Heron Lake, McAllister Lake, Navajo Lake, Bonito Lake, Quemado Lake, and Bluewater Lake. At Red River Hatchery Pond, reserved for children under 12, seniors 65 and over, and the handicapped, the bag limit is 4 per day or 4 in possession.

**Special trout waters:** Most special trout waters require artificial lures and flies that have a single, barbless hook. These waters have special bag and possession limits.

All trout waters require a trout validation stamp, but this is not required for anglers under 12 years. Since bag limits and some regulations are subject to change, consult current New Mexico Fishing Proclamation for up-to-date regulations and waters with special rules.

# Warm-Water Fishing Regulations

**Bag limits:** Black bass (largemouth, smallmouth, spotted), 5 per day; walleye, 10 per day; crappie, 20 per day; catfish (all species except bullheads), 15 per day; white bass, 25 per day; striped bass, 2 per day; northern pike, 10 per day; all other warm-water game fish, 20 per day.

**Exceptions:** A special catfish limit of 2 fish per day is enforced at the following lakes—Burn Lake, Oasis Lake, Eunice Lake, Tingley Beach, Green Meadow Lake, Lake Van, Jal Lake. The above seven lakes are included in the Big Cat Program, started in 1993 to provide better fishing opportunities during the spring and summer months.

**Special black bass legal sizes** (largemouth, smallmouth, spotted bass): A 14-inch minimum size to keep, applies to the following lakes— Brantley Lake, Caballo Lake, Cochiti Lake, Conchas Lake, Clayton Lake, Elephant Butte Lake, Springer Lake, Santa Rosa Lake, Sumner Lake, and Ute Lake.

**Other special size limits for black bass in possession:** Bill Evans Lake, 12–16 inches (legal keeper size, under 12 inches or over 16 inches); Bluewater Lake, 14 inches minimum size in possession.

# New Mexico Boating Regulations

All vessels on New Mexico Waters are subject to inspection. A vessel's registration number must be printed on each side of the vessel, and the certificate number must be on board when the vessel is in operation. Boaters may register and obtain titles from their nearest New Mexico Motor Vehicle Divisio office. Registration certificates are good for three calendar years and expire 31 December of the third year. It is required that all vessels be inspected for first registration or titles, and proof of ownership is required.

**Registration Fees (three-year period)**
Class A (under 16 feet in length): $28.00
Class 1 (16 feet to less than 26 feet): $36.00
Class 2 (26 feet to less than 40 feet): $47.50
Class 3 (40 feet to less than 65 feet): $51.00
Vessels over 65 feet: $66.00
*There is a special out-of-state fee for those individuals without an out-of-state registration.

Complete information on park regulations, boating rules and boat safety and equipment requirements is available at local park headquarters or from New Mexico State Park and Recreation Division, P.O. Box 1147, Santa Fe, NM 87504-1147; (505) 827-7465.

# Wilderness Use and Travel Etiquette

Each year thousands of people spend their vacations and weekends in forested wilderness areas for hunting, fishing, hiking, camping and other forms of relaxation. The desire to escape urban congestion for periods of rest and relaxation has created a demand for forest recreation. This need has been met through the extensive development of national, state, and municipal parks. To some, wilderness areas are more preferable than developed parks, because they can enjoy more seclusion and fewer restrictions on their activities. Many of the more accessible wilderness areas have become overcrowded, and evidence of disrespect for the forests and the lakes and streams within them is everywhere: trampled meadows, human waste and litter, outdoor gear, and unsightly campfire scars.

The forests, and the lakes and streams within them, are preeminently the home of wildlife, for it is in the forest that wildlife finds protective cover and food. The number and quality of the fish population in the lakes and streams is influenced by the water's clarity and cleanliness. Trampling of the forest floor and its vegetation, cutting through switchbacks, and scattering of litter, human waste and garbage cause erosion of soil and pollution of streams, which become warm and muddy and ruined for many species of game fish. It is, thus, our responsibility to others and to future generations to leave no trace of our visits to these wonderful resources.

Proper wilderness travel etiquette helps everyone enjoy the wilderness in its natural state. The primitive atmosphere of the wilderness is the attraction that lures the true nature lover. Trees, wildflowers, and picturesque rock formations are for everyone to enjoy in their natural state. Picking flowers, collecting rocks, and scarring trees, are all illegal and prevent others from enjoying their outdoor experience. In recognition of the potential damage to these fragile ecosystems and their natural beauties, respect the wilderness by walking softly. As a courtesy to others, leave no trace of your visit and take away only memories.

# INDEXES

# INDEX OF VICINITIES

| VICINITY | ZONE | MAP KEY | ROUTE AND ACCESSIBILITY (All roads to vicinities below are paved) |
|---|---|---|---|
| Abiquiu, 51 | 1, NW | D8 | 23 miles north of Española on U.S. 84 |
| Amalia, 135 | 2, NE | A2 | 5 miles east of Costilla on NM 196 |
| Albuquerque, 5 | 1, NW | K7 | At intersection of I-25 and I-40; excellent highways |
| Beaverhead, 319 | 4, SW | K4 | Off NM 59, 75 miles west of Elephant Butte |
| Belen, 203 | 3, SE | C2 | 34 miles south of Albuquerque off I-25 |
| Bloomfield, 81 | 1, NW | B3 | At intersection of NM 44 and U.S. 64 |
| Canjilon, 55 | 1, NW | C8 | 12 miles north of Abiquiu off U.S. 84 |
| Carlsbad, 245 | 3, SE | L8 | Southeastern New Mexico at junction of U.S. 285 and U.S. 180 |
| Carrizozo, 223 | 3, SE | G4 | 64 miles east of I-25 at intersection of U.S. 380 and U.S. 54 |
| Clayton, 173 | 2, NE | D11 | 83 miles east of Springer via U.S. 56 |
| Clovis, 281 | 3, SE | D10 | 9 miles from the Texas border at junction of U.S. 70/84 and NM 209 |
| Costilla, 135 | 2, NE | A2 | 20 miles north of Questa via NM 522 |
| Cowles, 105 | 2, NE | F4 | 20 miles north of Pecos on NM 63 |
| Cuba, 27 | 1, NW | F6 | 55 miles northwest of Bernalillo on NM 44 |
| Dulce, 75 | 1, NW | A6 | In northwest New Mexico off U.S. 64 and NM 537 |
| Eagle Nest, 145 | 2, NE | D4 | 17 miles south of Red River via NM 38 |
| Española, 39 | 1, NE | H1 | 84 miles north of Albuquerque via I-25 and U.S. 84/285 |
| Eunice, 267 | 3, SE | L10 | 14 miles south of Hobbs via NM 18 and NM 207 |
| Farmington, 85 | 1, NW | B3 | On U.S. 64 at junction of NM 371 |
| Fort Sumner, 275 | 3, SE | D8 | 45 miles southeast of Santa Rosa on U.S. 84 and U.S. 60 |
| Gallup, 299 | 4, SW | A3 | Off I-40, 22 miles east of Arizona border |
| Glenwood, 323 | 4, SW | L2 | Southwest New Mexico on U.S. 180 at confluence of Whitewater Creek and San Francisco River |
| Grants, 295 | 4, SW | C5 | 78 miles west of Albuquerque on I-40 |
| Hobbs, 259 | 3, SE | K10 | 22 miles southwest of Lovington at junction of 62/180 and NM 18 |
| Indian Reservations Zone 1, NW | | | It is advisable to check road conditions to destination within reservations |
| Isleta, 10 | | C11 | 13 miles southwest of Albuquerque off NM 47 |
| Jicarilla Apache, 75 | | A6 | Headquarters in Dulce 23 miles west of Chama via U.S. 64 or from the south via NM 537 |
| Nambe, 46 | | E9 | East of Pojoaque via NM 503 |
| Navajo, 91 | | B1 | Headquarters in Shiprock via U.S. 64 |
| San Ildefonso, 44 | | E9 | 6 miles west of Pojoaque via NM 503 |
| Santa Clara, 42 | | E9 | Entrance 2 miles south of Española via NM 30 |
| San Juan, 48 | | E9 | At the northern end of Española |
| Zia, 14 Zone 2, NE | | H5 | 17 miles north of Bernalillo off NM 44 |
| Picuris, 123 Zone 3, SE | | F3 | About 1 mile north of Peñasco off NM 75 |
| Mescalero Apache, 227 Zone 4, SW | | H5 | 3 miles south of Ruidoso on U.S. 70 |
| Zuni, 303 | | C1 | 24 miles south of Gallup via 602 |
| Jemez Springs, 21 | 1, NW | G7 | 18 miles north of San Ysidro via NM 4 |
| Jal, 271 | 3, SE | M10 | 33 miles south of Hobbs at junction of NM 18 and 128 |
| Las Cruces, 335 | 4, SW | Q11 | 45 miles north of El Paso off I-25 |
| Las Vegas, 111 | 2, NE | K4 | 64 miles northeast of Santa Fe via I-25 |
| Ledoux (see map), 118 | 2, NE | I3 | 9 miles southeast of Mora via NM 94 |
| Logan, 191 | 2, NE | L11 | 24 miles northeast of Tucumcari via U.S. 54 |
| Los Alamos, 35 | 1, NW | F8 | 19 miles south of Española, then west on NM 502, 14 miles |
| Los Ojos, 67 | 1, NW | B7 | 2 miles north of Tierra Amarilla off U.S. 84 |
| Lovington, 255 | 3, SE | J10 | 28 miles northwest of Hobbs at junction of U.S. 82 and NM 18 |
| Manzano, 199 | 3, SE | C3 | 56 miles south of Albuquerque on NM 55 |
| Maxwell, 159 | 2, NE | D7 | 13 miles north of Springer off I-25 |
| Mora, 117 | 2, NE | G3 | 30 miles north of Las Vegas via I-25 and NM 518 |

| VICINITY | ZONE | MAP KEY | ROUTE AND ACCESSIBILITY (All roads to vicinities below are paved) |
|---|---|---|---|
| **Newkirk, 183** | 2, NE | N6 | 23 miles east of Santa Rosa; Exit 300 then north on NM 129 |
| **Pecos, 101** | 2, NE | K2 | 21 miles northeast of Santa Fe via I-25 |
| **Peña Blanca, 31** | 1, NE | H8 | Via I-25, then northwest on NM 22 |
| **Peñasco, 123** | 2, NE | G3 | South of Picuris Pueblo via NM 75 |
| **Portales, 287** | 3, SE | E10 | 19 miles southwest of Clovis at junction of U.S. 70 and NM 36 |
| **Questa, 127** | 2, NE | C2 | 22 miles north of Taos at junction of NM 522 and NM 38 |
| **Quemado, 309** | 4, SW | G3 | 43 miles west of Datil on U.S. 60 and NM 36 |
| **Ramah, 303** | 4, SW | C3 | 53 miles southwest of Grants on NM 53 |
| **Raton, 165** | 2, NE | B7 | 8½ miles south of the Colorado border at junction of I-25 and U.S. 64/87 |
| **Red River, 141** | 2, NE | C3 | 32 miles northeast of Taos via U.S. 65 and NM 38 |
| **Reserve, 313** | 4, SW | J2 | 53 miles south of Quemado on NM 12 |
| **Roswell, 235** | 3, SE | H7 | 40 miles north of Artesia at junctions of U.S. 285 and U.S. 380 |
| **Roy, 169** | 2, NE | H7 | 35 miles east of Wagon Mound on NM 120 |
| **Ruidoso, 227** | 3, SE | H5 | 41 miles southeast of Carrizozo via NM 37 and NM 38 |
| **San Antonio, 211** | 3, SE | F2 | Good, paved access off I-25 |
| **Santa Rosa, 177** | 2, NE | O6 | 114 miles east of Albuquerque off I-40 |
| **San Ysidro, 13** | 1, NW | H6 | 23 miles northwest of Bernalillo off NM 44 |
| **Shiprock, 91** | 1, NW | B1 | 29 miles west of Farmington on U.S. 64 and U.S. 380 |
| **Silver City, 327** | 4, SW | O4 | 54 miles northwest of Deming on U.S. 180 |
| **Socorro, 207** | 3, SE | E2 | 77 miles south of Albuquerque off I-25 |
| **Springer, 151** | 2, NE | E6 | 67 miles north of Las Vegas via U.S. 85 |
| **Tierra Amarilla, 61** | 1, NW | B7 | 12 miles south of Chama via U.S. 84 |
| **Tres Piedras, 71** | 1, NW | B9 | 29 miles northwest of Taos on U.S. 64 and U.S. 285 |
| **Truth or Consequences, 215** | 3, SE | I1 | 149 miles south of Albuquerque off I-25 |
| **Tucumcari, 187** | 2, NE | M10 | 168 miles east of Albuquerque via I-40 |

# INDEX OF LAKES

| LAKES | ZONE | VICINITY | ACCESSIBILITY FROM VICINITY TO LAKE |
| --- | --- | --- | --- |
| Abiquiu Lake, 52 | 1, NW | Abiquiu | Good access, paved, off NM 96 |
| Alice Lake, 165 | 2, NE | Raton | Good access off paved highway |
| Alto Lake, 230 | 3, NE | Ruidoso | In city; good access, paved |
| Asaayi Lake, 94 | 1, NW | Shiprock | Fair access, dirt/gravel roads |
| Aspen Lake, 96 | 1, NW | Shiprock | Fair access, dirt/gravel roads |
| Bataan Lake, 246 | 3, SE | Carlsbad | In city; excellent access by paved roads |
| Bear Canyon Reservoir, 330 | 4, SE | Silver City | Paved to turn-off, then uphill by gravel road |
| Berland Lake, 96 | 1, NW | Shiprock | Check Navajo tribal office on conditions |
| Bill Evans Lake, 328 | 4, SW | Silver City | Good access, paved roads |
| Bitter Lakes, 240 | 3, SE | Roswell | Good access, paved roads |
| Bluewater Lake, 296 | 4, SW | Grants | Paved access all the way |
| Bonito Lake, 228 | 3, SE | Ruidoso | Good access, paved road, off NM 107 |
| Bosque del Apache, 212 | 3, SE | San Antonio | Good access, paved roads |
| Bosque Redondo Lakes, 278 | 3, SE | Fort Sumner | Paved road access off NM 272, from U.S. 60 |
| Bottomless Lakes State Park, 242 | 3, SE | Roswell | Paved access all the way |
| Brantley Lake, 252 | 3, SE | Carlsbad | Paved access all the way |
| Burford Lake (Stinking Lake), 80 | 1, NW | Dulce | Check out interior road conditions |
| Burn Lake, 336 | 4, SW | Las Cruces | In city, good access on West Amador Ave |
| Burns Canyon Lake, 68 | 1, NW | Los Ojos | Good access, by dirt/gravel road |
| Caballo Lake, 218 | 3, SE | Truth or Consequences | Paved access off I-25 |
| Cabresto Lake, 130 | 2, NE | Questa | High-clearance pick-ups or 4-wheel-drive vehicles |
| Canjilon Lakes, 56 | 1, NW | Canjilon | 4-wheel-drive advised in wet weather |
| Carlsbad Lake, 248 | 3, SE | Carlsbad | Excellent access, within city, all paved roads |
| Carrizozo Lake, 224 | 3, SE | Carrizozo | Paved access off U.S. 380 |
| Chaparral Lake, 256 | 3, SE | Lovington | In city, paved access |
| Charette Lakes, 154 | 2, NE | Springer | Good access, gravel roads |
| Chicosa Lake State Park, 170 | 2, NE | Roy | Paved access; lake dry in 1994 |
| Chuska Lake, 96 | 1, NW | Shiprock | Good access off NM 666 |
| Clayton Lake, 174 | 2, NE | Clayton | Paved roads all the way to lake |
| Cochiti Lake, 32 | 1, NW | Peña Blanca | Paved to lake, good access |
| Conchas Lake, 184 | 2, NE | Newkirk | Access of paved and maintained gravel roads |
| Costilla Diversion Dam, 136 | 2, NE | Costilla | Access off paved NM 196 |
| Cowles Ponds, 106 | 2, NE | Pecos | 20 miles north of Pecos, paved all the way |
| Cutter Lake, 96 | 1, NW | Bloomfield | Good access via paved roads |
| Dragon Fly Lake, 18 | 1, NW | San Ysidro | Good gravel road 1 mile off NM 44 |
| Dulce Lake, 78 | 1, NW | Dulce | Good access, off U.S. 64 |
| Eagle Nest Lake, 146 | 2, NE | Eagle Nest | Good access on paved roads |
| Eagle Lakes, 227 | 3, SE | Ruidoso | On Mescalero Res. good access |
| Eagle Rock Lake, 128 | 2, NE | Questa | Good access off paved road |
| Elephant Butte Lake, 216 | 3, SE | Truth or Consequences | Good access off paved road |
| El Vado Lake, 62 | 1, NW | Tierra Amarilla | Good access off paved roads |
| Enbom Lake, 79 | 1, NW | Dulce | Off J 8, good access, gravel road |
| Escondida Lake, 208 | 3, SE | Socorro | Good access off paved roads |
| Eunice Lake, 268 | 3, SE | Eunice | Good access off paved roads |
| Farmington, Lake, 86 | 1, NW | Farmington | Good access off paved road |
| Fawn Lakes, 142 | 2, NE | Red River | Good access off paved road |
| Fenton Lake, 22 | 1, NW | Jemez Springs | Last mile to lake is dirt, rough, risky when wet |
| Glenwood Ponds, 324 | 4, SW | Glenwood | On Glenwood Fish Hatchery, paved access |
| Goose Lake, 141 | 2, NE | Red River | Steep, unimproved rough Jeep trail |
| Gravel Pit Lakes, 148 | 2, NE | Eagle Nest | Good access, off paved U.S. 64 |
| Green Meadow Lake, 260 | 3, SE | Hobbs | Good access, in city limits |
| Green Acres Lake, 282 | 3, SE | Clovis | Good access, in city, 21st and Main St. |
| Harold L. Brock Fishing Area, 120 | 2, NE | Mora | Good access off paved NM 434 |
| Harry McAdams State Park, 262 | 3, SE | Hobbs | Excellent access by paved roads |
| Hayden Lake, 79 | 1, NW | Dulce | Check road conditions before going |
| Heart Lake, 127 | 2, NE | Questa | 4 mile hike by trail from Cabresto Lake |
| Heron Lake, 64 | 1, NW | Tierra Amarilla | Good access off paved road |
| Hidden Lake, 182 | 2, NE | Santa Rosa | Paved, then ¼ mile rough dirt road |
| Holy Ghost Springs, 16 | 1, NW | San Ysidro | Good gravel 1 mile off paved NM 44 |
| Hopewell Lake, 72 | 1, NW | Tres Piedras | Good access off US 64 |

| LAKES | ZONE | VICINITY | ACCESSIBILITY FROM VICINITY TO LAKE |
|---|---|---|---|
| Horse Lake, 80 | 1, NW | Dulce | Reserved for Jicarilla tribal members and Dulce residents |
| Ice Pond, The, 24 | 1, NW | Jemez Springs | Poor access during inclement weather |
| Isleta Lakes, 10 | 1, NW | Albuquerque | Easy access, off NM 47, south of Albuquerque |
| Jackson Lake, 88 | 1, NW | Farmington | About 150-yard uphill walk from parking area |
| Jal Lake, 272 | 3, SE | Jal | In city, paved road access |
| Jicarilla Apache Lakes, 75 | 1, NW | Dulce | Check in Dulce on road conditions |
| Johnson Lake, 109 | 2, NE | Cowles | Reached by trail only, 8 miles from Cowles |
| Katherine, Lake, 109 | 2, NE | Cowles | Reached by trail, 8 miles up Winsor Creek |
| Laguna Larga, 71 | 1, NW | Tres Piedras | Primitive unimproved roads, 4-wheel-drive advised |
| Lagunitas Lakes, 71 | 1, NW | Tres Piedras | Primitive unimproved roads, 4-wheel-drive advised |
| La Jara Lake, 78 | 1, NW | Dulce | Good access off NM 537 |
| La Joya Lakes, 204 | 3, SE | Belen | Access off I-25, entrance roads dirt and gravel |
| Lake Alice, 165 | 2, NE | Raton | Reached by trail only |
| Lake Farmington, 86 | 1, NW | Farmington | Good access by paved roads |
| Lake Katherine, 109 | 2, NE | Las Trampas/Pecos W. | Reached by trail only |
| Lake Maloya, 166 | 2, NE | Raton | Good access off paved roads |
| Lake Roberts, 332 | 4, SW | Silver City | Good access off paved roads |
| Lake Sumner, 276 | 3, SE | Fort Sumner | Good access by paved roads |
| Lake Van, 238 | 3, SE | Roswell | Good access by paved roads |
| Latir Lakes, 138 | 2, NE | Amalia | Steep, no trailers, rough roads 4-wheel-drive required |
| Lea County Park Lake, 262 | 3, SE | Hobbs | Excellent access, in Harry McAdams State Park |
| Leasburg Dam State Park, 338 | 4, SW | Las Cruces | Paved access, Exit 19, off I-25 south of Hatch |
| Los Alamos Reservoir, 36 | 1, NW | Los Alamos | Off paved road, then 1 mile rough road to lake |
| Lost Bear Lake, 109 | 2, NE | Cowles | Reached by trail only |
| Lost Lake, 141 | 2, NE | Red River | Reached by trail only |
| Maddox Lake, 264 | 3, SE | Hobbs | Paved, then about 300 yards hike to lake |
| Maloya L. (Lake Maloya), 166 | 2, NE | Raton | Paved all way to lake |
| Manzano Lake, 200 | 3, SE | Manzano | Dirt 1/8 mile off paved highway to lake |
| Maxwell Lakes, 160 | 2, NE | Maxwell | Good access, off I-25 at Maxwell then NM 505 |
| McAllister Lake, 114 | 2, NE | Las Vegas | Good paved access |
| McGaffey Lake, 300 | 4, SW | Gallup | Good access, paved roads, then gravel |
| Mescalero Lake, 232 | 3, SE | Ruidoso | Paved to reservation, then check on conditions |
| Miami Lake, 156 | 2, NE | Springer | Paved roads, good access |
| Middle Fork Lake, 141 | 2, NE | Red River | Reached by trail, not detailed in this book |
| Monastery Lake, 102 | 2, NE | Pecos | Paved access to parking lot, short walk to lake |
| Morgan Lake, 94 | 1, NW | Shiprock | Good access, paved roads off U.S. 550 |
| Morphy Lake, 118 | 2, NE | | Rough road, 4-wheel-drive high-clearance vehicle |
| Mundo Lake, 79 | 1, NW | Dulce | Good access off paved highway J-8; on Jicarilla Reservation |
| Municipal Lake, 248 | 3, SE | Carlsbad | Excellent access, within city, all paved roads |
| Nambe Falls Lake, 46 | 1, NE | Española | Good access |
| Navajo Reservation Lakes, 92 | 1, NW | Shiprock | Check with reservation on conditions |
| Navajo Lake, 82 | 1, NW | Blanco | Paved roads, good access to lake |
| Ned Houk Memorial Park, 284 | 3, SE | Clovis | Good access, paved roads |
| North Fork Lake, 117 | 2, NE | Mora (Pecos Wilder.) | Reached by trail only |
| Nutria Lakes, 306 | 4, SW | Ramah | Dirt road; muddy during wet weather |
| Nutrias (Trout Lakes), 58 | 1, NW | Canjilon | FR 125, dirt/gravel road, hazardous when wet |
| Oasis State Park Lake, 288 | 3, SE | Portales | 7 miles north of Portales, paved access to lake |
| Park Lake, 181 | 2, NE | Santa Rosa | In city, paved access |
| Pecos Baldy Lake, 109 | 2, NE | Cowles | Reached by trail only |
| Pecos Wilderness, 108 | 2, NE | Cowles | No motorized vehicles to the lakes, trail only |
| Perch Lake, 181 | 2, NE | Santa Rosa | In Santa Rosa, good access, paved roads |
| Percha Dam Lake, 220 | 3, SW | Truth or Consequences | Paved, off I-25 South, good access |
| Pioneer Lake, 141 | 2, NE | Red River | Reached by trail, not detailed in this book |
| Power Dam Lake, 181 | 2, NE | Santa Rosa | In city, paved access |
| Pu-Na Pond, 124 | 2, NE | Peñasco | On Picuris Indian Pueblo, good access |
| Quemado Lake, 310 | 4, SW | Quemado | 20 miles south of Quemado, paved access |

| LAKES | ZONE | VICINITY | ACCESSIBILITY FROM VICINITY TO LAKE |
|---|---|---|---|
| Ramah Lake, 304 | 4, SW | Ramah | Fair access off paved road then gravel |
| Rancho Grande Ponds, 314 | 4, SW | Reserve | Paved access all the way to ponds |
| Red Lake, 95 | 1, SW | Navajo | Good access, paved all the way to lake |
| Red River Hatchery Pond, 132 | 2, NE | Questa | Good paved access off NM 515 |
| Roberts, Lake, 332 | 4, SW | Silver City | Good access, paved roads |
| Sandia Lakes, 8 | 1, NE | Albuquerque | Paved roads, then short distance on gravel |
| San Gregorio Lake, 28 | 1, NW | Cuba | Paved, then ½-mile hike to lake |
| San Ildefonso Lake, 44 | 1, NW | Española | Good access, on San Ildefonso Indian Reservation |
| San Juan Tribal Lakes, 48 | 1, NW | Española | Good access on San Juan Indian Pueblo |
| Santa Clara Reservoir, 42 | 1, NW | Española | Paved roads, then well-maintained gravel |
| Santa Cruz Lake, 40 | 1, NE | Española | Well-maintained dirt/gravel roads to lake |
| Santa Rosa Lake, 178 | 2, NE | Santa Rosa | Good paved roads |
| Shuree Ponds, 135 | 2, NE | Costilla/Amalia | Muddy in wet weather, 4-wheel-drive advised |
| Silver Lakes, 227 | 3, SE | Ruidoso | On Mescalero Apache Indian Reservation, good access |
| Six Mile Dam Lake, 250 | 3, SE | Carlsbad | Good paved and gravel road access |
| Snow Lake, 316 | 4, SW | Reserve | 4-wheel-drive high-clearance vehicles advised |
| Spirit Lake, 109 | 2, NE | Cowles | Reached from Cowles, by trail only |
| Springer Lake, 152 | 2, NE | Springer | Paved all the way, good access |
| Spring River Park Lake, 236 | 3, SE | Roswell | In Roswell, paved all the way to lake |
| Stewart Lake, 109 | 2, NE | Cowles | Reached by trail only |
| Stone Lake, 79 | 1, NW | Dulce | Good access, muddy in wet weather; on Jicarilla Reservation |
| Storrie Lake, 112 | 2, NE | Las Vegas | Good access, paved roads |
| Stubblefield Lake, 162 | 2, NE | Maxwell | Good access, paved and gravel roads |
| Sumner, Lake, 276 | 3, SE | Fort Sumner` | Good access, paved roads |
| Tingley Beach Lake, 6 | 1, SW | Albuquerque | In city, all paved roads |
| Todacheene Lake, 95 | 1, NW | Shiprock | Last $\frac{3}{10}$ mile, unimproved, deteriorated; on Navajo Reservation |
| Tres Lagunas, 182 | 2, NE | Santa Rosa | Paved, then about a mile on rough dirt roads |
| Tucumcari Lake, 188 | 2, NE | Tucumcari | Paved off I-40, entry on some gravel roads |
| Tutah Pond, 124 | 2, NE | Peñasco | On Picuris Indian Pueblo, good access |
| Ute Lake, 192 | 2, NE | Logan | Excellent access by paved roads |
| Van, Lake, 238 | 3, SE | Roswell | Good access, paved roads |
| Vermejo, 135 | 2, NE | Raton | Private, not detailed in this book |
| Wall Lake, 320 | 4, SW | Beaverhead | 4-wheel-drive vehicles advised, roads badly deteriorated |
| Whiskey Lake, 96 | 1, NW | Shiprock | 4-wheel-drive vehicles advised, unimproved deteriorated roads; on Navajo Reservation |
| Zia Lake, 14 | 1, NW | San Ysidro | Off NM 44, good access to lake |
| Zuni Reservation Lakes, 306 | 4, SW | Gallup | Some accesses good, check conditions at Tribal Office for road conditions |